INFLUENCERS WHO KILL

A TRUE CRIME COLLECTION

REAL STORIES OF ONLINE FAME AND FATAL CONSEQUENCES

MADISON SALTERS

Published in 2026 by
ULYSSES PRESS
an imprint of The Stable Book Group
32 Court Street, Suite 2109
Brooklyn, NY 11201
www.ulyssespress.com

Library of Congress Control Number: 2025930785
ISBN: 978-1-64604-805-2
eISBN: 978-1-64604-806-9

Acquisitions editor: Shelona Belfon
Project editor: Kierra Sondereker
Managing editor: Claire Chun
Editor: Renee Rutledge
Proofreader: Jan Hughes
Front cover design: Kyle Keigan
Artwork: female killer © Alex Segura; torn paper and grunge background from shutterstock.com

Printed in the United States
10 9 8 7 6 5 4 3 2 1

To Ree, who won our final game at my last book launch party,
but who also won every game we ever played with her.

To Gerry, whom we never got to play part two
of the one-shot with, knowing that all one-shots
among good friends inevitably will need more play time.

CONTENTS

INTRODUCTION

Don't empathize, don't villainize.

Those are the hardline rules I set for myself in writing—and in reading—about violent crime. They're necessary, even when they scream against every human tendency to play judge, declaring pardon or penance.

In true crime, hair-trigger reactions are common. Sympathy for killers is born from our understanding that the root of violent crime is often social or psychological—that it preys on and propagates around untreated mental disorders, substance abuse, violent childhoods, bullying, and economic hardship. Rarely do you get a wildly sadistic serial killer with sterling parents and meaningful friendships, who murders for "funsies." Most criminal backstories are layered, and the perpetrator is also a type of victim. But empathizing too hard can offhandedly glamorize cruelty, manufacturing a celebrity criminal while retraumatizing victims—too much sympathy for the devil drowns out those they put through hell.

Yet all violent crime can't be painted with the same brush. Killing is sometimes a *true* accident: sometimes the wild product of heat-of-the-moment, sometimes a result of self-defense. Some perpetrators grow to profoundly regret their crimes, devoting themselves to improvement. When nuance dies, blind condemnation leaves no room for the possibility of rehabilitation. Even for the truly guilty, living in the confines of prisons or parole can still be prolific and meaningful, especially for young offenders.

I did not always accomplish this neutrality. In Snow's case, the harrowing act seemed purely like a sloppy and heartbreaking accident—Snow's federal judge agreed. In stark contrast, writing Yuka's chapter, I was bewildered by the amount of exoneration her *victim* required against his would-be killer—he'd barely survived a stabbing only to be nationally reviled for his background as an orphaned sex worker. Randy, for me, was the unwinnable battle. His YouTube fame and fairy-tale world seem to insulate him among online fans, who view him opulently despite his vile racism, sexism, and homophobia—and deliberate mass murder. His rantings against non-white Americans were so blatantly horrific that they could not stand to be published.

The rest were more straightforward. David and Samantha, who had unfairly and coldheartedly taken the lives of good people, but who'd suffered so deeply in their own adolescences that it was only a matter of understanding *how* the pot boiled over, not *why*. Then there was the banal radicalization of Pekka, the untreated mental health of Trey, the attention-seeking Abagail, the furious unmooring of Nasim.

With each new case, each new underbelly, coffee didn't feel strong enough to get me through the thousands of pages of research materials—dairies, autopsies, government reports, and social media handles that were like bottomless pits. Documents and newscasts needed to be translated from Arabic, Turkish, Finnish, Japanese. There were hours upon hours of audio and video evidence, documentaries, and media that needed to be compiled and consumed. Primary source interviews were conducted, lawyers were consulted. This book is a stitching together of all avenues, even the dead ends—witnesses who remained anonymous, family members who couldn't bear to revisit horrors, contradictions that remain unsolved.

Outside of murder and its harbingers, this book deals with three other central themes: influencers, pop culture, and parasocial relationships. *Influencers* are simply people who have become more a "brand" than a true and complex person online. They often work under a new name or "handle" and are known "for" something unique to them—a vibe or aesthetic, a way of speaking, joking, or moving. They have riddled out a formula that convinces others to do, buy, or listen to what they say, inspiring audiences to mimic their looks, thoughts, and acts. A rebranding of peer pressure, with an *It* factor. Influencers are generally recognizable for an individual niche, be it fashion, travel, food, comedy, or otherwise.

In this book, you'll be introduced to nine influencers whose main playground was pop culture—video gaming, anime reviews, cosplay, mommy blogging, American cartoons, sketch culture, militant veganism, and even modern-day manosphere white supremacy. Some of these influencers were well-established at the time of their crimes, while others were just coming into their own. Some only became influential as a direct result of their stabbings and shootings going "viral." These influencers operated broadly on the net and on social media—YouTube, Twitter/X, Instagram, Facebook, OnlyFans, TikTok, online forums, and more—connecting with fans and contemporaries.

With each new generation, pop culture is inevitably blamed for bad behavior (though with little scientific or psychological truth attached to that stigma). It's often a case of old versus young, from the "Satanic Panic" of the 1980s, aiming its ire rather ridiculously at the harmless game *Dungeons & Dragons,* to the scapegoating of video gaming in the 1990s as causation for mass shootings. Often, pop culture is just a haven for those who feel *othered*—bullied or disenfranchised—to find community. Fads may be a convenient target, but they rarely have any violent impact on society unless they are inherently violent in *rhetoric* themselves, such as Pekka's modish rebrand of fascist eugenics. "Red pilling" and "almond moms," assuredly faddish, have done more harm than the entire game library of a Nintendo 64. Similarly, it's important to remember that pop culture doesn't earmark something as cool or uncool, but *collective*: yesterday's "uncool" trends often become today's mainstream—just look at the rise of comic book superheroes being redesignated from "nerdy" to "geek chic," with gym bros now sporting Captain America's gear to weightlift. So, this book does not aim to marginalize or point at pop culture as problematic—it intends to celebrate and introduce elements of it, while acknowledging that those communities were some of the most duped and betrayed by these offenders.

Finally, parasocial relationships are key to understanding many of the fan reactions in this book. A parasocial relationship is the completely natural phenomenon of someone having a one-sided bond, positive or negative—usually with a celebrity—where they know or think they know quite a lot about someone, but the object they are judging does not really know they exist. Humans are predisposed to form social relationships and to connect those relationships to emotional responses, developing either friendly or unfriendly sentiments toward someone they "know," even if only by word of mouth, or say, television interviews. You may know you dislike the person your best friend describes as hating at their job, without *really* knowing them, and without them knowing you. Similarly, you might adore a late-night host or actor whom you've been watching give interviews for years—you might even know their favorite color and some anecdotes about their kids that make you feel warmly toward them, like they're a good person and you'd be great friends were you ever to meet. Influencers prey on the parasocial—they create a context where you "know" them, or think you do. They thank fans personally and remind them that their support is what matters, which deepens the bonded feeling. They're "real," rather than celebrities, which intensifies the impression of possibility—maybe one day you *could* meet and be friends.

Parasocial relationships toward influencers are normal and generally not unhealthy—but in some cases, influencers created strong enough bonds with their audiences that ghoulish glamorizations of their crimes occurred. Some influencers *themselves* engaged in parasocial relationships, but with *fictional* characters, to their detriment. While it is natural for humans to use storytelling to relate to characters both fictional (admiring and aspiring to traits in books and movies such as heroism, sacrifice, and fortitude) and real, but larger-than-life (sports teams, for example, where fans bond emotionally to achievements that aren't their own accomplishments), humans mostly use storytelling to help think about what they'd do in any given situation: a zombie apocalypse, a natural disaster, an underdog moment, a romantic one. In contrast, the influencers' parasocial relationships to *fiction* were largely used as ridiculous justification for malicious intent. Wanting to be more like John Wick because you love dogs and hate injustice is one thing; deciding you *are* James Bond and you're therefore allowed to jump out of a plane and shoot people is something else entirely.

Finally, as you read this book, occasionally pause to ask yourself why it can sometimes be easy to romanticize great acts, whether "great" means splendid or awful. People who make an impact snag our curiosity, and those who commit atrocities tempt us to ask "why?" Without that, there would be no book.

Sometimes, we know why. Or else we glean the reality in the margins of the self-aggrandizing clues left behind. Many of these killers left their own eulogies. Their own manifestos. Most aimed for being edgy; all were self-important. As influencers, they left pages and pages of content, a carefully curated "them" for others to consume, some even after death. But let's slide off the public-facing mask and dig into the truth. Who they really were, or are now. In this book, you'll be introduced to nine cases. And in all nine, you may find yourself either empathizing with or villainizing the central protagonist. Ultimately, you as the reader should draw your own conclusions—after all, *influencers* thrive in the court of public opinion.

That is, in part, what makes them such likely candidates for crime. Attention-seeking personalities catering to an anonymous chorus of critical voices can lose themselves to infinite people-pleasing. Posting for likes and comments, validation, or money, or both, can become addictive. With enough fame, even they might buy into what they are selling—that they are famous, special, above the norm, and that they always need to be doing *more*, performing bigger and better. The pressure can get to them as surely as the celebrity can.

Also, be sure to consider, as you read, the usual cacophony of contradictions when it comes to crime and its perpetrators. Someone may barely seem capable of violence online, yet is, in fact, a salacious bully to their peers. When it comes to perpetrators, always believe the evidence over what they say is true. You may hear that someone *loves* their partner, or loves children, or loves their family—but if they use them as fodder and torment them, is that really so? Many of these influencers *talk* a big game but don't walk in the shoes they ask their audience to believe they fill.

When this book's subject was pitched to me, Snow's case was presented first—someone who'd pulled the trigger on an accidentally loaded gun while just trying to play around with friends. They were pretending to be the Penguin, a villain from *Batman*'s *Gotham* TV series at the time. A few months ago, my own partner had dressed up as the Penguin for Halloween. There was nothing inherently evil in that make-believe. The *evil* sat in the barrel of that Glock. We must ask not about hobbies, but about intent. Who meant to do what, and why—and how do they now feel about their actions?

In this book you will meet nine individuals. Snow, a cosplayer who accidentally took the life of a friend and may soon have any sentencing revoked (with good behavior). Trey, a man obsessed with guns and anime, who slew his family. Abigail, a mommy-blogger who put a sloppy hit on her hardworking husband. Pekka, a Finnish terrorist who shot up his school in the name of white revolution. Nasim, a radical vegan who opened fire on YouTube's California headquarters over perceived slights. Samantha, whose rage born from harrowing childhood exploitation ballooned into fatal consequences against the kindest man in her life. Yuka, a red-light district worker who stabbed the object of her affection while he slept—for taking photos with other girls. Randy, a fantastically vicious murderer who believed he'd be reborn in a cartoon ghost world beyond the grave. And David, a professional video gamer whose disturbed upbringing seemed to set the stage for his gunning down of fellow gamers.

These stories span countries—the United States, Iraq, the United Kingdom, Finland, Japan. What connects them is ego. Big, overbearing, fanatical ego—serving as armor against deep insecurities that, once prodded or wounded, became a problem for anyone caught in the cross-hairs.

CHAPTER 1

SNOW, aka Snow the Salt Queen/ Yandere.Freak

Here's a motive: Hope it digs its way into your mind
Like a seed, it feeds on hope, until you're taking lives
Recognize my face, with one of different pairs of eyes
A body has been discovered—Looks like your friend has died
Oh, look at you tremble (tremble), Did you think that you'd be okay?
You peasants forget that this is all a killing game! I'm always watching
So, will you accept your fate? Make it flashy, for the viewers
OR IT'S FUCKING LAME!
There is no hope and soon you'll see, lives come and go, Kill and show them out there.

—"Fall Into Despair," HalaCG

This is a theme song from the horror line of video games called *Danganropa*, in which a cutesy young woman named Junko Enoshima features as the main antagonist, striving to reach her goal of spreading despair across the world, targeting her closest friends first. She is manipulative, two-faced, and homicidal. She is also the character Snow most strongly identified with and often dressed up as.

A note about names and pronouns in this chapter: The following case concerns the death of Helen Hastings, who went by the pronouns "she/her" and "they/them" before her passing at the hands of a friend named Snow. The family of Helen Hastings replied to initial outreach but declined to comment regarding the case. Therefore, to the best of our knowledge, "she/they" is accurate at the time of printing, and "she" is used in this chapter to differentiate Helen from Snow. However, "they" is preserved where used by original sources for Helen.

On public record across years of pretrial filings, legal proceedings, and official documentation, Snow variously went by "she/her," "they/them," and "he/him." Snow's current pronouns at the time of this writing are "they/them." Pronouns cited in sources from quotations, news media, documents, or public record have been updated to reflect this, regardless of original terminology. "[Sic]" is not used in these cases.

Additionally, Snow went by their dead name at the time of Helen's death. A "dead name" is the name assigned at birth to a person who has since transitioned to another gender or identifies as nonbinary, who has changed their name to reflect their identity. (This can also refer to anyone who changes their name and no longer wishes to be referred to by their given name.) The text respects Snow's current name and does not use the dead name, though all primary sources utilized it at the time of the incident. As a result, all instances of a text, video, or other sources citing the dead name have been updated here to "Snow" without use of [Sic].

As a note to readers, though Snow is a *part* of their original legal name, this is not considered a dead name. There has been some confusion in various reports surrounding this. To be sure of accuracy, we reached out to Snow's pretrial attorney, Brent Mayr, who kindly clarified/confirmed, "First, their name is Snow and their pronouns are they/their/them. We appreciate your concern on the correct name and pronouns.... Snow is a mononym."

Iceberg Lounging

2014's hit television show *Gotham* told the gritty story of a young Detective Jim Gordon in the eponymous city, back when Bruce Wayne still had on training wheels. It explored the origin of Batman before the cowl, featuring many members of his future rogues' gallery in the nascent throes of villainy.

At the climax of the first season's finale, "All Happy Families Are Alike," Robin Lord Taylor's Oswald Cobblepot—better known by his criminal moniker "the Penguin"—limps across the screen unloading a semi-automatic rifle into a crowd of mobsters and cops as a dark remix of his violin theme hurtles against the cacophony of concussive gunfire. He is wreaking a methodical vengeance on those who, moments ago, had him on the ropes—literally strung up for execution.

When the assault rifle runs dry, he hefts it aside in favor of a fallen Taurus PT92 pistol. The underdog villain approaches an unnamed man who throws his hands up in surrender, begging Cobblepot, "No... *please.*"

The Penguin summarily shoots him in the head at close range. Killing him.

In this scene, the Penguin plays both antagonist and unexpected antihero. The dead young man is merely a footnote; scenery that got chewed. The Penguin's story will continue across stepping stones like these for five seasons, the character's popularity only increasing with each new tidbit of drama or cruelty. This was in no small part due to Lord Taylor's portrayal being one of the first *attractive* on-screen adaptations of the gangster, with less the crude caricature of clubfoot, less the protruding belly, and less the hooked nose of the character's typical signature look. Instead, Lord Taylor's version leaned pretty boy, a '90s punk rock haircut wafting into pale blue eyes, his teeth yellowed just a tad by the makeup department, a sideways attempt to imply he might not be a Hollywood movie star. The carnage in the character's wake was largely glorified, forgiven, or excused by fans fascinated with the glamorous take on the character.

Snow was one such fan. They more than enjoyed the character—they wanted to look like him, move like him, dress like him. Villains were Snow's favorite type of character to embody, a lifelong fascination for someone who played dress-up professionally.

Helen Rose Hastings was nineteen years old on January 17, 2021. *Gotham* was playing on Snow's television in the living room of the house at Soft Pine Road in Houston, Texas. Outside, the COVID-19 pandemic was ravaging the globe, making house parties like this one rare. Inside the quaint four-bedroom A-frame with its beige brick façade, white moldings, and real, working fireplace, seven friends were deep into an evening of vodka sodas and marijuana. Some lived at the house full time, some part time, and others were just visiting.

Snow, twenty-three at the time and a full-time resident at Soft Pine, was showing off a Glock to the group. It had belonged to an ex-boyfriend, but it wasn't uncommon for Snow to take it from its case and parade it around. On this particular night, drunk, excited comparisons between Snow gripping the flashy weapon and the Penguin with his charismatic on-screen violence came easy. In a bit of roleplay taken too far, or a suggestion too well followed, someone egged Snow to aim the gun at them, just like the Penguin did at his enemies. Snow, pretending to *be* the Penguin, did so. They pointed the gun at one friend, then at another: Hastings.

It is unclear whether Helen had also asked for Snow to point the muzzle her way, with some witnesses saying yes, others saying no, and Helen's mother, who wasn't present, saying it would have been totally out of character for Helen.[1] But maybe *not* out of character for a Gothamite, spurring on a crime lord in a bit of inebriated playacting.

"Ooooh, shoot me!"

"Oh, okay."[2]

---

1 E. J. Dickson, "They Were Close Friends and Cosplay Stars. Then Snow Killed Helen," *Rolling Stone*, October 21, 2021, https://www.rollingstone.com/culture/culture-features/cosplay-tiktok-manslaughter-yandere-snow-helen-hastings-1234452.

2 "Marilyn Burgess," accessed April 30, 2025, Hcdistrictclerk.com, https://www.hcdistrictclerk.com/Edocs/Public/CaseDetails.aspx?Get=JT1fKyByn2YM0gG7S2MBS+gWJuDwUCuiFirpxsEv3z7ap1B7o08J3vDiyzVNk0I1RSdLNi9D9ZOiUGR9nM4lJXpJkTGOK6klPHELiFFSBFeVK6h+chrak1flHVgo34rGHdPQ8wYBrElAfamjLPA3gHsGN5d4hgBnAvOrNmjBSuKWEiSqzigy%2fg%3d%3d.

Snow took aim, from close range, at Helen's head—then pulled the trigger. A bullet fired, lodging in her skull. The bleeding was immediate and effusive. Helen hit the floor.

Scrambling and screaming, the housemates phoned for an ambulance and began applying first aid measures right away. Helen didn't die instantly, but the wound had rendered her brain-dead by the time she reached a hospital. Effectively dead, Helen was kept on life support until January 18, 2021, for the sake of organ donation candidacy. Helen's mother sang to her right up until she let her go. She was removed from life support and slipped away, almost like a secret being lost to the wind. Her death would take months to be discussed in the open—her school friends, awaiting her back at Oberlin College, would have little idea what had happened. There was no news media coverage around the shooting. And Snow would seem to carry on as if nothing had changed, peddling online content to legions of fans after only a short break.

Snow hadn't known the gun was loaded. It was purely a tragic accident.

Or so the story goes. It was what witnesses agreed on. Their united word was convincing enough to persuade a judge and a defense attorney. The case was never tried by a jury. But once the events of the evening finally came to light publicly, the internet at large felt very differently. The line between amateur online detective and actual law enforcement would begin to fray, with public opinion set firmly against Snow.

This was largely due to a series of disturbing videos uploaded online in the months that followed Helen's slaying that scandalized the community Snow and Helen had been a part of. Namely, that of cosplayers, video gamers, convention-goers, and anime fans. A popular cosplay model before news of the shooting went public, Snow had their share of scandals and detractors throughout their public-facing career. But the gory tone-deafness of those now-deleted videos turned the tide strongly against Snow. It led many to ask, how could an accident be followed up by such seemingly unhinged and unsympathetic behavior by its perpetrator? And how could such a catastrophe occur in such a close-knit group of young adults—peers who were like family?

> All happy families are alike; each unhappy family is unhappy in its own way.
>
> —Leo Tolstoy, *Anna Karenina*

> This foundational quote of the *Anna Karenina* principle, for which the *Gotham* episode featuring the Penguin taking charge was named, expresses the idea that it is possible to fail in many ways but succeed only in one. Consequently, to achieve success, every possible disaster must be avoided. Victory is difficult and singular; but dysfunction and despair are simple and common.

A Place to Belong

As a public figure, Snow was no stranger to controversy. From accusations of money scams to complaints of grave defacing, once Snow found online fame, infamy was its dogged bedfellow.

In their heyday, spanning the 2010s and culminating in 2021 after the Hastings slaying went public, influencer Snow boasted more than 1.6 million followers across multiple online handles, mostly on TikTok and Instagram.[3] They posted reels and hosted live video chats, raking in comments by rapt audiences. They went by the handles Yandere.Freak or SnowTheSaltQueen, as well as a few others, including BadGuyIncorporated. Their content mostly focused on cosplay and vlog-style narration of tips and tricks for costuming and makeup, and less frequently, the airing of public drama: complaints and defenses surrounding their own erratic behavior. Snow gained a passionate following for their impressive costumes and dark skits donning those costumes, but some followers came for the controversy and spectacle: hate-watching.

Snow had their fair share of white knights to defend them on every post and live feed, patrolling their narrative spaces and carefully guarding their image. Graced with easygoing, conventional good

3 Anna Bauman, "TikTok Star Accused of Fatally Shooting Houston Teen in Tragic Mishap at Batman Watch Party," *Houston Chronicle*, October 28, 2021, https://www.houstonchronicle.com/news/houston-texas/crime/article/TikTok-star-accused-of-killing-friend-in-Houston-16569432.php.

looks and an engaging, cavalier attitude, Snow was a fun watch, striking the right blend of innocent and edgy. Blond, slim, wide-eyed, and flighty of hand and voice, Snow reeled viewers in by talking a mile a minute, with perky or bizarre sound bites overlaid on mostly dark skits when they weren't live.

Of course, Snow also endured a fair share of online "flaming": brutal comments stemming from the overcritical nature of online parasocial relationships. Sometimes these were cruel, and sometimes they were a fair critique of Snow's offbeat actions. But detractors are something every online denizen is used to. Post a video of a puppy, a baby, or what you ate for dinner, and when enough strangers take notice, the comments section will inevitably bloat with critique on everything from the way the dog is being held to the dishware being used to the commodification of children in the modern day. Comment sections often devolve into armchair psychology, personal moral philosophy, and a spelling bee all packaged into a weird nexus of anonymous judgment. The snide side of the internet—the consequence-free ability to simply be *cruel*—leads many to play arbiter on strangers' personalities and motivations. Some of Snow's viewers tuned in specifically to mock, deride, and speculate. They were less on a fact-finding mission than on a mission to find someone to aim their vitriol at.

What both the pro- and anti-Snow encampments shared in common was a mania around the persona Snow crafted in their videos. Snow always leaned into controversy. Drama materialized around them, and rather than ignore rumors, Snow often doubled down by reacting to speculation. And while it could not have been pleasant to have the condemnatory eye of internet hordes upon them, it was undeniably lucrative; content was Snow's bread and butter. So rumors and public altercations, however hostile, kept up the tempo of views and introduced the act to new audiences who wanted to rubberneck the melodrama. And what was helping rile up these masses in Snow's comment sections? Cartoons. Specifically, Japanese anime and video games.

Snow's main cultural export was cosplay videos, in costumes inspired by anime and games. Their cadence often tapped into the vein of weird, ominous, and provocative. They invited onlookers to be disturbed: goth, a little frenzied, often *violent* when dressed up. When Snow spoke as themself and outside of cosplay, the effect was more laid-back: a makeup-loving, fast-talking (often, their videos were sped up), jittery young adult who seemed energized and even puzzled by all the attention, pulling cutesy or hyper faces while monologuing. Their cosplay choices and personae were a darker story.

Cosplay is a portmanteau of "costume" and "play." It's the word for dressing up as a fictional character from television, comics, movies, and books—often a beloved or favorite character. From elaborate wigs and stage makeup to detailed props and contact lenses, costumes can be as simple as a fifty-dollar purchase on Amazon for a polyester facsimile of an anime character or as complex as a multi-thousand-dollar handmade extravaganza for entry into an international competition, French-stitched and 3D printed with lighting rigs. Once little-known and even stigmatized, today, cosplay is an open secret and even a capitalistic playground. Popularized by hundreds of thousands of attendees to anime and comic book conventions worldwide, cosplay has become more than a phenomenon; it's become a business juggernaut.

The hobby is most often engaged with by eager fans live and en masse at sci-fi, anime, and comic book conventions worldwide, regardless of age, gender, or race. The explosive growth of cosplay "con" culture can be tracked by one of the United States' biggest anime conventions, Anime Expo Los Angeles. Its inaugural year of 1992 boasted only 1,725 attendees[4]; by 2025, that number ballooned to a mind-shattering 410,000 cartoon devotees, creating over $100 million dollars in *local* business revenue alone. Attendees donned wings spanning over three feet or foam swords larger than their bodies, eager to shed the work week and strut their stuff as Sephiroth, Hello Kitty, or Spider-Man, attending photoshoots and nightly raves as villains, schoolgirls, and heroes rather than as accountants, lawyers, or baristas.

Cosplay is often thought of as a Japanese cultural export due to its popularity with fans of anime and manga (Japanese comics).

4 Charles Solomon, "Mainstream Call of Anime," *Los Angeles Times*, July 2003, https://www.latimes.com/archives/la-xpm-2003-jul-01-et-solomon1-story.html.

But its roots are in American sci-fi culture—in conventions bulwarked around the *Star Trek* and *Star Wars* franchises, and really taking off in the 1980s. The word itself is attributed to Nobuyuki Takahashi, first published in the Japanese magazine *My Anime* in 1984 to describe what he'd seen in Los Angeles at a sci-fi convention, World Con.[5] At that point, the cosplay movement was only just starting to gain steam at Japanese comic conventions such as Comiket and was referred to as "Hero Costume Operation" or *kasou* (imaginary).

With anime going mainstream in the West beginning in the late '90s, then ballooning into a billion-dollar industry by the 2020s, cosplay went from an embryonic movement of geek-chic annual meetups on technicolor convention hotel carpeting to a way of life for some people. For many serious cosplayers, the con circuit makes up the majority of their social event calendar, and their friend groups are often attendees. Much of their annual vacation planning is mapped out against those schedules, traveling cross-country or internationally and paying for convention tickets and hotel stays to attend an event, where they'll spend even more money on merchandise. They drop huge sums on costumes, makeup, wigs, and photoshoots, spend free time crafting and styling, and assign their in-group to various characters and do test runs and meetups. And anywhere there's enough money and enough enthusiasm, something becomes a career option.

Career cosplayers such as Yaya Han,[6] or Jessica Nigiri,[7] who have millions of followers each, have turned their costuming lucrative, transitioning it into book deals, advertising, paid voice acting, and brand deals. Even with the expense of needing to output several costumes a year to present new and exciting looks online and for fan receptions, the benefits can outweigh the expense for those who "make it." Cosplayers like Japan's Enako, who once made the equivalent of nearly $100,000 in just two days of doing meet-and-greets

5 Achim Runnebaum, "The Origins of Cosplay," *Japan Daily*, August 4, 2019, https://japandaily.jp/the-origins-of-cosplay-6598.

6 "Yaya Han - Cosplay Galleries, Supplies, Ideas, Book," n.d. Yaya Han, https://www.yayahan.com.

7 Jessica Nigri (@Jessicanigri), Instagram, accessed April 30, 2025, https://www.instagram.com/jessicanigri.

at a Tokyo convention,[8] have earned over $1.5 million in one year[9]—and Enako has more than a million fewer followers than Nigiri's 3.7 million.[10] These powerhouses have worked with McCalls, JOANN fabrics, Nintendo, Sega, and the SyFy channel. These are not numbers or collaborations to sneeze at. This is "nerdom" at an astronomical level of social and fiscal dominance.

These idols make their cash, essentially, by living in a tango with copyright laws. They embody the characters and sell calendars, autographs, T-shirts, and even salacious photos dressed and acting as a character. They are hired to work conventions "in-character," serve as masquerade judges, or even host TV shows—all due to their popularity with their gobs of admirers. They bring attention to the properties from which they cosplay and are even sometimes hired by the production companies to sell it live. Like a Disneyland cast member dressed as Snow White interacting with excited fans at the theme parks, these people transform themselves and bring the magic directly to the enthusiasts, who, in tandem, treat them as if they really are the character. And just like at a Disney park, it doesn't matter if they're not *really* Snow White; for a few hours, they might as well be.

Of course, another way to make money—if you're popular enough—is with online content. This was what Snow was doing, on Instagram and TikTok—climbing the ladder to try to compete with the big-leaguers. But that particular sandbox was high-stakes and *extremely* competitive, with a "mean girl" laser-focus on attractiveness and accuracy. It was also highly addictive. The slow creep toward mini-celebrity makes the cosplay rat race especially cutthroat.

When cosplayers begin at local conventions, they get their first taste of the adulation that comes with transformation. People who recognize a cosplayer's costume might rush up in joy, begging to take photos of or with them, saying how much they love the character and the outfit. In this moment, the person is treated as if they

---

8 Max Chang, "Japanese Cosplayer Claims She Made $100,000 in Two Days at Anime Convention," NextShark, September 16, 2016, https://nextshark.com/enako-cosplayer-japan-money-comiket.

9 Gank Content Team, "How Do Cosplayers Make Money in 2024?" Ganknow.com, April 1, 2024, https://ganknow.com/blog/how-do-cosplayers-make-money.

10 えなこ (Enako) (@Enakorin), Instagram, accessed April 30, 2025, https://www.instagram.com/enakorin.

are their favorite character, or like they have sudden newsworthiness. In what other hobby can one essentially walk a red carpet with eager photographers complimenting them, fans screaming for them, offering gifts of pins and ribbons and free drinks simply for existing, in clothes? Like a night at the Oscars, many cosplayers don the most expensive outfits they own and spend hours on their hairstyles and makeup to get everything just right. They indulge in modeling-style photoshoots and post their photos and videos online for likes and gushing comments. The endorphin rush is unique.

But beyond the attention, cosplay is also uniquely appealing for people who want to experience being someone other than themselves for a while. For those who find their way into comics and cartoons through feeling *othered*, it's addictive to suddenly have built-in friends in the form of the people dressed as the *character's* friends. And with enough supporters and clout, cosplayers may even begin to feel like they *are* the magical girl or a mecha pilot they're playing dress-up as. The layers of addiction to praise, transformation, popularity, camaraderie, and playing pretend leaves many looking for the next fix.

The numbers don't lie. According to Konvoy, a gaming investment group, the compulsion has created an industry worth $4.8 billion as of 2023, projected to grow to $8.7 billion by 2033.[11] Cosplayers are currently in the millions, with nearly 30% of those ranks being found in the US. While the biggest segment of cosplayers are women in their twenties, the hobby is also a refuge for nonbinary and gender-questioning people, as it presents a form of escapism, role-play, and gender play, with folks often cosplaying their opposite gender. For some, cosplay isn't about being someone else for a day—but about wanting to feel like *themselves* for the first time.

The cosplay community is often considered a welcoming space for all types of individuals. Most cosplayers make or buy one or two costumes a year, but a whopping 25% of cosplayers manage five or more.[12] The two main drivers of growth in this market, where big spending is nearly a must in order to participate, are time spent online

11 "A Fast Growing Market of High Spenders," Konvoy,com, September 15, 2023, https://www.konvoy.vc/newsletters/a-fast-growing-market-of-high-spenders.

12 "A Fast Growing Market of High Spenders," Konvoy.com.

having a "digital identity," and escapism, according to Konvoy's data. This is a key to understanding the way Snow used the hobby versus the way that Helen did. Snow relied heavily on cosplay as a career choice (their digital identity), while Hastings used it as a way to forge community and find a place to belong outside of the bullying she'd endured in school (escapism).

It's also vital to understand both the allure *and* the competition Snow was facing down, and largely besting, when producing content and creating their own cosplay identity as a "brand." To be noticed, they needed a niche. And Snow's niche was being "*off*-brand"—they were the villain character, the twisted soul, courting political incorrectness. This was signaled by their online handles: @yandere.freak and @SnowTheSaltQueen. A yandere character, in a Japanese context, is someone who seems sweet and thoughtful on the outside but inside is violent, hostile, and sometimes even psychotic and murderous. It's a portmanteau of the Japanese words for "sickness/illness" and "lovestruck." Whereas to be *salty*, in English slang, is to be angry, or unreasonably upset; and they were announcing themselves the undisputed Queen of it.

For Snow, cosplay was a job, and for Helen, it was a hobby. Nonetheless, they'd met and bonded through it. They also both used it as an expression of gender. Cosplay can feel inclusive for people who are gender-questioning, gender-fluid, or transgender. Zach, a gender-fluid cosplayer from Virginia, noted about their own experience in cosplay, "When I was in high school [in the] early 2000s, just above the Bible Belt, [the] LGBTQIA+ community was less accepted than it is today. I was going through a time where I wasn't sure of my sexuality and it had me start questioning my gender.... [Cosplaying] was the first time I had worn anything atypical for a male.... I don't think I would have ever explored my gender without the positive part of the experience." Rachel, another cosplayer hailing from Maryland, added to the dialogue, "...I could use [cosplay] to explore this idea that maybe I felt better as a girl. [In 2006], I cosplayed Chi from *Chobits*.... As I walked around in this cosplay, my whole world changed. I felt happy.... I would swap back and forth cosplaying guys and girls.

I had fun with both, but it helped me to confirm that this was not a phase, Rachel was real and Richard felt like a total lie."

Cosplay in the early aughts was still thought of as the realm of serious nerd culture, with the negative stigmatic side-eye that implies, but the tides were beginning to turn. One article, especially unhinged in retrospect and published in the *Washington Post* in 2000 by staff writer Hank Stuever, crowed: "It's a combination of giant-eyed heroes and junk worship—... Two remarkable differences between [cosplay] and conventions of other genres are that there are at least as many girls here as guys, and there is more racial and ethnic diversity.... The anime kids seem cool, self-assured, uninhibited.... There may be some social marginalization going on here, like always, and these kids may yet entertain thoughts of blowing up the school ... [But] if you were 16 again, you'd want to date the girls dressed like Sailor Moon ... [Yet] animes are quite sad and poetic, almost pessimistic. These cartoon characters are not afraid to die and are frequently stabbed to death; those who are left behind shed noble, subtitled tears."[13]

Stuever's implication that one might want to *date* a geek without a *She's All That* makeover moment does predict the rise in idol-worship around popular cosplayers. Princess Leia costume fantasies were still the butt of jokes as recently as the television show *Friends*; but by the 2020s, there would be real competition—and fame—to be found in portraying a character fantasy better than anyone else. Better dressed, better photographed, better looking. The vestiges of someone who almost made it big live on in the shambled remains of Snow's online handles—now mostly deleted, privatized, or archived—which read like a video scrapbook of someone who was nearly famous before infamy got its arctic grip on them instead.

13 Hank Stuever, "What Would Godzilla Say?" *Washington Post*, February 14, 2000, https://www.washingtonpost.com/wp-srv/style/feed/a49427-2000feb14.htm.

Kinning the Villain: Wigs, Kittens, and a Graveyard

Almost every cosplayer worth their salt (pun, perhaps, intentional) is "known for" a particular character or costume. Often, if a cosplayer becomes heavily associated with an anime or game character, they'll do all variants of their costumes—from every new season of a show or new installment of a game, every weather-specific look for spring or winter, from a *yukata* for summer festivals to the bikini donned in a swimsuit scene.

The more a cosplayer becomes known for a particular character, the more jealously they tend to guard their identity around that character. The pressure to be the best version or to embody the fictional personality by bringing them to life can get intense. Especially in the early 2000s and among younger cosplayers, before the body positivity movement spread to cosplay communities more robustly, this often meant the cosplayers who gained recognition were thin, conventionally attractive, and formed the most like an anime character: tall, androgynous, wide-eyed, and often, fair-skinned. This had racist and fatphobic overtones for Western costumers, especially as Japanese media was producing so few compelling characters outside of a fair-skinned and skinny mold, leading to the formation of exclusive cosplay "groups" where the key factor was fitting the image. The more a cosplayer "looked the part" and the more well-known they were as a character (profiles were built up online, photoshoots were posted to blogs, forums, and socials), the closer they came to being the penultimate version—the version that all other cosplayers were compared against, famous within the community. For cosplayers on this level, it had been a battle to the top, so whether they were actually snobbish or just came off that way was often a blurred line. Accusations of elitism ran rife among the most popular sets of cosplayers.

For Snow, that character was Junko Enoshima, from the horror game series *Danganropa*. It is what their "yandere" handle was in reference to. Junko is a happy-go-lucky, bubbly youngster who seems to have deep empathy for other people. But the course of the plot twists and reveals her to, in fact, be the *antagonist*, responsible for locking her peers in a school and forcing them to play in a death match against each other, observing with sick joy as her classmates are butchered.

Snow purportedly defended their portrayal of Junko with jealous cattiness, going so far as to neg other's interpretations. It would have been punching down; Snow was viewed as one of the best Junkos on the circuit. But Snow was partly so protective because they related to Junko *deeply*.

Of the character herself, Junko's creator Kazutaka Kodaka said,

> Recently, I feel like more bad guys in games are given a harsh background of some kind that explains their evilness in the present day. But that feels like cheating to me. I felt like the most dangerous thing about Junko would be that she doesn't have any reason to do the things she does. So, I incorporated that into her character all the way through the game ...[14]

Junko is a despair-junkie who houses multiple personalities. A saccharine persona, a vulgar persona, and even one with crippling depression. Another is her murderous *Monokuma* persona, taking the shape of a mascot-like teddy bear in two-tone black and white. Junko's "true" self is apathetic and unhinged, manipulative and cruel, extremely violent, impulsive, and clever.

Quotes by her in the game and the accompanying anime released after the success of the game franchise include,

- Sure they were trash, but still ... you don't see this many people die at once without feeling *something*.
- To show the world the murders taking place at this school, which was meant to be a symbol of hope.
- So I'm hopelessly attractive? Hopelessly brilliant? Hopelessly athletic ...? ... I'm the hopelessly perfect ultimate human?
- Couldn't you just *die*?

14 Jacob Chapman, "Interview: Danganronpa Creator Kazutaka Kodaka," Anime News Network, July 22, 2015, https://www.animenewsnetwork.com/feature/2015-07-22/interview-danganronpa-creator-kazutaka kodaka/.90760.

In 2015, at the Game Developers Conference, Kazutaka added more insight into Junko:

> Junko has multiple personalities.... [including] Genocide Jack.... I wanted to create a character who was evil because they were evil, who only wanted pure despair. Without the possibility of redemption; they are bad and that's it. That's the kind of character I wanted to do ... The truth is that many girls want to dress up like her. If you read her dialogue, you think "Wow, what horrible things she says." But still, people want to be like her.[15]

Snow was the type of person Kazutaka was surprised by. Snow *so* strongly identified with Junko that their Instagram bio read "IRL Junko Enoshima" at one point. (IRL meaning "in real life.")

Many cosplayers and role-players try to avoid what is known as "bleed," which is associated with method acting. In taking on the mannerisms, expression, and sometimes even voice of a character to act them out for skits and photoshoots, performers sometimes begin to act like their characters even outside of costume or gaming, letting the character's personality and emotions "bleed over" into reality, coloring the way they act, react, and interact as themselves, or prompting them to still pretend to be the character outside of conventions, role-play, or cosplay. This is worsened in communities where bleed is encouraged—namely, where someone might be admired for embodying a character and replying "as" them, or in groups where there's sometimes shared bleed, with people's social interactions built on established *in-character* structures. This is especially so when people first meet while in character and only *afterward* meet as themselves, with only the shared experience or interest in the hobby as the grounds for friendship. Bleed can be dangerous if the person experiencing it negatively reacts to other people as if they were also characters, aiming the antagonism or bitterness their character feels for another *character* on the *person* embodying them after that person has shifted out of playacting.

---

15 Hyrule-enciclo, "El desarrollador Kazutaka Kodaka habla sobre la creación de Danganronpa - Koi-Nya.net," Koi-Nya.net, March 14, 2015, https://web.archive.org/web/20210121213300/https://www.koi-nya.net/2015/03/14/el-desarrollador-kazutaka-kodaka-habla-sobre-la-creacion-de-danganronpa; in translation from Spanish, possibly in translation from Japanese. Translation is as close as can be managed.

Most bleed is innocuous. An example of harmless bleed might be if a *Star Trek* cosplayer jokingly calls their car the "Starship Enterprise" or says they are having an "illogical" human emotion due to their half-Vulcan upbringing as a joke when excited about something. *Dangerous* bleed would be telling one's girlfriend when she is crying and upset that you do not understand *her* human emotions because you are half-Vulcan, and she should be less emotional. Harmless bleed might be bossing around a friend dramatically while matching the unique mannerisms, voice, and facial expression of *Gotham*'s the Penguin, letting them playfully complain what a harsh mob boss you are. Harmful bleed is shooting someone in the head as the Penguin in your living room.

Bleed can often be unintentional and positive—for anyone who has ever read a book or watched a film or TV show and gone "*that is so me!*," that is the point. Fiction encourages humans to empathize with the real world by identifying with characters in situations we may face daily, or may never have to face. Storytelling is supposed to teach us compassion. When small children pretend to be Disney princesses or one of the Power Rangers, they do not actually think they are those characters. But they're finding characters they relate to and wish to be more like, and in group play, inhabit their space and traits (compassionate, heroic, courageous) and identify members of their social group the same way; *you're the smart and shy Blue Ranger, and I'm the responsible leader—the Red Ranger!* Sports enthusiasts do something similar: they cheer and boo and put their emotions on the line for accomplishments they share with the larger-than-life athletes they root for, forming an identity around team fandom, villainizing other squads, picking a favorite player. However, they rarely think they *are* Micheal Jordan or Wayne Gretzky.

It's when the feeling of *that is so me!* becomes overwhelming that a deeper link called kinning may develop. Kinning tends to cross a line, being inherently somewhat unsettling, as it implies that a person feels they truly either are a character, or else that the character is real and speaks to them or through them. It can be a low-kinning: simply relating to the character; or high-kinning: feeling a strong, inseparable link between yourself and them. In serious cases, people feel that they embody them. In that context, it can feel strange and othering when "outsiders" claim that same character through cosplay or role-play, leading the kinned individual to feel annoyed, jealous, and angry. Kinning is not typically as serious as a deep delusion, but it does make cosplayers possessive of "their" character, who becomes an integral part of their social structure and their way of responding to the world at large.

Snow was known by the community to be particularly domineering about the character of Junko. They were the apex Junko in their friend group, and in an ironic twist (because Snow made money by styling and selling Junko wigs for other cosplayers), Snow was said to disparage other cosplayers who took on the character over the way they looked. Snow did, it is important to mention, allow others cosplaying Junko into their social group, but this was only when they'd take on a different persona from *Danganropa* themselves.

In a report by *Rolling Stone*, Megan Gross—who had dated Helen Hastings in high school—described parties at Snow's house as eccentric, saying there were a mix of people there that were either self-diagnosed with dissociative identity disorder (DID; known colloquially as multiple personality disorder) or who felt strongly kinned to their characters. They'd slip into these alternate personalities easily, changing the way they spoke, acted, and moved, and occasionally becoming aggressive or physical as their character, or "alter," called for it. "There was a lot of bouncing around between identities, and they enforced each other's issues with identity."[16]

While it isn't atypical in cosplay circles to have parties that revolve around character identities, claiming DID without diagnosis would be taking it a step too far. Snow kept a list of their alters public, ranked in order of how close they felt to them. Distressingly, many of them were villains.

In an adorable TikTok of Helen,[17] she dons a dark green curly wig and drawn-on blotchy freckles and lip-syncs to a song while cosplaying Izuku "Deku" Midoriya, the kind and dauntless protago-

16 Dickson, "They Were Close Friends and Cosplay Stars."

17 Helen Hastings (@helencosplay), TikTok, February 19, 2019, https://www.tiktok.com/@helenscosplay/video/6659773609969454341.

nist from *My Hero Academia*. In comparison, one of Snow's publicly listed alters was Himiko Toga from the same show. Toga is an unstable sadist whose power is transforming into anyone whose blood she ingests. Toga was violently in love with Deku.

Other characters Snow gained a following from making content as were Harley Quinn, the jaunty *Batman* villain; Bill Cipher, the demonic antagonist from *Gravity Falls*; and Yuno Gasai, a violent murderer in the anime *Future Diary*. When they cosplayed as heroes or good-coded characters, their content nonetheless skewed edgy. As Hatsune Miku, the innocuous *Vocaloid* singer, they lip-synced to the lyrics, "I'm the girl you'd die for. I chew you up and I spit you out"[18] In another video, cosplaying as gamer-turned-defense-pilot Hana Song from *Overwatch*, Snow lip-synchs the aviatrix going, "*Bam Bam Bam*!,"[19] firing at the camera with their hand.

In yet another TikTok, Snow speaks over prerecorded audio in a bloodied nurse's outfit, asking, "Do you target people who have been mean to you, or unkind?" Snow replies to their own question with, "I kill people I like."[20]

Controversy began to swirl around Snow's off-color content long before Helen's death, when several community members felt Snow crossed a line with one of their *Danganropa* music video and photo shoots—which featured Snow and friends being disrespectful at a local graveyard.

They lay on hallowed ground in costumes, put their feet up on graves, and sat on headstones for risqué panty shots. It was also reported, though not substantiated, that Snow, in their short-cut dress, was sitting on headstones without any undergarments on at all.[21]

While none of this qualifies as necessarily illegal—they didn't vandalize graves, enter restricted areas, or steal—it's bad manners in

---

18 Snow (@yandere.freak_fp), "Snows Hatsune Miku cosplay" TikTok, June 20, 2021, https://www.tiktok.com/@yandere.freak_fp/video/6975964590911819014.

19 Snow (@snowthesaltqueen.fp), TikTok, August 19, 2023, https://www.tiktok.com/@snowthesalt queen.fp/video/7269026691715058977.

20 Snow (@snowthesaltqueen.fp), TikTok, February 18, 2023, https://www.tiktok.com/@ snowthesalt queen.fp/video/7201550096817786117.

21 The Hot Box, "The Sordid Story of SnowtheSaltQueen," YouTube, October 2, 2021, https://www.youtube. com/watch?v=bNYTq7zCnUQ.

a consecrated space where mourners put their loved ones to final rest. This seemed obvious to the internet at large, which went into a furor over it. Rather than the cosplay group apologizing for their actions and pleading regrettable ignorance, Snow's first major controversy erupted around the group doubling down. Their cameraman posted a multipart defense of their behavior, noting that it wasn't criminal, they hadn't bothered any visitors, they'd selected graves not called on recently, and they wanted to pay their respects to the dead by capturing the beauty of their headstones with their own cosplay art. The videographer finished the defense with, "That video was bomb tbh y'all just wanting to be mad."[22]

West Hill Cemetery management was so distressed by the videos and the thousands of views, comments, and outreach from concerned citizens that they made a formal response, with the foreman at the time, Clinton Daniel Jr., writing, "I assure you we didn't and wouldn't give anyone permission to do anything like this." Superintendent Jimmy Mrozinski added, "I have already located one Instagram account mentioned and gave a stern warning on it for them to stay out of the cemetery or they will be arrested for violating city ordinances within the cemetery."

It is common for cemeteries to have their own rules, which the group may have violated. And though the group impressed upon their online followings that they didn't vandalize any graves, they *did* stand on them, placing boots and partially bare backsides on time-worn headstones. While the cameraman let audiences know that they only selected graves that were 100 years or older, they precluded the information that such graves in Sherman, Texas, include that of an enslaved girl tattooed by her slavers, sixty-six victims of a devastating tornado buried en masse, and the "father" of the city of Sherman itself, who relocated the Grayson County seat to there. These are lives and legacies to be remembered and respected, not besmirched, and often such headstones require the most care and upkeep.

Unfortunately, there exist records of Snow being not quite so respectful as their friends argued they were. Snow posted an

22 The Hot Box, "The Sordid Story."

Instagram story with a photo of a tombstone in the shape of a lounge chair and captioned it "My future tomb stone," then another of their face after they'd gotten home, with a written prompt to fans: "petition for when I die a hoard of junko cosplayers/kinnies to party on my grave." Snow also posted content mocking those upset about the shoot and wrote on Twitter that they'd be taking payments via PayPal to interrupt funerals with improvisational monologues. In the pantheon of teenagers being glib, this didn't seem so terrible; but later, reworked into the context of having fired a bullet into a friend's head, it felt sinister.

When the non-apology didn't go over well, Snow conducted a TikTok live addressing the controversy—while putting on makeup. In surviving footage that has been reposted, Snow states, "There's been RAVES at graveyards! But apparently, it's like a whole thing you're like not supposed to like touch the gravestones.... I didn't know there were so many god damn rules about graveyards, like, *oh my god*.... I still don't understand why it's wrong."

Snow's next controversy was pet related. They had found a pair of sick stray kittens and posted a link to their PayPal asking for donations to help with their care. Several people made allegations that Snow was lying, that the cats weren't ill, and that Snow had pocketed all the money. These allegations didn't seem to be based on anything except perhaps lack of updates or proof that the cats were being cared for and suspicions of a side hustle. Again, Snow would take to TikTok live to address the situation while applying makeup.

> I swear to god, if you bring up the kittens right now, I'm going to lose my fucking shit. I've been in and out of the animal hospital for like two fucking weeks with those cats. I did everything I could to save them and I DID manage to save one of 'em. I literally caught a parasite from them. Like, I—it was a contagious parasite TO ME and I CAUGHT IT.... You can eat my fucking ass.... I donated 700 of my own money and only raised about 200.... I will *end you* ... especially the fact that the person you're getting that information from, I know who they are, and I *know* what they've done, and if you knew the kind of things that that person has done, you would not be following them. I mean I may be

problematic or whatever, but I didn't go around literally telling people to *kill themselves*.

It seems likely that Snow really did help the cats, having kept one of them and having a traceable history of both caring for strays and asking for donations to do so—though not receiving much help in that regard. Perhaps the graveyard fiasco could have been ended by providing an apology, or perhaps an apology would have been belittled as too little too late, or insincere. Perhaps the cat storm could have been avoided by posting vet bills and bank statements more quickly. Perhaps they should not have thrown "shade" onto a random third party, smearing an unnamed person to add layers to the drama. But online arguments still meant views, and Snow was getting thousands and thousands of views—a hate click is still a click, after all—and they were mostly surrounded by supportive friends.

When friends did *not* support Snow, however, they might be in for revenge. In one case, when Snow was uninvited from attending an 18+ panel at a convention following a bitter feud with one of the guests, a former friend named Dolly Lace says Snow allegedly reported the panel to the convention for having underage attendees in the audience.[23] This is a major accusation at a convention, where 18+ panels might involve sexual content. Snow, though, who drank alcohol with friends under the age of twenty-one, would have been motivated more by retribution than concern if this were the case.

Dolly Lace added troubling context to the story:

"[Snow] was never invited.... and was actually blacklisted because they bullied one of the panelists to the point of suicidal thoughts and called them 'dead girl walking' whenever they made a reappearance at conventions. My cohost and I banned Snow from attending for the safety of the panelists, and Snow knew this. Snow tried to enter anyways and was denied entry, as expected. They got pissed, then went around lying, saying I personally invited them to my panel just to humiliate them. They then went to security saying there were minors in the panel and we were drinking. No one was drinking, and the only minor was a seventeen-year-old who was given permission by [the convention] to be in the panel room ... given their birthday was in

23 Dickson, "They Were Close Friends and Cosplay Stars."

two days. But because of Snow's scene I had to remove them from the panel. Also, the panel was 18+ due to language. No sex. No drinking. No explicit content.[24]

Despite these major blips, much of the angry discourse around Snow in the cosplay community was centered on the character of Junko herself. In a TikTok by cosplayer @AderuKitten (Adelle), Adelle comes on screen wearing a Junko wig and says, "I wasn't playing around. I need about three more of these to style these *correctly*, but I'm coming for your brand, bitch. So watch out. Let's see who the real Junko is."[25] Adelle's video is labeled: "Whos the salt queen now huh. Steal my shit and get hit. #snowthesaltqueen."

Nearly fifty people replied, looking forward to the showdown between them.

This feud, from what can be pieced together from online videos, seems to stem either from Snow's possessiveness of the character or—in what would become one of Snow's biggest online hullabaloos—Snow taking commission money to style Junko wigs for other cosplayers, but leaving some paying customers feeling ripped off. Many people wanted "the" Junko Enoshima to style their wigs, even at the cost of $300 a pop, but were disappointed after their payment was made. Wigs arrived late, were accused of being sloppily done, barely styled, or too flat. Adelle also began selling styled Junko wigs—for $200. Her mention that "I need about three more of these" referred to additions of more clip-on hair to make Junko's wackily voluminous side ponytails—a jab at Snow's wigs, as people complained they were too thin and inaccurate.

In another video by Adelle, she pokes direct fun at Snow's profile bio while dressed fully as Junko, with an audio overlay that says "I am *THE IRL* Junko Enoshim. She is me. I am her. KINNING!" The video was labeled "fuk u snow."[26]

---

24 Dolly Lace through Instagram with the author, January 7, 2025.

25 Adelle (@aderukitten), "Whos the salt queen now huh. Steal my shit and get hit," TikTok, June 3, 2019, https://www.tiktok.com/@aderukitten/video/6710735626473311494.

26 Adelle (@aderukitten), "Fuk u snow" TikTok, July 6, 2019, https://www.tiktok.com/@aderukitten/video/6710735626473311494.

Several commenters replied, some saying Adelle was a better Junko, some saying Snow was better, and some confused as to why comparisons had to be made at all. Adelle would then upload several more TikToks discussing her Junko wig commissions. Commenters seemed to confirm that in this duel of wig stylists, Adelle was winning:[27]

@noomnooom: it looks better AND is cheaper?! WOW

@beebuzzez: 100 less than snow and a thousand times better

@lolrockemoji: @snowthesaltqueen look at this wig and look at yours, take notes ✍

Adelle continued to post more videos and captions calling out Snow. But when did controversy over a *wig* really begin to bubble over? It came after Snow first posted about opening commissions on the social media site Tumblr. Their fee was high: $175 for materials and $125 for labor. Cosplayer and YouTuber @StarDere, with 4.5k subscribers, was one of the customers to excitedly place an order. They were a huge fan of Snow and truly looked up to their cosplays, especially that of Junko. They would later post a video about the ordeal,[28] with the description, "you could say I'm a bit ... salty."

It has been viewed more than sixty-five thousand times.

"Snow was my favorite cosplayer ..." Star begins before going on to explain, very cordially, what their experience was like. The wig took longer to make than quoted, and it was difficult to get in touch to ask for updates from Snow, who only communicated through socials but was so popular that messages got buried. Snow then turned off their account for a time as something of a publicity stunt, according to Star, with rumors swirling that they'd been kidnapped.

Star and a friend reached out again and again to ask about the wig's progress—it had been prepaid for—but also with some concern about Snow's whereabouts. When the wig didn't arrive on time before Star had to leave home to travel, they feared it had been stolen. Some of her winter holiday parcels—shipped to Star's

27 Adelle (@aderukitten), "My wig commissions will be $200. This wig was a practice wig. Message me on insta 4 commissions!" TikTok, July 7, 2019, https://www.tiktok.com/@aderukitten/video/6711034019414281478.

28 Stardere, "The $300 Junko Wig," YouTube, August 20, 2019, https://www.tiktok.com/@aderukitten/video/6711034019414281478.

dad—*had* been filched from their doorstep when she was out. The information about the theft was shared with Snow, and since it couldn't be verified whether or not the wig was among those stolen packages, Snow finally replied—offering to remake the wig at the reduced cost of $135.

At this point, Star thought the only issue was that the wig had not arrived in a timely manner, and Snow did not communicate quickly. She assumed if it had arrived on the date intended, before her departure, she would have been present to collect it, and this issue would never have occurred. Nonetheless, she agreed to pay for a replacement wig. But then, to her surprise, a box did arrive with the *original* order. The second wig had not shipped yet—and, as it turned out, would never arrive at all. This would mean that Snow perhaps knowingly allowed a second wig to be paid for without notifying the customer that the first hadn't even been sent before the thefts, then simply allowed the first to arrive in place of the second, raking in the cash for both.

But Star was mostly alarmed by *how* the wig arrived: in a small Amazon box with the individual parts in plastic Kroger grocery bags. It didn't come on a wig stand or with anything to keep it safely shaped correctly, as might be expected of a cosplay commission. It came with six individual clips for two ponytails, not assembled. Also in the box were wefts, but with no explanation of how to use them or how to combine the wig parts. As far as Star could tell, minimal effort went into styling the wig, and all of the parts could have been bought as-is, except for perhaps the fringe on the base wig, which Star said was poorly and unevenly done. The wig looked nothing like Snow's own, not having nearly the same volume, because it was unstyled.

In a later edit to the video's description, Star adds, "SO just found out my friend also bought a DDLC club cosplay from snow but [they] still haven't provided?? apparently [Snow] ordered something 'in the wrong size' and then ghosted.... bro I'm mad." There being three mishaps in a row was unlikely. People felt Snow was grifting the community.

Snow then went onto their @Yandere.Freak TikTok profile to respond to some of the criticism. Snow would give a very credible explanation for how to properly use what had been sent to Star, and how to make it look like their own version of the Junko style. The only issue with the video is that it's of Snow explaining how to assemble and coiffe the wig—something that, if you are hired to create a custom character wig, should be done by *you*. Snow alleges that a refund was offered to unhappy customers, but customers wanted to keep the wigs.

Another YouTube user—@TheHotBox, with nearly 180k followers—documented many of the Snow controversies. He also clearly had his own beef with Snow—in a video entitled "The Sordid Story of SnowtheSaltQueen," uploaded after Helen's shooting,[29] he alleges that Snow falsified legal documents. Snow sent him a cease and desist letter attached to an email, which @TheHotBox posted online, concerning defamation and libel. It reads, in part, "The defamatory statements include, but are not limited to, the following: Rape accusations." There is never any explanation as to where Snow's accusation has come from or what it is in reference to, but the quick response showed Snow was very aware of public opinion, kept an ear to the rumor mill and was willing to get litigious over it—falsified or not.

Snow lived a fairly tumultuous life in the public eye. Yet despite all controversies, they still had more defenders than detractors. And above all defenders, there was the inner circle.

I'll Be the Hero and No One Can Stop Me

Helen Rose Hastings grew up in urban Texas, the fifth child of Philip Hastings and the first child of Susan Rosenberg. Her parents both worked at Baylor College of Medicine as highly regarded geneticists. Baylor is part of a large campus in the heart of Houston, sitting on the edge of Hermann Park; 455 acres of green grass and flowing fountains, a stone's throw from the Museum of Natural Science.

The couple had Helen late in life, with Philip already old enough to potentially have been a grandfather, gray at more than just his temples at sixty-five and having had four sons and three wives before

29 The Hot Box, "The Sordid Story."

Helen came along.[30] Susan, by contrast, was just over two decades younger, but still at a difficult age to fall pregnant for the first time. She developed a serious pregnancy complication that led to the decision that Helen would have to be her only biological child—as first reported by *Rolling Stone* when she shared Helen's story with the magazine.[31]

Susan has since stopped giving interviews. She kindly considered it for this book, but ultimately chose not to follow up. It makes immediate sense—Susan lost the child she'd worked so hard to bring into the world that hot and humid July 2, 2002.

Helen was a beautiful and intelligent child, English and Greek and Jewish in origin, with round cheeks, bright, sparkling eyes, and a bowed mouth. She was small in stature and remained so to adulthood, only managing just a few centimeters over five feet in total. Helen in Hebrew means "light" and in Greek is "shining," like the face that launched a thousand ships in *The Iliad*.

As a youngster, Helen launched *herself*—into new activities as well as around the globe on her parents' work trips, visiting Europe and Asia before she was thirteen. Back at home, she tackled sports, extracurriculars, and even the performing arts. She loved to sing and climb and play music and build and learn. Helen gained a particular interest in Japan on a trip to Tokyo, where she became convinced that Japan needed more women in STEM. She'd grasped a salient point; as recently as in 2023, Japan ranked *last* within developed nations in gender parity in STEM, mainly due to gender bias surrounding motherhood.[32] Japan has just one female for every seven male scientists and only 16% of women in university major in these subjects, despite school-age Japanese girls scoring third highest globally in science and second highest in math. Helen thought she might be able to do something with her life that could help balance the scales.

---

30 "Philip J. Hastings, Ph.D.," BCM.edu, accessed April 30, 2025, https://www.bcm.edu/people-search/philip-hastings-22827.

31 Dickson, "They Were Close Friends and Cosplay Stars."

32 Mariko Katsumura, "How Japan Is Encouraging More Women in STEM Studies," World Economic Forum, July 17, 2023, https://www.weforum.org/stories/2023/07/japan-encouraging-women-into-stem.

Socially aware, culturally competent, warm, and talkative, she seemed on track across the board. Helen was engaged in *living* life, had a stable family background economically and educationally, and was being raised in a solid school district with plenty of hobbies to engage her mind. Her only gripe seemed to be that with four much older half-brothers—Jeffrey, Jeremy, Adrian, and Simon—she'd never be the big sister or have a sister.

Then middle school struck, and with it, a number of issues began to seethe to the surface. First, Helen began to discover her sexuality—that she was pansexual, attracted to all genders—and later on, her own gender fluidity, switching to using both the pronouns she/her and they/them. But once publicly outed as nonbinary and pansexual, school life became difficult. This was compounded by remaining naturally small as her peers shot up around her, making her a ripe target for bullies. Then there was her developing misophonia, too: a condition that makes loud or overlapping sounds almost unbearable, rendering socializing in big groups arduous. Side effects of misophonia can be embarrassing, causing sufferers to sometimes have over-the-top physiological or emotional responses, becoming "crazed" by noise, flying into fits of panic or rage, even hurling themselves out of rooms to escape the noise. The stigma against her deepened as she literally fled social situations or sat wincing through groupwork.

Helen then began to suffer from panic attacks, worsened by a budding depression triggered in her teen years. She developed an eating disorder, perpetually unhappy with her propensity for retaining body fat.[33] By high school, her mother had her enrolled in Fusion Academy in an attempt to counteract the mounting challenges. Fusion is a one teacher to one student private school chain that prides itself on a personalized education for students "with learning, social, or emotional differences."[34] Classes at Fusion can cost as much as $5,280 per course, *per term* for advanced placement (AP)

---

33 Helen Hasting (@helencosplay), "We done called ourselves out" TikTok, August 16, 2020, https://www.tiktok.com/@helenscosplay/video/6861656004858301701.

34 "Fusion Academy Campuses: A Private Education Community," accessed April 30, 2025, https://www.fusionacademy.com/campuses.

classes. A typical student will take up to fifteen classes across three terms, meaning that anyone who particularly excels and takes six AP courses in a year could be looking at a tuition of more than $68,000 for just one year of secondary school.

There was no doubt that Helen was a capable youth, despite any setbacks. She would eventually gain admission to Oberlin College, which has just a 33% acceptance rate. 78% of the Oberlin student body applies with a GPA of 3.7 or higher, with its students tending to be in the top 5% of their graduating classes.[35]

Helen's parents were determined to give her a good future. Their efforts didn't always rub Helen the right way, as she remarked on a TikTok video that she was left with "mommy issues." As she aged—as with many a teenager—there was friction at home. Her family was a loving one despite any friction and supportive even through tough times. There was, however, a sense of distance—perhaps because of the busy jobs or advanced age of her parents. When Helen turned eighteen, she made that distance physical, preferring her friend groups to her parents' company. But the remoteness was never total. Even when she moved out, the family still shared holidays and joyrides together. Especially Helen and Susan.

But Helen's shifting identity and priorities meant that in tenth grade, when through local anime conventions she met Snow—a winsome and popular then-genderfluid cosplay idol—it was like the clouds had parted. They became fast friends, and Helen—who felt she could explore her gender and hobbies in the rarefied constellation of community that revolved around Snow—became a defensive comrade. She stood by Snow through every controversy, her loyalty unwavering. She didn't see any red flags, only green for go, always seeking inclusion under the awning of Snow's popularity. Underage, she didn't mind being surrounded by drink or drugs when it was with Snow and their "cool" friends.

Snow, in turn, took Helen's side against an unpleasant ex, which only brought them closer. And Helen, just like Snow, made their own TikTok profile page based on cosplay content, using the handle

35 "Class of 2028 Profile," Oberlin.edu, accessed June 10, 2024, https://www.oberlin.edu/admissions-and-aid/class-profile.

@HelensCosplays. There, she filmed lip-sync videos in costume just like Snow did, and they both cosplayed from a lot of the same media—*My Hero Academia*, *Homestuck*, and *Danganropa*. In 2018 they shot a video together, which Helen tagged "#squadgoals." The first still-working video on her prolific TikTok is a duet with Snow.[36] Helen had found her community in these bright and rising stars. It made sense to want to emulate them.

But Helen was still very much an adolescent when she and Snow met. Her room in her childhood home was a sanctuary to her hobbies, with walls decorated in posters of Disney princesses, anime art, plushie keychains, and drawings that an ex-girlfriend had made. She was obsessed with her beautiful long-haired cat, Willa. Her bed was a mountain of stuffed animals she liked to cuddle to sleep—dinosaurs, whales, and rainbow hearts. She was becoming more herself each day, but "herself" was still a youngster then, still taking shape and looking for role models.

In high school, Helen had few friends outside her cosplay circle (who did not attend the same institution as her), but all that was about to change at Oberlin College. Newly eighteen, Helen's mom took her on a cross-country road trip to her new life in Ohio. She took to dorming like a fish to water, making friends and starting to find her people in the freshman class. Oberlin is known for its out-of-the-box thinkers, never minding a bit of quirk. When Helen texted the dormitory groupchat in search of milk to make a TikTok about boobs, someone readily provided. No questions were asked, no pause was given.

1,266 miles away from the place that had left her scarred and isolated, she had found a fit. Helen decided to major in neurobiology—but also in psychology and in art. One degree is hard enough, but triple-majoring is multitasking on a Herculean level. At Oberlin, it was clear Helen felt she could explore herself intellectually, trying a bit of everything before deciding on her future path.

The grassy lead-up to Dascomb Hall is dotted with violets when it's warm out. It houses 170 "first experience" students, and Helen was lucky enough to have a single room there to herself—a college

36 Helen Hasting (@helencosplay),"#duet with @snowthesaltqueen," TikTok, July 23, 2017, https://www.tiktok.com/@helenscosplay/video/253763794026397698.

luxury. The dorm had television rooms and lounges for students and even a World Cultures Wing. It was set up to encourage socialization and hosted events and theme nights to help freshmen find their group. And find them, she did. Helen swiftly had a close-knit unit form around her, making fast friends thanks to her zany wit and cheerful extroversion.

While she still shot some cosplay-themed TikToks, such as a costumed GRWM (Get Ready With Me), it was in her freshman year of college that her social media stopped being so largely about cosplay and started to be more about *her*. About Helen. Helen in her threadbare room with an explosion of laundry, paper boxes, and desk trinkets. Helen eating canned ravioli on the floor with friends, playing silly card games, and becoming a nexus for people on her floor. Helen starting to identify as a lesbian and having crushes on the young women she was meeting.

It was Helen in all her fullness and realness. According to her own self-descriptions from that time, that meant a girl with ADD, one who apologized often and suffered from depression and still struggled with panic attacks. Who was garrulous, loved helping, and who dyed her fluffy hair in bright pinks and purples. She played guitar and drums, listened to emo and punk music. She engaged in activism. She became known for her cool fashion sense and llama-themed socks.

She identified as hypersexual, was a voracious reader, and couldn't dance. She considered herself funny, drove well, enjoyed drawing and cooking, forgot things easily, was insecure about her body, played video games, and always gave too much of herself. She could be jealous and clingy, and she preferred bossy girls to shy ones. She had an infectious laugh that sounded like a cherub giggling, like bubbles of mirth, and it came easily; a quick-draw chuckle.

At the same time, Helen still struggled. In one TikTok post, she said the reason she wasn't dating was "because the last time I dated someone it was so traumatic that I have no memory of those two entire years."[37] That TikTok was posted two days before Helen would be shot by Snow.

Before leaving for college, Helen had lived for two weeks at Snow's place in the Houston suburbs, a place akin to a frat house given all the people, mess, and parties. It was chock full of pets, too. The year was 2020, COVID-19 was devastating America, and Helen had preferred to be quarantined with people closer to her own age than family; especially her father, who qualified as elderly during the pandemic, so any exposure would have proven a huge risk to his health. She'd find herself back again at Snow's house abruptly mid-semester in November of 2020, too, after her first semester on Oberlin's campus came to a screeching halt with the pronouncement that Ohio was shutting down in-person classes to curb the spread of disease. Virtual classes would fill the void until there could be a return to campus.

Helen planned to live at Snow's for the duration, her chances at normalcy stymied just as they had been gaining traction. She was set to return in late January.

In those couple of months, Helen made plans—safely. Outdoor celebrations with friends and family, convention preparation for future costumes, and poring over job opportunities at labs for the summer. There was an alfresco Thanksgiving. The stars bore witness to heart-to-hearts with her mom, who visited when she could.

On January 17, 2021, it was nearly time to return to Oberlin from the Wonderland of communal living with kinning costumers. Snow had been having vodka sodas and had a gun out. Though it had belonged to an ex who'd long since moved out, that evening, it belonged to the Penguin, the sinister Gothamite. Snow said they always took the magazine out when they played with the gun. Friends would say they thought all the bullets had been taken from the home by Snow's ex.

Bang.

Helen Rose Hastings was shot in the left side of the head, the muzzle of the gun almost right against her skin. Helen hit the floor

---

37 Helen Hasting (@helencosplay), "#stitch with @stephfabry haha and that's on abusive relationships," TikTok, January 15, 2021, https://www.tiktok.com/@helenscosplay/video/6918116937796996357.

face down and the group panicked. They grabbed a stuffed bear to stop the bleeding—perhaps the large plushie replica of Junko's Monokuma bear, used during her killing games. Snow rushed to get a towel. Paramedics and police were called. Helen was taken to the hospital as the witnesses filed outside to give statements. Everyone was cooperative. But shaken.

The hospital wanted three days to find appropriate matches for organ donations, but Helen's mother, Susan, gave them two. She sang softly to Helen as she lay, unresponsive—songs like "Hey Jude" and "Seasons of Love." Helen died on January 19, 2021, her hand in Susan's.

In a video Helen had uploaded to TikTok during her time at Oberlin, an audio overlay asks the subject to "put one finger down if you don't participate in cancel culture and [instead] let people grow and apologize for mistakes in the past." Helen gestures up at captions she'd written as they popped up, which read:

> Im close friends with snowthesaltqueen ive seen the harm cancel culture can do up close.[38]

Would Helen have forgiven Snow for what then happened? Her family thinks so.

Many of Helen's friends didn't hear about her death for some time. It was covered in *The Oberlin Review* on February 5, 2021. "Hastings was known for her laughter, enthusiasm, and compassion. Hastings was interested in helping treat misophonia..."[39] But they wouldn't know the reason for her death for months to come. Many assumed it had been suicide.

Status: Hiatus

The Oberlin bulletin's lack of immediacy and specificity meant that Helen's was a surprisingly quiet passing for a member of the Freshman community. Likewise, the incident was not initially given

38 Helen Hastings (@helencosplay), "Another one!" TikTok, September 9, 2020, https://www.tiktok.com/@helenscosplay/video/6870525204011961605.

39 Anisa Curry Vietze and Madison Olsen, "In Memory of Helen Hastings, College First-Year," *The Oberlin Review*, February 5, 2021, https://oberlinreview.org/22396/news/in-memory-of-helen-hastings-college-first-year.

media coverage outside of Oberlin, so word was mum on the convention circuit, where news usually passes like wildfire between highly communal cosplayers. Especially when it involves someone as public-facing as Snow, or something as brutal as gun violence.

Snow was a celebrity, in a sense, and there had been several witnesses at the party as well. But the news didn't seep through the cracks for a long, *long* time. There was no public funeral information, no vigil, nor any online obituaries. The major media blowout was still a ways to come. This was the brief quiet before things became *really weird*. When online rubberneckers learned the horrifying reality months later, *weird* would take on a *menacing* overtone.

Most of the criticism leveled at Snow wasn't for accidentally shooting a close friend. It was for Snow's behavior after the fact, which eclipsed silence and thundered its way into inappropriate.

Snow took a hiatus from social media after being released on bail, posting on January 21, 2021, to TikTok to allay concerns and rumors,

> I will be taking a hiatus, I'm unsure how long but I will keep you updated!

A hiatus by an online influencer is usually conducted when "real life" becomes too overwhelming to churn out content—which, for Snow, it certainly had. While people may have speculated what made the screen go dark, those who'd been to Snow's party didn't speak up—in part because the case against Snow was still being assembled and in part because the evening had been traumatic for them, too. As witnesses, it was their job to say less to the public, not more. And that was Snow's job, too—to only speak to police and lawyers, to mourn the loss of Helen, and to give the family their privacy. But then on February 10, something extraordinary happened.

> Hiatus is over! Expect more mikan tomorrow and please interact!!

Snow posted a video to TikTok featuring themself as the murderous character of Mikan, another yandere from *Danganropa*. More videos followed. One featured Snow as Anyo Aishi from the game *Yandere Simulator*, swinging a bat threateningly and then smiling and pretending at innocence, with a background smeared in bloody handprints. In another, also featuring a bloodied backdrop, Snow lip-syncs to a twisted overlay of "Do You Want to Build a Snowman?" from Disney's *Frozen*, but with the lyrics warped into "Will you help me hide a body~?" And another, this time of Snow as the homicidal villain Toga, singing along to "The Red Means I Love You" by Madds Buckley: "And goodness you're bleeding / What a wonderful feeling / You're down and you're pleading / My head is just reeling / The red means I love you!"

This content was very much on-brand for Snow, so no one batted an eye initially. But once what had happened that January evening went public, nearly ten months later, the tone-deafness of posting murder-glorifying and violence-happy content hit the cosplay community like a truck. The reaction was both volatile and viral. Snow became enemy #1.

Just days after Helen's death, Snow was also posting pay-to-view content to their Patreon platform, most of it not G-rated. For Snow, content was a job, and taking time off meant losing income.

So in November of 2021, when the internet outside of the convention community caught wind of the story after breakout reporting by *Rolling Stone*, people began searching for Snow online and found profiles littered with disturbing content—outrage swirled. People wanted to know: What did happen that night? Was Snow guilty of a crime, or was it a terrible accident? And if the latter, why did Snow seem so devoid of empathy or shame? Once the greater community found out, the niche cosplay community and Helen's Oberlin friends weren't far behind.

Deputy Margarita Nolan with the Harris County Sheriff's Office Homicide Unit was assigned to investigate what *had* happened that night. The incident took place at 12007 Soft Pines Drive, a pretty family home with four bedrooms, four baths, and a balcony overlooking a cheery green lawn. With plenty of hang space, it was the perfect spot for young adult friends to chill.

At 1:30 a.m. on January 17, Deputy Nolan took over from Constable R. Glick, who had overseen Helen being taken to Houston Northwest Hospital. There were six witnesses for Glick to question, including Snow. They were kept separate to see if their statements corroborated or contradicted. They made audio recordings of each witness, then compiled them in detailed police reports.

The Story, According to ...

Snow. Snow told the police that Helen had been visiting over a period of months. Snow had been drinking since much earlier in the day than the others, who had all gone out to Galveston, an amusement park city with a pleasure pier in Texas. Snow had also been doing marijuana. Snow admits that by the evening, everyone was drinking, though Helen, at just eighteen, was underage. Snow at the time was twenty-two.

Snow had played with the gun before. It was a great cosplay prop and, according to them, the ex had taken all of the bullets with him when he'd left the relationship and the house. While still together, he'd also instructed Snow on how to take the magazine out so the Glock couldn't lethally fire, no matter what. Snow thought they had taken the magazine out.

The youngsters had been playing pass-around with the gun for two or three hours as they drank, slowly becoming very inebriated, but no one was frightened, as they'd had no issues with the weapon prior. Then Helen jokingly asked Snow to shoot her, and Snow pulled the trigger with one hand, assuming nothing would happen. It had been making clicking sounds beforehand, up to four times while firing nothing. They were shocked when, instead of clicking, it dislodged a bullet.

Everyone in the room had touched the gun that night, but it had mostly rested in Snow's own front pocket. When police asked who'd shot Helen, Snow took immediate responsibility, saying they hadn't been paying enough attention and that it was all their fault. They had wanted to look similar to the Penguin character on the TV. The gun had never fired with them before.

Snow attested that they'd also pointed the gun at themselves. A friend, Danielle, came up and asked to be shot before Helen. Helen had gone next.

> Defendant stated [they] did not remember putting the magazine in the gun and stated [they] might have been really drunk and might have put it in not thinking anything of it.

But the gun had also been on the counter, when it wasn't in Snow's pocket. So other people could have messed with it. Snow hadn't seen anyone else touch it beforehand.

Danielle. Aged nineteen at the time, Danielle had been at the house since Thursday, January 14, to hang out with Alyssa, another friend who lived there. She was in the kitchen when she heard a bang. When she returned, Snow was screaming, then said they'd shot Helen and it was an accident, that Helen had been saying "Shoot me, shoot me!" Danielle agreed they'd all been playing with the gun beforehand, which had been taken from the garage.

As Snow defended themself to the group, in shock, Alyssa had knelt to check Helen's pulse.

AJ. At age twenty-one, AJ had lived at the Soft Pines residence for two months. She didn't like the gun and told the group to be careful and to put it away. According to AJ, Helen said, "Hey, haha, put the gun to my head," and then jokingly asked Snow to pull the trigger. So Snow did. Everyone began to scream and cry, and 911 was quickly called. AJ said she knew that Snow possessed the gun, but she was unsure who else that night had touched it. She was standing behind Helen when the shooting occurred.

She unknowingly disagreed with Snow's description of events, saying she hadn't seen Snow playing with it or clicking it prior to shooting Helen. She didn't know why Snow went to get the gun or when they did so. AJ's testimony also contradicts the idea that everyone present was comfortable with the gun being out.

Alex. Aged nineteen, Alex also lived at Soft Pines and was on the sofa watching *Gotham*. She says that Snow, Helen, and Danielle all got up to go play around with the gun. She then heard the gunfire, saw Helen on the floor, and in astonishment, watched as they rushed to apply pressure to her head. Someone called 911. She said she only saw Snow and no one else really handling the gun that night, perhaps implying Helen and Danielle didn't get a turn, or simply that she hadn't observed it. She said Snow was keeping it in a pants pocket. When Helen and Snow were goofing around with it, she overheard Snow egging *Helen* on. She did not hear Helen ask for the gun to be put up to her head. She also didn't see Snow point the gun at anyone else, or herself. When asked why then this might have happened, she replied it was because their "friend group is wild, dumb, and does jokes all the time." She thought the last time the gun had even been taken out was in August of 2020.

Alex's statement seems to contradict statements that everyone played with the gun, that the gun was taken out often, and that it was Helen who asked to be shot at. Alex's statement is least in line with the rest.

Olivia. Another resident, Olivia, was twenty-one at the time. The group was watching television and being silly, and then she looked up and saw Helen face down on the floor and bleeding. She'd had headphones in and didn't see who had the gun or witness Snow point it at Helen. There was screaming and panic as friends got up to find something to apply pressure with. Snow was on the floor with Helen, and Olivia says she herself moved the gun away from Snow, then went to get the stuffed bear after making sure Helen was still breathing and had a heartbeat. Olivia attested the ex-boyfriend had taken the ammunition with him but must have forgotten to take it out of one magazine. She thought that perhaps the empty magazine had been exchanged for a loaded one, somehow.

She told the detective that she believed there were two magazines, and that the blank one was always the one loaded into the gun and there must have been a mix-up—but that no one had bothered to check if there was live ammunition.

Bailey. Aged eighteen at the time, Bailey was a guest at the party. She'd been into the *Gotham* role-play and requested of Snow, "Shoot me now!" Helen had said, "Me next, me next," while horsing around, according to Bailey. Bailey said that Snow took the clip out at that point, "so no one gets hurt." But that was earlier in the night.

Bailey admitted she didn't know who put it back inside. She'd returned to watching *Gotham* at the time of the incident. Startlingly, Bailey added that Snow must have known there was ammo in the clip, because they'd both seen it when Snow took the clip out for safety earlier. However, Bailey also firmly believed Snow did not know the clip had been put *back into* the gun.

It was because Helen kept saying, "Me next, me next," that Snow obliged at last. Bailey ran outside in a complete panic at the sound of a real shot ringing out.

In all these testimonies, there is some discord about who touched the gun, who moved it, and when. They all had different recollections of what Helen had said, if anything at all, and how the gun had come to be pointed at her. Most distressingly, they all had different ideas about who knew the gun had been empty versus full, and who knew the magazine was loaded versus empty. But they all agreed on the shooter, the accidental nature of the incident, the lighthearted intentions, and the fact that many of them—minors, quite a few—were drunk and high.

Fragmented memories are common, especially during traumatizing events, and none of the facts skewed differently enough to point to an intentional shooting, nor were the responses organized enough to imply they'd all "gotten their story straight." Perhaps they'd all heard Snow say that Helen had asked for it and incorporated that into their memory of events, but the fact remained that there was seemingly no motivation that justified purposely committing a senseless act of violence in front of so many witnesses. It was just drunken recklessness and kinning gone too far. Snow had hoped to cosplay-test a new alter of the Penguin and did so a little too well.

Helen's mother seemed to agree. After the *Rolling Stone* piece came out about that night, she took to her Twitter/X to post:

> Our daughter Helen Rose Hastings was shot by a drunk, stoned fool playing with a gun. no need to read.[40]

---

40 RosenbergLabBCM (@RosenbergLabBCM), "Our daughter Helen Rose Hastings was shot by a drunk, stoned fool playing with a gun. no need to read. Helen was 18, home from her 1st term @oberlincollege which she loved, excelled at, and had begun planned triple major in neuroscience, psych and art," X, October 24, 2021, https://x.com/RosenbergLabBCM/status/1452417423458684930.

Snow was arrested and bail was filed the same day, on January 18, 2021, in Harris County, Texas. The state filed at $30,000, but according to *VICE* magazine, it was paid at $20,000 by Snow's family, and Snow was released[41]—charged with second-degree manslaughter for "unlawfully, recklessly caus[ing] the death of Helen Rose Hastings."[42]

There followed delays in processing Snow's case, mostly to do with COVID-19 protocols causing suspensions of proceedings. Then there was a switch in Snow's legal representation when the family decided to pay for an attorney instead of accepting the state-appointed one.

Snow was born September 21, 1998, making them four years older than Helen and someone who should have been a protector and a mentor. Helen died at 5:08 p.m. on a Monday with no brain activity. Twenty-three days later, Snow was posting gruesome skits to TikTok for attention.

After posting bail—and on the condition that Snow would always appear in court on time, commit no crimes, and submit to any drug and alcohol testing—Snow was allowed to go home. They weren't considered a flight risk, or a danger to others, but because of what they'd done, they were not allowed to use or possess marijuana or any unprescribed drugs; they were not allowed to use or possess a firearm; and because alcohol was a mitigating factor in their poor choices that night, they were barred from using or possessing alcohol, up to and including any foods or oral products containing it. Mouthwash, for example, was off the table. Snow was also fitted with an electronic tracking monitor and given a curfew of 8 p.m. to 7 a.m., all days of the week. And as a matter of course, Snow was not to come in contact with or reach out to members of Helen's family.

But on August 3, 2021, Assistant DA Dana Nazarova filed a motion to revoke the surety bond allowing Snow to go free, citing *numerous* curfew violations, all in July of 2021. The assistant DA listed for the court that Snow had a dead GPS tracker three times,

41 Matthew Gault, "TikTok Cosplayer Killed Friend While Pretending to Be Batman Villain," *VICE*, October 1, 2021, https://www.vice.com/en/article/tiktok-cosplayer-killed-friend-while-pretending-to-be-batman-villain.

42 "Marilyn Burgess," accessed April 30, 2025.

their GPS had no connecting cell service for four or more hours seven separate times, and there had also been failure to check in to the pretrial monthly meeting. But bond remained granted.

In October of 2021, Snow's new lawyer, T. Bren Mayr, motioned to make conditions of the bond more relaxed:

> The condition that [the] Defendant submit to GPS monitoring via ankle monitor ... is unreasonable and unnecessary.... The Defendant is greatly in need of psychological assistance and treatment and needs to be able to meet with their team of treatment providers without the scrutiny of having their physical movements monitored.

Snow still agreed to conditions limiting drug and alcohol use, going no-contact with Helen's family (despite avowing a wish to reach out and help them cope with the tragedy), as well as not possessing a firearm. The motion was granted, and both curfew and electronic monitoring were lifted. All treatment records were then sealed in October of 2021.

Another motion to revoke Snow's bond came in December of 2021, this time from Assistant DA Conner Bree Tichota. The concerns were more serious. "During the [drug and alcohol] test, Defendant attempted to provide a urine sample from condoms found inside their vagina. The Defendant, by attempting to falsify a urinalysis test, violated the conditions of [their] bond." The court decided it needed more information and did not ultimately rescind bond.

Eventually, the whole matter of the shooting was settled as positively for Snow as their team could hope for. Snow entered a plea of guilty, and there was no formal jury verdict nor any trial. The state recommended a sentence, agreeing that it had been a negligent accident, and accepted deferred adjudication with strict supervision and service as remuneration to the community.

In other words, if Snow stays out of any trouble, they will have *no* criminal record after five years, thanks to entering their guilty plea no-contest. They also must complete the conditions of service laid out by the court. Everyone involved—including Helen's mother—believed that jail for a young person also harmed by the act they'd committed wasn't the answer. Snow has the chance to never be a convicted felon, to have what happened wiped off of official records, though they can never escape it in memory. Should Snow violate the terms, however, they are liable to be convicted of the offense—which carries a maximum prison sentence of twenty years.

The cosplay community was less forgiving than the Texas legal system. In late 2021, TikTok sleuths began to determine what had really happened to Helen, which was no easy feat.[43] There had been odd silence from Helen's family—there hadn't even been a funeral open to friends to attend.[44] The parents did not speak out against alcohol abuse or gun violence. There were no vigils set up. In all of this, Helen's father is as a phantom, appearing in truly no discernible parts of the story, from Helen's ride to college to those final bedside moments in the hospital—most likely due to his advanced age, not for lack of devotion. Meanwhile, Helen's friends at Oberlin still thought that Helen had taken her own life; no one disabused them of the notion. For Snow, it was business as usual—not just online, but also in person. Snow began attending conventions again—ones in their immediate area that did not violate any of the terms they'd agreed to.

But when news began to seep through the cosplay community of what Snow had done, almost a full year after they'd done it, Snow began getting called out in comment sections and quickly shut down their socials. After shutting Snow down online, cosplayers then aimed to do the same in person and began writing to conventions asking that Snow be barred from attending. Technically speaking, Snow will—if they follow all court orders—not be guilty of *any* crime sometime in the latter 2020s, when their name is cleared by successfully performing the terms of their deferred adjudication. They will have no record, and the tragedy will be—legally speaking—behind them. The cosplay community was not willing to let bygones be.

Adding distressing context, it is alleged that some cosplayers have *seen* Snow break the conditions of their bond. In the explosive *Rolling Stone* exposé about the aftermath, cosplayer Dolly Lace stated that

---

43 Gigi Ewing and Ella Moxley, "Student Helen Hastings Killed in Gun Accident," *The Oberlin Review*, October 8, 2021, https://oberlinreview.org/24880/news/student-helen-hastings-killed-in-gun-accident.

44 Elizabeth Hawk, "Choose Respecting the Dead," *The Oberlin Review*, 2021, https://oberlinreview.org/23765/opinions/choose-respecting-the-dead.

they'd perceived Snow in attendance at Anime Matsuri in Houston get so drunk that security had to help them into a ride-share:[45]

> Snow got upset that a piece of their cosplay broke and took it out on an entire bottle of vodka. They were heavily intoxicated and stumbling through the con, which got noticed by security and they made them get an Uber.[46]

And the internet never forgets. Former fans were reposting snippets of Snow's TikToks and OnlyFans posts, grisly and gory and chillingly heartless within the new and horrifying context of felled friends. When Snow's lawyer, Mr. Mayr, was asked about Snow's motivation for gritty posts like these following Helen's death, he replied,

> As is commonly recognized, different people react to trauma in many different ways. Disassociation is one of those common reactions and, for Snow, their actions were entirely consistent with this ... Snow didn't discuss the tragedy with even their family and others close to them. Cosplay was also, in simplest terms, Snow's occupation and source of income. They used it to pay their rent and to feed themselves and their roommates. Because of the mental trauma they experienced, the strict bond conditions, and the isolation caused by the pandemic, however, Snow had no other way to earn income to support themselves.
>
> Much of the content that was posted was done by Snow's friends. Snow passed their phone and social media off to them to post content that had been produced prior to the accident so they could continue to earn money to pay their bills. Snow didn't make new content until they absolutely had to months later in order to continue paying the bills. There were times where Snow would break down crying mid filming and have to redo makeup and take breaks in order to push content out like they had been before. During these times, Snow went into a total dissociative state where, in their words, their mind "wouldn't let [them] remember what had happened." Without the help of mental health professionals, they likely would have continued on like that for a very long time.
>
> It has to be made clear that the last thing Snow would ever do, or intended to do is malign or disrespect Helen. The trauma had such a

45 Dickson, "They Were Close Friends and Cosplay Stars."

46 Dolly Lace through Instagram with the author, January 7, 2025.

powerful impact on Snow that they could not accept—and did not want to accept—the reality of the situation.

This might have been hard to swallow for some. Snow came from a background of support and reliability (their high bail was posted same-day, their legal team was upgraded) but also one of transience and difficulty. While Snow had been looked after financially, they had a difficult time in everyday life, suffering from dyslexia, mental health issues, and an uprooting caused by a divorce and swapping schools. They had gotten their first taste of fame and success cosplaying as Batman's Harley Quinn back when TikTok was still Musical.ly. But the more popular they got, the more they were called a bully, and the more they were bullied in turn.

Of course, Snow was an easy target. They fell into the trappings of early cosplay exclusivity; simply by existing and doing their craft well, they made people feel bad about themselves. They were additionally scoffed at for having a Patreon filled with lewd photos cosplaying minor-aged cartoon characters, though Snow only sold those when they were not a minor themselves. But it was seen as bordering on peddling pedophilia, even though the characters were fictional and the model was an adult—detractors argued it sold the fantasy of barely-legal.

But the defense team and the courts saw sending Snow to jail as piling "tragedy upon tragedy." Despite what it looked like online, they said that Snow was suffering deeply from PTSD following the incident, and that a lot of the acting out was Snow's attempt to cope.

Though refusing to speak directly, citing mental health concerns, this book was able to shed a light on some of Snow's point of view through Mr. Mayr, Snow's lawyer, with Mr. Mayr answering some of the most pressing questions regarding the case:

Salters: Joining the case, did you feel positively about the outcome at first?

Mayr: I felt positive about the outcome at first because, by all indications, this was nothing more than a tragic accident and Snow had a lot of positive character traits that confirmed that.

Salters: Can you share anything about why Snow made some errors during their bail time, according to public record, which included substance use and dead ankle monitor batteries?

Mayr: This was one of those things attributable to the pandemic and the isolation it caused.... There was a lot of miscommunication and misunderstanding at first with the agency responsible for supervising Snow's conditions of bond.... As for the alleged substance abuse, there was also some miscommunication and misunderstanding. Although Snow was initially ordered not to consume any alcohol, drugs, or controlled substances not prescribed to them, the orders were amended at some point thereafter and it appeared that condition was left off. Although Snow unequivocally abstained from the use of drugs or other illegal substances, they did consume a small amount of alcohol prior to a urine test (that would have tested for alcohol). That led to another alleged bond violation. Once the ambiguity was pointed out and cleared up, again, the judge agreed to let Snow remain on bond, where they continued to comply with their conditions, including monitoring to ensure Snow was not consuming even alcohol. Snow continues to maintain sobriety to the present day.

Salters: Can you shed any light on Snow's feelings for the victim, their family, and how Snow is coping with this terrible tragedy?

Mayr: Snow has spent and will continue to spend each day of their lives thinking about Helen and her family. In Snow's own words, they "miss Helen more than anything, thinking of her, and dreaming of her." Snow keeps a memorial for her with Helen's things that her parents allowed Snow to keep in their house, including pictures of her and art she drew. Snow sees it and grieves her loss every day.

Snow recognizes that any pain they feel is only a fraction of what Helen's family and friends have gone through, and Snow wishes they could do anything to take that pain from them. Snow further recognizes that Helen's family and friends are good people who never deserved to lose the wonderful person she was. Snow is adamant that they will carry Helen's loss until the day they are gone.

Salters: Is there anything that gets lost in these narratives that you think people really ought to know, or that sensationalism gets incorrect?

Mayr: We appreciate respected journalists and authors like yourself reaching out to get the "real story." When the story broke, there were a lot of individuals trying to act like journalists, offering nothing but speculation, unconfirmed rumors, and baseless opinions. People who knew Snow or claimed to know Snow attempted to act like experts into their mind when they had no idea what Snow was going through or experiencing. This was nothing more than a tragic accident involving two friends who cared for and admired each other. Snow admittedly engaged in reckless behavior that they will regret for the rest of their lives. They accepted responsibility and were held to account in a just and fair manner.

Salters: Were there any difficulties with the case for you?

Mayr: None. Getting to know Snow and the people in their life was an absolute pleasure. I saw a young person with a lot of regret and sorrow, but an incredible motivation to make amends, accept responsibility, and move forward with their life in a positive manner. They were an easy client to represent and advocate for.

Salters: What did the judge say, if anything, regarding the decision? Was it largely agreed this was a terrible accident?

Mayr: I think the decision to place Snow on deferred adjudication community supervision reflected the judge's recognition that this was indeed a terrible accident caused by an unintended act. The judge, in the end, had very little to say but seemed very confident this was the right outcome.

Salters: Why did Snow's ex leave a gun at their place? How long had it been there about?

Mayr: We can only speculate.... Snow and their ex broke up on very bad terms after being together for six years. The breakup was very sudden and there was a lot on their minds other than their possessions. We guess that in his haste to gather up his possessions and move out, he forgot about the gun. Snow did not discover it until well after he left and learned from others that he had taken the ammunition.

Salters: The police report says several witnesses were watching an episode of *Gotham* at the time, and that Snow was playacting as the Penguin from the show when the tragedy occurred. Can you shed any light on that?

Mayr: As a cosplayer, Snow was always watching shows with the mindset of who they would be able to dress as and make content of. Snow felt attached to the character, Penguin, and thought his aesthetic and personality would be cool to make a costume out of. That night, Snow found some clothes that resembled his and put on a "closet cosplay" just for fun to experiment with the character. Their other friends there were deciding what other *Gotham* characters they'd like to cosplay when the accident occurred.

Salters: Is there anything you can share about Snow's hopes for the future beyond this case?

Mayr: Snow has never shared this publicly but [has] given me permission to share. Originally, in the aftermath of the accident, Snow had no future plans. Snow's plans were to "join Helen." It was only by the intervention of Snow's friends at first and then later mental health professionals that Snow was able to deal with the grief and envision a life that went on without Helen. Now, years later, Snow is still a bit wary of the future. Snow was never a far-future thinking person, but now has come to terms with what they want in life. Snow wants to be in a stable place, providing a good and happy life to those closest to them. The people in their life have always been what has made life worth living for them. Now, more than ever before, it is always on Snow's mind to keep them safe, stay away from dangerous activities and people, and to tend to their emotional needs. In Snow's perspective, there is nothing more important than making sure they are happy and fulfilled. The only future Snow sees for themselves is one that they have with them.[47]

47 Brent Mayr via email with the author on June 11, 2024.

Future Plans

On Friday, August 2, 2024, after the interview with attorney Brent Mayr, I received a text message:

That's the one you're writing about, right?

The text linked to a "PSA" posted to Instagram stories and making swift rounds that Snow the Salt Queen was back. It linked to @Feral.Jinx, a profile on TikTok. The profile did indeed seem to be Snow, who'd otherwise shut down the majority of their public social platforms in 2020 and 2021. Once again, the internet was in an uproar. This time, it came with the question: Did reaching out to them via their lawyer have this effect?

Likely not. It turned out that Snow's plans for the future still involved cosplay. Starting in 2023, Snow began to make a gentle—mostly private—climb back onto social media in costume, primarily using OnlyFans—a website where subscribers can pay for often-pornographic content—and Patreon, a subscription service for supporting artists in exchange for content. Snow's content advertised "Lewds," or lude content.

Snow's return to socials was to help support their participation in the LFC—the Lingerie Fighting Championship, a face-off of scantily-clad, mostly female cosplayers. In a video posted by @MikeLarkin92 in October of 2023, LFC conducts an interview with Snow about their upcoming entry onto the roster. In it, Snow falls back on their old cosplay lineup—Harley Quinn, Junko, and one new costume, Jinx: a mentally unbalanced terrorist from the animated series *Arcane*. They talk about their favorite grisly horror movies, flail excitedly about themed underwear, complain about their boring normal job, and show off fan art of themselves as Junko. They also talk a little bit about high school, and when the interviewer calls himself a member of the "get along [with everyone] gang," Snow retorts, "I wasn't like outwardly aggressive really to anybody I really feel like, except the people who were just mean. But unfortunately, you know, on one hand I'd like everybody to get along, but on the other, some people are just mean...."[48]

The interviewer uses the pronouns she/her for Snow—perhaps a shape Snow was forced into to participate in the LFC. They discuss collabs and conventions. It's an uncomfortable conversation, but Snow plows through it with an almost pixie-stick-fueled excitement, plus the touch of mania they've always been popular for. It's the same old public-facing Snow persona.

In December of 2023, YouTuber @Gorg14 did a round-up post investigating why Snow was back online and in cosplay, noticing that Snow's paywall-locked social media (such as Patreon or OnlyFans) had remained quietly active throughout the years, never really turning the lights completely off.[49] This hearkens back to attorney Mayr's note about it being an income source for his client. Snow's Patreon at that time started with $1 monthly subscriptions for "safe for work" content and went upwards from there—offering "base level sexy," "light sexy," "very sexy," "extreme sexy," "god tier sexy," and finally "The Archive™ of the Sexy" for $450 per month.[50]

In a rare show, Snow *did* reply to @Gorg14 about their motivations for joining LFC, saying "My life had turned into me going to my cheap paying job 40–50 hours a week, eating junk, and not sleeping enough ... [my friend] suggested LFC both as a means to get myself motivated again, and to get healthy so I don't slip back into old bad habits...." When he follows up to ask if Snow's considering a full return to social media, they replied, "I honestly don't know, ill probably feel it out as I go tbh."

The friend who suggested the LFC to Snow was most likely Farah Fatherless, who'd helped introduce Snow to the League, dressed as Harley Quinn, but in lingerie. While Farah is a full-time LFC fighter, it doesn't seem like Snow's inaugural fight ever occurred, nor did Snow

48 Michael Larkin, "The Lingerie Fighting Championships Podcast-LFC Prospect Snow the Salt Queen," YouTube, October 19, 2023, https://www.youtube.com/watch?v=EGeI53XQXoM.

49 Grog, "SnowtheSaltQueen Has Returned to the Internet," YouTube, December 3, 2023, https://www.youtube.com/watch?v=LQ4eNF-1vio.

50 "Snow the Salt Queen," Patreon, August 29, 2022, https://www.patreon.com/yanderefreak.

make it onto a permanent roster, despite their briefly stated goal of being a pro wrestler.

On Instagram, @snow_the_salt_queen's profile says "My pronouns are Your/Majesty." They posted LFC content there, but the cosplayer they paired off with for their preliminary bout has since deleted their account. Snow's OnlyFans account, @redactedanarchy, is no longer active, but their handle @snowthesaltqueen is, with a subscription priced at $35/month.

Snow's "ONLY PUBLIC" account now appears to be on TikTok at @Feral.Jinx. As of May 2025, it's become a fairly active page, blooming from almost nothing. Snow posts videos of themself—just as often not in cosplay as in it—with songs by bands like Nine Inch Nails and Marilyn Manson, ditties like "Pretty Little Psycho" by TRILLZ and "Boogie Woogie Poo" by Cody. On a birthday post, in September of 2024, they were dressed as the villain Toga Himiko again.

Some of their most recent new cosplay content on TikTok has been of Mahito from *Jujutsu Kaisen*, a sadistic and childish demon spirit. In one clip, an audio overlay tells Snow as Mahito, "Someone ought to put you in a mental hospital." Snow, as Mahito, replies in audio overlay, "Someone ought to put you in a *box*, Grandma." The comments read: wonderful, incredible, amazing, *I love you*. Another is Misa Amane, a murderer from *Death Note*. Comments include: Cutie patootie, absolutely stunning, beautiful, perfection, your jawline is so sharp, *slaaaay*.

On February 28, 2025, Snow posted a TikTok saying "we still out here kinning."[51] It is suffused with villainous characters. Kinning, again, is deeply relating to the thoughts, feelings, and personality of a fictional character—such that in some ways, maybe all ways, someone feels that they *are* the character. Snow rarely replies to comments. But on the kinning post, they do reach back to someone named Sophie, who playfully noted Snow's character choices mean they wouldn't trust Snow with a drink order, implying they might spike or poison it. Snow replies:

51 feral.jinx (@snow.the.salt.queen), "It's 2025 and we still out there kinning," TikTok, February 28, 2025, https://www.tiktok.com/@feral.jinx/photo/7476551764863503647.

10/10 I would drink it
—@feral.jinx

Their most recent repost, at the time of writing, dated from May of 2025, was a clip from the animation Rick and Morty, featuring a version of the character Rick tied down and beaten to death by fists until his brain matter shows and his facial skin begins to burst and peel. As of May 2025, Snow's @Feral.Jinx profile bio reads: "In Tomura we trust. Snow, 26, Cosplayer. Im real guys not a fanpage." Tomura, from *My Hero Academia*, is another mass murderer.

Even if the internet has a long memory, beauty sells. Snow still has plenty of "simps" in their comment sections and, in fact, on their TikTok, almost all of the remarks fawn over their attractiveness and talent. Just as before the tragedy, there seemed a great many people who wanted to be in Snow's orbit. But there are the occasional accounts that haunt those same pages to remind them they're a "murderer" and that seethe at them to get lost, innocent or no.

Outside of the firing of the Glock, other victims of Snow's bullying still feel silenced. Dolly Lace is one of them:

> Snow told me to kill myself and made it a point to find whatever cons I was going to and cosplay my favorite character just to upset me because they were quote 'better than me' due to their following ... They have an obsession with things being canon and would make fun of those who didn't fit their idea of the perfect cosplay. This included race. They would tell [people of color] that their skin color didn't match the character.
>
> They fetishized gore and violence and use[d] to have the quote 'fight me I dare you' in their Insta bio just begging for people to do something they didn't approve of. They also literally believed they were fictional characters and anytime they did something shitty they'd blame it on whatever cartoon or anime character they felt like being that day. They literally bit someone ... and said Bill Cipher from *Gravity Falls* made them do it.
>
> Even before the incident with Helen, Snow was just a walking red flag full of violent mannerisms and an obsession with death and killing. Snow prided themself on the drama they caused which is why they went by Salt Queen. Another person they really traumatized who was

> actually close with them was [REDACTED].... Snow liked to think they owned them....
>
> I felt like no one believed me about how dangerous they were. I was blatantly told that the abuse and harassment I was experiencing wasn't real and I was making it up. Snow sent their followers to attack me time and time again and toxic behavior like this is what ultimately led to me deciding to retire from cosplay and conventions last year. Unfortunately, people like Snow are still around and history will just repeat itself because clout is more important than morality.
>
> I warned people Snow would hurt people. I was a broken record about it since 2016 and no one believed me beyond Snow's other victims. It took someone losing their life for people to reflect on the concerning and insanely dangerous behavior Snow displayed.[52]

Ironically, Helen Hastings loved snow—specifically, the snowfalls of Ohio, so magical to her as a native Texan. One snowy day at Oberlin, one of Helen's friends did something amazing in her memory: She painted a rock.

At Tappan Square on Oberlin's campus, there sit three large stones. One, of particular importance, was painted in block letters with the name AIDEN DAY, an Obie senior who had died of myeloid leukemia before graduation. One of Helen's first freshman friends, Elizabeth Hawk, decided to spray paint Helen's name and the dates of her short life on the other side of Aiden's name. Then, there, she held vigil.[53]

She felt betrayed and disappointed by the adults involved in Helen's story—that there hadn't been enough of a statement by the college, that reporting on what had really happened was slow, that there was no funeral for friends to attend and mourn, there had been no transparency, no eulogies. So, she gathered friends of Helen's around four candles she'd lit on the ground by that stone with her name, candles that struggled in the blustery winter weather. She would upkeep the stone like a grave, for months.

52 Dolly Lace through Instagram with the author, January 7, 2025.

53 Hawk, "Choosing Respecting the Dead."

And then a Girl Scout troop painted over the names of the dead young people, of Helen and Aiden, in white. And the campus didn't support Hawk when she fought back, instead siding with the Girl Scouts who'd chosen that rock over other blank ones as part of their incongruously named "choose kindness project." The article Hawk wrote on the incident is called "Choose Respecting the Dead."[54] It is about kids being "forced to pick up adults' slack" and the difficulty of achieving a sense of *permanence* when there isn't help. "Helen deserves better."

On May 27, 2024, Oberlin College held a commencement ceremony. The Alumni Medal was given to Nancy Dandridge Cooper, class of 1951, for the formation of the Status of Women Committee and for being an administrative liaison for the college's first LGBT organizing community, the Gay Union. The class of '75's Dr. Kathryn Anastos was awarded an honorary doctor of science degree for research in HIV/AIDS treatment, especially for women. A lot of this aligned with Helen's interests. She would have liked it—and she should have been there on that day, in that year, graduating—perhaps—in three distinct majors. Tackling STEM cell parity and making art.

Board of trustees chairman Chris Canavan would mention Helen in his remarks, saying she was there in spirit, crossing the stage that day with the rest of the Obie crowd.

They're Gonna Tell Stories About Us One Day, Kid.
—Oswald Cobblepot, *The Penguin*

54 Hawk, "Choosing Respecting the Dead."

CHAPTER 2

TREY SESLER, aka Mr. Anime

Flying home down the I-10...
Nobody knows, not your parents, definitely not our group of friends,
If I get out of this Ford, I'll be in Waller County
I just hope that she will get me there
All I know for sure is I'm going way over 90...
I miss the good times in the FFA
Inside jokes and the out-of-town trips, I miss everything.
—"Waller County," Charlie Cope

Awwww shit...
And if you fight tonight you gon'ta—
Waller County Jail. Hey.
Waller County Jail. Yeah.
Waller County Jail.
—"Waller County Jail," MC Sante

These are the two most famous (yet little-known) songs about Waller County, Texas, a place studded with controversy—and the town where Trey Sesler grew up. The FFA is Future Farmers of America, and its events supported by the local high school Trey attended. Trey himself drove a Ford. In its introduction, "Waller County Jail" sports a cameo by local sheriff Troy Guidry. It is the same jail where Trey Sesler was held awaiting his murder trial for the slaying of his family.

A Waller Welcome

Waller is a tight-knit community inland of the Gulf of Mexico in the Lone Star State. Deeply Americana, it boasts livestock competitions, rodeos, mutton busting, and it even crowns a few lucky teens "BBQ royalty" each year, with pageantry and sashes. Hovering around three thousand residents, its bona fide cadre of characters feels scraped off the editing room floor of television network the CW, with all the neurosis and charm of fictional towns like Stars Hollow, Smallville, and Capeside.[55]

Waller is more than the initial impression it gives—an old cattle settlement with blue collar pride and a Stepford smile, squat houses set far enough apart to make that smile gappy, sunken rusted rail lines and flat-tired Fords hunkering into overgrown lawns like modern sculpture art. It's home to football royalty, small businesses built on grit and expertise, and the kind of neighborly warmth that regards birthdays and high school reunions as notable and newsworthy. Waller's mayor, Danny L. Marburger, has served for forty-five straight years. He has a bachelor's degree in agricultural business and has managed fertilizer sales for twenty counties in Texas. He's a lifetime director of the Houston Livestock Show, president of the Waller Lions Club and an advisor to the local Wells Fargo Bank, the high school rodeo team, and the Waller County Historical Museum, plus a board member of the regional hospital. Those who are active in the Waller community wear many hats; almost all of them Stetson style with a cattleman crease.

A look at his recent mayoral race gives a picture of small-town idiosyncrasies. Marburger won his election against two other candidates in 2024. One was Shawn Blackmon, who on his "Meet the Candidate" page stands before a Marine flag and greets prospective voters with "Howdy! Most of you know me.... I'm a true born and bread [sic] Texan." The other was Simon Loche, whose misspelling of his home state of Louisiana in his public-facing biography prefaces

55 The CW Network, LLC, is an American broadcast channel. Stars Hollow is the fictional town featured in the show *Gilmore Girls*. Smallville is the fictional town in *Smallville* and *Superman & Lois*, and part of the *Superman* universe owned by DC Comics. Capeside is the fictional township in *Dawson's Creek*.

his political credentials as a real estate broker who enjoys horseback riding and sports cars.[56] One hundred and thirteen people voted in that election[57]—less than 4% of the population. Danny won, with sixty-nine of those votes.

The county has one newspaper, *The Waller Times*, with a website that boasts, "We've reached almost 5,000 facebook fans!"[58] Its website links to no live *or* archived articles. It says it publishes weekly on Wednesdays. *The Waller Times* was once housed in an unintimidating boxy concrete office near the city's main commerce artery. It has only two noted staffers: a founding editor and a guest columnist. Across the street from where the pair heralded the news sits a pair of corroded railroad tracks, and to the immediate right is Snowflake Donuts, famed for their "Kountry Boy" boudin kolaches—rice and pork sausages wrapped up in flaky dough, a proud Texan on-the-go breakfast. To the news building's left, along a yawning main street, are several moldering antique resellers, no-nonsense auto part shops, and a drowsy gas station. Waller is clearly marked by poverty. Still, some signs of hope rattle onward.

The Texas Central Railway (TCR) runs a scar-mark of rail tracks through Waller, the feeble remains of an 1876 expansion to carry agricultural goods toward the coast. They'd put a plan in motion in 2020 to paper over older routes and cleave new ones with the state's first high-speed rail, modeled on the *Tokaido Shinkansen*—the famed bullet train connecting Tokyo to Osaka in Japan. In 2022, the railway won the right of eminent domain—and with it, the right to seize land for the project.[59] While many Texans rallied against the idea, which would connect Dallas to Houston—239 miles, approximately the distance from New York City to Kennebunkport, Maine, or a three-

56 "Meet the Candidates," WallerTexas.gov, accessed April 30, 2025, https://www.wallertexas.gov/elections/page/meet-candidates.

57 "City of Waller General Election Unofficial Votes," The City of Waller Texas, May 4, 2024, https://www.wallertexas.gov/sites/default/files/fileattachments/election_information/page/2785/unofficial_votes_-_city_of_waller_2024.pdf.

58 "Waller Times," WallerTimes.com, accessed April 30, 2025, http://www.thewallertimes.com/index.html.

59 Timothy Malcolm, "Texas Leaders to Propose Statewide High-Speed Rail Authority," *Chron*, September 14, 2024, https://www.chron.com/news/houston-texas/transportation/article/texas-high-speed-rail-train-19765054.php.

and-a-half-hour drive for Lone Star Staters—Amtrak joined forces with the TCR and secured federal funding in 2024 to push forward with their dream liner. It might have a positive effect on a place suffused with surface sociability but pockmarked by decades of hostility and paucity, bringing in fresh commerce and opportunities for languid youth hungry for their shot.

Though Waller is a fairly diverse community made up of mostly families with children, the average salary around the town middles out at about $42k a year per family, with single men having an average income of around $30k and single women at just $21k, per census data. Some 18% of the population rests below the poverty line—especially affecting children and young adults, more than any other demographic. The high school tries to bolster its students against that poverty, pouring funding into hands-on agricultural training, a competitive computer science team, and an array of sports—from a women's wrestling squad that won titles in 2008 to the men's football club playing in a 10,000-person stadium, alma mater to several National Leaguers. Waller's a football town; Amy Adams Strunk, a partial owner of the NFL's Tennessee Titans, is a notable resident.

Waller High School, home of the Bulldogs, serves multiple local municipalities and is situated at the center of tracts of farmland. One graduate, Trey Eric Sesler, would go on to become a famous YouTuber—and the infamous murderer of his father, mother, and brother on March 20, 2012. Trey was also a foiled would-be school shooter. But he wasn't the first young person whose sense of purpose was consumed by drudgery and lack of mobility in Waller. Unable to keep a steady job, unable to apply himself to secondary education, but capable of buying a gun and training to use it, he'd fall into an angry malaise, directionless—and he'd take out those big feelings on those closest to him, at gunpoint.

For a suburb with such a low population, Sesler's isn't the only tale of bad blood. Waller is scarred by an incredible amount of disturbing crime, especially involving local police. In 2024, a federal jury found a Waller County District Attorney investigator, Alex Kassem, guilty on charges relating to the transport of heroin and cartel money across state lines in his police vehicle.[60] (Ironically, a "liked" post on his still-active LinkedIn reads, "let me tick some people off.... Did you get drug tested today? Thank you Florida, Kentucky, and Missouri, which are the first states that will require drug testing when applying for welfare. Some people are crying.... Repost this if you'd like to see it done in all 50 states!"[61])

In a more horrific national scandal, the death of a woman named Sandra Bland took place in a Waller County jail cell. Bland, who was pulled over by state troopers in 2015 for not signaling a change of lanes, wound up dead of apparent suicide while held in detention. Bland had been due to start a new job at Texas A&M University at Prairie View. A young Black woman, she was bodily threatened by white officer Brian T. Encinia, who arrested her on a trumped-up charge of assaulting a public officer after pulling her over. He menaced her at the traffic stop, saying, "I will light you up."[62] Sandra was booked on July 10, 2015, and placed in a women's detention facility, where three days later she was found hanging in her small cell, a plastic trash liner around her neck.[63] While ruled a suicide, the lies told by the officer, the undue harshness of the punishment for such a menial traffic offense, and the fact that she was not granted suicide watch after confessing to previous attempts on her own life (her emotional distress aggravated by being unable to pay her $500 bail) set the country alight with the racial injustice. Protests erupted nationwide, and an ongoing debate on police violence gripped headlines with #BlackLivesMatter.

In 2019, suspected workplace murderer Evan Lyndell Parker also committed suicide by hanging while in holding in Waller, dying of his injuries days later in a hospital. In 2017, a female inmate

---

60 William Melhado, "Former DA Investigator Faces Heroin Trafficking and Money Laundering Cases," *The Texas Tribune*, last updated February 28, 2024, https://www.texastribune.org/2024/02/27/waller-county-alex-kassem-drug-trafficking.

61 Beth Anne, "I AM ALL FOR THIS LAW..." LinkedIn, 2016, https://www.linkedin.com/feed/update/urn:li:activity:6083725020100579328/.

62 David Montgomery, "Sandra Bland, It Turns Out, Filmed Traffic Stop Confrontation Herself," *The New York Times*, May 7, 2019, https://www.nytimes.com/2019/05/07/us/sandra-bland-video-brian-encinia.html.

63 David Montgomery, "The Death of Sandra Bland: Is There Anything Left to Investigate?" *The New York Times*, May 8, 2019, https://www.nytimes.com/2019/05/08/us/sandra-bland-texas-death.html.

complained of sexual assault by a male inmate carrying out "trustee duties"—duties typically performed by officers that are assigned to trusted prisoners instead. Also in 2017, allegations were made that a female inmate, Chelsea Schehr, was taken into custody on a domestic dispute arrest, and had her clothes taken because she'd been placed on suicide watch—during her menstrual cycle. She was not granted underwear, tampons, or a sanitary napkin.[64]

Notwithstanding this tawdry record, Elton R. Mathias, DA of Waller County from 2007 to 2023, and then first judge of County Court from September 2023 onward, said of Waller, "I am most proud of the reputation that our county has developed regionally as a place where murderers, child molesters, and violent offenders know that they will face appropriate consequences."[65]

One such murderer who would face down those apparently appropriate consequences was Trey Sesler.

Small Town Royalty

Born August 3, 1989, "Mr. Anime"—Trey Sesler's online ego—was something of an early YouTube sensation, with the production value to match. Often filming from his bedroom or garage with backdrops hastily and unevenly hung to reveal bits of white wall behind slumping curtains, his dim lighting and lack of video editing gave viewers an authentic feel, lending his reviews a living-room chat quality. Just a friend, telling you his latest thoughts on what TV to watch ... or skip.

With more than 4,000 subscribers and over a million upload views, Mr. Anime had the numbers to be considered a popular reviewer of cartoons from Japan, often consumed in the States dubbed or subtitled into English. Almost all of his videos had over

64 Carol Christian, "Mom of Woman Kept Nearly Naked and Bleeding at Waller Countyjail Says Suicide Watch Inappropriate," *Chron*, last updated April 27, 2017, https://www.chron.com/news/houston-texas/texas/article/Woman-says-suicide-watch-at-Waller-County-Jail-11102942.php.

65 Waller County DA, "District Attorney Mathis Resigns, Accepts Appointment as First Judge of County Court at Law Number Two Effective 9/1/23," WallerCountyDistrictAttorney.com, August 23, 2023, https://wallercountydistrictattorney.com/district-attorney-mathis-resigns-accepts-appointment-as-first-judge-of-county-court-at-law-number-two-effective-9-1-23.

1,000 views within just a week of posting.[66] These were fairly heavy numbers for the years he worked, when anime was still fringe and Western reviews and rankings of it were embryonic. Trey's review style seemed unscripted, almost stream of consciousness, which locked horns with some of his more heavily produced video movie content, but which made him feel accessible. Despite the low production value, Trey actually did have a knack for filmmaking, skilled at special effects and PiP effects.[67]

Alongside his reviews, he posted rants, video game playthroughs, short movies, and tutorials. His tutorial videos were the first place where spectators might have glimpsed some of Trey's more disturbing inclinations and growing obsessions. A self-described aspiring director, Trey liked to make brief films, often violent in nature or horror-based, featuring shoot-outs, thefts, and killer Christmas trees. In that vein, he uploaded a series of discordant SFX tutorials to explain how he gave his films their brutal look—including a squib test for electro-explosive currents and one on how to make bullet wounds and ballistic firing look realistic.

His gun content would grow to be his most distressing. But that would come later, like a storm, in sudden cracks of lightning across his regularly scheduled uploads, signaling a bigger problem on the horizon. It began raising eyebrows too close to the slaughter of his family to save them.

Trey Sesler's family was in every way very typical.

Their house on 1616 Farr Street was a four-bedroom traditional with one floor and an attached garage, loft style, built in the 1990s. The Seslers would have enjoyed its tiny wood-burning fireplace in winter if the temperature ever dipped, while its tawny brick veneer and hearty slab foundation would have kept the air cool and circulating in the grips of summer heat. It had a small front lawn and a sizable backyard, kept brilliantly green, and only half-fenced. Inside the home, beige and white walls studded by low, arched windows

66 LensCapProductions, "Anime Haters," YouTube, Janaury 26, 2012, https://web.archive.org/web/20120131093406/https://www.youtube.com/user/LensCapProductions#p/a/u/0/LsYrvAYqRYs.

67 A PiP effect is an acronym for a "picture-in-picture" effect, a video overlay where there is a secondary, often partial video on top of original footage which can play simultaneously. Trey used PiP effects to "interact" with anime characters in his videos.

made it a breezy space, if monotonous. It had the look of care about it, tidy and welcoming to guests.

Trey's father, Lawton Ray Sesler Jr., worked at the local elementary school, teaching the fourth and fifth grades. He was a community favorite even as a boy himself, when he'd visit the homes of friends and amuse their parents with his antics and jokes. His own teachers in high school noted that he was "shy, but aggressive ... an outstanding young man."[68] He bloomed into a fine adult that locals were eager to have their own children learn under. Solidly built and handsome, with a chiseled jaw, bright eyes, and a beaming smile that only softened and became more encouraging with age, Lawton Jr. was a compassionate and exceptional teacher. Parents fought to get their youngsters into his class, where he imparted a love of learning, employed loads of silliness, and pulled his humor from a well of almost infinite patience. To imbue a love of STEM in his students, he'd often dub himself the "mad scientist," using that persona to add fun to mandatory experiments and difficult subject matter. He sometimes subbed at the local high school that both he and his two sons had attended.

Rhonda Dee Sesler, nee Wyse, was a newswoman. She worked with the *Brenham Banner-Press* and *The Waller Times*—she was a go-to for loading up papers for distribution. The type of woman who sustained strong friendships from childhood, Rhonda took to motherhood as easily as she had friendship. She was wildly supportive of her children and their dreams. When Trey, her youngest, began showing an interest in videography, she willingly made appearances in his YouTube films at his behest. By the time she was in front of Trey's lens, her once-jet hair had grown ocher with age, her sharp eyes were hidden behind lustrous frameless glasses, and the low, piercing brow of her teenage years—inherited by Trey—was hidden behind fringe bangs. Acquaintances described her as kind and humorous, with a knack for wordplay, cooking, and baking—a wonderful match for Lawton Jr. She was a year younger than him, almost to the day.

---

68 "Lawton Jr., Rhonda, & Mark Sesler |2012| Guest Book," CanonFuneralHome.com, March 20, 2012, https://www.canonfuneralhome.com/guestbook/1428788.

They welcomed their first son, Mark Alan Sesler, on September 5, 1985. Since his birth was on the last cusp of summer and close to that of his parents, it made for a wonderful exclamation point in the couple's annual traditions. Both Lawton Jr. and Rhonda celebrated their birthdays in August—and now they had a reason to extend the festivities. For four years, their little family was resplendent in love and laughter. Then, on August 3, 1989, they welcomed their second and final child, Trey Eric, into the world. Their household complete, August now absolutely stuffed with revelries, Trey would be about five years old and Mark nearly nine when they moved into the house at 1616 Farr Street. Mark would have sharp memories of the move, and Trey less so. The need for four bedrooms—three for the family and one for guests—felt evident as the boys grew bold and noisy. The boys' teachers would remark how very much Lawton Jr. and Rhonda adored their children and wanted the best for them, how dedicated they were to them. And for a long time, it showed.

Mark was Waller's average young man in every way that counted. He was popular enough at school, having a firm group of friends, not in any way an outsider. His teachers at Waller High described him as extraordinarily kind and gentle, willing to pitch in with theme nights and always happy to snap photos for the school. He would have weekly parties at friends' houses and was the consummate drummer in his group's *Rock Band* squad, their video game of choice. He was tall, with sandy hair and a softened version of his father's face, all the edges rounded out.

Trey was much more his mother's boy, at least to look at him. He had thinner, light eyes with a low, thick brow hanging over them like an awning, and a cut-across fringe, wavy like his mother's, but a warmer chocolaty brown. He seemed perpetually unable to either fully shave his five o'clock shadow once it grew in or to properly cultivate the facial hair, leaving his face patchy. Still, there was something charismatic and beseeching in his look; his smile felt self-conscious, and he gave the impression of supplication due to his low brow bone.

If there was any early jealousy of his elder brother, it didn't show. They were great friends, de facto partners in crime ahead of Trey's actual crimes. They both loved their family pets, a tabby cat and a rabbit. They played *Mortal Kombat* and other fighting or collaborative games together. They worked at the same grocery store as teens, shot videos, and had an overlapping friend group. Even as Trey—well-liked enough at school to have plenty of his own friends—gained a modicum of popularity as a YouTuber, it never seemed to go to his head. He never acted as if he were better or more special than Mark, nor felt inferior to him. The same seemed to go for Mark, whose less popular YouTube channel @TheMajor0 boasted itself as an "extension of Lens Cap Productions," Trey's videography team name and Trey's YouTube handle for Mr. Anime.[69] Mark, with just over 200 followers at peak, had only one curated playlist—Favorites, which featured thirteen videos, all by his brother Trey.[70] He himself was a supportive fan, clearly.

The family as a unit especially came together and sparkled during the Christmas season. The lawn at 1616 Farr was so bedazzled and decked out in myriad lights, displays, and blinking cascades of winter scenes that it became famous countywide. A 2008 photo montage on Mark's YouTube channel, titled "Lens Cap Christmas," showed the property in all its splendor. Though blurry, the pictures capture the great effort that went into the decoration, with swirling green trees made of rope lights, a lit candy cane lane, bushes strung tightly with an overlay of warm white fairy lights, blue glowing icicles hanging from the eaves of the roof, a striped candy cane arch, lawn strewn with stars, an igloo, a wreath, and a pair of deer, all luminescent.

But the festooning didn't end there. The Sesler house also sported a star above the door, a crucifix, a snowman, individual candles, bulbous multicolored holiday lights, ornaments, and loads and loads of string lights dripping blindingly across the property in warm and cool tones in a rainbow riot of color. Anything that could be swathed was, with a "more is more" approach that must have come with an astronomical electric bill. When the photo montage switched to video, the hundreds of lights flashed and blinked at tremendous wattage.

---

69 TheMajor0, "Favorites," YouTube, accessed April 30, 2025, https://www.youtube.com/playlist?list=FLFeCA3CdXItXmd8t5GtI9Mw.

70 TheMajor0, "Favorites."

The video credits Mark, then twenty-three, with the decorations, taking over from his father, Lawton Jr., who took the festive photos. It also gives special thanks to their mother Rhonda.

The lawn was so locally famous, it was covered by Texas-based news website CHRON on more than one occasion. Writes Nancy Arnold in 2010—in mid-November, no less—of both the display and the state of greater Waller:

> There is a tad more holiday spirit in Waller this year. I gauge that by the holiday lights—and there are some spectacular displays.... Lawton Sesler, on Farr Street just south of Waller Street, is carrying on the family tradition. I think he may have even added some bling to his display.... I wonder if this indicates a return to some sort of normal? I do hope so. That grim look that folks have been wearing for the past year or so needs a change.... To be honest, though, there hasn't been a whole lot to smile about since early 2009. Job cuts, salary cuts (I've had that!), higher costs in the household essentials, skyrocketing health care, including insurance, and prescriptions; the list could go on and on."[71]

Further back in 2005, Nancy from CHRON had noted,

> I was telling you last week about some of the more decorated yards in town, including the Sesler yards. Apparently the lighting genius is hereditary, because Lawton sent a message giving credit to the right artists. He said his oldest son, Mark, decorated his yard, and his youngest son, Trey, worked on his dad's yard just down the street.... kudos to the Sesler bunch for maintaining family traditions.[72]

And again in 2006:

> Take a drive on Farr Street just south of the school and see what Lawton Sesler has constructed. Very bright and colorful.[73]

It was a generational ritual that began with the Sesler grandparents, from whom Lawton Jr. had inherited it. He took it over from

71 Nancy Arnold, "Waller Wonders: It's Looking Like An Economically Healthy Christmas," *Chron*, December 15, 2010, https://www.chron.com/neighborhood/article/Waller-Wonders-It-s-looking-like-an-9475237.php.

72 Nancy Arnold, "Waller Wonders," *Chron*, December 14, 2005, https://www.chron.com/neighborhood/article/Waller-Wonders-9860873.php.

73 Nancy Arnold, "Waller Wonders," *Chron*, December 6, 2006, https://www.chron.com/neighborhood/article/Waller-Wonders-9602016.php.

his own father, Lawton Sr., in 2005—to the initial lament of the CHRON. "Lawton Ray Sesler's yard on Farr Street was 'the' place to see lights a-blazin. Then one year he just decided to retire from the decorating game.... Lawton, just a block north, who had grown up with the elaborate displays, decided to carry on the family tradition, much to the delight of passersby, and now his whole place is a work of art."[74]

2008, the year of the video that would allow the display to live on long past its creators, was also one of Lawton Jr. and Mark's final Christmases. The decked-out lawn video is overlayed by an almost oppressive musical choice: Bach's Fugue in G minor, which in retrospect rings out like a funeral dirge. The video, shot by Trey, though it was Mark who posted it, features jarring close-ups that feel almost distressing as the organ music ramps up. Which might be the point.

One year later, Trey would film his first short horror movie. Christmas-themed, about a murderous yule tree that uses a chainsaw against its victims. Taking something merry and bright and twisting it into something dark.

From the Sesler home, it was only a short walk down the street to Trey's paternal grandparents' place, where the secondary light display still sometimes went up, and only a slightly longer walk to the middle school both Trey and Mark had attended. There was plenty of parkland nearby, and they were only seven minutes by foot to Main Street—two by car. By all accounts, between the hardworking and ethical parents, the close-knit brotherhood of their sons, and easy access to farmland and friends, this was an idyllic upbringing for young men. They were middle-class for Waller, had no troubles at home, and had their futures ahead of them.

Trey was upbeat, polite, had hobbies that occupied him, and he loved his family. His YouTube channel produced fairly innocuous content and it chugged along rather successfully. In fact, onlookers appreciated his frank point of view and zany personality.

But Waller remains a hard city to excel in, even if you're looking to excel online. Trey, a clearly bored teen, had mostly only Main

---

74 Nancy Arnold, "Waller Wonders," *Chron*, December 7, 2005, https://www.chron.com/neighborhood/article/Waller-Wonders-9843763.php.

Street at his disposal, with its tattoo parlors, nail shops, and brewing company (for minors, soft drinks only), where the tax services are in the same building as the wax services. There's a salon, a single dry cleaner, and plenty of dusty maws of land for lease. The only restaurant on Main Street, owned by the same family that owns the brewing company next door, is Eji's, serving American cuisine, a lot of it "scratch made." Not yet opened in 2015, it's a modern bright spot on the otherwise tumbleweed street.

Despite its derelict state, there seems to be a sense of superiority about the town, one that exists now and existed then. Eji's serves the "Waller Cobb" salad, like it's a known delicacy—though the only thing that seems to make it different from a regular Cobb is Gorgonzola instead of blue cheese. Newsmen and politicians alike brag about how many years they've lived in the county, like it's a by-the-yard competition. Texan pride is real and almost seems to lash out, scolding those not local or not Texan *enough*.

In that vein, *The Waller Times* columnists' biography page boasts of one writer, "She is excited about being able to bring her folksy musings to what she calls 'the hometown crowd.'" And, "Because of family and career, she took a several-year sabbatical.... [For her beat,] she takes an amusing look at events close to her—family (much to their chagrin!), friends ... but she also tackles serious subjects ... from time to time." It lists, with names and relationships, which of the columnist's family members live in Waller, almost like poker chips to cash in for social credit. The next profile lists the journalist's husband and church, along with congratulating her on fourteen years of residence in Waller. It goes so far into her family tree, rather than her own accomplishments, that it lists the names and jobs of her children's *spouses*. (It does remark that she won awards for writing back in high school, though she is now old enough to be a grandma.)

This is a place where it would be easy for a young man, disillusioned and with no solid provincial prospects, to become lost and lackadaisical. Even violent. Add to this a difficult medical diagnosis Trey was to receive, and the problem boiled over.

Introducing ... Mr. Anime!

In the video entitled "LensCapProductions Introduction,"[75] Trey Sesler pretends to look around his front lawn for a moment before "noticing" the camera and giving his audience a wave."Oh! Hi, everybody. My name's Trey Sesler.... I'm most notably known for doing the Mr. Anime review series, and some know me for short films.... My Mr. Anime review series has been the most popular, so far, of everything I've done on the LensCapProduction's channel. I've had a lot of help, I've had a lot of great friends help me. Like the cameraman!" Here, he shows off his friend—a shy, laughing boy with a bowl cut, who waves—then talks about his YouTube statistics—50% of viewers from the US, 50% from Europe, mostly England and California. He implores those watching to please "spread the videos to other people who may like anime reviews, short films on low budget, special effects tests, or just me ranting and talking to you!"

LensCapProductions was launched by Trey in 2004 and was indeed most popular for its anime content. It reviewed trendy and niche shows alike and was known for being offbeat thanks to Trey's strange brand of comedy, often dark. In his *FLCL* anime review, conducted from on his floor, Trey talks while covered in cobwebs with a grim reaper figure and scythe in the background, noting to the audience that they're Halloween decorations. He's interrupted more than once by a machine blowing smoke into his face, which he won't verbally acknowledge, then finally shows his hands on camera, which have previously been off-screen. One hand is revealed to be giant, skeletal. He forges ahead as if nothing is amiss. A phone rings, providing another interruption. Trey ends on a cliffhanger, mid-sentence, and a trumpet plays over a loop of himself.

Oddly, his reviews never ran very deep, neither critical nor analytical nor even particularly educational. He tended to review anime with darker, more ruthless themes, but as a casual everyman. Trey even often mispronounced the names of the Japanese characters in the shows he'd watched; a cringey trait that would certainly invite

75 LensCapProductions, "LensCapProductions Introduction," YouTube, May 18, 2009, https://www.youtube.com/watch?v=WkD51F4h9Qc.

examination by 2025. ("What's up with these names?!" He laments in one video. "Well, here's my excuse. I'm American, I'm not supposed to do anything right!") The reviews were rarely probing examinations of art, story, or character arcs, and they rarely went over five minutes. They included pearls of insight, such as:

> I was impressed with this particular show ... pure cinematography shit right there. (*FLCL*)
>
> She has a bunch of porno and ... they all involve little girls. So she's a little girl herself and she's playing games that involve little girls and bad things. Um. UM. I'm really at a loss for words.... [there's] the anime club members at school: fat loser, and then that guy with the stupid-looking hair, and then there's that guy who looks like a faggot. (*My Little Sister Can't be This Cute*)
>
> The naked girl has a very dark, dark past. Turns out this girl is a vicious, strange, mutated human murderer. (*Elfen Lied*)

He actively engaged in bias, telling viewers what *he* liked, not what they might enjoy. He gave *Elfen Lied* a 10/10, despite its infamous ultra-violence. But Trey decided *not* to recommend *Higurashi no Naku Koro ni*, a murder anime featuring children brutalizing one another, with scenes of stabbings, maggot-infested wounds, and nails ripped off with pliers as torture—for not being scary or graphic enough.

Trey's videos featured a running gag in which he argues with Inuyasha, a dog-man warrior from the eponymous television series. He often curses at him, and they threaten each other with violence. He menaces the character with guns and flamethrowers that he has on hand—real, not props, even if the target is fictive and animated. Weapons would grow into a trademark of his channel. Reviews needlessly featured shotguns, handguns, and steak knives as props to black comedy. Videos sometimes end with someone off-screen being shot—also meant as a gag. "Kids are supposed to be destructive, they're supposed to want to shoot things," he says in a review of *Evangelion*, an apocalyptic robot show about forced teen conscription, while opening a can of beans. "Any kid would jump at the opportunity to get in a giant robot and blow the hell outta something."

The intro to many of the Mr. Anime videos was a rote one, featuring Trey in his room, innocuously enough, reading manga in different positions. It shifts abruptly to him shooting someone through the chest using a real gun and fake blood, his brother punching someone, and finally shows Trey kicking someone in the face, their body falling over a table. The reel is overlain with guitar music and ends with Trey pushing up a white bar that says "Mr. Anime Reviews" in red and black. A later opening on the channel would cut to Trey shooting someone in a medical mask who has their hands up in surrender, then to Trey's shocked disembodied head, a bookshelf full of manga on shaky cam, and finally, a cute shot of a pet rat—that he'd later kill. He also had a cheesy, sitcom-style opening with '90s television–style close-ups of him giving head-shaking smiles. It seemed try-hard enough that its edginess was dulled.

Trey's sense of humor was a hit, especially with male viewers. He received more than 170 comments on his overrated anime video, and rising levels of follower engagement inspired him to keep at it. He even began to implore his fans to send donations so that he could afford a more high-def camera for his content. The production value of his videos began to increase, and he began to post videos featuring his own scripts and directing. These were less popular—mainly because they were so strange, like a B-movie reel trying to be Rob Zombie.

A short film he titled "Action movie clip" shows Trey wandering his yard with a pistol in hand, when he's approached by another actor in all black, also toting guns. Trey fires, blood spatters. The next man he "shoots" staggers and sprays blood against a windowpane of his parent's home. The viewer briefly glimpses the idyllic backyard he grew up playing in: a swing set on the terrace, a wooden playhouse, wind chimes—not exactly the usual scenery for a snuff film.

In "Shootout,"[76] an almost six-minute video, two robbers (one played by his brother Mark) decide to steal the wallets of a pair of friends outside having a chat. All four actors pull out *real* guns and have a staged shoot-out across the lawn. A fifth person emerges from

76 TheMajor0, "Douglas Fir Trailer," YouTube, December 27, 2008, https://www.youtube.com/watch?v=5Jla207wlr8.

a trailer and is shot immediately. All four gunmen then receive bullet wounds to the abdomen, but the chase continues, past a wooden signboard with a large Confederate flag painted onto the side of a childhood clubhouse. (Texas was a Confederate state in the American Civil War, and today the flag is seen as a racist dog whistle.) Bottles of beer burst into scattered shards in the shoot-out. When only two gunners remain, one hides behind a barrel marked "fuel." Mark, seeing the barrel begin to leak, slugs it with rounds until it explodes into an inferno. He thinks he's won until the other gunner escapes immolation, only for Mark to realize he's out of bullets. The last man, played by Trey, headshots Mark's character, killing him instantly.

On Mark's YouTube page, a preview for "Douglas Fir"—Trey's Christmas horror film—stars Mark, Ryan Gaddy, and another young man, Chris Salazar.[77] Female actors never seemed to feature, outside of a cameo or two by the boy's mother, Rhonda. The blooper reel for "Douglas Fir"[78] features the kids having some jovial behind-the-scenes moments while shooting the scare-flick. It's clear they've used the Sesler Christmas lawn ornamentation to stud the film. In the extended B-roll footage, we get a glimpse of the Sesler home's living room with its bulky television and warm trappings, while Trey practices his facial expressions on camera.

In addition to including his friends and family members in videos, Trey was gregarious with fellow YouTubers, advertising them openly. In "Mr. Anime Updates/Plugs," he shouts out other channels, including "blowshimselfupdude," who he says posts great rants. He plugs his brother as well, but Mark was less serious about YouTube and would never reach Trey's popularity.

Very Bad News

Despite his bizarre cinematic shorts, Trey was considered a successful early reviewer and vlogger within his niche. Though his videos had what would now be viewed as a sort of antiquated charm—feeling

---

77 TheMajor0, "Favorites."

78 TheMajor0, "Douglas Fir Bloopers/Extras," YouTube, January 10, 2009, https://www.youtube.com/watch?v=5h46esINRi4.

more akin to an old film reel than one of today's shiny, focused, and heavily edited TikToks—Trey's work was robust enough that it even inspired collaborations and conversations with other pioneers of anime news, channels like MagnusX1 and Al's Anime Reviews. He uploaded frequently, with 318 videos on his main YouTube channel, which carried the byline "Subscribe and Wink =)."

But after Trey graduated high school, things started getting darker on his channel. He began posting more complaints—about social stigmas and the attitude of certain anime fans—as well as more unsettling bloody SFX content. Then came the rifle content—no longer playacting scripts and fiction, Trey started to post videos about the guns he himself owned. He tested his aim in empty lots with a more somber and serious persona than he'd had online prior. He said he wanted to go from being the "anime guy" to being the "gun guy."

Trey also seemed to manifest beef with certain *types* of people and would broadcast his distaste. In the clip "Anime Haters," he goes on a rant that he's apparently wanted to give for a "very long time." Directed toward cynics who mock anime-obsessed *otaku* like himself, he says, "Fuck you, anime haters." And he gives two middle fingers to the camera. Trey would go on to express a dim view of nationalism and borders, calling strong jingoism "laughable" and saying such people ought to "lay off."

His SFX tutorials also slashed a jagged line through his otherwise upbeat content. In "How to make a bullet hit," Trey describes how to fake someone getting shot. Methodically, head cut off by the camera angle, he fills and seals a Ziploc bag full of Halloween "blood" purchased from Walmart, then fastens the bag to his own torso. He tapes a firecracker beside it, directly onto his skin. Heading outside, he lights the firecracker with a match and pulls a white tee shirt over the blood bag and the explosive. It detonates, making a wound like a gunshot, tearing through part of the shirt as a wet red stain slowly blooms across his torso. The effect is *effective*.

With drab sarcasm, he stares into the camera and says, "*Ow*. It hurts so bad."

Another tutorial, entitled "Knife in chest effect," opens with Trey lying on the ground, fake blood spouting from the wound of a butcher's knife in his chest, metallic and gushing darkly against his white button-up. He clearly had a fascination with the look of violence. He suggests that, to make a stabbing look real, one should cut a knife in half and place a mound of play dough above where they'd want the wound to be, then stick the blunted end into the putty through a shirt, and *voila*.

In another video, "YouTube and Copyright," Trey grumbled over the same struggle that would later motivate Nasim Aghdam's violence at California's YouTube headquarters. That the hosting giant had the power to stymie creators' earnings by restricting views over objectionable content. Then, for no reason, he then shifts to talking about his fictional next-door neighbor, Inuyasha, before taking out a revolver and shooting someone off-screen. Again, this is intended as humor.

Trey affirmed that he made a living for himself via YouTube, meager though it must have been. It was a frightening time for reviewers because YouTube was taking down videos and suspending accounts over copyright violation issues, which Trey felt ignored fair use claims. It affected his ability to share music, imagery, and clips from shows in his evaluations. He called it the "YouTube Iron Fist Policy." "They have to cover their fucking ass," he'd admitted, but he thought they'd gone too far in hitting creator's purse strings. It was another ill omen.

In October of 2010, Trey ramped up the gun focus in his videos. "Get your rifle with flashlight attachment ready, because today I'm gonna review the zombie epic *High School of the Dead.*" Trey moves swiftly from reviews of anime *with* guns to reviews *of* actual guns and live ammo. In September of 2011, he posted a video of himself entitled "9mm rifle test."[79]

> It's Mr. Anime. Or you can call me Trey.... the guy who does all the gun stuff now.

He slurs his words and looks cagey as he hefts a black Hi-Point rifle into the frame. He talks about its affordable price point and different magazine clip types before noting,

79 LensCapProductions, "9mm rifle test," September 6, 2011, YouTube, https://www.youtube.com/watch?v=7jX1Vr21VUE&list=UUqtZg9i1IpbvEvQ-50qc9Mg.

> I have here a very classic 995.... It shoots 9mm rounds.... You can also buy an optional fifteen-round magazine, but you know I like really big clips, so I wish it came with like, a fifty.

He's performing this one-man stick-up under a concrete bridge at a public underpass, but one that's fairly overgrown and deserted. In the harsh daylight it's grimy with dirt mounds, cragged rocks, unkempt weeds, and locals' abandoned oversized trash—moldering couches and armchairs left upside down in the muck. Trey goes on to show himself shooting at a line of Dasani water bottles some eighty feet away, from two distinct camera angles. He nails all three bottles in one trigger pull each. It's one of his better filmed and edited videos, and his aim is exceptional, assuming there's no fibbing on the cutting room floor. He then moves on to an abandoned blue sofa, derelict and devoid of cushions. "What I'm going to do—and this is pretty childish and ridiculous—is blow up the couch to the best of my 9mm's abilities." He then fires recklessly into the settee multiple times from close range until he falls back in an exaggerated starfish pose. "Whoa! I wouldn't wanna be sitting on *that* couch right now."

Under that same bridge, he also filmed a test of a .22 pistol.[80] He shoots an aluminum bottle three times, surprised that the gun doesn't jam.

In Texas, no age limit is imposed on the purchase of ammo, no license is required, and no records are kept of who purchases ammunition or where. At around twenty cents a round for some 9mm ammo brands, Trey's hobby was more affordable than one might assume. Texans may carry long guns without a permit, and it is an open carry state. So his weapon-toting wouldn't have aroused much suspicion in greater Waller.

In an August 2011 video, "Gunshot wound to the head," Trey showed users how to use scar wax, liquid latex, eye shadow, and fake blood to make a "fairly legitimate" headshot SFX. "I don't know how I'm still talkin' with a nasty wound like that," he says, presenting a close-up of the gory, finished product on his own skull to the camera.

80 LensCapProductions, ".22 pistol test," YouTube, September 1, 2011, https://www.youtube.com.watch?v=ylumhDX6emY&list=UUqtZg9i1IpbvEvQ-50qc9Mg&index=41.

In another 2011 video, this one a skit entitled "Ambushed,"[81] a man in a white skull mask tries to kill him with a gun for watching anime. Instead, Trey—as himself—shoots him in the chest with a handgun, sending a spray of blood across his garage. Then he shoots a second masked man armed with a long sword. "Aw, man, I got all these bodies to clean up," Trey laments. In yet another video, "Molotov cocktail accident," a flaming cocktail is thrown at a person standing innocuously by a tree—that person explodes. The video is only three seconds long. His videos grew more brutal, less sensical.

In a rare bit of introspective content, Trey steers away from the "whacky" physical violence and gets personal in "My thoughts on NEETs." NEET, a Japanese acronym for people not currently engaged in employment, education, or training, is considered derogatory term in Japan, where not contributing to society casts you as a burden on your family and community.

"Technically, since I do a little bit of Googling, I don't totally consider myself a NEET," he begins jokingly.

> But this word is somewhat of an insult over in Japan.... NEETs are looked upon as, you know, the lower range of society. Like, think about it. They're not employed. They have no education prospects. They're not doing any training. So, they're just sitting around really doing a bunch of nothing. A lot of people are playing video games, uh, people like myself are wasting time on YouTube.... Hahahaha.

Despite the forced laughter, he is clearly speaking to his own worst anxieties.

> As for me, a NEET? Nooo.... Mr. Anime can shake it." Despite that feint, Trey then begins to wistfully relate to the plight of the NEET. "There's people that are aspiring artists, there's people that are aspiring reviewers, like myself.... I would absolutely love to make a living off reviewing anime.... I don't think that NEETs are losers.... But I think there's a large majority of NEETs out there, working from home like I am. They're trying to make it, they're trying to do something with the talent that they want to do. So you know what? To hell with whoever says ['NEET'], or status 0.... Fuck that shit. It's nothing but propaganda.

---

81 LensCapProductions, "Ambushed!," YouTube, April 20, 2011, https://www.youtube.com/watch?v=Ejb6ds1l8iY&list=UUqtZg9i1IpbvEvQ-50qc9Mg&index=48.

Trey, by this time a recent graduate who'd dropped out of college with no further educational expectations, set up a donation fund for purchasing new video equipment. To do so, he put his full and real Waller address on the internet in the hopes that strangers would mail him money. Remarkably, some did. He needed the cash, and badly—despite his dream of working in film one day, Trey wasn't progressing. His style wasn't becoming more nuanced or skilled, and his living situation was becoming uncomfortable. He switched between staying at his parents' and grandparents' houses while he worked delivering pizzas, using the same tired backdrops and odd gags to churn out online content. His brother, meanwhile, was moving on to better things.

In December of 2011, Trey asked friends on Facebook to visit his YouTube channel and click on ads to "help me build my income." He portrayed being upbeat about his delivery job ("about time" that he was working out of the home, he'd said), but his employment was not full time, stable, or fulfilling for him.[82] In fact, he'd flubbed a series of jobs. He worked at an ice-cream parlor, a campground, a gas station, and even a go-kart track. He was desperate, but either unwilling or incapable of holding anything down, despite that desperation.

The embarrassment of his setbacks was compounded by the comparative success of his brother, which Lawton Jr. found frustrating. Trey had no plans to move out of his family's homes, not after being unable to hack it at Blinn College, dropping out after just two years. Blinn is a community college that advertises its main virtues as affordability and speed of gaining credentials. Mark, on the other hand, had graduated from Sam Houston State University in 2010, earning a degree in business administration. SHU is ranked among the top US colleges for positive social mobility, its graduating classes made up of 50% first-generation students. Lawton, a teacher, and Rhonda, a wordsmith, would have been proud of son Mark's accomplishments and were openly concerned about Trey.

---

82. "Trey Sesler (22) Shot and Killed Three Members of His Family," MyDeathSpace.com, March 22, 2012, https://mydeathspace.com/article/2012/03/22/Trey_Sesler_(22)_shot_and_killed_three_members_of_his_family.

Trey also began to suffer from health issues. On December 11, 2011, he posted a video called "Very Bad News, Please Watch," in which he wore a pair of sunglasses and made the announcement that he'd been diagnosed with pneumothorax, a partially collapsed lung. "If you're religious, I'd appreciate if you prayed for me." This is one of his only videos featuring capitalization across the title, showing just how grave a topic he considered this to be. Pneumothorax can be so mild as to be asymptomatic or life-threatening enough to require surgery. It is caused by air filling the space between the lung and the chest wall. In his video, Trey touches his sunglasses constantly, noting his eyes are swollen. Perhaps he is holding back tears or has recently cried. Or perhaps he has the rare complication of orbital emphysema—air trapped in the tissue surrounding the eyes—that sometimes comes packaged with pneumothorax.

Trey alleged that air was leaking from his lungs and that they ran the risk of collapse. "It's not an act, it's 100% happening, and I'm pretty disturbed about it." Considering that his brother watched his YouTube channel, it's likely the diagnosis was true, as it would be odd to lie where he could easily be called out on it. But it's notable that he doesn't show the wheezing, fatigue, or bluish tinge common to the condition. He does, however, speak very haltingly.

Perhaps being faced with his own mortality and a good deal of physical agony and restriction pushed him over that edge, for he would deliver others' mortality to them, cruelly, just a little over three months after that video post.

Trey's final video, "Mr. Anime's new job!" was taken down due to a privacy claim by a third party, as was its predecessor, "Mr. Anime is planning something." The fact that the videos have even been scrubbed from internet archives like the Wayback Machine might imply that they were used eventually by the court as it presided over his multiple murder hearing.

In "Mr. Anime's new job!" Trey eerily brags, "I have some pretty good news. I found a full-time job in a department I'm interested in, which is film." He insists industry people finally recognized his talent. "I'm still going to be doing [YouTube] videos.... I want to thank you for sticking with me and watching the channel. Everything is going really good." He then announces a multiweek break while he adjusts to the new work schedule, adding that he might post some vlogs. What else he was planning, he didn't say.[83] Of course, it was all a lie anyway.

The video ends in a split screen, where two versions of Trey chat together. "Mr. Anime season two, we've had some good history," says the Trey on the right, while risibly eating a sandwich and smacking his lips. The effect is unnerving. "But I'm gonna be gone for some *work.*"

The video "Mr. Anime is planning something," uploaded around the same time, is uniquely shot on webcam in his room, using his MacBook rather than his video equipment. It's more sinister for this reason; and again, it feels personal. In it, Trey announces he's going to reward himself with a two- to three-week break and will be cutting back on anime reviews. He plays up how many viewers he has, saying it's more subscribers than ever, that he's been noticed by *real* professionals, thanks to his devoted fans, and he wants to thank everybody.

In reality, his numbers hadn't changed significantly. How much was donated via his mail-in fundraiser or ad clicks is unknown, but it was never enough to buy that new equipment. The sun was, in fact, setting on his brief heyday.

> I got more subscribers than ever, I got more views than ever, and everything is going really good.

Everything is going really good echoed across his final two videos. Long-time viewers now sensed something was wrong.

God, Please Forgive Me

Sometime between 2008 and 2010, Trey became enthralled by the 1999 Columbine school shooting, which had shaken America's foundations and ignited a national conversation on gun violence. But for Trey, the incident was a power move that held endless fascination. From then on, and especially in the colder months of 2011,

83 Michael Hall, "Mr. Anime Is Planning Something," *Texas Monthly*, January 21, 2013, https://www.texasmonthly.com/articles/mr-anime-is-planning-something.

he dedicated an inordinate amount of his time to reading about all types of mass killers, various school shootings, and American serial murders.

He had gone down a sick rabbit hole—and the more he researched, the more obsessed he became with outdoing those infamous murderers. He began planning how he could accomplish their missions better, mapping out where the killers had gone wrong and reworking their plans to maximize as many mass casualties as possible, even using aerial photos and live footage to map target zones as if it were a tabletop simulation strategy game.[84] These gruesome diversions chronicled his growing interest in mass killing on a more general scale—murderers who had targeted strip malls and supermarkets, not just schools. It spiraled from fantasy planning into real prep: Trey was looking into what locations *in Waller* could result in the most loss of life if attacked by a gunman.[85] He began training with his firearms and amassing an arsenal.

Trey watched a documentary on the Columbine tragedy *fifty times* at his grandparents' house in Hempstead, memorizing it. He became obsessed with the Virginia Tech shooting of 2007 as well, a university campus attack with another disgruntled young man who'd left a manifesto and carnage in his wake. Trey felt he could improve upon even his favorite killings, what with his cache of six guns and his nearly 500-pound car—which he planned to ram into a crowd to begin his dream massacre, racking up a high number of casualties early on.[86] He thought he might target the middle school within walking distance of his childhood home, or his old high school—maybe he could even do it during Waller High's homecoming football game, usually

---

84 Anita Hassan, Susan Carroll, and Lindsay Wise, "Conflicting Pictures of Waller Killings Suspect Emerge," *Chron*, last updated March 24, 2012, https://www.chron.com/news/houston-texas/article/conflicting-pictures-of-waller-killings-suspect-3432744.php.

85 Lindsay Wise and Carol Christian, "Shooting Suspect Studied Serial Killers, Massacres, Officers Say," *Chron*, last updated March 22, 2012, https://www.chron.com/news/houston-texas/article/shooting-suspect-studied-serial-killers-3427179.php.

86 Dr. Todd Grande, "Trey Sesler (Mr. Anime) Case Analysis | Deep Desire to be a Killer," YouTube, May 19, 2021, https://www.youtube.com/watch?v=M8Q59Y8TQTM.

played in September and well-attended.[87] That, he figured, could have maximum impact. According to Trey's own future testimony, one strategy he'd planned to employ was sneaking across the field, then opening random fire on hometown fans. He hoped the pandemonium of desperate escapees as bullets cracked and parents screamed would lead to more injury than his gun could cause, as people shoved and panicked, making bodies pitch over steep bleachers and tumble down fraught stairwells, only to be stomped on by fleeing mobs.

Just as he lied to his followers online, likewise, he told local friends not to worry—he was working for Google, selling advertisements, living with his grandparents. He said he aimed to move back into his old house with his parents, mostly because they had a better Wi-Fi connection for his video uploads.[88] He seemed to be future planning. Yet, according to what Trey himself later admitted, he was unemployed and stewing in his borrowed room, cooking up horrors—he couldn't even make it a few days without dreaming up some violent action he felt compelled to complete.[89] Listless and now caught up in his own lies, he looked with fierce longing toward what he now felt he *had* to do. His path was alarmingly clear. He was going to shoot up a school from which he'd graduated.

There was only one problem. If he did that, his family would be besmirched for all time. Waller, close-knit and neighborly, wouldn't hold to their bosom the family whose son took their own children. If Trey was going to do this, and do it right, he couldn't let the shame and degradation of it blow back onto his beloved kin. So ... he had to kill them first, he decided. To save them from his planned misdeeds.

Other than Trey's startling obsession with guns and his newfound interest in school shootings, there were further signs of a curdling psyche. He'd make prank calls to police and set a series of small fires in town. He began to use animals as target practice—a family pet went missing, but no one put together that gruesome math. He'd start

87 KHOU Staff, "Waller Man Confesses on Tape to Murdering His Family," KHOU.com, last updated September 17, 2012, https://www.khou.com/article/news/waller-man-confesses-on-tape-to-murdering-his-family_20161021103604243/339660444.

88 Hassan, Carroll, and Wise, "Conflicting Pictures of Waller Killings."

89 KHOU Staff, "Waller Man Confesses on Tape."

to have outward friction with Lawton over his stalled life, and he texted Rhonda regularly, begging help for his deteriorating mental health.

In a call he'd made to the police two weeks prior to the shooting he'd carry out, Trey reported that he'd heard a bullet whiz past his head while sitting and relaxing in his backyard. But he wasn't calling for help or backup. He was calling to let them know he'd gotten his own guns and was ready for anything—ready to take someone down.

In another troubling incident, he'd phoned an old high school buddy of Mark's, a police officer named Michael Mathes. He wanted to know about Kevlar body armor—specifically, how involved someone would have to be in the sale and purchase of it to catch the notice of police. He said he'd found someone selling it and wanted to know if he should report it; more likely, he wanted to know how much Kevlar he'd have to amass before he'd be slapped onto a watch list.[90]

On March 20, 2012, Trey left his grandparents' house, where his arsenal was stockpiled, and traveled to his parents' home on Farr Street, arriving a little before 5:30 p.m. The workday was done and everyone was home—including Mark. Trey killed Rhonda first. He coaxed his caring mother into the garage with him, where he had a loaded shotgun lying in wait. He shot her several times, at point-blank range.

Then, there was no turning back. Feeling—in his own words—that he'd already committed to the action, he had to complete it. After all, there was no laying down his weapon to meander into the house and declare to his father and brother that he'd killed his own beloved mother and to beg their forgiveness. There was no coming back from it now; no quitting.

From inside the home, Mark called out, "I don't know what you're doing out there, but it's really loud!"

Trey switched to a Glock .22 and made his way into the house, shooting Mark twice in the hallway—once in the head. Mark, panicked but not dying on impact, veered into their bathroom, pulled the door closed, and locked it, trying to hide from the onslaught. In

90 Hassan, Carroll, and Wise, "Conflicting Pictures of Waller Killings."

the adjacent master bedroom, Lawton—who'd been napping—woke up and called out. Trey smoothly shifted into the bedroom and killed his father. Then, he returned to the bathroom, shooting through the door and kicking it open, only to find Mark already dead—curled up in a fetal position on the floor. Slab counters and cool white tile were slicked red. No longer just SFX.

Trey circled the house again, this time to "double tap" his family members—a brief, brutal, accurate way for him to "mercy kill," firing more slugs into their lifeless bodies with a high-powered rifle.

"I didn't want anyone to be suffering, lying on the floors for hours moaning and groaning, so I was like, I've got to retrace with a more powerful weapon and shoot them again,"[91] Trey would later say.

From there, a frenzy came on. What he'd done and what it meant began to sink in. His precious family—the people who had nurtured, supported, and cared for him. He'd *murdered* them. He began to ransack the house, shooting and toppling furniture, destroying as much of the roof and the interior as he could. His bloodlust and its twin agony of personal loss crashed against each other and he doubled down on the horror of the situation, stalking the once-happy home to kill all the family pets—the fish in their tanks, a ferret, his father's pet birds, and the harmless gray tabby kitten with the wide eyes who could be seen cuddling his hand playfully in some of Trey's YouTube videos.[92] He overturned tables, stabbed knives into cabinetry, and threw a general fit.

Then, he lay down in the garage and took a nap beside his mother's torn and unresponsive body.[93] The exhausted son was seeking comfort one final time. At some point, deep in sorrow over his own actions, he scrawled messages across the walls and doors of the house with a black marker, even etching some statements into the wood at knifepoint:

> WHY DID I DO THIS?
> I LOVE MY MOM, DAD, AND BROTHER.

---

91 KHOU Staff, "Waller Man Confesses on Tape."

92 Dr. Todd Grande, "Trey Sesler (Mr. Anime) Case Analysis."

93 Dr. Todd Grande, "Trey Sesler (Mr. Anime) Case Analysis."

I MISS MY MOTHER, FATHER, AND BROTHER.
GOD FORGIVE ME, BECAUSE I CANNOT FORGIVE MYSELF.

The hysterics continued. He went into town. He shot indiscriminately at edifices and around businesses and schools. He went hunting for more helpless wild animals, squirrels and birds. And then he debated shooting up Waller Middle School, going so far as to sit outside the institute for a while before diverting to a friend's house. This had all been for the purpose of attacking a school—but in his grief, perhaps his bloodlust lessened, and the reality sank too far into his bones to allow him to continue his spree any further.

Not long after the initial incident, a neighbor would call the police to report the noise of gunfire at the Sesler house. It must have been quite a din, as they would have been used to hearing bullet rounds and firecrackers and the shattering of glass from Trey and Mark's skits. It was a clear day, a robust 80 degrees in the last thrall of a Texas winter, and sound carried. But whatever the police found on their outside inspection of the house didn't raise the alarm. No one answered the door when they knocked. With the sun still high at 5:30 p.m., they must have been met with warm quiet. The bodies hadn't yet begun to stink.

That was Monday, March 20, 2012.

Tuesday rolled around, and developments became more distressing. Someone had left messages that the Seslers wouldn't be in to work that day. Trey hadn't returned home to his grandparents, and most telling of all, no one was able to get in touch with Rhonda or Lawton. The family was in the midst of a personal tragedy at the time, with Lawton's father in palliative hospice care. They had end-of-life planning to do for the eighty-eight-year-old, who suffered from a terminal illness.

An aunt of Lawton Jr.'s tried calling the house. Only static greeted her on the end of the line. So, concerned family members contacted the police next, asking that they conduct a welfare check. The Sesler family had yet no idea how much deeper their budding sense of loss would grow.

When police visited a second time, it was around 1 p.m. on Tuesday. Officer Mathes was on call and unnerved by the earlier discussion he'd had with Trey regarding Kevlar. When knocking produced no reply from anyone inside, the patrolmen searched the perimeter. Officer Mathes leaned in at the window of the master bedroom to try to see against the glint of the sun on the glass, and there spotted the lifeless body of Lawton Jr. The officers quickly entered the house, which read like a nightmare zone—the stench of death, streaks of dried plasma, ravaged rooms, drawers with gutted contents. Shell casings were everywhere—more than a hundred of them. Floating above everything were those eerie pleas for mercy in block letters and black ink. A confession, of sorts. Officer Mathes immediately recognized that Trey's body wasn't among the fallen family members, nor was his beloved 2010 slick black Ford Mustang parked outside.[94]

Police issued an arrest warrant for Trey Sesler and went on a manhunt, finally spotting his Mustang parked in a friend's driveway in Magnolia. Trey was still sitting in it, driver's side, silent and still. He'd convinced himself to end the violence with just his family wasted, even if the point of those intimate murders had been to spare his family from his next ones. When police later asked him why he'd changed his mind, having found plenty of credible evidence that he'd planned on a mass killing, Trey answered, "Maybe what happened was just ... too real."[95]

In case he'd implicate himself on more charges, or in the case he might be a danger to himself and others, police initially watched him for a long while, ready to take action when Trey did.

But all he did was sit. Sit in the car, staring straight ahead.

Trey was finally apprehended by Texas Rangers, federal marshals, and Brazoria County SWAT officers at 9:30 p.m., arrested on charges of suspected capital murder. He was taken to Waller County Jail and held there.

His brother had been just twenty-six, his mother fifty-seven, and his father fifty-eight when he'd executed them. All so young.

94 MyDeathSpace.com, "Trey Sesler (22) Shot and Killed Three Members of His Family."

95 KHOU Staff, "Waller Man Confesses on Tape."

There was an immediate riot of interest around the case, with Waller residents demanding justice. The eccentricity of the matter did nothing to ease latent fears—that notable and beloved residents were dead and their butcher had intended the same for Waller's kids. The fact that Trey had been something of a minor online celebrity pushed media outlets into a frenzy, casting him as a malignant psychopath as they criminally profiled him ahead of trial. Out-of-town interest poured in, conclusions were Olympic pole-vaulted to, and in the *newsworthiness* of it all, the reality of the people involved got lost.

These media profiles spoke very little about mental health, but Trey had been suffering. He used recreational drugs to self-medicate, amphetamines and oxytocin, and was on additional drugs prescribed by doctors.[96] And he was drinking heavily, which had a mind-bending effect when combined with the Seroquel and Xanax he was taking. Seroquel is an antipsychotic.[97] Mixed with alcohol, it causes an increased sedative quality, weakened cognitive function, and impaired judgment. Mixed with Xanax, it has the potential for increased neurological effects and heightened psychosis. Trey's mental health had dipped badly, and his formula for release from his own demons was so potently dangerous that his father and his brother had both independently told friends that they had fears Trey might one day take their lives.

His decision to do so was rash, though. He'd made it just half an hour before he carried it out, half-baked and fully cocked.

In an eight-hour interview by Texas Rangers after his arrest, Trey confessed: "The thing about my family is I would protect them with my life, but at the same time, if anyone was going to hurt them it would be me." Why them? "They were the first immediate human targets in my sight. If I was going to go out and do anything, they would have to go.... And I'm like, there's my opportunity. Go ahead. Go get 'em."[98]

---

96 Lindsay Wise and Anita Hassan, "Police: Man Charged In Waller Deaths Planned Columbine-Like Attack, *Chron*, last updated March 21, 2012, https://www.chron.com/news/houston-texas/article/police-man-charged-in-waller-deaths-planned-3421875.php.

97 Dr. Todd Grande, "Trey Sesler (Mr. Anime) Case Analysis."

98 KHOU Staff, "Waller Man Confesses on Tape."

Though his reasons for the killings kept shifting under interrogation, ultimately the police accepted that it was out of some misplaced honor to his family—to spare them his greater evils. His bail was set in the millions, and he was placed on suicide watch.

The community was shattered by loss. But in the turmoil, Waller tightened its ranks. Instead of turning on one of their own, as Trey assumed might happen, friends of Trey's from school refused to call him a crazy loner, instead tempering the outside news stories of this wild incident with their memories of him as kind-hearted and congenial—so at odds with what he'd done.

Older community members decided to dedicate the Waller High School class of '78 reunion to Lawton Jr. Memorials popped up. Support for the remaining family members outside of Trey ramped up, too.

Erdie Sesler, wife of the terminally ill Lawton Sr. and mother of the slain Lawton Jr., found grace in her heart for Trey. According to Trey's lawyer, she was the real hero of what was otherwise a horror story. Her husband, Lawton Sr., died just three days after son Lawton Jr. was murdered, but she still visited the jail regularly and prayed for Trey and even set up a plan for his care to continue after her own death, once he was incarcerated. Her husband and son were both buried at the Canon Funeral Home in Waller, one interred on Wednesday and another on Saturday of the same week.

Speaking with Trey's attorney, John Franklin Blazik, about the case, Edie's fortitude, and public response, he noted,

> There was so much publicity. The media was just ravenous.... I was afraid that the publicity would just be overwhelming and there would be a lot of pressure on the district attorney to seek the death penalty.... they had images of him pointing rifles at cameras, because he had been prolific about posting.... so they had all sorts of violent imagery of him published in the media, and that scared me, that people would just get carried away by that.[99]

Attorney Blazik had informed the grieving widow that the media circus could continue for months if the state decided to seek the death

99 Interview with John Franklin Blazik, October 3, 2024.

penalty, which seemed almost certain. So elderly Erdie picked herself up, overcame her deep heartache, and went to speak to the DA personally—to save the grandson who hadn't shown her own son any mercy. She argued in favor of life in prison without the possibility of parole if Trey pled guilty. All to avoid death row and the stress of curious outsiders descending in droves on the town of Waller. All out of compassion. The DA, moved by her, agreed.

"Just a lovely lady.... It was very devastating to her, she was in mourning during all of this." Attorney Blazik, now retired, shared a photo of himself and Erdie on the day the guilty plea was entered. She looks steadfast and sure, but there was also an effervescent kindness about her face. A softness, despite the hard reality. She would tell the attorney that she'd joined a support group for surviving family members of serial killers, to bring meaning to the chaos. "She told me that provided something for her, some community that she could go to to get some support."

Positive and brave, Erdie stayed in touch with Attorney Blazik until her death in 2019. She visited with Trey regularly. After she passed, Erdie's daughter (Trey's aunt) would continue to provide for Trey, as Erdie had arranged.

"His family loved him," Mr. Blazik said in an interview about the Sesler case for this book. "They were very angry for what happened, they were very hurt, it was tragic. You know, I don't think anyone forgave anybody, but there was an understanding on the part of the family that Trey was seriously mentally ill. And I think they knew that before, and after, this episode." Erdie, who could have shunned him for compounding the loss of her husband with such a gross personal tragedy, instead found it in herself to work with the grandson she had left, flaws and all.

"I think the fact that his family encouraged him to accept the life in prison sentence was helpful to him, make him feel that his life was worth living, even if he was in prison ... [the DA] listened to grandmother, and [the DA] was concerned about his community.... I think he kind of resented all the press from Houston and the media trying to make a spectacle of everything. These people, Trey's parents, were so intertwined with the community, this was—they were not some strange figures, some strangers getting killed.... They knew lots of people.... everybody knew everybody, so I think a lot of people in the community were heartbroken."

Outside of the community, people also felt loss because of Trey's YouTube popularity. They saw it as a sad betrayal by Mr. Anime. What they didn't see, Mr. Blazik points out, is the human suffering Trey endured and will have to live with for the rest of his incarcerated life. "There were lots of people on the internet that had some knowledge of Trey Sesler.... They had harsh reactions to all this. [But] that's just the nature of thing.... He will always be in prison until he dies, and you know, he'll have to live with the consequences of what he did. It'll weigh on him."

As a last word, Attorney Blazik reminded, "His mental illness was severe, he was on medication, he was getting psychiatric help but whatever it was it wasn't enough to prevent him from acting on these severely impaired impulses ... and of course the fact that he was armed to the teeth. That was a mistake on the part of the family. They should have realized that with his mental health situation.... he should not have been allowed to have weapons. But we don't have anything in Texas to prevent that, you can be mentally ill and arm yourself to the teeth—everything's fine."

In a photo from the day Trey entered his guilty plea, he poses with Erdie and Blazik. Trey looks like he's put on weight. Maybe, in prison, he'd finally focused on bettering himself a little, forming healthy habits, if by force. In the snapshot, Edrie has an arm around him and a hand on his shoulder. Attorney Blazik is providing that same comforting support for Erdie. Erdie was a community pillar, and a pillar for her ruined family. Because of her, Trey Sesler remains alive.

Trey is currently serving out a life sentence with no possibility of parole in the Terrell Unit in the unincorporated Brazoria County. Following the death of David Owen Brooks to COVID-19, the accomplice to pedophile and murderer Dean Corll, whose crimes against twenty-eight boys were considered some of the most infamous in Texan history (Brooks himself was a victim of Corll), Trey Sesler is now the unit's most notable inmate.

CHAPTER 3

ABIGAIL WHITE, aka Mitzee Lewis

You can drive all night
Lookin' for the answers in the pourin' rain
You wanna find peace of mind
Lookin' for the answer
Funny how it seems like yesterday
As I recall, you were lookin' out of place
Gathered up your things and slipped away
No time at all, I followed you into the hall
Cigarette daydream
You were only seventeen
Soft speak with a mean streak
Nearly brought me to my knees
—"Cigarette Daydream," Cage the Elephant

This is the song Abigail White chose to overlay on a TikTok featuring one of the darkest facets of her young life: the multiple assaults she'd survived at the hands of a family member. When the lyrics "you were only seventeen" play in the video, she amends the lyrics with subtitles that note "11," indicating she was not even yet a teenager when the rapes began.

(This depicts a real-life story of spousal abuse. If you are experiencing abuse, there is help. Call the national abuse hotline at 1-800-799-7233.)

Chipper

On October 21, 2022, Abigail White was sentenced to life in prison. It was a fast sentencing, moving through the court system in just seven months, with jurors in agreement after only twelve hours of deliberation. The verdict was murder.

On March 24, 2022—Abigail's last day as a free woman, far from the closing remarks of Justice Fraser in the Bristol Crown Court—she'd been down at the Horseshoe public house for a couple of hours, fueling up on rum and Cokes. The pub was just a three-minute car ride from her home on Chipperfield Drive in South Gloucestershire, England.

Alfie Pike had been happy to give Abigail and her former paramour, Bradley Lewis, a lift home after their night out. They'd been among a big group of friends, all locals, but when the scene curdled alongside spilled drinks and raised voices, it became clear that they'd better go—especially as Abigail had been drinking heavily by then, her mood turning foul and raucous. Alfie was worried for Bradley, who was a close mate. He'd wanted to see the pair back safely, since it was past dark and they had little children waiting on them. He'd hoped his being there might also prevent the barroom squabbles between the pair from hitching a ride home with them. Abi had a wild temper.

When they arrived at Chipperfield Drive, Alfie quietly offered to take his friend back to his own home, after seeing Abi to the door—Bradley lived in town with his mother. Or, he offered, he could take Bradley anywhere else he wanted to go. Anywhere, away from Abi and a situation they already knew to be unsafe and unstable. In fact, by court order, Bradley wasn't even technically allowed inside Abi's home, a home they'd once shared—for his *own* safety.

Bradley turned down the offer. It was a decision that shortened his lifespan to only minutes.

"I'm dead when I get home," Bradley had murmured under his breath to Alfie when they'd neared the walkway of the brown and beige concrete-brick house. Abigail's place, which had once been Bradley's, too, was on a winding street dotted with carbon copies of the same home, most with high walls or fences protecting mealy strips of yard suffused with dilapidated children's playhouses or abandoned gardening projects. The yards were sprinkled with sagging soccer nets, deflated plastic pools, loose red scalloped shingles, rusted oil drums, and giant wooden cable reels serving as makeshift tables. Abi and Bradley's property, in contrast, was neat and tidily green, with only two brackets of fencing having gone sideways. They were, by the look of it, the local Joneses everyone was meant to keep up with.

Surrounded by overgrowth and underdevelopment all around, their plot of land looked practically royal for their young ages. At just twenty-four and twenty-two years old, respectively, Abi and Bradley had an orderly lawn attached to a multi-bedroom home that was their own, where three young children were kept warm and cozy among pink teddies and Peppa Pig stuffies. A dream many couples still strive for in their early thirties and later. It was an advantage afforded at least in part by the flash-in-the-pan riches Abi had made as a popular OnlyFans model. She was known fondly online as "Fake Barbie" for her filler-plush lips, voluptuous chest, and long, bottle-blond hair. Her body was her selling point, but as competition grew—both from other online content creators and for her lover's attentions—her rage grew along with it.

That three-minute drive to Abi's home was the last time Alfie would see Bradley Lewis alive. Bradley had correctly predicted his own homicide, knowing well what his ex-girlfriend was capable of. But he wasn't an oracle or a diviner. He knew Abigail could hurt him because she'd done it before. In fact, her physical, mental, and emotional abuse of a man younger than herself and far gentler—a man with a large network of friends and family throughout Bristol that knew him as courteous, gregarious, and devoted—had become so overwhelming that Bradley decided it was time to break things off.

"I don't want to be with you anymore, Abi."

It was a refrain he'd delivered often, and again earlier that same day, in a park with one of Abi's friends nearby to hear it, after they'd had a heated phone argument in the morning. It was not his first attempt to break things off, but he'd seemed more sincere about it this time around. That frightened and infuriated Abi. In a perfect scenario, they would have parted ways then to handle their wounded emotions separately. Bradley's, timid; Abi's, uproarious.

Instead, Bradley showed up to the pub that night at Abi's behest, against the advice of friends and even a governmental agency. And then, he'd gone home with her.

The shocking details of their toxic relationship would play out in court over phone messages, witness testimony, National Health Service records, cruel TikToks, and social services archives.

Abusive Behavior

Kingswood, in South Gloucestershire, England, is a cozy urban burrow on the outskirts of Bristol, which looks less metropolitan than it does Grimm's fairytale-meets-just-plain-grim. Its residents don't brag of it very much, but they do take pride in its solid nature: a few good shops, a café or two, and a nightlife that promises lukewarm draft beers at barstools until the lights go off at around midnight—sometimes earlier.

It has a wee stone church with a wide red door and graves dating from the early 1900s. Its local banks look pinched from fantasy movies about wizards and high elves, an effect enhanced by stone reliefs advertising the likes of the "Old Flower Pot Inn" from 1890. There's a central clock tower in brass and red brick, plus the occasional sheep ambling by. Its high street, in contrast to the warm fabulist classical buildings, is squat and offers England's typical fare for bargain diners and beer drinkers: kebab, fried fish, and something pretending to be pizza. A few decades earlier, the area was rougher around the edges, split between the right and wrong side of the tracks—though in Kingswood's case, that refers to its prolific bus lines, not rail. Its businesses dodder along, with graffiti peppering dreary streets and many "To Let" and "Wanted" signs up near office buildings corroding in disrepair. New locals complain of a lack of entertainment or green spaces as the population has been on a steady rise, bringing in more families each year as mounting costs in nearby, more urban areas drive Britons to look for more budget-friendly options.

Bristol, nearby, has ever been the more exciting choice—but excitement comes with its price tag.

1998 was a busy year in Bristol. It opened its red-brick Tobacco Factory Theatre in the ashes of lost industry after Imperial Tobacco—which employed a staggering 40% of the local workforce—relocated elsewhere in England, leaving the building, and its workers, abandoned. It became a flourishing space for the arts and for low-priced coffees. An International Balloon Fiesta was held, sending hot air balloons majestically careening over Ashton Court. Her Majesty the late Queen Elizabeth II and then-Prince Charles paid a visit. The Church of England ordained its first female priests at Bristol Cathedral. Young people were indulging in frenetic underground raves with loud counter-cultural music, driving white collar parents *nutso*. Abigail White was born.

Hers was a rocky life from the start, as her family was wholly unfit to care for her. When she was only two years old, her father began mercilessly beating her mother, often in front of baby Abi. This was her earliest example of a romantic partnership and her earliest model of communication style, characterized by his rage and physical assault. By age four, her mother had had enough of that abuse, and the two split up. Her mother dated around before finally marrying a man that Abi would come to know *far* too intimately.

Abi's stepfather began to sexually assault her before she was even a teenager, acting out perversions on her and manhandling her body. Whether her mother knew about the abuse or not, she was incapable of protecting her young daughter. Confused by the attention and coaxed into compliance by the revolting older man, Abi was too young to really comprehend what was happening to her.

In her own words on TikTok years later in June of 2021, she overlaid the following text on a video of her in a tank top singing along to "Cigarette Daydream":

> Me feeling "lucky" when my step dad used to secretly let me stay up late with him and make me feel "special."[100]

---

100 Abigail White (@mitzeelewis), "Me feeling 'lucky' when my step dad used to secretly let me stay up late with him and make me feel 'special,'" TikTok, June 28, 2021, https://www.tiktok.com/@mitzeelewis/video/6978864195114650885

It was hashtagged: #rape. TikTok unhighlighted the hashtag, making it unsearchable. Adding illness to injury, *rape* is considered a censorable word on much of social media because too many people use the term to indulge in fantasy, rather than to engage with survivors' narratives.

Despite Abi having thousands of followers, that post garnered only one comment in 2021:

You've got through it so strong 💪🖤

It was from Brad, her then-boyfriend, on the handle @LewisFamily4. Comments since have been more to the tune of:

@alfiedowing5: lol im glad

Brad's comment has 10 Likes. @Alfiedowing5's, celebrating her childhood rape as penance for her later crime of murder, has 18.

As a child, Abi was shuttled from home to home until she eventually landed in foster care for a stint. From there, she was taken in by her grandparents, moving yet again. Displaced, abused, and abandoned by those who should have provided for her, she was prescribed medication for depression before she'd even turned thirteen. In school, Abi had a difficult time focusing and keeping on the straight and narrow, what with all the upheaval she'd endured. While still underage, she embarked on her own early romantic relationship, clearly affected by what her stepfather had done. Her first partner should have been someone in her age bracket whom she could grow alongside, learn from, and rely on. This first major attachment should have helped fill in the cracks in her foundation surrounding communication and consent. Instead, in the not-unexpected pattern of an abused child selecting a companion who will also engage in patterns of intimate partner violence (IPV), she began an amorous relationship with a man in his thirties.

With such a broad age discrepancy, and the age of consent in England being just sixteen years old, there's almost no doubt that this relationship qualified as grooming—the sexual predation of vulnerable victims, often built through gaining trust by giving seemingly supportive attention and then slowly normalizing exploitation. For

Abi, who'd already endured so much, the line between acceptable and unacceptable or unexpected behavior would have been thin. Survivors of childhood sexual abuse are likely to exhibit signs of post-traumatic stress disorder, schizophrenia, and often engage in recreational drug use.[101] For Abi, that drug was cocaine.

The result of these negative, uprooting, and sadistic environmental factors triggered borderline personality disorder (BPD), which largely went untreated. BPD is classified as a problem with producing serotonin, leading to aggressive behavior, depressive episodes, and trouble reining in destructive urges. When not genetic, it can often be caused by improper brain development in early upbringing, especially mitigating factors that affect the child's mood (when they feel frightened of expressing joy, or unsafe expressing unhappiness to caregivers), anxiety around long-term planning (after the loss of home, guardian, school, or due to exposure to food scarcity), or an atmosphere heavy with aggression, anxiety, and fear. This can impact the brain chemistry severely, even changing the brain's structure as it bends to accommodate high levels of cortisol, impairing emotional function and cognitive regulation. This especially affects the hippocampus (resulting sometimes in reduced ability to tell past from present, or retain memories), the prefrontal cortex (affecting impulse control and rational decision-making), and the amygdala (like pressing on a fear-response button, it can cause overblown, defensive emotional responses).

Sufferers of BPD have difficulty regulating feelings, exhibiting self-control, and making wise decisions. It is a hallmark disorder of childhoods pockmarked by intimidation, physical or sexual violence, emotional manipulation, neglect, and protracted stress. Abi checked every box for the early environmental factors flagged by the UK's National Health Services (NHS).[102]

---

101 Helen P. Hailes, Rongqin Yu, Andrea Danese, and Seena Fazel, "Long-Term Outcomes of Childhood Sexual Abuse: An Umbrella Review," *The Lancet Psychiatry* 6, no. 10 (2019): 830–39, https://pubmed.ncbi.nlm.nih.gov/31519507.

102 "Overview–Borderline Personality Disorder," NHS.uk, last updated February 12, 2019, https://www.nhs.uk/mental-health/conditions/borderline-personality-disorder/overview.

All of this made Abi extremely volatile, especially around her main triggers—rejection or abandonment, especially where it concerned family or men.

On the other end of the spectrum was Bradley Lewis. His home life could not have been more different, and neither could the personality that blossomed from an environment of positive reinforcement, healthy boundaries, and sustained schooling. Born about two years after Abi, Brad was a cheerful boy raised in a warm and comfortable family home with adoring parents and a cluster of close friends. He was all skinned knees and grass stains as he devoted himself to soccer, being a huge fan of one of London's local teams, the Premier League's Chelsea F.C., having played himself up through junior club.

Brad was handsome, athletic, and a gentleman. Parents Steve and Rachel were terribly proud of their boy, with his tousled dark hair, dimpled smile, and his keen work ethic. "He'd do anything for anybody," his father said of him, after he passed. "And that is shown by his popularity ... because of what a popular, thoughtful, helpful person that our son was.... Brad would now be saying, 'That's enough now, Dad. Just shut up.'"[103]

He was modest, too, apparently, not one for garnering too much praise. He had a sweet, cheeky sense of humor and a sentimental streak for family—parents, siblings, and eventually, his own children.

Brad had attended and graduated from Saint Stephen's Church of England Junior School, an institution focused on the "British values" of mutual respect and tolerance, with interfaith teachings and inquiry-based learning. The school's educational approach poses questions and gives students the freedom to research, study, and express themselves as they build unique answers, more open-ended than rote, promoting cognition. It's a school with World War focus weeks and a World Book Day costume competition, which blasts confetti on children's graduation days, gives out Orator of the Week awards, and has student rock bands take the stage to Change the World. The dean shares Hot Chocolate Fridays with lucky students, and children are

103 BistolLive, "Steve Lewis, Dad of Bradley Lewis, Speaks Outside Bristol Crown Court after Abigail White Jailed for Life for Bradley's Murder," Facebook, October 22, 2022, https://www.facebook.com/watch/?v=3352703188341954.

encouraged to scrawl poetry on their desks with washable markers. On special days, the lawn even boasts a bouncy castle. The school awards house points and invests in its robust theater and athletics department—locals are particularly proud of the competitiveness of Saint Stephen's boys' soccer team, which performs well, so placement on its roster can get competitive. Students who attend Saint Stephen's do so in a dapper uniforms: smart blue jumpers and light gray bottoms. Daily, they tuck into healthy warm lunches. Parents and siblings are even invited to themed dinner nights at the school.

In other words, Saint Stephen's is a community and a refuge—a place for students to develop healthy and curious.

Brad and Abi grew up close in distance, yet so far apart from one another by every other measure. In different worlds within the same England.

They met as teenagers, and when Bradley was sixteen, they began to date. From late secondary school onward, Brad showed tremendous interest and determination in trade work and began apprenticing as a flooring installer. Abi, for her part, got into a budding online platform: OnlyFans. Launched in 2016, the London-based company offers subscription services to individual content creators, taking a cut of the profits. Users pay to view the content on locked profiles, then can buy extras and add-ons based on what each individual content creator has on offer. Though the site plays host to a number of musicians and gym gurus, the content it is famous for and peddles to a worldwide consumer base is pornography.

OnlyFans has been characterized by the online community at large as a safe, creator-led platform for sex work and sexual content, hailed as an ethical place to consume consensual pornography, where 80% of spending and 100% of content direction is in the hands of the creators themselves—models, mostly. Unlike other pornography websites, which get accused of content or wage theft, human trafficking, and revenge porn, OnlyFans largely skirts these issues by putting power in the hands of the models.

Users on OnlyFans make money through pay-per-view, customer tips, and subscription services, offering saucy pictures and erotic short videos that unlock for fans willing to pay more. Some models even allow commissions or one-on-ones, where users can tell them what they want, and the model privately delivers. Its work-as-you-like, when-you-like framework makes it a flexible option for those who want to make side money but have irregular time off to create content.

With positive reviews pouring in from users who could directly access kinks they were into and models they liked, as well as it being a secure platform for sex workers that wanted to be the primary beneficiaries of their own body work, OnlyFans' popularity exploded along with the ever-high demand for porn. From 2016 through 2018, the userbase increased from ten million to 100 million, then increased even further during the COVID-19 pandemic, when live entertainment was shuttered and thousands of people lost steady work and turned to distractions and online intimacy.[104] While OnlyFans' most-subscribed-to users can earn up to one million dollars a month, and relatively new users can expect to earn around $150 a month, OnlyFans has become so saturated with content in recent years that the mean annual payout was only $1,300 per creator as of 2023.[105] That means that the average user earned less than an urban *monthly* living wage for a *year's* worth of work more recently.

But OnlyFans persists. Creators shoot their shot. That's in large part because OnlyFans (also called "OF") isn't just for classic sex workers. It hosts workers from every professional background, from high school teachers who use it as a side hustle to supplement the cost of classroom supplies in the United States, to doctors trying to fund their clinics for underprivileged patients. Even celebrities are on board—actress Bella Thorne, singer Cardi B, and *Real Housewives* reality star Denise Richards all have or have had accounts.

OF caters to every possible curiosity, whim, and fetish. People pay to watch women bottle their own bodily fluids and gases, act out perverse fantasies made up as cartoon characters, show off their post-eating belly bloat, pretend to be puppy dogs, humiliate opposing sports teams' fans while dressed in hometown jerseys and

---

104 Barry Elad, "2022 Onlyfans Statistics, Users, Usage, Earnings and Alternative," EnterpriseApps Today.com, last updated June 12, 2024, https://www.enterpriseappstoday.com/stats/onlyfans-stats.html.

105 Todd Spangler, "OnlyFans 2023 Financials: Porn-Friendly Site Payments Hit $6.6 Billion," *Variety*, September 6, 2024, https://variety.com/2024/digital/news/onlyfans-payments-2023-financials-revenue-creator-earnings-1236135425.

dominatrix gear, overeat messily, show off intergenerationally with parents appearing in the same videos as their adult children, or even actively pretend to suffer from the flu, all to get voyeuristic users off.[106]

Online, Abi went by the name Mitzee Lewis and was nicknamed Fake Barbie. Her look changed over the years due to her multiple pregnancies, but she was a beautiful girl throughout, with knockout hazel-green eyes. Often, she'd bleach her long hair to a platinum blond and overdraw the lip liner on her augmented mouth to complete her doll-like trademark look. At first, the gimmick worked. She made the equivalent of more than $60,000 in one year on OnlyFans.

This was a fairly good commission, and the job allowed her to stay home, which was convenient for a young mother. Abi would have three children with Brad across their six-year relationship, two girls and a boy.

In addition to OnlyFans, Abi—at handle @mitzee, whose social tagline was "Come and have fun with me 😈"—had active accounts on AdmireMe, Twitter/X, and Instagram, along with a public Amazon wishlist that included kink items, sex toys, coffee makers, hair care products, candles, and lingerie that fans were encouraged to buy her.

Some of her content was a disturbing outlet for the trauma she'd suffered. In one Twitter/X post, as Mitzee, she's seated on a countertop posing in a revealing crop top and shirt, with the description, "Daddy I've been so bad at school today 😇 come and punish me." On her @mitzeelewis handle she wrote, "Have you got a man [or] are you taken? Anyway.... What difference does it make 🙊😈." In another, this one a cry for help, on November 6, 2020, she posted to Twitter/X, "I have major daddy issues," followed by a second post, a filtered selfie with the description "On my way to a dick appointment with my very lucky man."

She also had a fair amount of female/female content for the male gaze, posing in lingerie and asking for girl/girl hookups with a suggestive tongue-out emoji or making out with a girlfriend live, dressed as a devil while the friend dons cat ears: "I like girls, too 💦."

---

106 Zachnading, "18 Unique and Remarkable OnlyFans Accounts That We Didn't Believe Existed," Ebaumsworld.com, January 19, 2022, https://www.ebaumsworld.com/pictures/xx-unique-and-remarkable-onlyfans-accounts-that-we-didnt-believe-existed/87080780.

She wasn't shy about uploading videos of herself and Brad, either, or herself and other partners.

Her relationship with Brad, it turned out, was sometimes open and almost always fraught. The money, however, came easily. At least for a while.

Subscriptions to follow Abi started at just $5 a month on the OnlyFans platform.[107] On November 7, 2020, a user commented, "Looking fucking amazing. Them recent fully naked ones 🥵. Bristolian accent turns me on to fuckkk—dying to see more of you and your BF fucking."

Most of her content, as she became a little older and gained weight over the course of her pregnancies, utilized heavy filtering technology. Uncensored content for public consumption consisted mostly of edited selfies of her in a good deal of makeup or teasers of her with other women. On TikTok, she posted a lot of mommy blogger videos—or vlogs—which were all comedy and bliss, until the content abruptly turned darker. Until it turned against Brad.

Her first public posts featuring Brad were gooey and thoughtful, reflecting a beautiful parenting partnership between the pair, who weren't married but seemed to be deeply in love and committed to their children. Abi would post photos of her and Brad with a giggling child, or fawning videos of their sweet babies, or she'd post public appreciation for her partner. One TikTok read, "The best daddy you could ever ask for 😍🥺. He wanted a princess after our two boys." This was overlain on a photo of Brad beaming down at a bundle in his strapping arms, with a tiny pink knit hat on her infant head—their daughter Dolcie.

But slowly, by degrees, the rosy picture they had together began to lose its color. Abi could be abusive—emotionally and physically—and felt Brad was controlling about money. When the OnlyFans revenue began to dwindle, her take-home pay dipping to around $12,000 a year (less than a fourth of what it had been in her heyday), the fights ramped up. Abi, who was also posting pornography of herself with

107 Emily Crane, "Fake Barbie" OnlyFans Model Abigail White Guilty of Murdering Ex after Breakup," *New York Post*, last published October 21, 2022, https://nypost.com/2022/10/21fake-barbie-onlyfans-model-abigail-white-guilty-of-murdering-ex.

female partners and was actively seeing other men, was furiously jealous whenever Brad would go on a date with another woman. It was a semi-open secret between them that Brad might be doing so but should not say so. Whereas Abi was allowed to flaunt and even capitalize on their open relationship, Brad had to be silent. At first, Brad had tried to be honest about other women he was seeing, but Abigail's habit of demanding retribution curtailed that. Abi also despised the fact that Brad had another child, outside of their relationship, a daughter named Scarlett with a partner named Leah. It took away from Dolcie being *his little princess*, in her eyes only—Brad was a doting father to *all* his kids.

In fact, as a father, Brad was nearly faultless. He was avidly involved in the lives of his children, all under the age of seven. He took his eldest children to school and daycare, provided a steady presence, and was a positive influence. Physically strong, he often lifted his children up, carried them in his rose-tattooed arms, fed them, hugged them, and played with them. Laughing with his babies, Brad was a dream. Handsome, with beachy blond hair, a thin moustache, and blindingly blue eyes, he kept an even temper and a steady paycheck. He gifted his children genetically with their messy blond heads and big, toothy smiles.

He let the kids make messes. When they spilled his instant coffee all over the kitchen floor, he jokingly posted a video to TikTok saying, "Have kids, they said. Coffee cake anyone?"[108] The mess apparently came from doing the "tiger pig dance" too hard, a marketing gambit by the Subway sandwich chain in the UK challenging families to do fun and silly dance-offs. He danced, where others might cry over spilled milk—or coffee beans, as it were. He posted an homage to his daughter Dolcie to Kiefer Sutherland's "Song for a Daughter," with photos and videos of the two of them shopping, cuddling at the playground, and in a ball pit. It featured snippets of her with her big brothers, too, so as not to leave them out. (Perhaps he was unable to post so openly about Scarlett thanks to Abi, or perhaps Leah was

108 Bradley Lewis (@thelewisfamily4), "coffee cake anyone?" TikTok, October 18, 2021, https://www.tiktok.com/@thelewisfamily4/video/7032068407759588613?lang=en.

more private, not wanting her baby's face on social media. Abi had no such qualms, often posting her toddlers publicly.)

The profile for Brad's TikTok, in a sweet tribute, was named for his family (without Scarlett) at handle @TheLewisFamily4, and his bio read "Abigail <3 Archi – Logey – Dolcie." Again, he may have been browbeaten into keeping his daughter Scarlett's name off the line since Abigail trolled TikTok often. Notably, he had no discord with Leah, whom he was still seeing at the time of his death, and who mourned him thereafter. Abi's TikTok, by comparison, consisted of mostly "thirst trap" enticements and, increasingly, content tinged with abuse toward Brad. In one of her TikTok postings, at handle @MitzeeLewis, she wrote of his supposed infidelity, "Why cheat on me when we can **** her together and make her walk home?"

The infidelity was only supposed because, in addition to the open relationship, over time, Brad more and more unambiguously wanted to leave Abigail. That led to the fateful day he worked up the nerve to really tell her so, and Abi's wild response—stabbing him in the heart in the hallway of their home, killing him in front of their eldest son.

A Case of Love Bipolar

Abigail had always been emotionally volatile, but with Brad the training wheels came off. She loved him and was obsessive about him, but in equal measure she sometimes seemed to despise him. Her key wish was to control him. His, increasingly, was to escape her.

A number of emotional blows had made the ground beneath Abi's feet shakier than usual. She'd endured the miscarriage of a child before Dolcie, which sent her into a desperate melancholy. And as Brad drifted away from her as a partner, as his world opened to kinder and more stable options for romance, Abi's ire became chronic and uncontrolled. Mutual friends all knew the relationship was deeply toxic. But maybe strangers did, too. Abigail left clues on her social media, especially on her TikTok.

In one video, she wrote, "When your man pisses you off so you report him to the GV 😂." GV, in this case, was short for "government"; an extreme reaction, also likely based on a fabrication, to punish him for her annoyance. In another video, she'd written, "When god gives you men that you have to watch go to court to watch either get sent down or nearly sent down…#jailboy." This seems to imply that either she got Brad in trouble with that government call, or else, he got himself in trouble and she wished to publicly humiliate him for it. Or perhaps, again, it was merely a fabrication designed to shame him.

And in another:

> When I stop taking my meds and have a bad bpd episode 😂😂

—to the lyrics from Katy Perry's "Hot and Cold" chanting,

> Someone call the doctor, got a case of a love *bipolar*.

On and on the videos went:

> When she tries to touch your man in a 3some,

featuring footage of her threatening the supposed girl. (Brad had replied to this one with laughing emojis.)

"Played the tinder notification and he passed obviously 🔪," she wrote, over a video of Brad half-naked and half-asleep. The Tinder game is designed to check if a partner recognizes the sound of a Tinder match, meaning they're using the dating app to cheat. When Brad doesn't react, it proved he hadn't been using Tinder to meet women, so he'd "passed" her test.

More and more, meaner and meaner:

> We all know a dickhead called…BRAD LOL.

> If my man ever got with someone else…UGLY DOG, UGLY DOG, UGLY DOG.

> Told him I was going out for a jog…little does he know I've got to meet the girls for some wine and snaxx.

While Brad became the focus of much of her content, this focus was jealous, controlling, and purposefully debasing. But Brad wasn't the only one she posted about inappropriately. Unfortunately, and though almost certainly without malice, her children were made into hapless targets of her boredom and inability to parse what was suitable for children, which may have been understandable, considering her own childhood. Abi posted a video of her seven-month-old daughter photo-manipulated into singing Cardi B's song "WAP," a title abbreviation for "wet ass pussy." Due to the child's age, the lyrics aren't too unsuitable by far. She also posted a video of her young son in a shirt that says "Dad is SUPER," but dancing to that same song, extremely concerning considering the boy's young age.

A phenomenon called trauma bonding often causes abuse victims to side with and even defend their abuser. So, perhaps unsurprisingly, on Abi's channel, Brad's comments and reposts had been wildly supportive. He replied positively to any post he did check in on, calling Abi one of "my angels" when she'd post with Dolcie. He commented on a photo of the ultrasound of their miscarriage with a crying face. He did not make a public peep on any of the disparaging or belittling posts aimed at him, to complain nor defend. He didn't disagree with Abi online. Ever.

The pair suffered three miscarriages between the birth of their second son and Dolcie, who wasn't even three years old when her father died. She was the apple of his eye, though he loved his sons and other daughter dearly as well. In late 2010, Dolcie had been a difficult birth, brought to fruition only to suffer from seizures in the first months of her life, forcing her admission to the children's hospital. When Brad couldn't be at her side due to work, Abi texted him a photo of Dolcie covered in IVs. He texted back, "Makes me so sad seeing that photo. My little warrior. Give her a big kiss from daddy."[109] Despite Brad's devoted tendencies as a father and his nearly boundless forgiveness as a partner, Abi had crossed a line beyond online ridicule into genuine mistreatment behind closed doors. Sophie Webber, a friend of Brad's, received a desperate phone call from him one time after Abi found out he'd "cheated" on her, the court would hear at Abi's eventual trial. "Help me, Sophie, she's trying to kill me, she's trying to stab me, she keeps beating me up, she's hurting me."

Abi *was* hurting him.

She'd stabbed him in the arm already once and in the leg another time, leaving a large gash and a scar. One of the two stabbings took

109 Abigail White (@mitzeelewis), "Heart breaking [broken heart emoji] my princess forever," TikTok, October 10, 2020, https://www.tiktok.com/@mitzeelewis/video/6884560869284416769?lang=en.

place just a week before she'd ultimately take his life. At the hospital, when he received medical, care, Brad lied both times and said the wounds came from work, explaining them away as an accident—as abuse victims often do.[110]

Her intimidations came regularly, and they often skewed brutal. She threatened to stab him in the face or to kill him. She threatened to murder his mother, the friends and family members he loved, and any other woman he'd slept with outside of her. She threatened to destroy him.

Clearly, these were not idle threats. Aside from actually brutalizing him, she openly admitted on TikTok to calling the government on him for 'pissing her off,' as noted. Any time he tried to leave, she pulled out this same arsenal—and more. She threatened to kill *herself*, incapacitating him, as he didn't wish to be the reason his children went motherless, nor did he want to endanger his own family and friends by leaving them alone in the miasma of Abi's temper.

The situation became so sour that Social Services had to be called in and an official declaration was made that, for safety reasons, Abi and Brad couldn't live together anymore. Brad moved back in with his mother, but against the order of the governmental agency, began to frequent Abi's home again. Perhaps coerced through emotional manipulation, perhaps due to his desire to be with his children (it being the responsible thing for him to care for them and take them to school), devotion put him constantly in Abi's orbit and warpath, primed to be prodded back into the home. It all came down to control. Abi wouldn't *let* Brad leave her—and the more she was able to get away with, the more liberties she took. If he took too long to text back, she'd fly into a rage. If he didn't do exactly what she wanted, she'd become explosive.

Abigail admitted to friends that she felt Brad only told her the truth if she threatened him with physical violence. In some ways, that was true. Though they both partook of outside sexual partners, she demanded absolute fidelity from Brad. When he didn't live up to her

---

110 "'I'm capable of killing him'—OnlyFans model in voice notes before murdering boyfriend," ITV.com, October 21, 2022, https://www.itv.com/news/westcountry/2022-10-21/i-am-capable-of-killing-him-voice-notes-of-onlyfans-model-who-murdered-man.

double standard, he lied to reduce her ire. When she henpecked him into telling the truth, needling for details and beating him at times, he'd eventually give in and reveal that he'd been seeing other people. Abi would then inform him that he owed her penance to—according to Justice Fraser, who passed sentencing at the eventual murder trial—"make it up to [her]." He lied to protect himself, most of all, because the penance was never pleasant.

Brad remained a gentleman throughout the relationship. While eventual court documents would show that he could be controlling about money and sometimes was defensively aggressive, Abi was never injured. Witnesses and friends had never seen Brad do anything but put his hands up to protect himself against her onslaughts. If Brad ever was in any way abusing Abi, she would have just needed to call Social Services, and he would have been removed from her premises, under their formal directive.

Abi had some awareness of her own propensity for evil. She knew that she suffered from borderline personality disorder, and she knew it was worsening. She'd reached out for mental health support in the weeks leading up to the incident, but no help was given to her. That particular system failed her, as so many had before.

In a voice recording that would later be played for the Bristol Crown Court, Abi called a friend and said of Brad, "Obviously I have no limit when I get angry and like obviously he said that I need help with that. Because people are genuinely saying to me: one of you are going to end up dead. Like, and I fully believe that I'm quite capable of killing him if he hurts me again ... or I'm going to end up being in prison. I don't believe a fucking word that comes out of that boy's mouth. I have to beat the fucking living daylights out of him for him to tell me the truth and he still don't tell me the truth. He only tells me the truth when he thinks I'm going to fucking kill him. Like when I get a knife out. Like when I fucking stab him.... I just don't get this kid.[111]

---

111 "Family of Man Murdered by 'Controlling and Violent' OnlyFans Model Speak Out," ITV.com, October 21, 2022, https://www.itv.com/news/westcountry/2022-10-21/family-of-man-murdered-by-controlling-and-violent-onlyfans-model-speak-out.

And then Brad, still recovering from her stab wound to his arm, said he was leaving her.

That Night

March 24, 2022.

It happened often, Brad telling Abi he meant to leave. He was perpetually trying to. He was frightened of her, but equally frightened of what she'd do if he made good on it.

This time, he seemed seriously convinced it was what had to be done, but he still bowed when she pressured him to go to the pub that same evening—and then after, to return home with her.

Brad, in a way, was also a child victim. He'd begun dating Abi when he was just sixteen and she, eighteen. While it might seem silly to attest that this counts as proof of toxic grooming, it's important to consider that Abi had experienced negative age-gap power dynamics for most of her life, aimed at her, the younger partner, and that people often mimic and internalize attachment styles—including negative ones. Even with sixteen being the age of consent in England, some sexual behavior, such as sexting, or the sending of pornographic texts back and forth, remains illegal under the age of eighteen, due to the Protection of Children Act of 1978. Though there is no proof that Abi and Brad engaged in such behavior, it is notable that Brad was still considered a minor under the edict of some laws when the two began dating, and also notable that Abi began to exploit Brad for monetary gain (though consensually) on her OnlyFans by broadcasting their sex once he was of age. Considering the abuses Abi suffered as a child under the thumb of overbearing authority figures in the guise of romance, and considering the dictatorial relationship she had with Brad, their age gap is not irrelevant to the picture.

The abuse may have been more insidious for Brad. Abi was simply mimicking much of what she'd endured—but for men, it's often difficult to recognize and accept that they are being abused or overpowered by a female partner. Outsiders likewise often have trouble sympathizing. (Though Brad's friends, it must be said, were more understanding than Abi's entire support system had ever been while she was growing up.) Since men are less often the target of abuse than women or children, a built-in stigma adds weight when they consider what to do. Men are less primed to tackle exploitation, less educated on how to handle it. So, as with many abuse victims, Brad didn't manage to follow through with his intentions of leaving Abi that night or any other. Her over-the-top behavior, which seemed so egregious to other patrons their final night at the pub, had all the trademarks of intimidating a weakened partner into compliance. All-gender victims returning to their abusers share a lot in common with Brad's situation. They do it for resources and for their children; a shared home and shared offspring are the penultimate resources. The victim is usually "programmed" through continued bullying and negative feedback to feel worthless, and these feelings increase when the partner is infuriated with them. They've been badgered into accepting cruelty as a sign of passion—that their partner needs, wants, and adores them too much to let them go, like the flames of rage are just the opposite side of the coin from love. Especially if violent bouts are soothed over in sex, which Abi prided herself on being so gifted with. Public humiliation is another factor in deciding to stay—abuse victims are often silent, while abusers publicize what they deem to be the failures of their partners. Additionally, it can be difficult for a man to see the mother of his children, who raises them with tenderness, as a monster—and difficult for outsiders to see a man as being less capable than a woman when it comes to physical altercations and defense.

However, Brad and Abi's shared friend group absolutely did see the warning signs. Far from thinking Brad could take care of himself, they felt the relationship was poison and encouraged Brad to escape—especially and crucially that night at the Horseshoe. They gave phone numbers and offered rides in the opposite direction.

Brad arrived at the Horseshoe pub at 6:30 p.m. Abi had already had a whole bottle of wine, some mixed drinks, and—in the pub's bathroom—cocaine. The first thing she did was scream at him. She scolded him so loudly that it caused a bar-wide scene. He turned away to get a drink, shrinking from the harshness of her words. In a move that would be even more of an affront to her, he then refused to step outside and speak with her one-on-one, terrified to be alone with Abi. In retribution for his disrespect, Abi punched and slapped him—when several friends and even a stranger stepped up to shield him, she spat in their faces. Someone called her a bully, and she began to rave at Brad for not sticking up for her. She then poured her drink on someone before slapping one of Brad's protectors, a man she did not know. That man would slap her right back.

Another man, the friend of Brad's she'd spat at, excused himself to keep from doing the same.

Abi would call 999—the UK's 911—to report the man who'd hit her, saying she'd been attacked, ignoring the fact that she'd struck him first. She must have realized her error eventually, because she hung up when the police began to ask more probing questions. When authorities called back, she provided them with a fake name.

Bradley's friends, seeing the state Abi was in, leaned on him not to return with her to the home at Chipperfield Drive. But one of their children was present with Abi at the pub, and eventually Brad felt cajoled into leaving together with Abi and their boy. Abi had been in a terrible mood all evening, argumentative with other pub-goers even before Bradley arrived, frustrated by his tardiness. Friends had told her to take her behavior down a notch, to no avail. So loud was her bellowing that night that patrons in the parking lot outside had heard her before they'd seen her.

At some point Bradley escaped to the bathroom and broke down into wracking sobs. Visibly distressed, he was repeating, "I'm dead when I get home," over and over—the same refrain he'd make later to Alfie. Expressing his terror, he told friends who followed him that he wanted badly to leave Abigail but was afraid she'd commit suicide if she did, pinning that on his conscience. He'd expressed earlier to the friend at the park that his main stressor was being hunted down by Abi if he left her. The dual terrors of murder-suicide hung over him like a shroud.

Unsure what else to do, a male friend offered to buy him a beer. Abigail knocked over that beer, spilling it on Brad, and announced they were leaving.[112] A newer friend of Bradley's passed him a mobile number to call in case he needed anything that night, like help leaving.

At 7:50 p.m. Brad, Abi, and their child left the pub with Alfie Pike. Abi was still drunk and high. They would have reached home at around 8 p.m. At 8:10 p.m., Abi phoned for an ambulance. She then ran out of the house screaming, calling for a neighbor's help, panicked and weeping.

Earlier on the very day she'd murder him, she'd posted to TikTok a video of herself smacking the air in front of her like one might spank someone, with a text overlay reading "Me with his homeboy when I find out he cheats."

Hours later, she'd kill.

Assassins Get Paid, Luv

Once inside the house at Chipperfeild, Abi and Brad had told their son, Logan-Leighton, to go upstairs and off to bed. Brad was lingering in the hallway of the ground floor, perhaps waffling over his decision to stay. Abi wandered into the kitchen, where she spotted a big carving knife. She grabbed it and headed back into the hall, where she would plunge it into her ex-boyfriend with little ceremony—effectively ending their argument.

Abi rammed the knife nearly three full inches into Brad's chest as he stood there, helpless in shock. Her attack found an opening between frames of his ribs, pressing into his thoracic cavity, and the tip of the weapon lodged itself into his heart. It was the same kitchen knife he'd used to help make family dinners for his three children.

Brad collapsed. When he fell, Abi hustled to call for an ambulance, as the reality of what she'd done and what it would *cost* her settled in. Not just a boyfriend, but also her freedom.

Abi also hustled to clean up the scene. She used a mop, a T-shirt, and some washing-up liquid to wick up some of the blood—an attempt to change the thumbprint of the crime. After going into

112 Geoffrey Bennett, "Bradley Lewis Heard to Say: 'I'm Dead When I Get Home' Shortly Before He Was stabbed," *Bristol Post*, last updated October 11, 2022, https://www.bristolpost.co.uk/news/bristol-news/bradley-lewis-heard-say-im-7690061.

hysterics and yelling for a neighbor, she then called a friend, Laura Watkins via telephone, and immediately laid claim that Brad had stabbed *himself*. It was a desperate accusation she'd repeat when police arrived—that Brad had tried to take his own life and had turned the knife on himself.

"He's going to be okay, he's going to be okay, tell me he's going to be okay.... We are going to be together," she'd whimpered to Laura over the receiver.[113]

When police and paramedics arrived, she told them adamantly, "I did not stab Bradley." She stood fervently by the story that he'd self-harmed and committed the brutal, soon-to-be life-ending action on himself. It was a statement undone in part by the one key witness to the crime—their three-year-old son. Logan-Leighton observed the stabbing and would later tell the court, "Mummy stabbed Daddy."

Only in July of 2022, more than three months later, would Abi change her tune. She finally reversed her statement to authorities, admitting that she'd stabbed Brad but twisting her motivations to press for leniency, in an attempt to give herself a pass. She told the jury that she'd only meant to *startle* Brad, not to kill him. She would still stand trial for murder.

"We were arguing, and he was pushing me and were in the hallway. I went into the kitchen, and I seen the knife on the side, picked it up and walked back towards Brad. I went over to him to shock him, to scare him with the knife and before I knew it, I had stabbed him.... I picked up the knife in anger and upset, but I didn't want to hurt him or kill him," she told jurors at Bristol Crown Court. But they were not convinced.

Jurors were treated to her side of the story, however, told in part through forensic psychologist Dr. John Sandford, who'd have sessions with Abigail on behalf of the court. He'd determined that there was some credibility that Brad could be domineering over their funds or even manipulative at times, but he also determined that Abi both had a personality disorder and that she had engaged in the

---

113 "Woman Knifed Boyfriend in the Heart Then Said He'd Tried to Kill Himself," ITV.com, October 11, 2022, https://www.itv.com/news/westcountry/2022-10-11/woman-knifed-boyfriend-in-the-heart-then-said-hed-tried-to-kill-himself.

assault while fully aware of her actions, despite drugs and drink. There were mitigating factors in Brad's lying about his unfaithfulness and its emotional impact on Abi, and in Abi's clinical inability to control those emotions. But the judge ultimately determined it was Abi who was the truly coercive and scheming party.

In his sentencing remarks, Justice Fraser said on October 21, 2022, that the jury had reached the verdict that Abi had indeed intended to cause serious harm that night.[114] That she was invidious, toxic, and domineering. She was sentenced to life in prison with eighteen years before consideration for parole by the court, on the charge of manslaughter.

Mitigating factors that subtracted from her minimum time before consideration for parole were the exploitation she faced as a child, her mental disorder, the lack of medical help she had received for it, and her calling 999 right away when Bradley was mortally wounded. Factors adding to her sentence were her lying to the police and framing Bradley for his own demise, her attempt to alter the crime scene, the intent to do egregious harm to her victim, her history of malicious violence toward him, and the fact that she'd committed the act in front of their small son, now bereft.

"There are a number of TikTok videos where you sought to humiliate [Bradley] and boasted of your use of violence against him," The Lord Justice said, pointing out that the devoted family man had been the object of cruelty long before this final act of viciousness.

Brad had been given urgent treatment at the scene that calamitous night and taken to a nearby ICU, but had died of his wounds in the small hours of the next day, March 25. More than 800 people attended his wake and funeral, with vigils held countywide. Friends described themselves as "gutted."

After the reading of the trial verdict, thirteen adult family members crowded around Brad's mother, Rachel, and his father, Steve, who read a statement to the press.[115] "[Bradley] loved his children. Loved, unfortunately, the woman that ended up taking his life.... You know,

114 "The King-v-Abigail White," October 21, 2022, https://www.judiciary.uk/wp-content/uploads/2022/10/R-v-White-sentencing.pdf.

115 BistolLive, "Steve Lewis, Dad of Bradley Lewis, Speaks."

[a] number of people [have been] in touch since what's happened to Brad, and those people are still grieving today." Steve would talk about Brad's best qualities, his own grief, and how his son would often tell him to stop fussing over him, "And [I'd give] my famous sayin' ... '*That's my boy talking.*'" He noted with rueful pride, of whenever Bradley would humbly steer conversation away from himself. His father called what his family must now endure the *real* life sentence. Life without a precious part of themselves, and for so many others, life without a dear and sweet friend.

> Proof of [how beloved Brad was] was shown by the hundreds of people that attended his funeral and events arranged in his memory. His popularity has also been shown by the memorials that are on display in various locations in South Gloucester. We are, in a sense, lucky as a family to still receive overwhelming support from everyone that knew Brad ...

But he ended the statement in a chilling manner.

Even after all the mitigating factors of Abi's childhood were taken into account, Bradley's father informed reporters, "[We] have secured the fact that my grandchildren, Brad's children, will all be looked after until at least they're 18.... And, rightfully or wrongfully, I have to thank Sherry and Tony. I know that's Abigail's mum and stepfather, because they're the ones that have taken on the children. And in the future, they will be ensuring that I spend time with my grandchildren, which is going to be a great memory ... for us, of our son."

Tony being Abi's *new* stepfather, and a far better one, one can only hope.

Scarlett, Brad's fourth child, would continue to be cared for by her mother Leah, who'd given a grief statement to the court, expressing how the loss would impact them as well.

After the verdict, Abi's story should have quietly hummed along in spates of unremarkable jail time, with Bradley living on through his children's goodness. But in the latter half of 2023, something curious happened on TikTok.

For a short time, someone using Abi's @MitzeeLewis account—ostensibly Abi herself, though how she did so from jail remains mysterious—began replying to public comments on Abigail's old TikTok posts. Many theorized she'd somehow snuck a cell phone into the prison or gained access to one (not, in fact, all that uncommon for incarcerated persons) or that perhaps a friend was weaponizing the account, either talking for Abi through it, or *as* Abi for a lark.

Her TikTok's comments sections, post-trial, became rife with users calling her out as an abuser and a murderer, and replies to her posts were outlets for the outpouring of anger and grief from the public. A public, this account pointed out, that didn't know Bradley or the children and thus had little reason to demonize or sympathize.

The responses coming from the @MitzeeLewis handle for that short burst in 2023 are not paragons of compassion or repentance, but instead, bite-backs brimming with sass and snark, crudely doubling down.[116] If truly written by Abi, they are startling in their pitilessness, even where they do occasionally self-reflect:

@✞Maroun Francis✞: She doesn't have any remorse. 😵😞

@Mitzeelewis: I do

@Skye: 🖤 Your just so so cruel! I hope you have a hard time where ever you end up!! 😡

@Mitzeelewis: Nope loving life hun 😘

@L.🥀: Fingers crossed she gets what she deserves in prison 

@Mitzeelewis: Yes thank I get a comfy bed and food is great

@Missnicola dunn: Her children have to grow up knowing she killed there father who has her babies now hopefully that are in a loving home

@Mitzeelewis: Yeah they still in my home it's very cosy 😁

@Chosen.: Girl you don't deserved the children. Is a shame that they have an assassin as a mom.

116 Abigail White (@mitzeelewis), "Me with his home boy when I find out he cheats," TikTok, March 25, 2022, https://www.tiktok.com/@mitzeelewis/video/7078963074501283078?lang=en.

@Mitzeelewis: Assassins get paid at least love.... My man just emptied my pockets

@Shan: rip Brad God bless 🖤

@Mitzeelewis: Fuck off Shannon 😁

CHAPTER 4

PEKKA-ERIC AUVINEN, aka Sturmgeist89/Naturalselector

When you turned your head in class
With your eyes like this and your head like this
Tauno and I switched places
When you were in the cafeteria after school
The gang sat around and robbed the place
At the cash register, they exchanged glances
Bom-bo-bom-bo-bom bom-bo-bom-bom-bo-bom
I'm so young, I know I'm young, I know I'm young
But I'll take it, I'll take it, I'll take it.

—Translation of "Nuori Rakkaus," by Rauli Badding Somerjoki, with guitarist Pekka Järvinen

In his hands are the toys you gave
To fill his heart with delight
And in the ring stands a circus clown
Holding up a knife
What you see and what you hear
Will last you for the rest of your life
And it's sad, so sad ...

—"Circus Left Town," Eric Clapton

Pekka-Eric Auvinen was named for musicians Pekka Järvinen and Eric Clapton, having been born of music makers himself. Pekka-Eric's father, Ismo Auvinen, was a guitarist; his mother, Mikaela Vuorio, sang, played, composed, and wrote lyrics.

Natural Selection

Within commuting distance of the national capital of Helsinki sits the pretty, old ironworking and farming lands of Tuusula, Finland, scoured by yawning lakes and thickets of alder trees, often blanketed by snow. A blustery landscape festooned with bursts of juicy red rowan berries, whipped by damp winds carrying the muffle of overlapping birdsong from wrens and pipits.

Houses in Tuusula are usually bright and airy, nestled in personal little coves of nature. "Safe" is a word that comes to mind when observing the terraced residential blocks, with log houses hewing a skyline beset with sunset pinks and golds. Children's bedroom windows, looking out onto such idyllic scenes, are havens of sanctuary for play and study.

Finnish children are often raised with a strong focus on independence, recreation, and personal freedom. They are incentivized to develop their own hobbies and opinions, to be upfront with parents, and even to openly disagree with them. Corporal punishment is illegal, and there is less societal pressure to succeed in school than in other countries, with an overarching emphasis on peer community-building, gender equality, and personal fulfillment over individual achievement. Play is seen as one of the best ways to learn, and autonomous play is warmly encouraged.

All of this means that a child who is very comfortable at home, in the security of their own bedroom in Tuusula, might be expected to be quiet and self-governing all day long, reading and gaming and slipping outside to enjoy nature on their own, and then equally expected at times of togetherness—family trips and meals—to be outspoken and contrarian, raring for lively debate. Such behaviors wouldn't sound alarm bells for Finnish parents. They wouldn't assume that their quiet child was in his bedroom radicalizing himself, that when he enjoyed films and games alone, it was mostly for the gratuitous violence, that he was spending study hours convincing himself of the worthlessness of humanity as he pored over the work of serial killers and eugenicists with admiration. Or that while flirting online, his main attraction lay in hurting and belittling women, or that when he went into the surrounding forests, it was with a gun not intended for hunting *game* but other young people, or that when he discussed politics and philosophy, his opinions were rooted in an acrimonious revulsion for mankind and not just teenage rebellion and angst.

Outside the home, though, is where such a young man would rub up against the grain in the wrong direction. At Finnish schools, parental and even institutional oversight is more scant than in other countries, but peer groups are strong correctors—yardsticks of acceptable and unacceptable behaviors. If a child or teen cannot get along with same-age social groups and instead has an adolescence pockmarked by increasing ostracization and derision, their adult lives are almost certainly not shaping to be easy, fulfilling ones. Peer respect, strong friendships, and healthy romantic attachments are vital to the early independence Finnish teens have. Many migrate to bigger cities by the age of nineteen and take advantage of free education and affordable housing. They move in with friends and begin to structure their lives for entry into the workforce, embarking on romantic relationships where men and women might be more equally expected to take on the burden of homemaking and finances than in other nations. In these close-knit and mature groups, true outliers—those who go beyond independent or unique personalities and veer into the "unacceptable"—are viewed with suspicion and often rebuked for their strangeness.

It is therefore very possible for a moody or aggressive Finnish teen to seem normal to their parents over discordant dinner conversation, while suffering immensely for those same asocial traits during school lunch hours.

On November 7, 2007, in one such idyllic pastoral home in Tuusula, in one such teenager's whitewashed room filled with afternoon light dappling shelves full of books and trinkets, there sat a letter. It was addressed, "Dear mum and dad and brother."

When Ismo Auvinen found the letter, his son Pekka-Eric was already as good as dead. It would take him ten hours to fully pass after having shot himself in the head in his school's bathroom, after which he would not wake again. His other victims did not last as long, and the suffering of those who did not die instantly from the wounds he'd inflicted upon them was greater.

Pekka-Eric had taken eight lives before his own, in a school shooting that lasted almost a full hour. He had roamed the halls of Jokela High School, firing into windows and television sets, executing fellow teenagers with head shots, terrorizing cafeterias and courtyards, stalking stairwells and bathroom stalls, and pouring petrol gas on locked doors to set them alight. His deadly campus shooting was only the second in Finland's history.

A year later, inspired by Pekka-Eric, would come its third, the Seinäjoki University school shooting. Pekka would have been sincerely proud to know his legacy lived on in copycat killings. That was, after all, his fondest wish.

In his suicide letter to his family, Pekka-Eric described a bleak existence, seemingly devoid of promise for the future. Newly eighteen, at this point he would have been expected soon to graduate, move out, get a job, and further his education, or join the armed forces. Instead, after a middling school career and failing to qualify for Finland's mandatory conscription (disqualified by the military for reasons of mental health), he planned an extensive attack on his hometown, hoping instead to be the only thing he now could qualify for, in his opinion—memorable.

At first, he was torn between shooting up a shopping mall or his own school. He'd been inspired by the Myyrmanni mall bombing of 2002, carried out by nineteen-year-old Petri Erkki Tapio Gerdt, where seven had died and 159 were hospitalized. The choice of his school didn't seem especially motivated by personal vendetta, only a desire for the fame that came from murdering young people and his esteem for other school shooters. Or, perhaps any shopping malls of merit were simply too far away—almost forty-five minutes by car, much longer by the bicycle he rode.

The night before the attack, he agonized over little edits to the online manifesto he'd later make public, planned as his final and lasting mark on civic discourse about school shootings and a look into the deep recesses of his mind. It was as if in being a killer, Pekka thought he'd suddenly transform into someone unique and interesting.

His parents knew him as a stubborn boy who, once his mind was set, did not easily budge. Pekka had convinced himself that the world was an insignificant place; he was disillusioned with humanity, with life, and with living it. He'd turned his own loneliness and social awkwardness into a philosophy, assuming segregation from his peers wasn't due to his extremist views or increasingly disturbed fetishizations, but instead because of his inherent, and rare, superiority to all other people.

He took the perceived bullying he'd endured and turned it outward tenfold, explosively and intimately, even speaking with some of his victims at length before slaying them. Jokela High School's headmistress, Helen Kalmi, encountered Pekka in the courtyard beside the school's scenic pond mid-rampage and tried to convince him to end his killing spree. He chatted with her, then had her kneel before him and shot her seven times, leaving her to die in slow anguish for over twenty minutes. Rescuers arrived while she still had a pulse but were unable to save her.

Pekka claimed in his final words to his online audience, and even to his schoolmates as he brutalized them, that he had a vision for a revolutionary world, one that he said was fairer.

A world that didn't include him, but that he'd contribute to by culling his classmates and leaving behind a manifesto outlining the twisted opinions and values that had warped him into the conclusion that murder was the peak of freedom and self-expression.

Pekka's laptop, also found in his room that November 7, close to his final letter, unleashed a warning just a little too late for police to catch up to. He'd arranged for a litany of social media posts to go live just before he attacked, ranging from footage of his target practice, to videos foreshadowing the location of Jokela High School, to moral screeds overlaid by metal music, to eerie apologies to other content creators he'd insulted or harmed in online flame wars or in private messages up until that point. His computer couched a browser history full of rotten breadcrumbs that led to his penultimate moment of horror. He'd stalked online forums and consumed old video footage of other school shootings, especially those in the United States, and was an avid and active member on school shooting forums. He had bookmarked footage from the Columbine High School tragedy in Colorado. Thirteen had been killed and twenty injured in that attack, which rocked American society and charged the dialogue on guns. He thought the perpetrators were akin to rock stars. He pored over the dairies and ethos of other mass killers as well, admitting openly online that researching serial murderers was one of his biggest hobbies.

Pekka also avidly admired the work of Finnish ecologist and extremist Pentti Linkola, who espoused violence as the only effective means for a minority population to hold influence. Some quotes by Linkola that inspired Pekka, from Linkola's book *Can Life Prevail?*, include,

> I could never find two people who are perfectly equal: one will always be more valuable than the other. And many people, as a matter of fact, simply have no value.
>
> Human brilliance manifests itself only in flashes, among rare individuals. For this reason, humanity as a whole is enormously destructive: the creation of something as devastating as Western culture, which is now allowed to spread throughout the world, offers sufficient proof ...
>
> The difference between a terrorist and a freedom fighter is a matter of perspective: it all depends on the observer and the verdict of history.
>
> I wish that death to mankind comes soon.

Initially, after the horrific event, police were baffled. Pekka seemingly had a normal upbringing and a supportive family, he had friends at school, and former teachers said he was mild-mannered and didn't get into fights. Yet all telltale signs of a disturbed and radicalized mind were boiling just under the surface, seemingly undetectable until that surface was scratched.

His online persona was proof of his rapid radicalization. Online, Pekka went by many handles on social media and internet forums—@NaturalSelector89, @Sturmgeist, @EricvonAuffion. His most prolific screen names were NaturalSelector, a callout to his beliefs in social Darwinism, and Sturmgiest89. Active on MySpace, IRC-Galleria (a Finnish social networking website focused on photos and short messages), Rapidshare, and YouTube, Pekka had online friends on each of these social sites, as well as on forums about the Columbine school shooting. He was especially active on a site dedicated to natural selection, an evolutionary theory postulating that species weed out weak genetics generationally through survival of the fittest. This forum, however, twisted the idea into the more "red-pilled" version heard so often today on incel and "manosphere" forums, websites devoted to far-right radicalization of men against women and society, blaming their lack of romantic success not on themselves but on unfair societal norms.

The ideas projected on these sites and forums were that perfect male "Chads" ("Alpha" males with genetic superiority and more raw sexual appeal) and discerning female "Stacys" (attractive, hyperfeminine women who prefer Chads) breed together, and even "mid" (average) women audaciously only want Chads, leaving all the less physically impressive male "Betas" and "Omegas" to fight over the few remaining women with little hope of success in scoring "high value" (attractive, submissive) partners. None of this, of course, is real social science. But paired with Pekka's belief that the weak can only overcome the genetically strong through brutalization, as espoused by Linkola, Pekka began to assure himself that any unpopularity he experienced in real life was due not to his many shortcomings as a person—a person who espoused eugenics views loudly, and got his jollies off to non-consent—but to his being above the beastly hordes of "normies" in terms of brainpower, which he could only express through force.

Pekka-Eric, who was admired more online than in school, was not yet a sensation. His status as a peak influencer, by his own design, would occur after his own death, and as a result of it.

Before his death, he was mainly relegated to being prevalent on the fringe. He was also known for getting into fierce online arguments with a YouTuber who went by the handle @TheAmazingAtheist. Atheist's channel, which featured critiques of religion but also pressing social issues, often blended intellectualism with a dirty mouth; he calls himself a "professional ranter," and still posts to this day.[117] A stout young man with loaded concepts and casual delivery, TJ Kirk—the American behind the moniker—wasn't taken as seriously when he uploaded a video ahead of the Jokela shootings, warning that the lurker behind the handle @NaturalSelector89 was a Columbine worshipper who had all the markings of someone who would reap genuine violence on his own community. He posted that video in June of 2007, just months ahead of the school shooting.

> We're always talking about ... warning signs and *could we have seen it coming*? ... Those are your fucking warning signs. Investigate those *fucking* people.[118]

The post originally featured a list of online handles, highlighting users TJ felt were the wrong blend of "threatening" and "shooter-obsessed." Though the video would be uploaded again with the handles removed for privacy, one of the people he'd originally flagged was Pekka.

In Atheist's comment section on that video, evidence remains of Tana, Pekka's then-online girlfriend, chiming in to gang up on TJ before both her and Pekka's accounts were deleted. The proof comes in the form of one of TJ's old but preserved comments:

> You know what's really funny, @Robin [McVeigh] (it sucks that you're too stupid to understand what I'm about to point out to you, but I'm sure Tana will get it at least), you and I offend each other with our moral codes in equal measure.

The user, @Robin, had taken on the last name of American domestic terrorist Timothy McVeigh for her screen name, and was arguing right alongside Tana. As they bullied TJ, other users chimed in to tell him he was overreacting. But TJ knew the score from personal experience. A loner and a metalhead, following Columbine, police had interviewed him in California—having identified *him* as someone who

117 "INTO THE FRAY," YouTube, accessed May 1, 2025, https://www.youtube.com/channel/UCjNxszyFPasDdRoD9J6X-sw.

118 INTO THE FRAY, "Columbine Killers, Mental Midgets & Social Darwinism," YouTube, June 7, 2007, https://www.youtube.com/watch?v=Pq56CjUA0C4.

might commit a school shooting.[119] He was quite the opposite of a school shooter, never condoning violence, but he *did* understand the unique blend of antisocial quirks and personal hardships that might encourage a young person with a chip on their shoulder to decide to destroy life. He knew how to recognize his own malaise in others, while also identifying what about them wasn't rooted enough in reality and empathy to make them dangerous. He himself hadn't succumbed to misanthropic behavior, but he'd come close enough in the worst days of his loneliness to know the qualities of someone who might.

On November 7, 2007, the day of the shooting, @TheAmazingAtheist uploaded another video, entitled "I Knew This Would Happen." In it, he said: "I warned you [this] would happen.... You criticized me for it, many of you said that *I* was being a bully.... Well, one of those *poor little picked-on morons* decided that he was gonna go to school and shoot up his class.... I warned you guys that these social Darwinist kids ... were dangerous." He'd go on to remind his viewers, "I went specifically head-to-head with this very kid who committed this act. I made videos directed exactly at him [like] my video 'NaturalSelector is a sub-par human'.... [I knew] he was going to just live out his little testosterone fantasy."

The video mentioned, the one aimed at Pekka, has since been scrubbed from the internet. The title, however, is fairly self-explanatory.

So, who was the Pekka-Eric of the comments sections on early YouTube, with his online supremacist girlfriend Tana, extolling the virtues of mass murderers?

On one of Pekka-Eric's YouTube accounts, where he sported the screen name @Sturmgeist89, he ironically espoused Nazi views—ironic, because he claimed to be against them. Blond, light-eyed, and a keen new member of the Helsinki Shooting Club, Pekka's screen name (meaning "storm ghost" in German) sounded like a nod to the Sturmabteilung—the Storm Troopering paramilitary wing of Hitler's Nazi party. These were the self-described "concerned citizens" who

---

119 Matthias Kremp, "Warnung vor Amokläufer schon im Juni," Spiegel, November 10, 2007, https://www.spiegel.de/netzwelt/web/schulmassaker-in-finnland-warnung-vor-amoklaeufer-schon-im-juni-a-516645.html.

took it upon themselves to guard Nazi rallies and violently advocate for Nazi propaganda, starting brawls in beer halls and harassing those with different viewpoints. Pekka thought of himself similarly, as something of a vigilante at the head of a movement for Finnish justice—a justice that he felt must sweep *violently* onto the scene and take its pound of flesh.

But as Pekka was avidly against any form of organized political party—including the Nazis, despite having so many opinions in alliance with them—it is more likely that this user handle was, in fact, a reference to the Norwegian industrial metal band, Sturmgeist, which, paradoxically, wrote songs from the Nazi perspective.

The Columbine High School shooters, Dylan Klebold and Eric Harris, had espoused and popularized tying school shootings to vicious world-weary industrial music, especially the work of German band KMFDM (whose name translates to "no pity for the majority"). They focused on the band's lyrics in their rants and in personal journals, widely publicized after they massacred twelve students, one teacher, and then killed themselves on their high school campus in April of 1999. Pekka, their big fan, also dressed up his videos with KMFDM music.

Online, Pekka also celebrated mass killers Timothy McVeigh and Seung-Hui Cho. In 1995, McVeigh bombed a building in Oklahoma City from within a parked rental truck, using a homemade bomb fashioned from agricultural fertilizer and diesel fuel. He killed 168 people and injured hundreds more. A loner who had felt browbeaten in school, he stood against systems of government and against bullies. He felt the US government was the penultimate bully after its hand in the Waco Siege of 1993 and in the Ruby Ridge incident of 1992, both of which had led to civilian casualties. Similar to Pekka, in high school he became handy with computers and hacked onto government websites on his Commodor 64, using a handle inspired by music, as he became increasingly obsessed with guns and racial superiority. He was convicted and sentenced to death by lethal injection, which was carried out in June of 2001, after he gave his final written statement—a copy of William Ernest Henley's poem "Invictus," translating to "unconquerable."

Seung-Hui Cho was responsible for the Virginia Tech shootings in April of 2007, just a few months ahead of Pekka's own atrocity. Thirty-two people were killed and seventeen injured on campus before the shooter took his own life. A native South Korean, Cho suffered from social anxiety and was bullied in school. Like Pekka, he had an increasingly vested interest in violent stories, idolized the Columbine killers, trained at a gun range, was obscene toward female classmates and teachers (even taking nonconsensual photos of their legs under desks), and abhorred religious institutions. Cho's qualifies as the deadliest school shooting in US history, perpetrated by a man who used the handle @QuestionMark, as if he were an unsolvable riddle. Cho set his manifesto to go public right before the brunt of his killings, just as Pekka one day would. Pekka went online to celebrate Cho's shooting the day it happened.[120]

In the autobiography Pekka would eventually post on his YouTube account, he described himself as a "cynical existentialist, antihuman humanist." It seemed to fit the mold of his favorite killers. His manifesto, which he sent out as a mocked-up press kit to other influencers, read in part, "I am prepared to fight and die for my cause. I, as a natural selector, will eliminate all who I see unfit, disgraces of the human race and failures of natural selection."

Poignantly, Pekka-Eric would thereby choose to eliminate himself.

The Young Life

How does a young Finnish boy get so bullied that he decides on the inherent worthlessness of human life? What made the Pekka-Eric story so attractive in media immediately following the shooting at Jokela was the image of a boy at wit's end, one who had mental illness that went untreated due to long clinic lines and drug shortages, one who had been persecuted by his classmates and then dumped by his cheating girlfriend in favor of another man.

Trying to make a villain relatable is a key conceit in any form of storytelling, it helps journalists peddle a more nuanced narrative and

120 "Jokela School Shooting on 7 November 2007 Report of the Investigation Commission," Ministry of Justice, 2009, https://www.turvallisuustutkinta.fi/material/attachments/otkes/tutkintaselostukset/fi/poikkeuksellisetapahtumat/SbmrFqAo3/Jokela_School_Shooting_on_7_November_2007.pdf.

helps comfort readers whose primary question is always *"Why?"* What could cause such a tragedy? How does an average person look a petrified peer in the eye and decide to shoot them just to watch them die, and call it grace?

Saying that the villain came from a loving and supportive background and had a relatively normal, easygoing life brings no comfort or closure. It allows little wiggle room for compassion or forgiveness. The fact of the matter is that in Pekka's case there was no romantic excuse for his actions. He was enchanted with murder, disenchanted with society, and committed one against the other, ruining families by robbing them of beloved members. Pekka himself grew up in a middle-class family with two loving parents who buoyed him, and a younger sibling with whom he shared a good relationship. They were a talented, artistic family.

Both of Pekka's parents were gifted musicians. Mikaela Vuorio (credited as Micco Vuorio) composed folksy rock music, jazz refrains, and sweeping ballads. A skilled lyricist, vocalist, and even guitarist, she sang her own poetry in a buttery alto across eleven tracks in her most celebrated solo album, *La Mia Grande Avventura* (My Grand Adventure).[121]

Her songs have been listened to thousands of times. It's likely Mikaela met husband Ismo—then with the stage name Big Papa Auvinen—through the music scene. Big Papa joined Micco's band for a television spot, where they recorded the song "Todellinen Rakkaus" (Real Love). To Big Papa's backup guitar, Micco sang in Finnish, "And once you fell, I could die ... and go."

Micco had long, crimped blond hair and a tight, sharp face, while Ismo was as stout as Micco was thin, also with wavy locks, milk tea brown and down to his shoulders. He'd often sport sunglasses, even indoors, wearing a suit jacket, while Micco opted for flannel and hair clips, making her look a bit punk rock and a bit '70s flower child. They soon became an unstoppable musical force: Micco sound-mixed, produced, and played bass, organ, and even piano

---

121 Micco Vuorio-Topic, "Todellinen rakkaus," YouTube, January 13, 2019, https://www.youtube.com/watch?v=xSjMBQiU76c&list=OLAK5uy_kn8Qgzsy4sKsmnPvfWvdvKk0Qnali1cfk&index=3.

eventually to formulate their sound.[122] But Ismo was no slacker. A cigarette hanging classically in his mouth and the leather strap of his guitar sitting pretty over a shoulder, he rocked his way onto nine of her albums.[123] Sometimes lending his expertise to producing, arranging, or composing, his main joy was in being the lead guitarist for boppy tracks. His pièce de rèsistance, for which he was the composer, was "Rolling with the Tide"; the album cover features him in his signature sunglasses, draped over the sunset-orange hood of a Cadillac Coup de Ville car, beside a lanky blond sporting flannel. Credited on this album under the alias Micco Milkowitz, Mikaela drawled along the tracks Ismo composed in unsteady English, her accent veering Oklahoman.

Big Papa Auvinen was included on Micco's albums as backup until he was finally included in her life as an equal. They settled into new roles as parents and embarked on two new and distinct careers—Mikaela's in hospital care[124] and Ismo's in railroad construction.[125]

They still produced music, of course. In 2000, when Pekka would have been about eleven, they were on one of Finland's main channels, Yle TV, where they performed live from a sound studio.[126] Yle TV is where Finns can watch news, sports, documentaries, and even *The Gilmore Girls*. A full-length song played there live would be a bright spot of familial pride. In Finland, music is a big part of the cultural weave of life, mixing classical and folk with metal and synth.

Music was a big part of Pekka's life, too. While his later tastes were influenced by Columbine killers' widely documented love of industrial bands like Nine Inch Nails and Rammstein, Pekka also enjoyed aggrotech, shock rock, and electro music. On his IRC-Galleria online

122 "Micco Vuorio – La Mia Grande Avventura," Discogs.com, accessed May 1, 2025, https://www.discogs.com/release/1660804-Micco-Vuorio-La-Mia-Grande-Avventura?srsltid=AfmBOor7cV2KD3CVBu9GsiLXjct8XsBPkTyfRSu8Y7Mt_rXjgCfXn9N3.

123 "Big Papa Auvinen," Discogs.com, accessed May 1, 2025, https://www.discogs.com/artist/5403778-Big-Papa-Auvinen?srsltid=AfmBOop1DwvNRzmK35cKbT7YzWaj8-FXdEjl_CMIP8UI87kr52phOe1V&superFilter=Instruments+%26+Performance.

124 Alexander Oey, director, *Pekka: Inside the Mind of a School Shooter*, 2014.

125 Wif Stenger, "Don't Blame Me, Says Girlfriend Who Split with YouTube Killer," *The Sunday Times*, November 11, 2007, https://www.thetimes.com/travel/destinations/europe-travel/lapland/dont-blame-me-says-girlfriend-who-split-with-youtube-killer-ss9bnxz0nns?region=global.

126 Rootsmusicandmore, "Mikaela Vuorio - Yle TV Live 2000 - Todellinen Rakkaus," YouTube, May 16, 2014, https://www.youtube.com/watch?v=cZL3LwoFit8.

profile, he listed Slayer, Prodigy, Suicide Commando, Hatebreed, and Suffocation as some of his favorites.

The Auvinen house was a quaint yellow clapboard with a red scalloped roof and a white door, a picket fence, a cobbled walk, and a small expanse of cheerful green lawn on either side. It was charming, earnest in its small messes, with bicycles often boyishly strewn on the lawn by the two brothers who had no fear of them being stolen. As a child, Pekka was often seen around the property laughing, playing with his parents, or hamming it up for the camera. The family living room had large couches, sturdy wooden furniture, framed family photos, and a preponderance of books. The family recommended reads to one another, with a heavy preference for nonfiction, and encouraged one another to try out authors that had resonated with them. Pekka was the most prolific about this, often steering his mother in particular toward his favorites.

There was no violence in the home, nor was there any substance abuse. The boys got on famously. If anything, Pekka's parents were stricter than the local culture dictated. They felt that schools were too tolerant of bad manners, and too many kids drank, smoked, swore, or bullied.[127] They had a preference for rules and order, though they weren't tight-fisted about chores or tidiness with their sons. Both boys enjoyed being outdoors, hiking or cycling, and the family composed music together indoors. The Auvinens unflinchingly allowed Pekka his space, too, which he used to recess into the more solitary hobbies of computers, books, and films.

There were no major, uprooting events to speak of—the Auvinens lived in the same home for a decade by the time Pekka turned eighteen, so he was used to his community, his house, his town, his school system. He had security and stability. The family had originally moved to Tuusula from Helsinki, which, while a bigger and more vibrant urban center, was still within easy commuting distance, with a railway station located just by the Jokela school. While Pekka wasn't smothered by his parents, neither was he a casualty of inattention. When he began to play overtly violent video games, his parents

127 "Jokela School Shooting on 7 November 2007," Ministry of Justice.

confiscated and resold some of the worst offenders, deeming them too gross for the boy.[128]

At school, Pekka did reasonably well in terms of grades. As he aged, he excelled in history and philosophy but began to struggle with science and physical education. Nonetheless, he passed all his classes. A former teacher said of Pekka, "He was never mean to anyone, or angry at anyone."[129] He'd never been in trouble with school officials. He had friends in his classes and no dedicated animosity toward anyone in particular. He was, however, picked on in small ways—ways that many school children get picked on without becoming mass shooters.

Classmates recall that Pekka, like his father Ismo, had something of a "uniform." Except, instead of dark sunglasses and a black ensemble, Pekka opted for a checkered shirt, a brown leather jacket, and a somewhat risibly professional briefcase, forgoing a backpack. He always dressed painstakingly smartly, while his classmates were more casual. Students did occasionally poke fun at this, being so outside of the norm. That amplified the social anxiety Pekka was suffering from—an anxiety that Finland's healthcare system would be unable to appropriately counsel him on or medicate him for, due to national shortages. Pekka also blushed easily, which he was devastatingly self-conscious of, especially at school.

There were more marked signs of Pekka's inner turmoil as he got older as his grades declined, and peers began to distance themselves. One friend, Tuomas Hulkkonen, said Pekka became withdrawn in the months leading up to the shooting. "I thought that perhaps he was a bit depressed, or something, but I couldn't imagine that in reality he would do anything like this."[130]

The brunt of any school bullying, it is suspected, comes from peer pressure to conform to *moralistic* norms. In the months leading up to the shooting, Pekka began espousing social Darwinism and

---

128 Peter Langman, "Two Finnish School Shooters," SchoolShooters.info, February 1, 2016, https://schoolshooters.info/sites/default/files/two_finnish_school_shooters_1.1.pdf.

129 Oey, *Pekka*.

130 Roger Boyes and Marcus Oscarsson, "Finland Digests Report Into Youtube Killer Pekka Eric Auvinen," *The Times*, February 26, 2009, https://www.thetimes.com/article/finland-digests-report-into-youtube-killer-pekka-eric-auvinen-knlvf67pfnj.

bragging that he'd bought a gun—a fact his parents say they didn't know, though they were aware that he was a member of a shooting club. His emerging despotic interests startled his classmates, and as his online world became his preferred space, he began expressing himself as aggressively in person as he did online. He spoke with chilling enthusiasm about extremism, fascism, and his .22 caliber pistol. Peers found him increasingly off-putting, his takes belligerent. They recoiled. In other words, the bullying or isolation that Pekka-Eric experienced was largely a movement of his own making. Classmates disassociated from him the more loudly he radicalized and the more intimidating he became.

As he began to skew heavily and fervently extremist, his casual conversations at school would even begin to include his regard for mass shooters. This behavior became so consistent that, in August of 2007, students began flagging Pekka to the school's youth worker. His peers were worried about what he might do—his conduct felt threatening, shaded in violence and suicidal ideation. In October of 2007, just months before the shooting, several more reports were submitted.[131] Pekka had been asserting the ominous notion that people would soon die in the "white revolution." (Though most likely a reference to the conservative "White movement" of the Russian Civil War in the early 1900s against the socialist Bolshevik government, called the "Reds." But the racist overtone is also undeniable.) The head teacher was informed and agreed to keep a careful watch on him.

A youth worker spoke with Pekka on three separate occasions, but at every meeting, he was calm, polite, and cognizant. Already the age of majority, Pekka was able to block the social worker from bringing any concerns or reports to his parents. The last time Pekka and the youth worker would speak was in November of 2007.

Pekka's parents, eager to defend their son, laid down unsubstantiated claims of more severe bullying in a short television interview they agreed to give more than a year after the mass murders. "They attacked him and threw him across the halls and things like that....

131 "Jokela School Shooting on 7 November 2007," Ministry of Justice.

[They] pointed a laser pen at his eyes," they'd insist. They do not mention on this interview any actions they, the school, or Pekka took surrounding these allegations.

But Pekka did suffer from loneliness, despite his online friend groups. He felt daily embarrassment in public spaces over his short stature (he was just under 5′5″) and could be anxious to the point of debilitating shyness in crowds. Over time, he even began to fear compulsory social situations, terrified of applying for part-time work. His parents made sustained complaints to the school that Pekka was being bullied—the school disagreed, finding no real evidence of this and biting back that it was the Auvinens' strange behavioral norms inside the home, outlandish and outdated, that made life difficult for Pekka at school.

The school may have been on to something. So adamant were the Auvinens in their perception of Pekka's schoolmates as bad eggs that Mikaela would actually phone other students' parents directly, to complain about their children. Those families in turn, not taking kindly to accusations, would warn their children not to hang out with Pekka, as his parents were annoying. This was even noted in the official Jokela School Shooting Inquiry by the Finnish National Government.

Ismo and Mikaela said the opposite was the case. According to the couple in their televised interview, they went around *begging* other children to be friends with Pekka—which, if true, must have felt deeply humiliating for the adolescent.

Desperately, his family wished to equate severe bullying with Pekka's loss of purpose and his acceptance of radicalism. Truthfully, bullying is fairly common in Finnish schools, and Pekka's didn't seem to be all that severe. His feeling othered was at least partly due to his progressively racist, sexist, and malevolent rhetoric.

Nevertheless, his school had made attempts to help after Pekka self-reported bullying. Though staff did not observe any bullying, they did notice a drop in Pekka's socialization and his thinned-out peer group. There were internal discussions that led to classroom-wide discussions regarding bullying, moderated by the head teacher who Pekka would later kill. But Pekka was mostly mortified by any attempts to help; even after he'd reached out for it, he staunchly wanted the matter kept quiet. When students were questioned by teachers about what was going on, they'd reported that Pekka wasn't being "bullied" but was sometimes teased, admitting to some unkind ridicule. The "horseplay," as the kids put it, was mainly name-calling and taunting, never physical. It was most often aimed at his style of dressing and his belief in forceful eugenics.

In a progress meeting, Pekka told the school that everything was going well again, that he hung out with friends, chatted with people in the cafeteria, was doing well in group work on class projects, and had plans for the future that included matriculating into college to study psychology, philosophy, or history—subjects that had always appealed to him.[132] The case seemed to have improved, or at least normalized. It was also a lie.

Pekka had also briefly received help from Finland's national medical system. He was diagnosed with a phobia of social situations as well as an anxiety disorder. In Spring of 2006, he was prescribed SSRI medication to increase the effectiveness of his body's serotonin absorption, to improve his overall mood. But he soon needed a higher dosage in order for the drugs to work. He also did not combine the medication with therapist's visits, which was recommended for success. Finland requires rigorous follow-up and progress-tracking for minors, but, because of the perceived lack of severity of his case, combined with an overburdened mental healthcare sector, there was difficulty assigning Pekka time with a therapist—so he mostly called in prescription refills by phone. For over a year, until January of 2007, his parents requested that Pekka be admitted into the Adolescent Psychiatry Outpatient Clinic, but their entreaty was turned down on the basis that there weren't enough resources to waste them on such a mild case.

Pekka took his medication only sporadically, not in the dedicated way he needed to for the SSRIs to be effective, and by late 2007, stopped taking them all together. His behavior from there began a slow creep into the erratic, moods swinging from serene to aggressive and back on a dime.

132 Langman, "Two Finnish School Shooters."

The contradictions are admittedly rife. Students, teachers, and staff say that Pekka wasn't really bullied, but his parents, Pekka himself, and existing documentation indicate that he was. Pekka was called in turn a good student and a calm student, but also a student phobic of social situations and essentially companionless. Yet he was also somehow a struggling and fitful student, one with close peers who noticed minute changes in his behavior, wildly social online and abrasive enough to feel threatening. He wanted help and didn't get the therapy his family petitioned for, but then also did not take his medications or appreciate intervention on his behalf. His parents say he was without evident issues, yet tried for over a year to check him into a clinic for mental health. He was deferred from mandatory service on the basis of how he had acted during his medical examination, for fear he was mentally unfit; yet the school doctor concluded he simply needed to go outside more and get exercise.

Much of this follows the narrative of hyperbole, that frantic search for what was broken and could have been fixed in Pekka before his misdeeds. In truth, despite his relatively normal and free upbringing, Pekka himself was growing inexplicably darker.

Outside of music, many of Pekka's other hobbies were disturbing in retrospect. While there is an entire meme culture built around the idea of young women unwinding after a long day of work to eat ice cream and binge-watch true crime documentaries, Pekka's interest in true crime bordered unhealthy. He was obsessed with researching murder scenes, criminal motivations, and the victims of serial killers, only to plot how he could have done a better job. He studied deep ecology, natural disasters, eugenics, and ecofascism. He enjoyed movies and video games with violent themes—*Natural Born Killers*, *James Bond*, and *The Godfather* franchise captivated him—and in his own words, the bloodier the better. He enjoyed sarcasm and dark humor.

When it came to the opposite sex, his interests turned more twisted still. A self-described BDSM aficionado, his tastes skewed less kink and more nonconsensual. On his laptop, police would later find dozens of photos and video clips of women in situations where they were either being raped or actively attempting to escape sexual assault. Often, these included fully or half-naked women bound, gagged, habitually strung up, always struggling.

He had written his own sexual daydreams down, privately. They included the abduction of young women, a fantasy of dragging them away somewhere and forcing their submission. His sexual appetite did not stay in the realm of healthy play but had dark undertones propped up by his philosophy that the weak only get what they want through physical violence and force.[133]

On his IRC-Galleria profile, he admitted that he despised gender equality. In his private videos, later found by police, he narrated his ideal situation for sex:[134] "She would try to struggle, but she would feel the knife on her skin and surrender to me. She would be totally dominated and helpless and then I'd fuck her like an animal!... [Women] are cheating whores, lying sluts, and manipulative bitches. They are best when they are dominated, bound, and gagged." He overlaid his misogynistic video fantasies with music by the band Rammstein about stalking women; a nod to the Columbine shooter's use of "Weißes Fleisch" by the same band, with its theme of the rape of a school-aged girl.

His caprices, luckily, were to remain just that. Though he wore a mantle of toxic hyper-masculinity in his writing—the domination and subjugation of the weak through violence, the taking of women by force, the notion of his intellectual dominance, his contempt for *lesser* men—in reality, he was a panicked little boy clinging to his basest impulses and hating himself for his shortcomings. Hardly the pinnacle of machismo, he'd even recently lost a girlfriend who did not ultimately agree that she had *been* one.

In the summer of 2007, before the shootings, Pekka's "girlfriend" went by the handle "Tana Scheel" online. A seemingly graceful Dane who shared his love for violent flicks and his dislike of organized religion and who also made inflammatory online videos about social Darwinism, they exchanged comments and messages and realized

133 Langman, "Two Finnish School Shooters."

134 Tomi Kiilakoski and Atte Oksanen, "Soundtrack of the School Shootings: Cultural Script, Music and Male Rage," *Young* 19, no.3 (2011): 247–69, https://journals.sagepub.com/doi/pdf/10.1177/110330881101900301.

their world views had a lot in common. Namely, their matching opinions that the masses were brutish and stupid. After the killings, many people finger-pointed Tana as being one of Pekka's key motivations—that she'd broken his heart by meeting another man that same year, dumping Pekka just months ahead of the attack.[135] That had been the final straw for him, theorized many netizens in another attempt to make sense of his cause for violence. Really, it was just misogyny packaged in another format.

Tana had been an *online* girlfriend only. The pair was young. Both teens who had never met in person, nor who even lived in the same country. If she were aware that Pekka had romantic feelings for her, which it's almost certain she was, then it's likely that she did not reciprocate them. As Pekka's idea of romance had a lot of overlap with assault, it was maybe wise of her not to have. Of course, whether she really "cheated" on Pekka and "left" him, or simply wanted to engage less with an online companion she'd never had any intention of meeting, one can't blame Tana for Pekka's actions—nor, perhaps, for not wishing to date a man capable of killing his peers, who had lurid dreams of holding women hostage in caves for the purpose of breeding superior humans by force.

Early into to the eventual police investigation, Tana received death threats and hate mail placing the blame on her. Her response on her public YouTube channel was, "Many people are rejected without then going out and committing murder. He was not crazy, and this is not about me."[136] She'd note that while Pekka was "not a psychopath or a sociopath" and "was not bullied or picked on," in her estimation, he was fighting against the burden of severe mental illness.[137]

Nonetheless, a number of dark and bizarre internet theories popped up around Tana, including that she was a member of a European royal family or connected to one, that her privileged education at an elite boarding school meant she was connected to wealth and privilege on an unthinkable scale while she condemned those

135 Stenger, "Don't Blame Me, Says Girlfriend."

136 Stenger, "Don't Blame Me, Says Girlfriend."

137 Steve James, "Finland: What Are the Social Roots of School Gunman's Murderous Rage?" WSWS.org, November 23, 2007, https://www.wsws.org/en/articles/2007/11/finl-n23.html.

below her, and she was even accused of mind-controlling Pekka into the shooting on some Finnish blogs.[138] As if she exploited Pekka by some witchcraft, with Illuminati-level power and privilege.

Tana, years after the shooting, flat-out rejected the idea that they'd been a couple at all. She stated to Empirics Asia, a collaborative crowdsourcing educational website, that he'd actually been obsessively stalking and harassing her. In that same interview, she also misquotes the number of his victims by more than 200%, which either suggests she was not close enough to him to have remembered the news about the shooting, or that she assumed with the distance of time his crimes had been even more heinous.

The truth of Pekka and Tana's relationship probably rests somewhere in the middle. They had never met in reality, and the likelihood that they ever would have is slim. She did, in fact, attend Switzerland's most elite private high school (costing more than $100,000 a year for a boarding student), and she did exchange messages with Pekka espousing similar repugnant viewpoints for shock value. Their once-romantic relationship was previously confirmed by Tana, and by others in their circle, directly after Pekka's crimes, but Tana's denial of it now is probably a product of age—that what was serious to a couple of teenagers who felt alienated at school and liked putting on airs online without ever seeing each other's faces was nothing like a real romance. They had not even shared phone calls, much less held hands or stolen kisses. But just as Tana, as a teen, had classified them briefly as a couple, Pekka had certainly felt that they were. He sent her a message after finding out about Steve, her new boyfriend, stating, "my heart and mind [are] hurt and broken.... Because you are still the woman I love (I never had these emotions towards anyone in my sad and boring life). You made me free. You freed me from my prison of emotional apathy. But all this is killing me from inside."[139]

Regardless of the nature of their relationship, it would seem unlikely that a romance built on white nationalism and online sensationalism by two teens in separate countries was destined to last. One was bound for university in a country even farther away and had spent

---

138 Stenger, "Don't Blame Me, Says Girlfriend."

139 Oey, *Pekka*.

high school swaggering around the cream of European society, while the other had no prospects and was too anxious to apply for steady work, so he'd fallen back on idly plotting mass murder. When asked outright, "Can we actually meet some day?" Tana's reply to Pekka had been, "I don't know, we'll see."

At first, the breakup of their "situationship" even seemed to be going all right, nothing for either of them to feel bothered by. Tana wrote to Pekka, "NaturalSelector, I will always like you, I mean you are (and were) my best friend even before starting something else. That's not going to change," and Pekka had replied, ":-) okay well good."[140] But that quickly soured and descended into immaturity and insult.

> **@NaturalSelector89:** You "are with" Steve? You are his "girlfriend," and he "won your heart"? ... I have seen how you send messages to each other.... You know why I have pains and why my heart and mind [are] hurt and broken.
>
> **@NaturalSelector89:** You only care about your fingernails, rich and spoiled little girl. Have a happy life together, weakminded worthless bitch and superdupersuperdupermegasuperhypersuper aryanman :D Sieg Heil to your hilarious relationship (I'm sure it lasts long like her every other relationship in the past (LOL)."[141]

Tana's new boyfriend eventually replied to him:

> **@AryanRevolutionary8:** Get off her channel, you little cockmonger. No one gives a shit what you think or the simplistic views you have. You are nothing, your thoughts are generic, you are immature, pathetic, a joke. I've actually laughed at you when I think about the bullshit you peddle as provocative or scary. You are scared and small-minded. You fucking sicken me. Piss off, you jealous little boy.
>
> **@NaturalSelector89:** How are you and your bitch? She sure is a cheap whore :P

Certainly, comments like the one from Steve, or the videos from TJ, calling Pekka subhuman were more hurtful than anything happening at school. Yet, in an amazing display of self-awareness

140 Oey, *Pekka*.

141 Oey, *Pekka*.

and responsibility—perhaps because Pekka knew he was on death's doorstep by his own fashioning—in the days leading up to the murders, Pekka sent apologies to Tana and TJ.

Tana replied, "If you want me to accept your apology, then do it correctly. You said that shit publicly, be a man and apologize publicly. I unblocked you, but I can't take your fucking mood swings anymore. If you go off like that again, that's it." He wrote back to her, "I am actually sorry for everything and also sorry that I have been behaving as lame as I did...." Before going out, armed, to Jokela, he added in a final missive to her, "I guess it is time to say goodbye now. I have my destiny to fulfill. I'm serious, I'm quite sure I won't be talking with you or anybody else anymore since I'm probably dead when you read this."

He then sent a final apology to TJ as well.

Since he'd planned to release many of the videos foreshadowing the tragedy, he sent out apologies like a harbinger, even leaking his manifesto ahead of the shooting at 11:45 p.m. on November 6—the night before. One website, Albaani.org, that received Pekka's "media packet" with his motivations, managed to publish a warning. It even posted some of what Pekka had uploaded, calling it "attack information" and piecing together who the attacker was, where he planned to attack, and judging accurately the time of the attack. It's unclear whether the police were called, and what, if anything, they did.[142]

The warning post was so accurate, the moderators having read and listened through all of the content Pekka had released publicly and then to them privately late in the night, that it even correctly guessed Pekka would be armed with a .22 caliber Sig Sauer Mosquito to massacre his fellow students. The moderators also clearly knew his plan to shoot up a school was in order to go down in infamy. Pekka made that very clear in one video included in the press packet called "Jokela High School Massacre 11/7/2007," which used "Stray Bullet" by KMFDM as its background music—a shout-out to the Columbine killers.

142 Jack Malvern, "Prediction of Killings Posted Hours Before Attack," *The Times*, November 7, 2007, https://www.thetimes.com/article/prediction-of-killings-posted-hours-before-attack-0wkb6nw025z.

Pekka uploaded all the documentation about what he planned to do and why to a RapidShare server just minutes ahead of leaving for school in the morning. Police would later comb through the full media package he'd left online, which contained pictures, videos, and the long-winded manifesto in English. They'd eventually make forty-six videos from his computer public.

The videos showcased the mind of a supreme egoist. Pekka, pointing a gun at the camera to KMFDM music. Pekka firing his gun in the forests around his home. A reel of narcissistic photos of him posing with his gun. An animated version of his manifesto. His sexual fantasies. Fascist propaganda. A clip from a video game of him killing women in a toilet stall. Several clips of him shooting in games. Tributes to the Columbine shooters. Footage of Jewish female athletes being captured, bound, and gagged. Clips of Marshall Applewhite and the 1997 mass suicide of his cult, Heaven's Gate, where the brother of *Star Trek's* Nichelle Nichols had died, hoping to be taken to heaven on a UFO.

By doing all of this, Pekka could at last exert some control over his life. He would own, shape, and distort the narrative, laying a foundation for future enthusiasts to research him on *his* terms, assuring that his declarations would be combed over again and again. After all, he'd been planning the shooting for nine months. The plan, as he'd written it, was to cause chaos, destabilize society, and kill as many as possible. He meant to die in the action, and he hoped his scheme would be remembered and copied forever.

We Miss You So Much

There has been discourse, investigation, and psychological study into why a young person would choose to carry out a school shooting—what inspires someone to turn against their peers. Many studies conclude there must be some of the following mental comorbidities: psychological issues that worsen one's feelings of isolation; seeing one's self as socially marginalized; lax scrutiny by authority figures; dynamic assurance by some greater force that violence gives them scarcely felt control; and easily accessible guns within their society.

The usual aim of such attacks is to reverse a perceived social order where the shooter is "lesser"—less powerful than popular peers, less authoritative than teachers or staff, less worthy in the eyes of those they are sexually attracted to, and the observation that they have an inferior sense of humor or intellect when compared to their peers. Such individuals seek to upgrade their position through violence. As such, it is more likely for males to be school shooters than females, as physical dominance is more often a masculine solution to problem-solving, self-assigning a kind of heroism to taking violent action. In the US alone, 98% of all mass shooters were men as of 2021,[143] and in Finland, 90% of juvenile homicides were committed by boys.

In Finland specifically, juvenile male shooters plan their actions more meticulously than adult perpetrators and are on the whole more brutal, with revenge most commonly aimed at same-age peers.[144] Like Pekka losing Tana, most shooters experience a loss before leaning into violence, especially the loss of a close relationship. Other indicators are failure in home or school life (such as Pekka's tanking grades or deferral by the military) or losing status within a social group (such as Pekka's peers increasingly distancing themselves from his odd behavior).

For Pekka to carry out his plan, he needed a gun. In August of 2007, he went to a shooting range in Helsinki and practiced his shot, thereafter joining a club. In early October, he applied and was rejected for a high-powered gun permit with the Järvenpää Police Department. They were suspicious of his need for a Glock 17 just for his application's stated purpose of shooting at his new club now and again. In late October, he reapplied for a less powerful firearm, and that application was approved. On the application he even whined that the smaller caliber .22 would barely allow him to enjoy himself. He said it was the minimum possible option that could still *maybe* work for what he *intended to use it for*.

Just days ahead of the shooting, on November 2, 2007, he purchased a .22 caliber Sig Sauer Mosquito and ammunition, then

143 "Mass Shooters," TheViolenceProject.org, accessed May 1, 2025, https://www.theviolenceproject.org/mass-shooter-database.

144 "Jokela School Shooting on 7 November 2007," Ministry of Justice.

practiced his aim in the woods by his house. His gun had a ten-round capacity, and he had bought 500 rounds of ammo.

Then, on November 7, he put the gun, a knife, matches, and a fifty-ounce plastic bottle full of petrol and lubricant into a shoulder bag, checked his social media one last time, played a game, made a few final tweaks to his manifesto (already uploaded), said goodbye to his father (his mother and brother had already left), and a bit before noon, left home to go kill his classmates.

Jokela High School is an upper comprehensive compound, sprawled along a large, idyllic pond at the culmination of a dead-end street. It has inner and outer courtyards, three floors, and zig-zagging corridors. It features eight entrances and exits. In other words, it's a difficult landscape for police to infiltrate easily.

On the day of the shooting the pond and grass were all iced over, as it had just dipped into freezing temperatures. The school was packed, and as it was lunchtime for many students by the time Pekka arrived, the cafeteria was especially busy. Jokela had about 450 students and fifty teachers on campus. Pekka had bought a bullet for each of them.

He had skipped his first classes to play around online but arrived at about 11:42 a.m., entering the upper-secondary school and shooting his first victim in the head, who was simply the first person that he saw. He'd timed the attack to coincide with the seventieth anniversary of the Bolshevik takeover of Russia (hence his "white revolution"), which, as bitter irony, had been a relatively bloodless movement of organized politics—a concept Pekka purportedly despised.

The shooting of his first victim would have immediate tragic consequences outside of the murder itself. As Pekka moved into a lavatory along the nearby corridor, several students noticed the body on the floor. Not acclimated to violence, and seeing the boy face down, many of them would assume he'd badly hit his head and had passed out. One would call the Emergency Response Center (ERC), and the school nurse would also be called.

Pekka, seeing the commotion—and hearing the phone call—bore his muzzle out from the mouth of the bathroom and shot his next two victims, students who'd gone to aid the first, and killed them instantly.

A third student, realizing that this was a live shooting incident, abandoned their call to the ERC and ran up the nearby staircase to the staff room to alert the teachers on break there. They made their point in a frenzy. The school nurse soon descended right into Pekka's crossfire as well, and seeing the carnage, began bellowing for students to flee—to save themselves. Another teen who had phoned the ERC—which did not realize just yet this had been upgraded from a low-level need for an ambulance to an active shooter situation—was also killed. Pekka then chased and hunted down the nurse, who tried to run, murdering her, too. He turned his gun on yet another youngster who had run with her and killed them also.

In less than four minutes, Pekka had killed six people.

The ERC operator heard the shouting and the gunfire but was having trouble identifying what was going on. There was panic on the line, bellowing, popping noises. A student shrieked that they saw a gun pointing through a door. Another call was placed to the ERC from a classroom nearby. Finally, they realized there was a live shooter at Jokela school.

From there, chaos. An education welfare officer, using the cell phone of the original ERC caller, picked up communications with them and was told they should stay locked inside the staff room for safety. Instead, some teachers left and began to shout instructions to hapless students, one bravely entering the mouth of the hallway where bullets had been flying to warn children not to make their escape in that direction. Another instructor ran to the cafeteria, full of students having their midday meal, enjoining them outside and ordering staff to lock the glass doors that stood between them and a rampaging murderer. Other teachers ran for safety.

The deputy head teacher was alerted by a female student of what was happening and quickly went to the head teacher, who crackled onto the PA system at 11:47 a.m., just minutes after the shooting had begun, to tell everyone to shelter in place and lock classroom doors. Fire doors were shut. Some people not in classrooms and unable to gain entry hid in storage closets and bathrooms and held their breath. Entire classes began escaping through windows. Phone calls and texts began to fly between rooms and floors. A few unfortunate cases thought the announcement was only a drill and stayed idling and chatting outside.

Pekka, still roaming the halls, began to scream, firing indiscriminately at walls and windows and shouting that he'd kill everyone. In the havoc, a student's mother came in through the same central entrance he had used—and in a startling display of mercy, Pekka simply let her go. She was not supposed to have been there, and so, she was not a target. Then he began pounding on and shooting through classroom doors, trying to force entry. Students who bunched away from the entrances or hid behind overturned desks would largely be okay. The doors held. One student sustained a bullet wound to his foot.

Pekka moved on. He sprayed his homemade lighter fluid over the walls of a corridor and tried four times to set the walls on fire. Luckily, inexpert, he couldn't get the fluid to ignite, and so didn't achieve his dream of sowing additional bedlam by forcing classroom doors open with flames and fumes. That would have allowed him to mow down more frightened teenagers as they fled the burning right into bullets. In his own words, Pekka had wanted his "marvelous attack on humanity" to feature "people dying, some in panic and others running away, some are maimed, smoke coming out the building.... fire ... spreading."[145] Instead, he was stonewalled.

Frustrated, he soothed himself by walking up two flights of stairs to the top floor, where he shot at a pair of best friends mid-conversation on a bench. Before they could comprehend what was happening, Pekka had leveled his gun at them and fired. One boy escaped. The other died.

It wasn't enough. Pekka moved to the canteen, where several students and staffers were still hiding, and was incensed to find they'd blocked it off. He demanded the glass doors be unlocked and even tried firing through the glass, hitting only wooden chairs and overturned tables. People inside escaped his onslaught by scaling up to high windows that led to a room behind the kitchen. He turned a gun on two teachers who'd run into him by chance while he tried to

145 "Jokela School Shooting on 7 November 2007," Ministry of Justice.

force entry, but they evaded him. One teacher ran outside and began to signal for students to evacuate. This poor missive led them directly into the path of Pekka's muzzle, so he abandoned the cafeteria to chase them into another room. There, they jumped from the windows to escape, and for some reason, Pekka allowed this, damaging the room they'd darted into only superficially.

While this was happening, the education welfare officer and the head teacher were outside by the pond. The head teacher, who'd made the announcement on the PA, paused to take a phone call from an official about the situation while her colleague moved to the car park to direct rescue vehicles. Pekka exited the building then, foiled by the cafeteria doors, agitated now and cursing loudly. There, he'd murder the head teacher, execution style, shooting her seven times after a brief, almost ordinary chat with her at gunpoint. But he did not shoot her in the head as he had with other students, instead making her kneel and then choosing to fire into parts of her body that assured her death would not be instantaneous, but agonizing.

Pekka moved on. Back inside, he went to the staff room, shouting that he'd kill all the teachers. He dared them to come out and meet their fate but none did, so he sniffed out a classroom with a still-open door instead. There, with students cornered, he shot at a television set, cracking it, and a window, shattering it. He yelled for stunned pupils to destroy school property, informing them this was a *revolution*. As they got up to begin doing as he said, the gunman was satisfied and moved on, not harming any of them.

Police arrived on the scene. Pekka opened fire, but failed in a fair fight of similarly armed combatants. Seeing that his game was over as officers began to enter the building, he moved into a boys' bathroom. No longer in a position of power as they shouted instructions to him, applying combat training and genuine physical prowess—traits Pekka had only been playing at by terrorizing unarmed underclassmen—he realized he would not overcome them. So, in a stall, beside a toilet, Pekka set his bag down and shot himself in the head. It was 12:04 p.m.

Pekka didn't die instantly. He died nearly eight hours later in a nearby ICU, brain-dead. Police managed to evacuate nearly 200 people in half an hour once on-site, and as students sheltered in place, unaware that the killer was neutralized, they began getting updates from *outside* of the school, over their phones from friends and family who were watching the news. At this point, many staffers already knew who the killer was. Students were beginning to learn as well.

The families of victims would have to wait a lot longer for confirmation. Pekka's own parents say they were kept in the dark about exactly what had happened until after their son was dead at 10:14 p.m. that night, barred by imposed ignorance from visiting Pekka's bedside at Töölö Hospital, where he took his final breaths.

The twelve ambulances that had shown up to assist victims didn't have much to do. Outside of just over a dozen minor injuries—mostly cuts and sprains from escape attempts—only three people who'd been shot remained alive after Pekka's rampage: the head teacher, who died almost immediately on-site during triage, the boy who'd been shot in the toe through a door—not a life-threatening injury—and Pekka himself, for whom death was a matter of when, not if. Doctors already knew there was no chance of recovery.

Everyone else he'd shot had been callously killed with no hope for resuscitation. He'd carried out the murders with a blank face—no empathy, just apathy. Paramedics tried revitalization techniques anyway, frantic to help, before being forced to pivot to the ghastly task of black-tagging Tuusula's dead children. Police, knowing the subject was delicate, only reported the two adult staff deaths in their first press conference. They sent a grief worker and a pastor to deliver the news to each of the families of dead teenagers, once their identities had been confirmed. Pekka's parents were informed of his involvement via phone, and of his death the same way.

Nine people were killed and thirteen more injured. From this barbarity bloomed the copycat violence that Pekka was hoping for. Eighty-six threats were made at Finnish schools in the nine months following his shooting, mainly by teenage boys, with thirty-four of them being credible enough to prosecute. It culminated in September of 2008 in the Kauhajoki school shooting, where ten students enrolled in vocational training at the campus of Seinäjoki University were killed. The gunman, Matti Juhani Saari, had purchased his firearm from the same vendor as Pekka had.[146] Years later, the Viertola shooting of 2024—perpetrated by a twelve-year-old victim of bullying—would hearken again to elements of Pekka's case. These boys were the ghostly echo of his odious legacy.

Pekka was hoping he'd be famous for his "work." And indeed, over 200,000 people viewed his online posts before they could be taken off the internet. They have been reposted by dozens of users since. In contrast, the stories of those who were lost and those left behind to grieve mostly sank into anonymity, for good or for ill, drowned out in the noise and fury of Pekka's manifesto. As is often the case with murder, the innocent victims were not cast as main characters.

There was Sameli Nurmi, aged seventeen, called "Same" by those close to him. He was the one sitting on a bench talking to his best friend, Joni, when Pekka turned the corner and opened fire. He and Joni had been friends since they were small, and they both vaguely knew Pekka as their unruffled senior. Sameli, a sweet boy who didn't think badly of others, hadn't felt any fear when he saw Pekka, not registering quickly enough his mal-intent. Same's phone would be overrun with texts in the hours after he was killed, asking after his whereabouts, friends and family frantically trying to find out if he was okay. He was beloved among his community.

There was Hanna Katariina Laaksonen Kinnunen, a twenty-five-year-old mother to two little children, aged just three and five. She had reenrolled in school to complete a certificate so she could get a better job to support her munchkins. The head teacher was a big supporter of women's education, so Hanna was right at home at Jokela, where she was supported in her dream for a better life—until hers was abruptly ended.

Ari Juhani Palsanen was another victim. Ari's father, Arto, was interviewed for Yle news live before he found out the fate of his eldest son. Ari was an older brother to siblings Tiia and Jani, and went to school with his younger brother at Jokela. Jani had made contact with his father by the time of the Yle interview, having escaped the building, but

146 "Jokela School Shooting on 7 November 2007," Ministry of Justice.

Arto had told newscasters, "I don't know anything about my other boy yet."[147] The thoughtful tousle-haired young man who'd enjoyed football and looked out for his siblings was dead at just seventeen.

Sirkka Anneli Kaarakka was the school nurse who'd rushed to offer first aid to the initial shooting victims, and who'd then rushed to warn students away once in Pekka's crosshairs. She was killed at forty-three years of age. Immature and angry young students across Finland who made threats to their schools over the next year in Pekka's shadow would often target school nurses in particular, following her death. The specter of prejudice against older women, the pall of Pekka's misogyny, hung like a gnarled shroud across her memory. She saved lives that day through her shouted directions to students; she died a hero.

Helena Kalmi, the sixty-one-year-old head teacher, had been a prolific textbook author in the sciences. She had studied philosophy and chemistry at the University of Helsinki, and was a chemistry teacher and vice-principal before becoming headmistress, working in education for thirty-six years. She was a member of the board of the Finnish Academic Women's Association and headed up a local soroptimist chapter, focusing on educational empowerment for women. As Pekka's final victim of the day, she left behind a husband and two sons.

In many cases, the heartache to families was so personal that details stayed that way—private. There was Mika Petteri Pulkkinen, seventeen at the time. Mikko Tapani Hiltunen, nicknamed "Mikkous," also seventeen, and Ville Valterri Heinonen, sixteen—the two were good friends. All three boys died just a few feet from one another, on impact. One had been the original victim, minding his own business on the way to class, and the others had rushed to help when they saw a fellow student on the floor.

After the massacre, students, families, and staff gathered by the Jokela pond late into the glacial night, leaving candles, flowers, and

147 Masskillers, "News broadcast about Jokela high school shooting. At 2:30, a man is interviewed, he has 2 sons studying at the school, he later found out that his older son, Ari Juhani Palsanen was killed in the shooting. (Sorry if the title is confusing)," Reddit, 2020, https://www.reddit.com/r/masskillers/comments/f4zvnu/news_broadcast_about_jokela_high_school_shooting.

letters, praying as wet snow rained down on them. There would be hundreds of candles cradled and protected in jars amassed along the banks, huddled together and zigzagging in all directions. Lights, blistering in solidarity.

One girl left behind a card nestled into the grass that simply said "Mikko, Ari, Ville, we miss you so much." It had a heart drawn on it.[148]

Idiocractic Selector

The manifesto Pekka left in his wake was the compilation of the unhinged, grandiose ramblings of a young man steeped in his own dissatisfaction. A coward's crowing, placing the blame for his own lack of self-worth on others, and justifying how he intended to take it out on victims who largely had not even known him. He entitled the diatribe: "How Did Natural Selection Turn Into Idiocratic Selection?"

He'd begun writing it in May of 2007 and put the final touches on it just minutes before riding his bicycle to the Jokela school, laying bare his twisted and cynical philosophy. The document is riddled with typos and exclamatory statements—clearly the writings of a struggling student.

Paradoxically, his ramblings prove that far from being unique (something his own writing strains and whines to assert: that he is special, different, *better*), Pekka was almost the textbook example of a mass shooter, desperately copying others who came before him. He put a disclaimer at the bottom of his screed, saying, "It's my fault! Not my parent's, not my brother's, not my friends, not my favorite bands, not computer games, not the media, it's mine," which closely matched the disclaimers on the manifestos of the Columbine killers. (It also, ironically, admitted that Pekka had friends.) Sycophantic, Pekka wrote with pride about how similar his name Pekka-Eric was to that of Columbine shooter Eric Klebold. He wrote this in his diary the way one might combine names with someone they have a crush on, but his was to a darker purpose.

---

148 Ian Traynor, "The Pupil Who Declared War," *The Guardian*, November 9, 2007, https://www.theguardian.com/world/2007/nov/10/schools.schoolsworldwide.

In the photos and videos that accompanied his manifesto, Pekka wears a black T-shirt emblazoned with the words "HUMANITY IS OVERRATED."

Pekka is perhaps best expressed in his own words. Below, some excerpts taken from his "grand" manifesto, as he wrote it, with his typos preserved:

> How Did Natural Selection Turn Into Idiocratic Selection?
>
> Retarded and stupid, weak-minded people are reproducing more and more faster than the intelligent, strong-minded people.... Homo Sapiens, HAH! It is more like Homo Idioticus to me! When I look at people.... I can't say I belong to the same race as the lousy, miserable, arrogant, selfish human race! No! I have evolved one step above!

He goes on to describe "mass delusion systems" that are at work in the world controlling people through religion, law, and mental health classifications. He describes how "groupthink" fences humans in, bending them away from what is natural, making them feel inferior, depressed, hateful, suicidal, and homicidal. One can extrapolate, from the pseudo-intellectualism parading as research and the ego parading as logic, that this is, in fact, a microscopic look at how *Pekka* felt, both in and toward society, rather than any true reflection of society itself. He was hostile, frustrated, and self-loathing. Humans, he says, are just another kind of animal.

While taxonomically correct, his classification of humans as *animals* was more akin to calling his fellow man *beasts*.

> Death and killing is not a tragedy, it happens in nature all the time.... Not all human lives are important or worth saving ... inferior (stupid, retarded, weak-minded masses) should perish.
>
> Stupid people [should be] slaves and intelligent people as free.... free and rulers ... [while] the robotic masses, they can be slaves.... The gangsters that now rule societies would of course get what they deserve.
>
> Of course there is a final solution too: death of the entire human race ... no one should be left alive. I have no mercy for the scum of the earth, the pathetic human race.

His manifesto does call the Nazi party just another brain-washing, likening them to governments and corporations, monarchies and the church, even as he shouts their rallying cry of "final solution." He feels democracy carries the same broken promises as any other system: the illusion of free will to enslave the weak. Pekka feels free of this involuntary slavery to a future as just another "human robot," by deciding to kill and be killed. His choice, he peacocks, is *action*.

> You can say I have a "god complex" sure ... then you have a "group complex"! Compared to you retarded masses, I am actually godlike ... Democracy is just the dictatorship of the moral majority.

He goes to describe three types of people in the world as he sees it—"Mass Humans," who make up 94% of the population, "Individualistic Humans," and "Manipulative Humans," who each make up 3% of the population. The latter two categories are the only types he feels have been bestowed with real intelligence, creativity, and self-awareness. He also estimates that at least 3% of the human population consists essentially of "vegetables," mindless nobodies. This hierarchy and its percentages are, of course, based on nothing but his own twisted perception.

> Hate, I'm so full of it and I love it. That is one thing I really love. Some time ago, I used to believe in humanity and wanted to live a long and happy life ... but then I woke up.... I just can't be happy in the society or reality I live.... Life is just a meaningless coincidence.... And I'm the dictator and god of my own life. And me, I have chosen my way. I am prepared to fight and die for my cause. I, as a natural selector, will eliminate all who I see unfit ...

Near the end of this denunciation, he posts a photo of himself holding a gun toward the reader, expression blank. The whitewashed walls of his room, lined with books, speak of a future that could have gone a very differently had he not applied himself to a crippling echo-chamber of hate-mongering, making heroes of mass murderers simply because he felt what so very many teens do—alone, different, unique, and also somehow so remarkably not-unique as to be overlooked, misunderstood, and cast aside unfairly.

> You might ask yourselves, why did I do this and what do I want. Well, most of you are too arrogant and close-minded to understand.... You will probably say that I am "insane" "crazy" "psychopath" "criminal"

> or crap like that. No, the truth is that I am just an animal, a human, an individual, a dissident … I don't want to be part of this fucked up society.… Human race is not worth fighting for … only worth killing.… Long live the revolution.… If we want to live in a different world, we must act.…hopefully my actions will inspire all the intelligent people of the world.… [even if I am] only remembered as evil.… It's time to put NATURAL SELECTION & SURVIVAL OF THE FITTEST back on tracks!

Finally, it ends with a photo of him waving goodbye.

Though this does sound like the god complex he diagnoses himself with, Pekka's tirade more closely resembles the lashing out of someone who feels like a bullied teen. It has all the hallmarks of a young, bruised ego: pseudo intellectualism, othering, and posturing to make one's feeling of worthlessness the fault and responsibility of others, to rebrand hurt as a hallmark of being special. In a world where Pekka had been cast at school as "Them" in "Us vs. Them," he had recast his "Us" as the intelligentsia, the "thinking" minority. And pre-knowing that his actions would be seen as evil, psychotic, and immoral, he attempts to manipulate the reader to reject the "Them," implying that should they agree with the "system" and not understand his motivations, they are among the "sheeple," the robots, the *slave*-class of people. They took the blue pill, they tapped out, happy cows at pasture paper-pushing their way through a meaningless life, puppeteered by bigger systems and fatter wallets. He tells the reader: Agree with me, or you're admitting you're an idiot. It's an effective game of chicken, as young readers of his "work" might not want to feel as if they are being called stupid.

Interestingly, studies show that boys in Finland who were both bullied and then themselves became bullies show the highest tendencies toward depression and suicide, more significantly than bullies or victims alone.[149] Pekka playing out his dark revenge fantasy after creating a gloomy inner world where the population he maligned as servants for the slaying fits nicely with this assessment. Again,

149 Anat Brunstein, et al., "Childhood Bullying as a Risk for Later Depression and Suicidal Ideation Among Finnish Males," *Journal of Affective Disorders* 109 no. 1 (2008): 47–55; https://pubmed.ncbi.nlm.nih.gov/18221788.

everything about Pekka proved he was the textbook definition he complained of.

Though Pekka defined himself as the kind of dominant, aggressive meta-human that he would like society to have more of; in fact, his "alpha male" brand of aggression—derision and gun violence—are not the markings of the most dominant male's traits. Truly dominant males *and* females, studies have shown, share three important qualities:[150] First, they are not *overtly* aggressive but instead are *defenders* of their resources and social groups, via *prosocial* helpfulness and voluntary benevolence. Next, they are *relationally aggressive*, harming others' social standing rather than aggressing one-to-one or with physical violence and intimidation. And finally, they attract social attention and collective aspiration; their peers want to be like them and are eager to be liked *by* them to elevate their own social standing. Sociability and authoritative generosity are, in fact, the hallmarks of the most dominant people in society.

By these factual standards, Pekka was a rather submissive type of man. But surely he must have felt that was so and hoped to transform that truth into a less bleak reality—not through working on his faults or toward a better future, but by making himself judge and executioner.

His lazy and defensive point of view is nonetheless very *attractive* for many young readers. So attractive, in fact, that after the atrocities Pekka committed, sympathy groups would form—for the shooter himself.

On a Facebook page entitled "Jokela Highschool Shooting Sympathizers," moderator Matthew Eugene wrote, "While we frown on the killing of high school students (there are many Finnish industry headquarters for example which probably would have made more appropriate targets), we sympathize with 18-year-old Pekka-Eric Auveinen as his beliefs and actions are an honest and sane reaction to the horrors of modern society ... there are many who view our current situation ... in an ultimatum perspective: We, because of our

150 Patricia H. Hawley, Todd D. Little, and Noel A. Card, "The Myth of the Alpha Male: A New Look at Dominance-Related Beliefs and Behaviors Among Adolescent Males and Females," *International Journal of Behavioral Development* 32, no. 1 (2008): 76–88, https://www.researchgate.net/publication/247779752_The_myth_of_the_alpha_male_A_new_look_at_dominance-related_beliefs_and_behaviors_among_adolescent_males_and_females.

own stupidity and selfishness, are at all times mere hours away from total destruction, we are killing our planet at an exponential rate, we value individual happiness over what is right.... WE ARE A CANCER ON THE PLANET AND MUST BE CUT DOWN TO SIZE. These actions will be universally denounced ... [but Pekka] will inspire people to 'rather fight and die than live a long and unhappy life.' We consider this point of view admirable in this dystopic time of unimaginable corruption and destruction."[151]

Sympathy for the shooter over the victims came from Pekka's parents, as well. Remorse and guilt are usually hallmarks for parents of young murderers who have to speak to the actions of their children to a cloying the public hurting for answers—but the Auvinens' nationally televised interview managed neither to be apologetic nor particularly empathetic, instead coming across as largely myopic and self-sympathetic. And YouTube commenters seemed to take their side:[152]

> **@eye_exist:** A lesson to learn: do not bully the weird quiet kids.
>
> **@hawrushe:** He was a victim as well.
>
> **@patrik4586:** Nice looking people, it's a real pity ... bullying is the cause here too.
>
> **@arlene19:** [Pekka] WAS bright and intelligent!! Eric and Dylan were pretty cool guys, they helped many of us and saved our lives. I'm sorry for everyone killed that day but now there are people who try to make a change to stuff like bullying.[153]

Of course, Pekka did not target his supposed bullies. He *was* one.

In the interview, Pekka's father Ismo shows off a video he has made, posted to YouTube on October 8, 2008, entitled "For Our Son." (After a decade online, it was removed from the host website.)

---

151 Timo Jaakonaho, "Finland Crime Shooting School," Getty Images, November 8, 2007, https://www.gettyimages.com/detail/news-photo/woman-looks-at-an-internet-webpage-of-the-jokela-highschool-news-photo/77798183?adppopup=true.

152 Ramnodest Ramndom, "Pekka-Eric Auvinen Parents' Interview 2008," YouTube, March 16, 2022, https://www.youtube.com/watch?v=stzHCyMgRnw.

153 Jaakko Heitanen, "Pysäyttävä haastattelu: Jokelan kouluampujan vanhemmat eivät osanneet aavistaa mitään – "Sieltä löysin Pekan jättämän viimeisen kirjeen," MTV Uutiset, May 8, 2021, https://www.mtvuutiset.fi/artikkeli/pysayttava-haastattelu-jokelan-kouluampujan-vanhemmat-eivat-osanneet-aavistaa-mitaan-sielta-loysin-pekan-jattaman-viimeisen-kirjeen/8136528#gs.inpkhy.

The video, which includes sweet family photos, ends with a picture of Pekka-Eric's gravestone, which is engraved with two peaceful deer in a forest. Ismo vocally defends his right to mourn and grieve in his own way, as a parent who also lost their child that day. Ismo attaches a disclaimer to the video, stating, "I don't accept school shootings. I don't promote violence."

The username Ismo chose was @finnbluus, Finnish Blues, though he now goes by @bigpapaauvinen. By 2017, Pekka's tribute video had 321,657 views.[154] As background music, it uses the song "It's a Long Road" by Dan Hill from the film soundtrack for *Rambo I, First Blood*. Rambo is the classical masculine armed fighter, driven by trauma, who uses guns and explosives against his enemies. It generates a disturbing association.

"I haven't really given guilt any room myself," said Ismo, in the interview. "I've had so much other stuff on my mind." Throughout the airing, the Auvinens hold fast to a small and endearing tricolored family dog, curious and bouncy. They carry that little dog around like a lifeline, clutching it often. It adds a layer of humanity and normalcy to an otherwise alien conversation.[155]

The interview footage originally aired on MTV3 and was translated by YouTube user @ramnodestramndom1237. It is the only video on that channel, which has just thirteen subscribers.

Mikaela said on that same interview, "Pekka was also a very kind and well-behaving guy. No one would have believed he could do anything like this."

The pair looked pained as they answered questions, insisting that investigators blamed guns when they should have looked into what really causes such tragedies—school culture and social pressure. Mikaela added, "Do we need to compete so much? Always grinding to get more wealth and prosperity, more of everything." Ismo forged on, saying he still feels stuck in that day, and mostly only thinks of his own pain. He remarks that's normal for a parent—grief for his own son

154 Johanna Sumiala, "Agony at a Distance: Investigating Digital Witnessing on YouTube," *Ethik in mediatisierten Welten* (2019): 131–45, https://helda.helsinki.fi/server/api/core/bitstreams/22c89c7f-58bf-4619-98d8-428597dfc74a/content.

155 Ramnodest Ramndom, YouTube.

above anyone else's. They keep a silver-framed photo of Pekka front-and-center on their bookshelves, visible within the TV camera's shot.

Blissfully, Pekka's younger brother is left out of the news.

The morning of the shooting, Ismo says he was on vacation from work and spent some time with both his sons. A friend of Pekka's from school called later in the day to ask if Pekka was home or if Ismo could locate his gun. Ismo says he'd had no idea Pekka owned a gun—but a bit like when the family said they had no idea Pekka had any friends, only to be phoned by one, this seems obtuse. They had at least known Pekka had an interest in guns and practiced his shooting.

Ismo found the receipt for the weapon later, hidden in a drawer in Pekka's room. But when he went looking for it at the friend's behest, he found the suicide letter instead, and went into shock.

The family says they were told at 5 p.m. on the day of the shooting that Pekka was in critical condition, but no victims were mentioned to them. They'd already, apparently, learned about Pekka's condition via the news, so it was strange that they were in the dark about the other victims. Perhaps they simply, somehow, were willfully unaware that Pekka had been the perpetrator, despite the phone call about the gun and the suicide letter. Perhaps they simply were holding on fast to hope.

"I could only see the situation from a fatherly perspective," explained Ismo. "I was just so worried about Pekka." But Mikaela interjected, perhaps realizing the statement read as unfair to other aggrieved parents, "Why couldn't Pekka spare the others and only take his own life?"

When asked if there had been any signs of violence or radicalization in their son, the pair answered awkwardly, with Ismo beginning to say, "I can't say I would have noticed," and Mikaela cutting him off to quickly correct, "Not in his behavior, no. Pekka was extremely calm and seemed happy most of the time."

The school and teachers had given positive feedback about him, they said. This again seems odd, since he was doing worse in school in the lead-up to the shooting, he was allegedly being bullied, and students were submitting reports about him. His parents had been the ones to push the idea that Pekka was anxious and unhappy, that other students were tormenting him. Though the school could not share the social worker's reports with Pekka's parents, it seems unlikely they'd report quite so sunnily on his progress.

Said Mikaela, "[They] gave us the picture Pekka was a very talented student—which was probably true—well-behaved, positive in every way." The only signs they had seen, in retrospect, were that Pekka had stopped paying attention to household chores and was reluctant to buy winter shoes, which he'd very much need by the end of November ahead of heavy snowfall. This became a sticking point between him and his mother, with Mikaela not understanding his reticence. But he hadn't planned to still be alive to need them.

The pair also quickly place blame on others outside of their son—the schools and its students, the bullying that Pekka went through, resisting what school officials said about the worst of it being light verbal teasing. "[It] got physical, different variations of mental violence, name-calling...." Mikaela fusses, as Ismo adds, "They shot him with an airsoft gun on his way to school once.... Wrote stuff about him on the whiteboard.... the whole class was laughing."

"In the end he was left with no friends," said Mikaela. "No one to play Playstation with. It was awful. Extremely rough couple of years."

This seems to maybe have been in reference to back in Helsinki, however, not after the move to Tuusula. Yet it contradicts the fact that he was more popular as a child and lost friends as he grew. His having no friends also contradicts Pekka's own words—and Ismo's—about it not being the fault of his friends, who called the Auvinens before even the police did, full of concern. Very little of these justifications seem to make sense, even within a short TV spot.

His parents go on to state that in 2006, Pekka began to suffer from panic attacks but that wait times of over six months to see a doctor doomed him—mental health services, or lack thereof, were also to blame. This seems a reasonable outcry, as surely Pekka should have been prescribed regular SSRIs and been seeing a therapist about his severe social anxieties, just as his parents had begged of the Finnish national health system.

Regarding his more radical views, Mikaela said that those did not come from the home—that, in fact, Pekka was the one who got *her* interested in social and ecological theory, not the other way around. Whatever the case may be, the reality is that Mikaela runs a very active far alt-right Finnish Twitter/X page under the handle @MikaelaVuorio. On it, she complains about the erasure of Finnish culture by *indigenous* peoples, and retweets posts by accounts suspended for radical and hateful commentary.[156]

She also makes fun of diversity initiatives (one might call that bullying); lambasts Middle Eastern communities in Finnish society; is an Elon Musk retweeter; bites back at Yle, the station that supported her music, by saying they should have their entire budget cut. She makes fun of families who don't dress well enough on Christmas; calls immigration into Ireland "ethnic genocide"; and talks about the age of "neo-stupidity."

It is, in fact, very easy to see where Pekka's values may have had their tiles laid. Again, he was not so remarkably unique—he seemingly was just parroting what he heard in his home, as much as he parroted what he read online and the actions of the disaffected youth that came before him.

As part of his final online screed, Pekka posted a profile of himself, sharing with an international audience the following, immortalized in time, in his own words,

> What do I hate / What I don't like?
>
> Equality, tolerance, human rights, political correctness, hypocrisy, ignorance, enslaving religions and ideologies, antidepressants, TV soap operas & drama shows, rap-music, mass media, censorship, political populists, religious fanatics, moral majority, totalitarianism, consumerism, democracy, pacifism, state mafia, alcoholics, TV commercials, human race.

156 Mikaela Vuorio (@MikaelaVuorio), "Tätä olen minäkin ihmetellyt pitkään. Esim. suomalaiset täyttävät kirkkaasti alkuperäiskansojen määrityksen jos ketkä. Julistautukaamme siis itse alkuperäiskansaksi - pelle-YK:lta sitä on turha ruikuttaa. On korkein aika tehdä se nyt, kun meitä suomalaisia vielä on!" X, May 16, 2018, https://x.com/MikaelaVuorio/status/996878357102030849.

Before he went and killed his classmates, Pekka played a final round of *Battlefield 2*, his favorite online game.[157] He had proudly completed 9,475 in-game kills and 234 suicides.[158] It was a blasé last moment of childhood play, tinged red.

His parents ended their interview by saying how tough all this had been on them, but that with the help of friends, family, and therapy they had been able to get back to their lives. They make sure to mention how annoying it was for them in the coverage that followed the shooting that neighbors told reporters that by moving into the neighborhood they had ruined the look of the street by allowing their boys to litter their pretty lawn with a slapdash of their objects: bikes and toys and garden tools. That's, they argue, is not *fair*—their lawn is fine.

It was an odd sticking point in an interview about Finland's dead children.

Pekka's cult of fame, the copycat threats and killers that followed, meant that as he'd intended, he became a greater influencer after his death—for all the wrong reasons. The Auvinen garden had not been all right. It had grown a rotten weed right into Tuusula's rich soil.

157 Langman, "Two Finnish School Shooters."

158 Langman, "Two Finnish School Shooters."

CHAPTER 5

NASIM AGHDAM, aka Green Nasim

Do you dare not to kill for passion
Not to wear bloody fashion
Not to sell your soul to the world of
Money, fame, blood and joy?
It's all a dead world.
Do you dare to be one in a million?
Do you dare to walk in an opposite direction
When you see the color of compassion?
Get your words out in any situation,
Help them see through.
—"Do You Dare," an original song by Nasim Aghdam

This song was written and sung by Nasim Aghdam for her pro-veganism YouTube channel. The music video for it features clips of her dancing in glamorous gowns and then as a disembodied head floating in the clouds, godlike. She'd interspersed these bizarre moments with short, disturbing videos of cows, pigs, bulls, foxes, seals, wolves, and other animals being slaughtered for food, fur, or fun. The suffering of these animals is assuredly upsetting. Nasim was an avid animal rights activist who wanted to bring more attention to animal cruelty. She'd go on to shoot three innocent strangers, with intent to kill.

Iran, 1996

> The right of citizens to change their Government is severely compromised by the leadership of the Government, which effectively manipulates the electoral system to its advantage. Iran is ruled by a group of religious leaders and their lay associates who share a belief in the legitimacy of a theocratic state based on Ayatollah Khomeini's interpretation of Shi'a Islam. There is no separation of state and religion. The clerics dominate all branches of government. The Government represses any movement seeking to separate state and religion, or to alter the State's existing theocratic foundation.
>
> — US Department of State, "Iran Report on Humans Rights Practices for 1996"[159]

Human rights committees have been established in the *Majles*, the elected Consultative Assembly, and also in the judiciary branch of the Iranian government. But they lack power. Human rights abuses are dog-whistled by foreign watch groups who face less peril in doing so than local minority factions bandied together to speak out against their erasure from public life. A dangerous uphill battle that, within three decades, would become a landslide backward. The fury of dogma would win out against tides of bloody protest, *sharia* law ripping its fingernails against the swell of women's bodies when in 2024 the *Nezam*[160] called for their removal from sight, posters featuring women's free-flowing hair cleaved off the walls of Tehran.

In 1996, it had only been seventeen years since Iran's Islamic Revolution overthrew the Pahlavi royal dynasty, turning Iran into a republic from the ashes of an autocratic imperial state. Women's rights had been in a state of slow erosion ever since, a loss less painfully felt as it was meted out in drips and drabs. Iran's displaced former imperial Pahlavi shah had been eagerly following the example set by Mustafa Kemal Atatürk in the neighboring predominantly Muslim country of Turkey, a popular and more secular model of leadership.

During his reign (1941 to 1979), Mohammad Reza Pahlavi promoted inclusion, unveiling, and enfranchisement for Iranian

159 US Department of State, "Iran Report on Human Rights Practices for 1996," State.gov, January 30, 1997, https://1997-2001.state.gov/global/human_rights/1996_hrp_report/iran.html.

160 The Nezam are the ruling governmental body of Iran, its state political structure.

women. He prescribed to these tactics sometimes violently. Under the shah, wearing *hijab* was forcibly banned; the even more modest chador was literally rended off of women protestors in the streets by state police. He called it his "White Revolution"—unrelated to the Bolsheviks, except as a title mostly reserved for "bloodless" revolutions that see power turned over with very little death. In 1963, for the first time, Shah Pahlavi's administration even gave women the right to vote. But when the shah was forced to flee to Egypt, his vision for Iranian women was unseated alongside his family. The religious revolution of 1979 that displaced him saw women abruptly lose their nascent voting power, now under Ayatollah Khomeini. Hijab hair coverings became compulsory. Whereas organized feminism had been a radical addition to Iranian life just a few decades prior, now, the country's freshly installed spiritual leaders saw merit in having women banned from public life entirely, regardless of the fact that these same women had helped conduct the business of their revolution. By the late 1990s, the theocratic sect was pushing women out of the workforce less coyly. The new Islamic Republic shuttered childcare centers to force mothers to stay at home and demanded the rigorous coverage of female bodies in public spaces, making many jobs impossible. They shortened the age of retirement for women, transforming them into early dependents, and banned them from learning over one hundred subjects at university, restricting career mobility.[161] Women were being relegated to mothers and sisters instead of doctors and lawyers, financially beholden to husbands and families. They fought back. But they were losing the battle in crumbs.

By 1996, the US Department of State noted that discrimination was enshrined by the courts in Iran, especially in matters of property or family disputes. A woman's testimony in Iranian court was, legally, worth only *half* that of a man's—meaning that if it came down to *he said, she said*, then officially speaking, what *he said* would always be correct. Families of female victims of violent crime were additionally responsible for covering a male defendant's costs for trial.

161 Mahnaz Afkhami and Erika Friedl, *In the Eye of the Storm: Women in Post-Revolutionary Iran* (Syracuse University Press, 1994).

Spots at universities for women were shrinking along with job willingness to take them on. Literacy was tanking, with rural women suffering more than their urban counterparts. Perhaps worse, contradictions ran rife. In 1995, for example, women were surprisingly given the right to be elevated to court judges—but female judges were barred from trying any legal hearings, effectively making it a "right" in name only. Women were expected to follow dress codes; but how conservative those were remained ambiguous and enforcement was haphazard and decided individually by local government and institutions like schools, workplaces, and social spots. This meant that punishments for infractions were just as random.

Others were also maligned by the Islamic State. Mainly religious and ethnic minorities, for whom only five seats were reserved in the 270-seat *Majles*—the likes of Armenians, Zoroastrians, and those of Jewish or Bahá'í faith. They were systemically discriminated against in housing, education, and employment, as sanctioned by the regime. Unflinchingly, the state forced public sector workers to do a screening that proved their adherence to Islam ahead of hire, and universities installed theological entrance exams featuring only Islam, regardless of the test-taker's faith. Religious minority sects, such as Sunni Muslims, also suffered under this system.

So to be a woman in Iran in 1996, and to be a Bahá'í woman at that, was no simple existence.

At seventeen, Nasim Najafi Aghdam was both. She had been fourteen when the Supreme Revolutionary Council gave special directives to effectively end Bahá'í participation in public life. It proclaimed that Bahá'ís should have their employment restricted, communities left undeveloped, lines of communication and financial support from abroad terminated, properties confiscated, places of worship seized, and they should be barred from positions of influence in Iranian public life.[162] They were forced out of higher learning, their public workers were summarily fired, and Bahá'ís were denied pensions, benefits, or unemployment. In some cases, they were even required to pay their salaries *back to* the Iranian government or face jail time.

162 US Department of State, "Iran Report on Human Rights Practices for 1996."

The silver lining to these draconian directives was that, by 1996, Bahá'ís were allowed once more to send their children to public school (previously restricted) and were given small food ration booklets—a pittance at best, but a stark necessity when jobs were scant.

At seventeen, Nasim was at an age when school was no longer permissible for her. Food, employment, and security were in scarce supply. So, her family—including a brother, parents, and her grandmother—immigrated to the United States, leaving behind a homeland that, in its furor, had abandoned them first. They'd settled on the West Coast, in Menifee, California.

Theirs was a cookie-cutter street where all the houses were different taupe versions of each other, with big jutting garages, dangerous arrays of pointed desert plants in stunted front yards, and repetitive gables cresting short floors, accessible by the welcome nook of a sunken front door. To the immediate right of their own beige home was a big, empty lot. Dirt as far as the eye could see was patched over in scorched, balding grass. A town ripe with American McUrbanism, but on a horizon of tumbleweeds.

Nasim did not yet know that this was merely the next home she would be expelled from. She ran with her family from tyranny and would one day leave Menifee ready to commit atrocity.

For her parents, California was a brutal second upheaval. Originally from Azerbaijan, they had migrated to Iran—whether forcibly or not is unknown. Azerbaijan, Soviet from 1922 until it declared independence in 1991, had a fraught relationship with the Bahá'ís, too. Soviets campaigned against the faith and expelled practitioners from their territories. In the Azerbaijan of Nasim's parents' generation, Bahá'ís were restricted from meeting in large groups, fundraising, performing outreach, or founding community childcare centers. Educational bans, mass arrests, and scattered executions took such a steep toll on the Bahá'ís, that they lost the numbers to qualify as an assembly in Azerbaijan by the 1960s, and with their minority Caucasus disbanded, they were left with little to no political power. In the early 1980s, the Soviet Union's KGB doubled down on violence against the community, with the faithful subjected to grueling hours-long interrogations in dimly lighted rooms, on flimsy "evidence," for the crime of being.

Whether Nasim's family had left by coercion, need, or will, Nasim herself was not born on her parents' native soil, the "land of fire" on the Caspian Sea, studded with its Caucasus mountains—but in Urmia, Iran, the "city of water." The population there would have been mainly Azerbaijani in 1979, the year of her birth, and Nasim would have grown up speaking Turkish, warm and dry in the shade of the Zagros Mountains.

Urmia was fairly diverse as far as Iranian cities went. Menifee, by comparison, must have felt worlds different with its impersonal fast-food chains and bizarrely empty commercial storefronts. Built as a "master-plan community" in the late 1980s, it was constructed to be largely residential, but by the 1990s, its mixed-use spaces still hadn't inspired Californians to give Menifee a chance when a number of more exciting cities—Irvine, Palm Springs, San Deigo—were just a few hours' drive away. Though it was curated to feature lakes, gardens, and playgrounds, Menifee's residents traveled outside of the city for work, play, and grub.

Still, there was the opportunity here for Nasim to grow into whomever she wanted to be. Yes, speaking English when she already spoke so many other languages—Farsi, Turkish, up to perhaps as many as six other languages total, at least partially—was a whole new challenge, and the cultural shift was not easy. But she felt up to the task. Nasim was driven. She was a devout vegan and an animal rights activist. She threw herself into health, fitness, and the pseudosciences of holistic wellness. She wanted to be famous. And she wanted to achieve that fame with an almost fanatical adherence to clip art, drumbeats, nylon cat suits, and '80s wigs. Luckily for Nasim, a young platform was just coming into its own at exactly the time that she needed it. The platform showcased videos, which allowed her to explore and solidify her "brand" over hours of filmed footage. It was called YouTube. When the host site monetized in 2007, Nasim was twenty-eight years old. Still living under her parents' roof in Menifee, she must have seen a golden opportunity for financial independence and celebrity—plus the ability to fund causes that were near and dear to her heart, expanding her brand as an offbeat video guru.

Why, then, on April 3, 2018, just before another birthday, did she drive to San Bruno, California, with a loaded gun and extra clips to kill as many YouTube employees as she could? It was a tragedy that could have gone much worse, eventually ending in just three serious injuries and only one death. Nasim's.

Freedom Fries & PETA Bread

In 2010, Nasim began to use YouTube in earnest as the main platform for uploading her unusual content. She was still living with family in Menifee, in her parents' palatial five-bedroom house, expansive enough to host family and any guests who came to call. It was perhaps a kindness that her parents did not expect independence of Nasim and were willing to support her financially. When she was in a creative mood, their home became a dance studio, a gym, and a backdrop for Nasim's art. She'd made those rooms a canvas for her videos, even spilling out onto the lawn and the driveway, using green screen technology sometimes, and sometimes giving audiences a full view of their house. In this way, in this space, she produced dozens of videos.

The content that Nasim uploaded to YouTube had a health and wellness bent, which tied in seamlessly with her veganism and staunch animal rights activism. Viewers had to squint past some of her channel's eccentricities to find that her platform, at its core, was about fitness and advocacy. She uploaded complementary content to her Instagram and Telegram handles, of which she had quite a few, and additional videos to her personal websites, which hosted some of her more intimate prose and salacious rants. Her handles were also separated by country: US, Turkey, Iran. And some by genre: art, advocacy, athleticism. In total, she had over a dozen.

Already well into adulthood, Nasim hadn't shown any signs of striking out on her own for higher education, career-building, or homemaking, and so she mostly dreamt up content in this little Californian oasis her family had adopted as their own. It was a pretty place to work, thanks to her mother, who kept the house neat and well appointed, its windows overlooking a simple, private garden where they could take tea surrounded by greenery, outlined by a protective wall. Beyond it, paved roads and dirt mounds stretched over the bend of Alta Mira Street, ironically named for its tall view, though it mostly showcased a sprawling vista of not-very-much. Nasim spent a good deal of time in her room, looking out at that expansive nothingness.

Nasmi's main roadblock online was that her successful persona was fractured across multiple YouTube landing pages, all in different languages (Farsi, English, and Turkish), and even across varied social media platforms and websites, making it hard to properly monetize. While her popularity on her non-English profiles was greater, a lot of the feedback she was receiving in those spaces was negative, with audiences tuning in to ridicule or mock her.

Her videos were a little bewildering, to say the least. Avant-garde in the extreme, Nasim's content was a rotation of trippy aerobic videos, staunchly pro-vegan jump-scares, a brick-a-back of clip art and MS-paint-drawn backgrounds, often with discordant musical overlays and edits that screamed *vintage*. Hers was a playlist rife with uncanny valley. If the color-riot brand Lisa Frank, a Richard Simmons workout VHS tape, and Clippy the Microsoft Word–helper tool shared a fever dream, this assuredly is what it would have looked like. It was a strange, but engaging, way to introduce heavy topics. Much of Nasim's platform revolved around veganism for the sake of animal rights, with some of her grittier videos even featuring live animals and detailing the cruelties they endure at human hands. These videos carried heavy overtones of blame, often equating meat-eating with outright murder. She balanced this with lighter wellness and workout videos, mostly featuring easy exercise or unusual recipes. Viewers were meant to mimic her and follow along. Finally, she also made quite a few bizarre dance videos that seemed to be inspired by the 1980s, tall hair and all, with jerky repetitive movements and neon sweat bands, sometimes featuring original songs she'd croon in her flat, monotone singing voice.

In skits, she often donned catsuits in bright colors and plunging necklines, always skin-tight, in camo or metallic leopard print—a kind of off-brand Cheetara from *ThunderCats*. At other times she accessorized her looks with an askew fedora while clutching a live chicken or rabbit. Sometimes she wore a wig in a comically towering bouffant, her expression dead serious, or carried a sword in the name of bovine sanctity. Sometimes she wore lipstick—but all over her face, like a children's art project. Viewers didn't know if all this was performance art, unconventional comedy, or engagement tactics for the sake of her advocacy work. But the mark she'd ultimately leave on the world would be more in line with some of her darker content.

Because Nasim had so many varied accounts per language and added new handles often, it's difficult to know her full subscriber count at peak, but assumptions can be made. On her @nasimnaja435 YouTube handle she had over 30k subscribers and had uploaded 127 videos. She certainly reached over 50k subscribers across her various other YouTube profiles. Her vegan activism Instagram handle, @Nasimsabz1, had 55.5k followers—she followed no one back. She even had a separate social profile for hand art. Most of her handles translated into some version of "Green Nasim," the green referring to her natural way of life. Her website, NasimSabz.com, also translated to Green Nasim.

Despite her large following and the upwards of nine million views her videos had across handles,[163] Nasim was still only earning a pittance. A fact that made her more and more frustrated over time, especially as that slight amount lessened. When put in context, those nine million views would have been across nearly eight years and at least four channels, lessening the impact of the number. By splitting her brand, she'd thinned her profits, despite reaching more of the world through content in multiple languages.

What her content across all platforms had in common was an almost comedic seriousness. Her off-key singing carried desperate solemnity; she'd dance in full-scale ball gowns by simply moving one arm vaguely or bopping a hip. In one video, Nasim painted ultra-fake blood on her face and carried a curved plastic pirate's saber

163 *Inside Edition*, "YouTube Shooter Vents on Website After Making Just Pennies for Videos," YouTube, April 5, 2018, https://www.youtube.com/watch?v=ubu557K-_T8.

to a 2009 PETA protest in San Diego to object Camp Pendleton's use of pigs in US Marine trauma training—the practice of instructing doctors on battlefield injury care using live animal tissue, because it closely mimics that of human tissue, to better prepare them for saving human lives. Animals are euthanized after the training. The subject itself isn't humerous at all; it's Nasim who looks vaguely like a Monty Python character come to life, baffling even her allies in the fight. She was a sight to behold, with crimson tears painted across her face and a huge, fake black mullet. But the look served its purpose—garnered attention. She was even quoted in the *Los Angeles Times* about the protest:

> Nasim Aghdam, twenty-nine ... dressed in a wig and jeans with large blood drops painted on them. "For me, animal rights equal human rights," Aghdam said.[164]

Had she left it at videos about veganism, even about vegan extremism, she likely would have continued to gather a more robust following of like-minded individuals. Instead, a lot of her content increasingly became just a little bit *strange*, tone-deaf of itself. In one of her videos, entitled "Exercise for Legs,"[165] Nasim pulls out all her best moves and gives viewers the penultimate look of what to expect from her channel.

The video is 1:40 long. It opens with Nasim walking onto a greenscreen to the sound of djembe drumming music, and the screen explodes in fire as she juts her hands out, turning the fire into large, pink 3D flowers. She is wearing a leopard print leotard. She turns quickly to the screen, makes a "four" with one hand, then a "two" with the other. For less than a second, there's a pop-up of a fake book with her on the cover, also donning leopard print, in front of the live version of her in the same outfit. The title reads "Veganism: Fall of Terrorism" in English and "Veganism: The End of Bloodshed" in Arabic, in the colors and pattern of the Iranian flag. She holds

164 Kristina Davis, "From the Archives: PETA Protests Use of Pigs in Military Trauma Training at Camp Pendleton," *LA Times*, August 13, 2009, https://www.latimes.com/local/lanow/la-me-pigs-training-20180404-story.html.

165 Andrés Tozado Mihano, "Exercises For Legs," YouTube, April 5, 2018, https://www.youtube.com/watch?v=sTNGPXbX07k.

up her hands in the British gesture for "fuck you." Tulips blast open, and suddenly viewers are with her in a bedroom, with an overlay advertising her various channels and handles.

She does a brief intro to the video, in Persian: "Show me an exercise to make the buttock muscles beautiful and happy," she purrs.

She then proceeds to speed-run eight different muscle-building drills for legs, the video badly spliced and none of her demonstrations feature correct form, pacing, or even instructions on how to do the workout so it actually targets the muscle groups the moves should be affecting. It's Nasim, not in gym clothes and in bare feet, with a mic pack strapped to her back, making unnerving *The Office*–style unblinking eye contact with the camera, counting quickly in Turkish over loud tambourine music as she does a facsimile of calf raises and hamstring curls. She is in full glam, with thick, expressive makeup. The video ends abruptly, with no outro, just a brief half-second clip of her in a purposefully racy freeze-frame pose from behind. Many of the clips were filmed from an angle to show off her backside in body-hugging lycra—odd, for content aimed at cultures steeped in religious modesty. The video, if posted in the 2020s, would likely be titled something more tongue-in-cheek, like #twerkin'out.

She often received backlash on her videos from Middle Eastern audiences. Unfortunately, Iranian audiences didn't "get" her, despite her pride in her heritage, and a lot of her engagement in that region came from people hate-watching her. Audiences found her content bizarre, especially her unnerving penchant for staring wide-eyed into the camera without blinking. Her titillating angles came off as ostentatious rather than sporty. Something about her persona struck people as "off," though they couldn't put a finger on why, and speculations in her comment section grew to such a fever-pitch that she felt she had to respond to her detractors.

She posted a short reply to some of the more hateful critiques, saying, "I don't have any special mental or physical disease. But I live on a planet filled with.... perversion and injustices."[166]

166 *Inside Edition*, "YouTube Shooter Vents on Website."

She also couldn't seem to pick a lane. Her Instagram profile listed her as an "Athlete Artist Comedian Poet Model Singer Host Actor Director Producer." In fact, she wasn't particularly prolific or educated in any of these professions. She posted no comedy except by accident, her personal training videos didn't qualify as athletic, and she acted and directed only her own YouTube shorts. She was both the most well-known and the most mercilessly ridiculed on social media in Iran, the country her family had fled. Despite that, it would be American life and culture she felt discontent with.

Compared to the persecution in Iran, her home in Menifee should have been a boon. Done in a coastal "Nantucket style," the interior featured deep cherry woodwork and sleek black modern appliances. A wrought-iron staircase shot up from the first floor, where her parents shared a lavish master bedroom with a his and hers vanity bathroom, then to the second floor, which housed the four bedrooms the rest of the family used. Flawless cream and beige knit carpeting tongued its way down the steps; precious family moments were captured in golden picture frames; florals were everywhere. The kitchen, which spilled in an open plan to a living room with a delicately embroidered white couch, had a wide island that allowed for group cooking. They had a separate sitting room, a fireplace, a pool table, and a backyard with a ping pong table, all beckoning recreational use. On the front lawn, sculptures of baby deer nestled in the grass, and the patio was shaded by an awning. The home was set up to accommodate pets, which fit Nasim's deep moral alignment with animal rights. Damask curtains, chandelier sets, and pretty antique furniture spoke to her mother's touch. It was a home that yearned to host visitors, that begged for family time. Seating was set up for at least seven wherever you wandered.

"If you are superficial, you will think it is heaven here. [But] you will see that it is worse than Iran," Nasim said of California.[167] Though she never expounded fully on what she felt was worse about it, some of her point of view can be inferred. Moving away from her native country in her late teens made assimilating to American culture

167 *Inside Edition*, "YouTube Shooter Vents on Website."

difficult. Veganism, too, must have been a tough platform in a city that boasted twenty-one fast-food restaurants in just forty-six square miles, priding itself on its burgers and carnitas. Her "green" alignment would have felt out of place among the Cadillac margaritas on offer—which, though named for its ingredients, might well have looked car-sized to anyone not used to West Coast Americana. Nasim identified as Persian and not American, and she felt most comfortable speaking in Farsi. Her English remained heavily accented, and while California is home to the largest migrant population of Iranians in the United States, they made up less than 0.4% of the population in Menifee, according to the general census at the time—meaning that Nasim stood out when she spoke. Her Bahá'í faith made her a religious minority almost everywhere she went, but also something of a cultural curiosity in the US, as her faith inspired her to become a vegan and prompted her to stay away from drinking and smoking. Bahá'í also forbids premarital sex and gossiping—the types of things most religions forbid but many religious people ignore when not under their parents' roof. In just a handful of years, Nasim would find ways to break the more serious tenets of her religion—the ban on carrying arms, strict obedience to the government, and even the highest Bahá'í crime: committing assault or murder.

In a slightly disturbing culmination of facts, two days after the 9/11 attacks by terrorists on New York's Twin Towers and Washington DC's Pentagon via the hijacking of four commercial aircrafts, Nasim applied to get her student pilot certificate to begin flight lessons from the US Federal Aviation Administration. She never ended up going through with the module.

Though Nasim was a radical when it came to animal rights, it was a compassion that did not extend to human rights, which the world was about to find out.

Make the Lie Big

Nasim's distaste for the American social landscape didn't compare to her unhinged animosity towards YouTube, but it was close, or at least they were entwined. Specifically, she became disturbed by YouTube's change in monetization practices in 2016.

On June 16, 2017, Nasim penned an email to YouTube's legal team. The subject was "Discrimination On Youtube." She posted a partial screenshot of it to her now-defunct website's index folder, NasimeSabz.com. While the entirety of her screed is cut off, the letter begins:

> Hi, This is Nasim.... There are discrimination and hatred problems against me committed by YouTube against my channel. My first YouTube channel ... was functioning well at first and my videos used to get views up after uploading more videos in Farsi and Turkish channels.

She does not show any more of the missive to viewers, but the comparative makes it clear that she is trying to draw an association between a loss of viewership and the uptick in her "foreign" videos, positioning, and branding. On the same website, she posted the response by YouTube's legal support team:

> This account appears to be active, and you should be able to access it. Learn more about recovering your account. Regards.

She writes in large, red letters over the purported exchange: "My email to youtube legal team. Subject is discrimination, but their response is about account activation!" Of course, there's no way of knowing what the rest of her email stated that the team might have been responding to.

Nasim was perhaps projecting some of her frustrations with her life in general onto YouTube. She'd been struggling with fitting in and was feasibly feeling revictimized by "the algorithm" for posting in languages other than English. Her prospects were stymied, and she had heavy reliance (or perhaps, delusion) on the notion that she could thrive as an influencer. While YouTube *can* penalize accounts for posting the same video content to multiple channels, the most likely culprit here wasn't Nasim posting for different native speakers. What set Nasim against the media giant came when its new advertising policy *did* hit her algorithm—due to her content itself.

On May 5, 2016, VidCon—the annual convention for brands, influencers, and fans of digital content creators and their platformers—hosted a brandcasting panel with YouTube CEO Susan Wojcicki. VidCon was the brainchild of John and Hank Green, the @Vlogbrothers on YouTube, who were catapulted into stratospheric and lasting fame thanks to their videos. (John Green is now a prolific author whose books have become major motion pictures. Hank Green is also an author, musician, and a cancer survivor.) There, in Anaheim, California, Wojcicki acknowledged that YouTube was growing larger than ever but was facing an uptick in competition, so it would be employing a host of new strategies to help bolster and monetize its *star* content creators. This included mobile live streaming to vie against Facebook and Twitter (now X), new tools for better incorporating and replying to fan commentary, and a help-desk setup for monetized creators.

What YouTube did not anticipate after VidCon was the backlash from smaller and midrange creators. YouTube was hoping the announcement would inspire creative ambition from its makers, prompting them to climb the rungs of profitability, as without them, YouTube cannot earn effective ad revenue. The better its key creators did, and the more staunchly new or middling accounts strove to expand their audiences, the more money they *all* made. What they got instead were mounting complaints. In a bid for transparency, YouTube had also announced that they'd let creators know when a video was being demonetized—and for what reason—rather than keeping users "in the dark" while promoting popular creators and content that already had significant viewership. The changes were meant to cull the site of some bad-faith sock puppet accounts, made merely to spam for views and game the system. Another announcement was that accounts that reached the minimum follower and view count and wanted to be monetized would be asked to sign up for the AdSense program and must agree to its terms and conditions and set their preferences. All of this, the company thought, would help users understand the process better so they could *do better* on the site. But many felt it was a betrayal.

A small but noticeable online controversy bubbled up around the moves, heralded by the hashtags #YouTubeIsOver and #YouTubeIsOverParty, with content creators discussing how demonetization could be used as a tool of censorship. Some threatened to leave the platform over the changes, calling it the "Adpocalypse." From the company's perspective, this was less about shifting rules and more about giving creators a *snapshot* of the rules that had actually already been in place, baked into the Terms and Conditions for hosting content on the platform. YouTube felt it had opened avenues of communication that encouraged better posting, ostensibly because the more monetized videos on the platform, the more YouTube earned as well. Users allowed to share in e-generated profits as part of its creator partner policy could make up to 55% of the total ad profits, more than the platform itself.

Since a user cashing in meant YouTube did, too, it had an active reason to discourage posts—unless they broke core rules that would upset advertisers or that brands actively didn't want their name associated with. Here is where many creators ran into difficulty. Content had to be "family friendly," but the slightly nebulous definition of family-friendly led to some videos being flagged without the creators understanding quite why. Outside of avoiding obvious pitfalls, such as avoiding obscenities or sexually explicit content, users would have to comb through guidelines to riddle out why content had been barred from profitability. YouTube's missives could be hard to parse. In fairness, these rules meant that the more popular the account, the more scrutinizing eyes were on it—making influencers more likely to run afoul of regulations and audience flagging. YouTube's policy would also demonetize channels with fewer than 1,000 subscribers and 4,000 hours of audience watch time. Nasim's channels would not have been affected by those quotas.

People who relied on the platform as a vital source of income were frightened that they might one day be the target of these directives, without forewarning, and could be dinged for demonetization on a dime. In reality, most, if not all, of these standards had already existed—just more quietly. And because the rules were sometimes vague and haphazardly applied, YouTube set up a system that allowed for re-review by a team member. It's not certain that Nasim used this system, but we can be sure that her letter to YouTube's legal team would not be the correct avenue for re-review.

Her fears of targeted censorship for being multilingual were very likely unfounded. Her fears around being unable to re-upload demonetized content with edits that made it monetizable again were more substantiated. But that wasn't on YouTube; it was on the audience.

Nasim was convinced she was the target of a take down from within. She theorized that it was either due to her mother tongue, or her evangelizing veganism—since animal abuse videos often suffered flagging. She frequently showed the brutalization of animals in the dairy and meat industries, which, while a reality, was nonetheless disturbing to viewers. More difficult still, her content readily veered into those clips without warning. In one music video, featuring an original song, a boppy tune was overlain with gauzy footage of her dancing and singing, interspersed with jittery clips of severe animal cruelty; wolves having their heads crushed, seals being clubbed, and pigs being hung upside down, screaming. Decidedly not "family friendly."

In September of 2016, a hashtag discussing YouTube's "disastrous" new honesty over long-standing policies gained more than 174,000 tweets in less than 24 hours.[168] But the fact remained that ad revenue choices were largely at the discretion of the advertisers themselves as opposed to just YouTube. Current demonetization guidelines have roughly the same warnings to content creators against foul language, violence, shocking content, and hateful rhetoric. Perhaps a little more inflammatory or difficult to parse are its warnings against videos that contain "controversial issues" (including self-harm, abortion, suicide, and eating disorders), "[use] keywords related to a sensitive event to attempt to drive additional traffic," and or which seem to carry bias: "reviews of cannabis coffee shops, head shops, dealers, dispensary tours, etc." YouTube largely says that videos that truly break these rules intend to profit from sensationalism or tragedy—that they don't demonetize educational content. In other words, someone won't be penalized for talking about their recovery from anorexia or drug addiction, but someone *might* be penalized

168 Joan E. Solsman, "Pause the #YouTubeIsOverParty: YouTube isn't Pulling More Ads from Stars' Videos," CNET.com, September 1, 2016, https://www.cnet.com/tech/services-and-software/pause-the-youtubeisoverparty-youtube-isnt-pulling-more-ads-from-stars-videos.

for monetizing an upbeat music video about a recent bombing. On a surface level, the rules are mostly reasonable and even somewhat easy to skirt. But lending credence to the idea that *some* censorship is at play, YouTube's "Advertiser-Friendly" guidelines page is often updated with warnings currently in effect. This includes, for example, those still in effect in 2025:

> March 23, 2022: Due to the war in Ukraine, content that exploits, dismisses, or condones the war is ineligible for monetization until further notice. This update is meant to clarify, and in some cases expand, our guidance as it relates to this war.[169]

This would mean that content by Ukrainian nationalists would be eligible to be monetized, while potentially that same content by Russian nationalists would not. A Russian nationalist could therefore complain that the website has bias against them. To some degree, all social platforms enable such biases as they relate to their own culture, having to take a moral stake in pertinent social issues. If a Nazi is offended that Nazi propaganda is censured from social media and that limits their freedom of speech, a common refrain is "good." Some ideas are intolerable in a safe and judicious society; some rhetoric is too violent, illegal, or even infringes on human rights.

But who decides what is intolerable? There is an ongoing conversation around social media and censorship that reached a fever-pitch in 2024 to 2025 as Meta (owners of Facebook and Instagram) bent their bias rules to be more open to intolerant comments, Twitter/X began expanding fact-checking to rein in opinion parading as fact, and Bluesky exalts more protective practices against bullying. Hearings have been held to see if social media manipulated elections by peddling misinformation over sock accounts, Grok AI technology has been both fascist and "woke" in its replies to humans, TikTok has been accused of being a tool for Chinese spying. Conservatives are more likely to ask for rollbacks in protections that limit free speech online, but conservative states are equally more likely to ban books for their content. YouTube's efforts are more cut-and-dry: Just because

169 "Advertiser-Friendly Content Guidelines," Support.Google.com, accessed May 1, 2025, https://support.google.com/youtube/answer/6162278.

you can say something, doesn't mean companies have to *pay you for it*. So, who is right?

With YouTube, the controversy largely blew over, as users understood that there wasn't any real upheaval in effect; this had largely been an effort to get creators to see behind the looking glass. Very few producers left the platform, the spark never growing into an explosion. But for Nasim, demonetization rules became a sticking point. It was a strange point of contention for her, not just because the rules hadn't really changed, but because while Nasim was popular, she was not popular *enough*—even with the staggering combined audience across all her platforms—to be making very much money on YouTube to begin with. At thirty-eight years of age, she was still living with her family, requiring financial assistance from them.

In one video posted by Nasim highlighting her Turkish channel, she tries to prove just how deeply demonetization is impacting her. She displays the analytics of a video whose title translates to "What I Ate Today: Eat Vegan." It had 336k overall views but only earned her ten cents that revenue cycle. SocialBlade, a site that tracks analytics, showed that June of 2016 was a difficult month for Nasim's central YouTube channel and biggest moneymaker, which led to her opening additional pages throughout 2017. These all trended upward in viewership briefly before tumbling down again.[170] This, she viewed as proof of the conspiracy against her.

But what do all those numbers really mean in terms of income? With one thousand views earning between a quarter of a dollar and four dollars in creator income, depending on the creator,[171] Nasim's video with 336,000 views *could* have made a minimum of $84—if, indeed, it was being monetized for all of the views. That's a far cry from the ten cents she alleged she had been paid, but also not that big of a fiscal hit. Even with the flat viewership Nasim had across her platforms, it's unlikely that she was making more than $11,000

170 "Nasime Sabz," SocialBlade.com, accessed May 1, 2025, https://socialblade.com/youtube/channel/UC-dWtG5_M6eXlhfSI14-38A.

171 Ben Collins and Kalhan Rosenblatt, "YouTube Shooter Repeatedly Posted Grievances About the Video Platform," *NBC News*, last updated April 5, 2018, https://www.nbcnews.com/news/us-news/youtube-shooter-repeatedly-posted-grievances-about-video-platform-n862791.

a year from being an influencer and may have even been earning as little as $1,000 a year on average.

Perhaps the perceived slight by YouTube meant that the career she felt she was working her way up toward, which would provide stability and freedom from under that Menifee roof, had been firmly pulled out from under her. In a video uploaded to her website, she'd furiously stated:

> I am being discriminated [sic] and filtered on YouTube ...

Going on, she explained, "So recently, they also attacked my Persian channel, Nasime Sabz; if you go and check my videos, you'll see that my new videos hardly get views and my old videos, that used to get *many* views, stopped getting views." Nasim holds her hand up in a *stop* gesture. "....because I am being filtered. *And*, another thing, they age-restricted my ab workout video. A video that has nothing bad in it, nothing sexual. Why they did that? Because it got famous and was getting many views. So, they age-restricted that video to keep it from getting views."

She'd continue, saying of YouTube's review response, "I contacted support team and they also said the same thing. There are some inappropriate things in your video ... videos like, uhh ..." Here in the video, there is an abrupt cut. "Many singers like Nicki Manaj, Miley, and many others have censored since so inappropriate for children to watch, don't get age restricted. But my videos, my workout video gets age restricted." She does not expound on what was flagged as inappropriate, and notably, does not opt to re-upload the videos removing what had been flagged.

> It's what they are doing to vegan activists. And many other people who try to promote healthy, humane, and smart living. People like me are not good for big businesses. Like for animal businesses.

Here, a bulletin flashes up in yellow and black:

> *They want you to be their slaves and not think outside the box they designed for you! Your knowledge is their enemy!*

"For ... medicine business," she says. "And for my other businesses. That's why they are discriminating and censoring us." Her English is halting, sometimes hard to discern, but her rage translates. It has the tinge of the conspiracy theorist to it: big business being against *the truth*. But Nasim herself seemed just as uninterested in truth, as she would prove later. After blaming xenophobia, big business, and anti-veganism, Nasim would move on to accuse YouTube *employees* specifically of putting age restrictions on her videos, calling it a form of sexism. She continued, "There is no equal growth opportunity on YOUTUBE or any other video-sharing site, your channel will grow if they want to!!!!! Youtube filtered my channels to keep them from getting views!"

Her zealous devotion to veganism was still a burgeoning concept in the United States, with only 0.5% of the population identifying as vegan.[172] "Most people ... cause violence and murder [against innocent animals] just like terrorists, either directly or indirectly," she said. "The whole world may mourn for the death of one person but ignores thousands of animals being tortured and killed every day!" This kind of incendiary statement may have felt extremist and tone deaf in the midst of the U.S.'s geopolitical "war on terror" era.

But her cries of sexism may indeed have been at least partly true, as her surrealist exercise and dance videos were often suggestive, even if that was not her intention, and sometimes went beyond suggestion into the realm of the obvious. Skin-tight suits with plunging necklines and fully visible backs may not have been against any American modesty laws, and certainly—as Nasim herself pointed out—she was more clad than many pop stars. But much of her following was Iranian. In fact, on one of her English YouTube channels, her following was a mere 5,000 people; Iranians and Turks made up the majority of her video viewership.

Iran's regime in 2025 ceased to allow YouTube in the country at all. A more liberal leadership had even suspended access briefly in 2006 for reasons of immodesty, political incorrectness, and sexually suggestive content. In 2016, the year of the VidCon announcements about monetization, Iran was banning 14,000 websites and online accounts *weekly* under the missives of Prosecutor Ahmad Ali

172 Lane, "How Many Vegans in the World? In the USA? (2023)," VeganBits.com, February 3, 2023, https://veganbits.com/vegan-demographics.

Montazeri's Internet Censorship Committee, stating that his committee felt Iran's "religious and national values" were under attack by foreign IPs.[173] During the bans, Iran also toyed with blocking the social site Telegram, where Nasim had been active.

Nasim also posted much of her content in Turkish. Turkey has blocked access to YouTube several times over the years, often long periods, for varied reasons. The ban was first ignited by Greek and Armenian content that insulted "Turkishness," according to the government in 2007.[174] Additional reasons for the blackouts since have consisted of political or social commentary not in line with the government's ideals, insults to ruling leadership, or uncomfortable footage of the Turkish military. Many Turks, undaunted, used DNS servers to gain access to the site during blanket bans, meaning its popularity never waned. While full access was restored in 2016, it blipped in and out to combat a viral video of Turkish soldiers being gruesomely immolated by Jihadists. Turkish viewership in general was more liberal than Nasim's Iranian audiences, but also applied their opinions more liberally.

So Nasim's content—which ricocheted from strangely sensual to often brutal in its condemnation of meat-farming industries—would not have suited the idea of "appropriate" for many of the countries she performed for, perhaps including the United States. Consider any online comment section on a video featuring a woman simply existing in yoga pants—the outrage that bubbles up from replies, from Georgia to Utah, over female bodies in anything skin-tight makes it obvious how Americans, too, might have found Nasim gyrating in a leotard "offensive." If that seems absurd, consider that in 2016, *The Washington Post* ran an article titled "Yoga pants are comfy. They're also an assault on manners and a nihilistic threat. The seductive danger of athleisure."[175] In 2018, *The New York Times*

173 Prosecutor Ahmad Ali Montazeri, who presides over the Internet Censorship Committee.

174 Ali Jaafar, "Turkey Bans YouTube," *Variety*, March 8, 2007, https://variety.com/2007/digital/news/turkey-bans-youtube-1117960760.

175 Kerry Folan, "Yoga Pants Are Comfy. They're Also an Assault on Manners and a Nihilistic Threat," *Washington Post*, December 15, 2016, https://www.washingtonpost.com/posteverything/wp/2016/12/15/yoga-pants-are-comfy-theyre-also-an-assault-on-manners-and-a-nihilistic-threatyoga-pants-are-comfy-theyre-also-an-assault-on-manners-and-a-nihilistic-threat.

posted an opinion piece entitled, "Why yoga pants are bad for women."[176] Policing women's bodies is as much a pastime in the West as anywhere.

Outside of sexism possibly being a latent cause for demonetization due to her clothing choices and more risqué style of aerobic filming being flagged as immodest by conservative users across countries (this matching up with the alleged support feedback that her videos were too erotic and not appropriate for all ages), in a cringingly ironic twist, it may turn out that a sizable portion of Nasim's monetized views were not of her own making. These views came from Turkey, after a famous Turkish YouTuber called @Yorekok made a video about her in Turkish, ridiculing her.

That video, from September of 2016, was entitled "YEŞİL in Wonderland," with YEŞİL being Nasim. His description for the video, translated, reads as follows:

> As you know, YouTube is a very strange platform. If you get lost in it, you are likely to encounter things you don't want to see. Let's see how our crazy girl Green Nasim plans to take place in our nightmares on her channel, which she runs like a horror movie.... Warning, it contains a high amount of nightmare fuel.[177]

@Yorekok, who as of 2025 has over 663k subscribers, reached over 800k views with this video. In it, he mocks Nasim's outlandish content, saying "I hope there is only one of these [types of people] on Earth." He cuts to some of her most risible tutorials, like "Vegan poop cookies in Turkish," to which he replies, "It is an interesting experience trying to eat something I shit out every day." He expresses admiration that she made the cookies look *so accurately* like they'd been defecated, but dismay at why she'd felt the need to do so. As with all of Nasim's content, her poop-cookie tutorial was steely-serious, not intended as comedy; this bewildered and delighted the online bullies that often dogged her.

---

176 Honor James, "Why Yoga Pants Are Bad for Women," *The New York Times*, February 17, 2018, https://www.nytimes.com/2018/02/17/opinion/sunday/yoga-pants-sweatpants-women.html?smid=tw-nytopinion&smtyp=cur.

177 "YEŞİL HARİKALAR DİYARINDA," Facebook, accessed May 1, 2025, https://www.facebook.com/watch/?v=1254254751318425.

@Yorekok then goes on to critique one of her workout videos, saying she looks like a "Catwoman fetish dress-up." Tongue-in-cheek, he adds, "The purpose of this video is definitely to teach my friends exercise, don't be fooled by this girl's outfit.... The video is educational and instructional, do not watch it any other way." Then he cuts to several images of men sweating, the meaning clear: that he definitely took the video to be purposely showing off something other than her athleticism. Next, he compares a creepily cut video of hers to a horror film, saying, "Rumor has it if you say her name five times, she appears under your bed..... Look into her eyes.... You can see the souls of millions of women who were burned and killed ... run away." He does appreciate her originality, but not before likening her to a witch and a psychopath.

Nasim never makes any public response to this.

Instead, in another screed against YouTube rather than her detractors, she posted the following in a garish yellow, black, and red font:

> BE AWARE! Dictatorships exists [sic] in all countries but with different tactics! They only care for personal short-term profits & do anything to reach their foals [sic] even by fooling simple-minded people, hiding the truth, manipulating science & everything, putting public mental & physical health at risk, abusing non-human animals, polluting environment, destroying family values, promoting materialism & sexual degeneration in the name of freedom...& turning people into programmed robots!
>
> There is no free speech in real world & you will be suppressed for telling the truth that is not supported by the system. Videos of targeted users are filtered & merely relegated, so that people can hardly see their videos!

Below this she shows more "proof" of being censored. A screenshot, taken on January 15, 2016, purportedly showing that she'd had over 182k views in the last twenty-eight days. Then a second screenshot from October 14, 2016, showing only 127k views. This is still a significant number and not quite as dramatic a drop as being "filtered" might imply. It also shows that in that time frame, her general unique viewership had increased from just over two million to 3.2 million, a noteworthy rise, and mostly on her English-content channel. In contrast, the diatribe goes on to show her Iranian channel. Over a screenshot of one of her videos that YouTube had disabled, Nasim writes,

> This video got age restricted after new close-minded youtube employees got control of my farsi youtube channel last year, 2016, & began filtering my video to reduce views & suppress & discourage me from making videos!

Translated, the video's title is "Abdominal slimming exercise with the breeze of an Iranian athlete girl." At this time, Iranian authorities were specifically banning the content of religious minorities, international profiles, and activist groups. In May of 2016, several female models in Iran were arrested for posting photos of their modeling on Instagram—without headscarves.[178] Minoo Haleghi, who had been elected to Iran's moderate reformist parliament that February, was then banned from holding office when someone posted a photo of her on Telegram not in hijab. The man who'd posted the photo was arrested, and Minoo was summoned before a court in Tehran.

In light of this, it is very likely that Nasim's profile was simply being repeatedly reported for perceived violations by Iranian viewers especially. Nonetheless, she increasingly blamed YouTube employees and the American mindset in general. She attended protests with signs that read, "YouTube Dictatorship Hidden Policy: Promote Stupidity, Discrimination, Suppression of Truth." She aimed derisive videos at Americans—in one, filmed in English, she dons a rare hijab with a chin covering in all black and asks her audience, "Welcome to freedom of speech! When it comes to freedom of speech, do you think that Iran is better than USA, or USA is better than Iran?"[179] She goes on to say, "In Iran they kill you by axe. But in United States, they kill you with cotton." This Iranian figure of speech refers to a slow and comfortable death, but death nonetheless.

---

178 Thomas Erdbrink, "Iran's Hard-Liners Crack Down on Models Not Wearing Head Scarves," *The New York Times*, May 16, 2016, https://www.nytimes.com/2016/05/17/world/middleeast/irans-hard-liners-crack-down-on-models-not-wearing-head-scarves.html?_r=0.

179 *The New York Times*, "Who Was the YouTube Shooter? | NYT News," YouTube, accessed April 4, 2018, https://www.youtube.com/watch?v=oNpzeIdOtlk.

Iranian commenters continued to grow bolder in their condemnations; they told her she was crazy and accused her of paying for fake followers on Instagram. But she remained laser-focused on the United States, the place making her so unhappy. "If you are superficial, you will think it is heaven here. You will see that it is worse than Iran."[180]

She posted ever-more-unhinged content, too. On her Iranian channel, she videoed a pair of realistic silicone breasts on a table, which she then rubs to illustrate a massage that is purposely evocative and does not seem in any way medicinal. In another video, she does the same with fake buttocks before dancing aggressively with a peach; in another, she suggestively eats a carrot before the footage suddenly cuts to her in bed wearing only a shimmering purple silk robe.

Her English-language channel matched her growing inflammatory vibe. In an upload entitled "Sultan Nasim," she parodies becoming sultan of the world, and her first order is that "Everybody must be vegan. And those who oppose this...will be sent to slaughterhouses so their meat will be eaten by the eagles and wolves." She copies multiple voice-overs of herself yelling "Sultan Nasim!" to feign an adoring crowd cheering her on. In yet another video, she stands before a green screen with multicolored 3D balloons and says, "What takes many people away...is balloon boobs and butts." She then steps away from the screen to show off her figure in a onesie with cutoff shorts and an exaggerated fake chest before she begins to dance and sing a song she's made up for the video, which goes—"Balloon boobs girl, balloon boobs girl, balloon boobs girl...." over and over again. Twistedly, Nasim herself posted misogynistic content, poking fun at the "sexual degeneracy" of women whose endowments are large and equating overt femininity with obvious stupidity, adhering to the Barbie trope of dumb silicone blonds.

Whatever hypocrisy she was blind to, Nasim felt like she was being silenced, stuck in a holding pattern—and she had to do something about it. She became so volatile that she began regularly arguing with her parents, and her sudden and irrational animosity

180 *Inside Edition*, "YouTube Shooter Vents on Website."

toward them forced her to move out, leaving home to go live with her grandmother in San Diego.

Nasim had also become obsessed with the idea that "not everything is as it seems." To prove to her viewers how easily fooled and manipulated people can be, in one video she donned a shirt with a plunging neckline, accentuating huge breasts cresting over the line of her V-neck. Her plump chest seems authentic when partially covered by fabric—until she pulls the chest piece off, revealing that it had been a costuming prop all along, molded plastic laid over her real body. This display of smoke and mirrors, she felt, served as proof of how easily people could be hoodwinked. A lot of her content skewed this way—telling viewers the ways in which they were wrong, misguided, stupid, or evil. It was rarely introspective.

Without giving others much grace, Nasim still courted her audience's empathy—she hoped they'd believe and care that she was being censored. She wanted them to buy into YouTube as a nemesis to freedom of speech. She even posted an infamous quote to liken YouTube to Hitler's regime. The quote described the key strategy that had helped Naziism find footing in Germany:

> Make the lie big, Make it simple, Keep saying it, And eventually they will believe it.
>
> —Adolf Hitler

In posting this, Nasim told on herself. The quote she attributed to Adolf Hitler on a post about misinformation is, paradoxically, by his henchman, Joseph Goebbels. She herself engaged in only minimal research before cluelessly passing along her misinformation. Quite by accident, she was the underline of her own point.

By January 16, 2018, Nasim could take it no more. Making videos about her victimization at the hands of big business wasn't enough. She felt that she must act. So, she legally purchased a gun while living with her grandmother. Then, on April 3, 2018, Nasim traveled to YouTube's headquarters by car, where she'd shoot three people—and finally, herself.

The Shooting Star

YouTube's headquarters in San Bruno is a massive complex, sprawling out onto Cherry Avenue like a set of eco-friendly Tetris blocks, built in undulating wave formation with sweeping staircases and glassy window-walled architecture that welcomes the rush of California sunshine. Framed by mountains and with partially organic rooftops blanketed in the flora of the savannah, it's a lively place to work. It is technology-forward, with spinning chairs, large fake plants to block out glaring midday light, treadmill desks, graffiti walls, a giant red indoor slide, stacked flooring to draw hot air up and out of the building, and plenty of meeting spaces. Upwards of 1,000 employees work there, mostly in sales and engineering. It's Silicone Valley, but with a streak of fresh-faced modernity.

12:46 p.m. was smack in the middle of lunch time for employees. Temperatures were in the '70s and sunny, so plenty of workers were taking advantage of the good weather and eating out on the verandas of the company campus. Tuesdays are a rough day in any week, so a good number of staffers were enjoying the chance for a break.

Nasim had parked her white 2006 Pontiac two-door and entered the YouTube campus through a parking garage. The courtyard didn't allow for nonemployee entry—ironically, as a security measure against active shooters. Armed with a Smith & Wesson 9mm semi-automatic, and clear-headed, she approached a patio and opened fire. She had ten shots per magazine and plenty of targets.

She'd only reload once. Twenty bullets fired, in total.

Glass doors shattered. The lobby became a shooting gallery. Nasim's indiscriminate firing into the crowd caused mass panic; employees inside the building who heard the commotion began barricading themselves in conference rooms and called for police. A fire alarm suddenly went off, sending some unfortunates scrambling dangerously out of the belly of the building onto the verandas, where bullets were flying. With all the noise, some had mistaken the emergency for an earthquake.

"Come get me!" Nasim shouted—or, in the clamor and confusion, it might have been "Come at me!" Mostly, people ran *away*. One woman would seriously injure her ankle in a bid to escape. Two other young women were struck by bullets. A male employee was also struck, critically. Everyone Nasim injured was under the age of forty—young, muddled, and now in blooms of agony and anxiety.

When the bullets dwindled, Nasim saved the last of them for herself. She turned the gun, placing its muzzle above her heart, and fired—ending her own life.

Police flooded the scene, and SWAT followed suit, with paramedics stabilizing those shot and squad cars blocking off traffic. Men and women in helmets and bulletproof armor swathed the area in caution tape and began their evacuation procedures—but by then the attack was over. Nasim had her misguided revenge, carried out by a gun hidden in her bag.

Police had the opportunity, just the day before, to stop her. They'd been warned.

After disappearing from her grandmother's house for two days, last seen by family on the afternoon of March 3, Nasim's father had called the San Diego police to report his daughter missing. She hadn't been answering calls or replying to direct messages, and then her phone was found left behind at the house. On the call with officers, the Aghdam men—Nasim's brother being there as well—expressed concern. Her father told officers that Nasim was very angry with YouTube, and he had fears "she might do something."[181]

A day later, her car's plates were spotted in Mountain View, California—more than a seven-hour drive from her grandmother's San Diego home, but only half an hour from San Bruno and the YouTube campus. It was 1:40 a.m. when police spotted her, sleeping in the back seat of her boarded-up car, parked outside of a Walmart, ensconced in a pink hoodie. Concerned officers ran her plates because cars in that lot late at night were often stolen vehicles. It was part of their evening routine to run checks. Nasim's plate number flagged the missing person's report, which noted her as being "at risk," but didn't expound upon why. The officers made calls to the

---

181 Holly Yan and Faith Karimi, "Youtube Shooter Visited Gun Range Before Attacking Strangers, Police Say," CNN, last updated April 5, 2018, https://www.cnn.com/2018/04/04/us/youtube-hq-shooting/index.html.

station that had filed the report, but the only additional information they could supply was that Nasim had run away with no notice to family. Nothing on record said she was violent, mentally ill, or suicidal. But "at risk" usually carries the meaning of being an immediate danger to one's self or others, so officers exited their vehicle to go chat with Nasim.

On the walk over to her, they reviewed next steps,

Officer 1, male: "So what are you supposed to do in these cases?"

Officer 2, female: " ...see what her story is, and then you'll get a vibe of whether she's a 5150 or not."

5150 is a Californian statute that gives authorities the right to involuntarily detain someone in the midst of a serious mental health crisis for up to seventy-two hours, for their own good or that of others. It's paired with a psychiatric hospitalization for that time period. In other words, they needed to make sure that Nasim wasn't suicidal—and if she were, she would be need to be taken in to prevent self-harm.

The police, who wore body cams, recorded the entire encounter, beginning with a simple rap on the car window.[182] Nasim crawled up to the driver's seat from the back, and though tired and replying tentatively to the officers, the entire conversation was cordial, polite, and seemingly forthcoming. Nasim looked small in that car, just 5'5" and very slender, her hair and wide eyes both jet black, sitting scrunched among a refuse of cleaning products, socks with cartoon animals, and red Solo cups.

She rubbed her eyes sleepily and opened the front door to speak with them, seeming untroubled by the confrontation, very tranquil. But she moved her key into her hand, as if for protection or to leave quickly if the conversation turned hazardous or concerning.

Officer: "Hey, so, you're reported as missing."

Nasim: "Missing?"

Officer: "Yeah. As missing, from San Diego?"

Nasim: "Yeah, I left my family."

Officer: "Okay."

Nasim: "So I don't live with them anymore."

---

182 *Mercury News*, "Police bodycam footage of Nasim Aghdam hours before YouTube shooting released (Full Video)," YouTube, April 13, 2018, https://www.youtube.com/watch?v=jYren919axg.

Officer: "Okay. Can I just ask, if you don't mind, why you left?"

Nasim: "We don't get along together, so I left."

From there, Nasim sits up a little more defensively, legs folded onto the driver's chair with her, and she begins to touch her hair frequently, a nervous tic. As the police officers move around the outside of the vehicle, it becomes clear that the car is truly packed with trash, its windows blocked for protection, showing that she'd certainly been living out of it.

Officer: "Were you just not getting along with your family?"

Nasim: "Yeah, with my father."

Of course, this was not entirely the case, as the home she'd left was her grandmother's. But she'd let officers know she had no plans to go back to her family and had no message for them. As she was very much an adult, this was well within her rights. She additionally agreed she'd left her main cell phone back at home along with some of her banking cards, but seemed unbothered by that. She said she'd come to Mountain View to look for work, despite having no friends or relations out that way.

She also said that the lot seemed like a good place to sleep, the town being safe. Then added that she wanted to "Get out of San Diego.... I have memories I don't wanna have. Somewhere new. New new new new—"

"Start fresh?"

"Yeah. Have no memories about the past." She became animated at this point in the conversation, waving her hand in the gesture for "no" almost aggressively. This was probably true from her perspective, and spoke to the agitation beneath the calm. But then Nasim abruptly becomes nervous about whether she is allowed to "live" in that Walmart parking lot. The cops assure her it's all right for now.

"Did you tell anybody where you went?" the officer asked, to which Nasim replied, "No, I've told nobody."

She insists she isn't off-grid, as she has another phone with her. The police ask if they can have that phone's number, and she says she doesn't know it—likely meaning it was new or a burner. But she does unlock the device and, with their help, looks up the number and provides it to them.

The second cop asks if she takes any medications, and getting a "no," moves on to asking a series of questions to determine the 5150.

"You don't want to hurt yourself, do you?" Nasim looks away and almost imperceptibly shakes her head no. "You don't wanna hurt anybody else?" The officer presses.

Nasim occupies herself by looking down at her now-bright phone screen and seems to mouth a word—maybe "no" again. But maybe she says nothing at all. It's hard to tell.

"You don't want to commit suicide or anything like that, right?"

Nasim taps at her phone without looking up for a long moment. "No."

"Okay."

The officer takes only seven seconds to ask these three questions. It is the least verbal and forthcoming Nasim will have been the entire tape. Nonetheless, she gives all the right verbal cues to prevent further prying, and the police seem to lean into everything being all right. Then the officer asks, "Are you ever planning on going back home?" Nasim finally looks the officers in the eye again and shakes her head "no," not once, but twice.

More police arrive. It is a whole lot of moths to the flame of *something* going on at a drowsy hour in safe, quiet Mountain View. "We just had to make sure that you were okay. We have to call your dad.... let him know that you're fine. And you wish not to be contacted."

"And where ... and where I am?"

"We have to tell him that we found you, right? Um, legally we have to do that ... we found her, she is fine, she left home because she doesn't want to be there anymore, and she doesn't want to be contacted. But that's all we tell him. Okay?"

The officer not pitching questions says under their breath to another, "You don't have to worry about 5150." Nasim will soon be removed from the MUPS list, California's Missing and Unidentified Persons Section. She's passed the questioning with flying colors. "Is there anything you want us to tell your parents?"

It is Nasim's last chance to leave some comfort behind for her parents, brother, and grandmother. She opts not to. "No ... nothing."

The encounter lasted about twenty minutes and was a fairly respectful exchange. Nasim passed muster on the wellness check, so the police were not within rights to detain her. She didn't express resentment, didn't refuse to answer, didn't exhibit violent or suicidal ideation, and didn't wish to be identified to her family. It isn't an uncommon occurrence for adults to flee their homes, or for families to invent a mental illness in an attempt to have officers retrieve them. Nasim seemed to be implying she wanted distance due to irreconcilable differences, and that she had hope for a future away from her father. Mountain View's police characterized the exchange as positive, saying, "Throughout our entire interaction with her, she was calm and cooperative."

Afterward, they'd call Mr. Aghdam to let him know they'd found Nasim and she was all right, but that she wanted no contact with him. Again, the Aghdam men warned authorities about the chip on her shoulder with regards to YouTube. But police deny they'd made the warning clear, with the department later announcing, "At no point did her father or brother mention anything about potential acts of violence or … lashing out as a result of her [YouTube] videos."

At around 3 a.m., though, Nasim's father called the police back. He explained that his daughter put out vegan video content and was deeply upset because she felt YouTube had done something to the videos. It was a relaxed call and, once again, officers didn't hear him attest to the possibility of truly violent acts. Nasim's brother would later tell CNN that it was *where* police had found her that had alerted them to her dangerous trajectory.[183] She was too far from home and too close to the target of her ire.

Later that morning, after the sun had crested, Nasim went to a nearby gun range and practiced her shot. She had a lawfully purchased handgun, but not very much experience to go with it.

It would be fortunate that she had such bad aim. With plenty of targets on the YouTube campus, the only person she ultimately managed to kill was herself.

The evening of April 3, 2018, after the incident, agents from the Bureau of Alcohol, Tobacco, Firearms and Explosives would conduct

183 Yan and Karimi, "Youtube Shooter Visited Gun Range."

a search of the Aghdam family's vehicles and their pretty Menifee home, search warrants allowing them to look for and gather any additional evidence. Her family would later make a public statement, apologizing for her actions and saying that they were in shock. Their main focus was now the victims, and they offered prayers for recovery and their deep and sincere regrets, calling Nasim's actions "horrific" and "senseless."

Poignantly, one of the employees on the campus the day of the shooting was Zach Vorhies, at that time a YouTube software engineer responsible for scaling the company's app. He'd skateboard away from the scene, past wounded victims, because the fire alarm had given the signal for people to escape the building when they should have sheltered in place. Blood and glass littered the courtyard outside the lobby and confused employees scattered to find different routes when they realized the emergency was a *shooter*—yet unsure whether it was an *active* shooter, *where* the shooter was, or *who* the shooter was as they fled in threadbare throngs.

Vorhies, who had also worked for Google for five and a half years, became a famous whistleblower whose LinkedIn experience at Google simply reads "don't be evil," Google's original company slogan.[184] He'd eventually walk out of the company with 950 pages of internal documents that he'd take to the US Department of Justice, accusing the company of extensive censorship. He alleged that "Machine Learning Fairness" had blacklists and secret rankings that allowed Google to manipulate public access and opinion, using distortion, promotion, and suppression to control narratives.[185] He even participated in a six-part docuseries about it, *Shadowland*, and helped produce a book called *Google Leaks*.

Google had purchased YouTube in 2006.

Vorhies' book was alternatively hailed as brave truth-telling from a corporate mole, and sneered at as conspiracy-theorist garbage from the mind of an embittered anti-Trump employee who then, in

184 "Zach (Senior Software Engineer) Vorhies," LinkedIn, accessed May 1, 2025, https://www.linkedin.com/in/zachvorhies/details/experience.

185 "Zach Vorhies," Amazon.com, accessed May 1, 2025, https://www.amazon.com/stores/author/B098HR2CFW/about?ccs_id=4ae3ea1c-2081-40a3-a5d2-859e1ef4ae0f.

a turncoat move, hypocritically went to work for the infamous anti-globalist site *Infowars* under far alt-right radio host Alex Jones during the COVID-19 pandemic. *Infowars*, blasted for its fake reporting, would declare bankruptcy in 2022.

The very thing Nasim had insisted was real—censorship, online manipulation—which had incensed her enough to attempt mass murder, it turned out, was being researched and hip-checked by the very people she'd pulled the trigger on that day. Unfounded or not, it turned out that at least one employee ducking bullets had shared similar fears. But those fears were not substantiated by her gun violence. She left innocents with bullet wounds and PTSD. In the end, Nasim only enacted one change for the social media giant: That YouTube would tighten its campus security from then on.

Directly after the shooting, news crews in Iran were on the ground gathering local feedback and sampling public reaction to the news. Iranian citizens were calling Nasim insane and, ironically, *too American*. In California, Nasim's family continued to make statements of remorse.

> I am so sorry for those people shot.... Hopefully nothing [will] happen to them [and] they get better.

The Aghdams also spoke with NBC news, confirming that Nasim hated YouTube because it had "stopped everything," leaving her bereft with "no income."[186] Everything her family would say after the incident was victim-centric, always putting the wounded in their thoughts and well-wishes, first and foremost.

The paradox of Nasim's work is that her platform said it hoped to protect animals and promote compassionate living, beauty, and art. But when greed poisoned her well, her "compassionate" vision crumbled, and she chose to shatter human bodies in retribution.

Today, in a quiet way, she is celebrated on some parts of the internet for showing people the same cruelty they show to animals. But even in reclassifying her selfish acts as *vigilantism*, even if strangers view her assault a wake-up call to a society on censorship, even if people felt her gun waving helped highlight biases in social media

186 Collins and Rosenblatt, "YouTube Shooter Repeatedly Posted."

or disparity in big business with a flash-bang—ultimately, she accomplished nothing so noble. She had suffered upheaval and indignities, and while she spoke empathy out of one side of her mouth, she exhaled cruelty from the other.

What Nasim did was shoot three unrelated people over essentially $84—three people she didn't know, who were enjoying lunch during their nine-to-five workweek. She, who said she despised the violent nature of humans, turned that viciousness outward in the most cowardly way possible—behind the muzzle of a gun.

Luckily, she was a poor shot.

CHAPTER 6

SAMANTHA NICOLE WOHLFORD, aka SimplyManic

I need the rush
There's nowhere you can hide before you die
Why won't you face me?
I can see the fear that's in your eyes
Where will you run? Where will you hide?
I see the blood drip from your eyes
Who will survive? Let's get it on
And we'll fight.
—"Immortal," Adema

My child arrived just the other day
He came to the world in the usual way
But there were planes to catch and bills to pay
He learned to walk while I was away
And he was talking 'fore I knew it, and as he grew
He'd say "I'm gonna be like you, dad, you know I'm gonna be like you!"

And the cat's in the cradle and the silver spoon
Little boy blue and the man in the moon
"When you coming home, dad?" "I don't know when"
But we'll get together then; you know we'll have a good time then.
—"Cat's in the Cradle," Harry Chaplin

"Immortal" played as the end credit song for Samantha Wohlford's video about a mass killing in a movie theater in Colorado. The song was written for the popular video game franchise *Mortal Kombat*, in which characters fight brutally to the death. Awkwardly, it was overlain with still pictures of herself and her young family.

"Cat's in the Cradle" featured in one of Samantha's candid vlogs called "road trip music," sung wildly off-key by the adults in the car, who were smoking cigarettes with windows rolled up. Inside the vehicle, breathing in the smoke clouds, are her young children. Samantha turns the camera around to herself briefly, joking, "Pity me. Pity me deeply."

(This depicts a real-life story of spousal abuse. If you are experiencing abuse, there is help. Call the national abuse hotline at 1-800-799-7233.)

After Midnight

It's after midnight, officially February 20, 2015, though no one tucked into the brown-and-white slatted house in Mount Pleasant is awake to know it yet. The day is in that crawl space of morning darkness ahead of the groggy winter dawn, which will roll onto the Texan landscape at 7 a.m. For night owls, it's still a thirsty Thursday evening on the town, urban centers alive with dancing and drinking across dimly lit nightclubs and cocktail bars. For morning people, who've long since burrowed into bed at a reasonable workaday hour, it's the small of Friday.

For Samantha Wohlford and Earnest Lee Ibarra Jr., it's a bit of both.

"Look at the time!" Sam had fussed when one day folded into the next and she and her husband were still lying in bed awake, tousled into one another, playing aimless app games on Ernie's phone. They had to be up before the sun—at 5 a.m.—for work. Sam chided her husband that they'd better get to sleep, then took an Ambien to get herself there fast.

It was incredible that pure exhaustion hadn't been able to sweep Sam away on its own, but she'd always been a *bit* of an insomniac.

She was also stressed from a string of bad-luck situations—totaling her car, a hose fire—not to mention the erratic schedules of her five young children. Sam's kids, already in dreamland under the brown shingled Mount Pleasant roof, were all below the age of seven and needed constant care. Sam often unwound by staying up late—past their bedtime—to grab a few hours to herself, smoking tobacco or filming YouTube videos until one, two, or three o'clock in the morning.

But *that* day had been an unusually busy one outside of the house. She'd given her gaggle of kids to a trio of acquaintances who'd taken them to cause havoc across the aisles of a local Walmart. This left Sam free to visit with a friend, Sharla, who was in the hospital ahead of a C-section. Those same acquaintances later dropped Sam and the kids back at the house, using Sam's car—as a thank-you, she decided to let them borrow the vehicle for a while, so they could drive Sharla home after her overnight stay at the hospital. One of the three was Sharla's current beau, a man named Johnny Rebel, and Sam liked him well enough and wanted to be helpful.

When Ernie got home that night from an exhaustive shift, they'd spent time together relaxing. They'd had their problems in the past, but things were looking up lately. They put the kids tenderly to bed then launched into their precious hours of adult-only time, exchanging all the mundane tidbits about their day that can feel captivating to a devoted partner. They'd been married nearly two years now, though dating on-again, off-again for much longer, and they were the type of couple that was always working towards being better—better communicators, better parents for their kids. They shared three children biologically, but all five in sentiment.

That night they made love. Then, they'd showered together, dotingly lathering one another up and rinsing one another off, paying no heed to that old adage that when two people share one jet stream, someone is bound to get chilly. Especially in the wintertime.

Finally, they'd hopped into bed to cuddle and game until Ernie's phone read exactly 12:01. One minute past was when Sam made the declaration that they *must* now sleep. With less than five hours left to carry them through the next day, they drifted off together. For the last time.

Jerking motion. Rough yelling. Sudden cold.

The blankets were grabbed off of Sam's body. She twisted as gravity and a rough hand dumped her onto the floor, sheer motion taking her, like a crumb being wafted off a napkin. Before she could register anything else, a knife was pressed in threat against her throat. Mind bleary from the sleeping pills, Sam didn't struggle as much as she could have, bewildered as a stranger's gloved palm repositioned the knife to the base of her spine.

Above her, sounds of a scuffle. Ernie was fighting off two—or was it three?—attackers. So much yelling, and the meaty sound of fists making contact with flesh. Ernie struggled, but the odds were too overwhelming. He joined his wife on the floor, doubled over, and the attackers bound his hands behind his back. Sam, too, was hog-tied with tacky masking tape in a vulnerable position, then gagged with cloth. It all happened so fast. The confounded couple, shaking, had just moments to take in their assailants—all of different heights and builds, wearing black, loose-fitting clothing. Ski masks, pants, shirts, gloves. No identifying features, just inky residues blotting out the happy peace they'd enjoyed just a few hours prior, looming violence in their broad stances, weaponry glinting with menace. All men.

Ernie was lugged away by two of the large figures, pale and thin in only his underthings. Sam was held in place. Nothing, for a few moments, and then Sam would hear shouting from downstairs and the telltale noises of a fight. But it wasn't a fair fight, with one man tied and the others armed. They were beating him.

"Luke, bring her down!"

What seemed like a lifetime passed before this order was shouted up, and Sam realized she was the only *her* in the situation. She was dragged down the stairs and manhandled into the space between their kitchen and the living room—the kitchen, where she liked to prep snacks for her little children, and the living room, where Ernie liked to play his video games. Joyful places, once littered with family memories, were now littered with the shattered remains of their front door. The entryway was one big gaping maw, stomped off its hinges to accommodate the break-in. Sitting amid the debris of wood and glass was Ernie, his face mottled with blood.

"Look at her," the two assailants instructed. Ernie, indignant and concussed, would not. They struck him on the back of the head with a pistol to tenderize his compliance.

Sam realized with a jolt that they were *fully* armed. Not just with knives. They'd been roughing her husband up with a gun as much as with their knees, feet, and hands, buffaloing him with firearms that sent a spray of gore where they landed.

"We'll hurt her if you don't."

Ernie looked up. Blood knotted his hair, split his lip, ran down his face and body. In his underwear he looked fragile. He'd always been slim, but now with two sweeping figures flanking him, with pain coiling him into himself, shoulders struggling inward, arms awkward behind him, expression unfocused, and skin streaked raw—his form looked diminished.

The man called Luke hooked his knife in against Sam's shirt and began to slice it off for Ernie to watch. She hiccupped in distress as her nightshirt was cleaved clumsily from her body and tossed unceremoniously aside.

"Isn't she pretty? Isn't your wife beautiful?" The man who seemed to be calling the shots sneered at Ernie's shrunken form. "You don't want us to do anything *bad* to her, do you?"

Ernie, in cold dread, shook his head no. They struck him again as Sam looked on, quivering and now half-naked.

"You can thank your dad for this!" The jeering man began to yell, over and over, starting up with beating Ernie again. "He took one of ours, so we're taking one of his!"

What were they talking about? Sam knew that Ernie's dad was a drug pusher, so maybe he'd missed a payment or a deal had gone awry, or he'd snitched on part of the network? But what did that have to do with them? Were they guilty just by relation? If that was the case, then were the children in danger, too?

After this next bout of violence, Sam was gripped by her bound wrists and forced onto her knees in front of Ernie. She was gagged, but Ernie managed to find his voice through the delirium of violence.

"Are the kids ... okay?" He'd had the same thought. Sam managed a nod. Her children were still in their beds, asleep despite all the noise. Or maybe hiding.

The ringleader towering above Ernie hit him again, affronted. "Don't you ever accuse me of hurting kids! How dare you." The irony of doing this to their parents, where those same kids could hear, it was lost on them at about the same velocity that Ernie lost a tooth. He was hit again, pistol-whipped with enough force that one went flying from his mouth in an undignified spray of blood. At least Sam was pretty sure it was a tooth she'd seen arc across the room. Hours earlier, she'd been kissing the mouth that now looked so pulpy and abused.

Having no idea what these men wanted, but sensing finality in the way they didn't pull their punches, Ernie docilely asked what he could do to resolve this. He offered them his truck, the most expensive thing he owned. Their leader laughed and asked if, instead, he could come up with $20,000 in the next five minutes. Despite the brutal reality of the situation, Ernie laughed, too. Of course, he didn't have $20k just lying around. He worked two jobs just to make ends meet. He had three children and supported two more. He'd even been looking for a third job.

When his laugh confirmed that no, he could not pay his father's supposed debt, the men roughly cut a piece of his hair off his scalp. Ernie had long, gorgeous dark hair, often held back in a flowing ponytail. He was a handsome man, almost soft-looking, with high round cheeks, soulful warm brown eyes, and a high forehead. With naturally super-arched brows, plush lips pointed impishly at the corners, and the sharp slender nose of a glossy magazine model, it was clear how Sam—who obsessed over pretty boy vampires like Lestat de Lioncourt or Damon Salvatore—might have fallen for this gothic prince who favored black clothes and always smiled wryly, like they were sharing a joke. An hour ago, sleeping beside Sam, he'd been beautiful.

Now, as they tossed the lock of hair at his heaving wife, he looked ruined. "This is all you're ever gonna have of him," they promised, smirking. "This is all you're gonna have left of him when we're finished."

Sam went into immediate hysterics. She began to scream around the fabric knotting into her tongue, gagging, trying to pull in air as the tears come hot and heavy. Panic gripped her lungs, dread and adrenaline making her shake in her contorted, half-naked pose. It was humiliation and sadism, a spiteful mockery. And it was their final moment together.

"Get her the hell out of here," the ringleader commanded as they hauled Ernie out through the gaping doorframe and into the cloudless night, onto their quiet property with lawn and trees sprawling far enough to swallow up any cries for help. No one could hear them. No one did, except for the captors themselves.

Luke, stuck with Sam back indoors, also began to panic. "Man, this isn't me, this isn't me." He'd make the sudden humanitarian decision to give Sam back her decency. He'd begin sawing and picking at her wrist bindings, using the knife he'd minutes ago been threatening her with. After getting the masking tape off, he shouted to her to go get a shirt on, and to "Hurry up!"

In case she got any bright ideas about going after Ernie, he pressed the knife against her throat one more time, briefly—as a reminder of what could happen should she fail to obey. Sam, frantic, found a pile of laundry in the living room and pulled on a fresh top. She hurried. Once the shirt was on, Luke bound up her hands again, then led her upstairs, back into her bedroom, pressing her to the floor and tying her ankles. "Don't move if you know what's good for you."

The assailants knew that Ernie had a phone—they'd found it at his bedside, and they'd taken it—but now Luke asked if Sam did as well. She shook her head no. Hers had fallen off the bed in the initial scuffle, and was half-hidden now, under the bed. Luke left then to ransack the house.

Spotting her phone, and hopped up on desperate adrenaline, Sam wiggled her way across the floor to pull it toward her—using her teeth around the gag to do it. It was hard, dirty work, face down in dust and boot prints, drooling around fabric. And then her heart stopped as she heard Luke's footsteps approach again.

Using her cheek to heft the phone aside, she elbowed a piece of plastic over it, also loosened in the initial scuffle. Then the man came back in, searched through drawers—ostensibly for valuables—and checked her bindings one last time.

Then all three men were finally gone, with Ernie in tow. Dead or alive, Sam couldn't yet say.

When the coast was clear, Sam used her chin to turn on her phone and dialed the first number on the recent calls menu: her mother's. She clicked the "call" button with her nose.

Luckily for her, her mother Rosie was one of those thirsty Thursday night owls. She was only just leaving a karaoke bar in a town about an hour away with Sam's sister Natasha. It was just past 2 a.m., but Rosie picked up and was greeted by muffled panic on the other end of the line.

When Rosie put together from snippets of garbled speech that there'd been some kind of home invasion, she quickly called Sam's aunt—her sister Ginger—and Ginger's partner. They lived less than ten minutes from Sam and would beat the hour it would take Natasha to drive Rosie out there, even going over the speed limit. She left calling the police to Ginger. Everything took on a sudden, eleventh-hour urgency. Ernie, Sam was saying, had been kidnapped.

Just a few hours later, Ernest Lee Ibarra would be dead. Murdered, execution style, after stumbling through some woods and taking a bad fall, cut down by a single gunshot to the back of the head, delivered by a man he didn't even know. Indeed, it was an extremely personal kidnapping, carried out by *three* men he'd never done any harm to.

That was because all the harm he'd done had been to *Samantha*, at least in her opinion. And no stranger to tall tales, Samantha would deliver the above narrative to police detectives that same night, scripted down to exactly what each assailant had said and done. It was all a lie.

Sam, in fact, *did* know who the three kidnappers were and what they planned to do. At the point she'd spoken to detectives that Friday, February 20, 2015, she still could have reversed the clocks and saved her husband's life. Delivering real information or giving a true confession could have potentially enabled police to locate Ernie in time to prevent the worst. Instead, doubling down, Sam texted her trio of accomplices from the police station to tell them to shut off Ernie's phone and ditch it—she'd overheard that the police were tracking it.

So Ernie wasn't dead yet when police arrived at the Mount Pleasant home and began to take in the disheveled state of the house—and its multitude of contradictory evidence. The wild goose chase of falsified information, in the end, was the final nail in Ernest Ibarra's coffin.

The story that Samantha Wohlford spewed to detectives left no emotional rock unturned in her dramatization of an evening that, in reality, had gone *very* differently. She'd always wanted to be an actress, so as she gave her statement to police she began to breathe hard and wail loudly and put her head in her hands, becoming agitated as she divulged each harrowing detail. She was displaying all the signs of real trauma, except she couldn't summon the most important one. She never cried any real tears while recounting the story of her husband's abduction.

She simulated crying, but couldn't make her eyes lie with her. Not until days later, when detectives told her they knew the truth—that she had orchestrated the whole thing. That they knew she was a callous murderer. Then, Sam cried real tears—for herself. Not for Ernie and not for their children, who through her crimes had lost two parents; one to death and one to jail.

No. She cried because now there would be consequences for her actions. Ones that affected *Sam*.

Mommy Blogging

On its welcome sign, Mount Pleasant calls itself "A Texas Main Street City." It would be less a Main Street and more a crossroads for Sam and Ernie.

Samantha Nicole Wohlford was born on August 28, 1989. She was the oldest of three siblings and assumed a doting, motherly role with them. Warm and gregarious, she was known as the life of any party, always friendly, outspoken, and wildly extroverted. She loved animals and grew up showering love upon the family's black Lab, handling their pet rats with care. Younger siblings Natasha and Darrell described her as sweet and nurturing. They all thought she'd make a wonderful mother. And soon enough, that would be put to the test.

Sam was also a typical American teen in a lot of ways. She liked television—especially vampire shows—wearing makeup—she carefully crafted her daily eyeshadow looks in bold colors—and had a lot of little, unique-*isms*. She was a little compulsive about organization and numbers, preferring even numbers to odd, and she could be mouthy. She hoped to be an actress one day, but in the vague way that some people hope to win the lottery—low effort, high optimism. She was waiting to be discovered.

Her family was close-knit and fun-loving. They enjoyed singing, dancing, partying, playing games together and pranks on each other well into adulthood. When Sam and her siblings were older, alcohol and smoking were major features of their family gatherings. They had the kind of fun sometimes more suited to a frat house—in one video Sam would post, she filmed her half-naked male relatives shooting each other with a cork gun, the shots becoming progressively more close-range and painful. "Be tough!" an older man says to a much younger one before holding a gun to his collarbone. "I don't know," the boy replies, unsure that he'd *like* to be shot. "Be tough," the man says again, and fires at point-blank range into his underarm. The younger man screams; Sam, off-screen, bursts into a fit of giggles. The men take turns shooting each other's naked flesh, screaming in pain, and laughing at each other.[187]

In high school, Sam fell very much in love with her senior year sweetheart, and just after graduation she gave birth to her first set of twins. According to Sam, though it cannot be verified, her younger sister was pregnant at the same time—which would have been an incredible burden on the family. With Sam's twins fathered by a likewise teenager, and with their relationship turning rocky over two years of dating, the boy moved on from Sam, abandoning her with

187 Simplymanic6075, "Grown men and cork gun," YouTube, October 21, 2012, https://www.youtube.com/watch?v=xgQxvjvLT38.

their two infant girls. At that age, children require ceaseless care, making any kind of school or even steady work a difficult prospect for their mother—even with the help of extended family.

Sam had never felt that her boyfriend was good enough as a partner or a father, but when he was gone, her financial struggles increased. She took on odd jobs, becoming a Mary Kay makeup consultant—a job with out-of-pocket start-up fees for supplies to upsell—and photographing newborns for a little extra cash.

Ernest Lee Ibarra Jr. was born on Christmas Day in 1985 to devoted mother, Randy Atchley. He had several adoring siblings—big sister Abigail, sister Tiffany, and brother Jimmy Jack. A calm and sweet little boy, the most trouble he got into was for falling asleep during class in middle school. Ernie had a habit of staying up late and reading, so in an ironic turn, his mother had to ground him briefly from his books so that he'd get enough sleep. An unusual sentencing for an American child, more liable to have phone, television, or video game privileges revoked for failing to meet parental expectations. Few children read themselves to exhaustion.

Ernie was a graduate of Mount Pleasant High School, which offered an incredible curriculum in the arts and sciences, including lavish theater productions, student newscasts with real teleprompters, a competitive athletics department (their Green Knights often stormed the field to victory), and an excellent computer and technology lab. When Ernie discovered computers—and along with them, computer and video *gaming*—he'd found his purpose. He devoted himself to the study of those bits and boards, taking computers apart and building them back up stronger and better just for the fun of it. He understood them.

Eventually, that fun would grow into professional ambition. Ernie went to college and received a certificate in technology and engineering—one he admittedly wouldn't get much use out of.[188] After meeting Sam, his life would become focused around making enough money to keep them afloat, rather than any of his dreams or passions. At least he'd still be able to engage with his main hobby, gaming, for

188 *Snapped*, "Samantha Wohlford," April 25, 2021, Oh! Oxygen, https://www.imdb.com/title/tt14501006.

pleasure. By the time he'd finished college, gaming was something of an obsession for him, his means of escapism.

Ernie had grown up in a brick house with a cheerfully bright red door and lots of love. Of course, his life had its share of complications, too. His father and his uncle were both drug dealers, known to the police; and Ernie would find himself in trouble with the law from time to time, too, gaining his own police record for assaulting an officer.[189]

Ernie met Sam at a tattoo parlor in January of 2008, when he was twenty-three and Sam was eighteen. Ernie was taken with her bubbly personality, her wide eyes and big lips, and the cute way she dressed in nerdy T-shirts emblazoned with band names or superheroes. Her neon gothic style—lots of black paired with tattooed eyeliner and bright, colorful eyeshadow, with red-slicked lips—appealed to him. And besides, she was a gamer, too. Or so she said.

Sam, for her part, liked how much he looked like a vampire with his pale skin and sweeping dark trench coats, liked his propensity for not talking very much, his arch and broody looks, his flowing hair straight off the cover of a drugstore trade romance novel.

Sam would have still been with her high school sweetheart when they met; possibly she was already pregnant, or soon to be. This means that Ernie would have known her throughout her first stint with motherhood, her first serious failed relationship, and he would have stuck by her as a friend. When "friends" became "more than friends," it was a case of opposites attracting with magnetic poetry: Ernie was the eye to her storm. They began hanging out and hooking up.

In 2011, Sam became pregnant again, once more with twins. Keili and Kaedin—a girl, and Sam's first boy—were born on September 1. Ernie would be a present dad, but his relationship with Sam was ambiguous. She often referred to him as "the kid's father" rather than as her boyfriend.

Ernie and Sam were involved long-term from there, but their romance was tumultuous. Much of the uncertainty around their level of involvement and how much they actually loved one another

189 "This is MONSTERS, "Samantha Wohlford: From YouTube to Murder," YouTube, October 19, 2023, https://www.youtube.com/watch?v=UxO-IxLkxXO.

likely stems from Samantha's habit of fibbing. She especially liked defaming Ernie—almost as much as she liked talking him up. So everyone in her life had a different understanding and version of who Ernie was, what he was like with her. She often complained that he was an absentee father; Ernie had the same complaint of Sam as a mother. He felt she was too self-involved, and despite being a stay-at-home mom, she didn't look after the kids enough. The two dated in a lazy fashion, as well—Sam still saw and even fell for other men. She openly remarked, after the birth of their twins, that she hadn't met the man she would one day marry yet. Ernie, apparently, wasn't in the running.

Despite that, in 2013, Sam would become pregnant again. Jareth would be her third child with Ernie, the first standalone, arriving just shy of two years after the second set of twins. Sam was twenty-four when she became a mother of five. To support the growing brood, Ernie became a woodworking specialist at a D-BAT facility, running the laser instrument that helped make baseball bats for America's children. On the side, he was a Little Caesar's pizza boy, collecting crumpled dollar bill tips and working late to satisfy drunk cravings and busy households.

In the summer of 2014, Sam called the police to say that Ernie had attacked her. Ernie was arrested on the charge, and an emergency protective order was issued against him for a short amount of time. Ernie's family to this day believes that the allegations of abuse were trumped-up. Ernie's mother, interviewed for the TV show *Snapped,*[190] explained that her son was always honest with her and admitted that he'd once thrown an empty cardboard box at Sam, but that was the worst of it.

But throwing boxes and being granted protective orders are certainly hallmarks of a toxic relationship. If Sam was lying, that lie was at least rooted in the tumult of the truth—that the pair fought often, and were perhaps violent—emotionally, if not physically. The court or police, at least, had found something credible in Sam's words. That time, anyway.

---

190 *Snapped,* "Samantha Wohlford."

One of the difficult things about those who lie about abuse is the great onus it puts on real victims to overtly prove what happens behind closed doors. There was likely some truth to Sam's allegations—she made them often enough against Ernie. In the one and only YouTube video on her channel to feature Ernie, he is aggressive and dismissive with her, cursing at her. But one might wonder why Sam would post that content at all. Seemingly, it was to show how brusque Ernie could be. Yet it ignores the fact that his terseness was caused by being filmed against his will in the first place, from extremely up close, while he was trying to relax. He'd made a line in the sand, saying he neither wanted to be featured on Sam's YouTube channel nor did he wish to watch it. She ignored his wishes, got in his face, and put the result online.

Filming him might have been a clear indication that she pushed boundaries, violating his comfort levels. His disinterest in her main hobby of videography and her hope for a career as an influencer or actress was, likewise, an indication that he was not supportive of his partner.

That said, it is very likely that Sam was overstating any claims of one-sided abuse as attention-seeking behavior. Clearly very unhappy, suffering from depression, Sam's main concern throughout her day was in collecting pity, praise, and outside validation. Chronically negative, almost all of her storytelling was in diatribe form, outlining villains (never herself) and the hero of the story (always herself). In Sam's world, in her words, almost everyone was a scoundrel.

A year before having her fifth child, in 2012, Sam turned to YouTube to help feed her addiction for attention—and potentially, if she could get popular enough, it would have the side benefit of providing a decent chunk of disposable income. Sam became a "Mommy Blogger"—a person who shares tips, tricks, and real-life advice and anecdotes about being a mother online—and amassed an audience of over 5k. She filmed her videos as if she were already famous, doing shout-outs to fans, giving instructions on how to send her fan mail and when she would collect it, and ending videos with "I love you all." Most of her content was no-budget, poorly lit, unedited monologuing. She'd often read from her own computer screen, flicking her dyed red hair and batting her eyes as she let loose rants best reserved for close friends or therapists.

When viewed in drips and drabs, her content seems innocuous enough. The difficulties of raising twins, tales of woe and wonder from family holidays and weddings, her worries and aspirations for the future. She was meant to be a "relatable" persona, lamenting having so much to do to get her household in order each day, providing cautionary tales of unplanned young pregnancies, and griping about misadventures in aging. Though she didn't have a lot of advice on any of those topics, or even sometimes any real lived experience—at only twenty-four, she was at an age many viewers were envious of, balking about the difficulties of getting old.

Sam's videos became known for more than just her frank talk about the difficulties in her life. Her makeup looks were her signature—plum or crimson lips, yellow or metallic purple eyelids festooned with exaggerated cat eyeliner, she always wore something fantastical on her face before facing off against the camera. Some of her videos amassed as many as 172k views. But watching her library as a whole and knowing the crime she would later commit, a different picture emerges from the footage than that of a candid, often zany, "momfluencer."

Sam's ability to lie was almost pathological; her care for only herself comes across like a cold slap. Mommy Blogger or not, it's clear she often put her children second and her husband (she and Ernie would eventually marry) down. Many of Sam's stories across her video library come across as unbelievable, the fabrications paper-thin. And her empathy? Totally lacking. Sam's complete shortage of compassion sings across her content like a canary in a mine shaft. Her favorite types of videos to make were gory news reviews or humiliating tell-all grievances against people in her life. Almost all of her posts featured martyr-like self-fawning and praise.

Her YouTube handle was @SimplyManic6075. Mania is an elevated state of activity and emotion that's markedly different from one's normal personality. It's usually associated with bipolar disorder, which Sam was not formally diagnosed with. Mania on its own is characterized by an extreme change in mood, usually from a low to a high, like dizzying joy and sudden bursts of motivation, or wild irritation and fury. Often, it's pocked with impulsive ideas not rooted in reality—such as the notion that one could become a billionaire athlete without ever having played a sport or become a famous vocalist even if one is chronically off-key. People with mania pour a good deal of their resources into these sudden bursts of inspiration, to the point of losing sleep as they pour themselves into the new mold of what they think they can or should be.

In this way, perhaps, Sam was telling her viewers something about herself. For someone supposedly dedicated to influencing and acting, she quickly dropped most of the ideas she announced on her channel—reading fan mail, unboxing gifts, doing makeup tutorials, pregnancy vlogs—often letting go of the promise of new types of content before ever even having posted first attempts. She was always galloping to the next idea, always pretending there was thirst for her insights in a new realm. But her audience engagement just didn't seem to support that idea.

A big schtick of Sam's was saying "so many people have asked for..." and then naming something that *supposedly* curious fans had contacted her about: questions about tattoos, raising twins, her jewelry, and her life in general. That seems very obviously made-up; she never cited any users asking such questions, and certainly these requests weren't filling her comments sections. She also only seemed to be asked questions about things that she *wanted* to talk about. When she begged viewers to make video responses to her content in reply, she became frustrated when no one did. Not even the supposed fans she'd produced her original responses for.

What others may have read as her "bubbly" online persona—when she wasn't ranting—perhaps instead was her self-described manic euphoria. Or, it was just her inflated ego and delusions of grandeur propped up by her easy way around a lie. Though not diagnosed with mania, it sounded edgy and gothic to have a username about it. She wore whatever mask fit to make her seem cool, mysterious, and well-liked.

Sam's YouTube channel is where one finds all of the contradictions that are so important to understanding who she was when she was still a free woman.

Simply Manic!

Sam launched the @SimplyManic6075 channel in 2010. It contains 88 videos and has netted almost a million views. But Sam also had earlier, less successful forms of social media.

Her Facebook page, back before the 2014 policy update allowing only real and verified names, was @Simply.Manic6075, now scrubbed from the internet. Her Twitter/X name, also scrubbed, was @SamNwohlford. In an odd move, she encouraged strangers to reach out to her via direct message on Skype, where she was @simplyemanic, promising that if enough people did so it would entitle them all to a live video chat with her. Sam even shared a PO box in her video descriptions, encouraging people to send letters and presents.

Rather incongruously, while Sam probably hoped that having a post office box just for fan mail or offering to reward those who sent tribute with her time made her seem popular and in high demand, the opposite was true. She didn't have enough fans obsessed with her to chase what truly famous people crave: *privacy*. She clearly had high aspirations and a low sense of threat to share her locational information online and expect to be sent snail mail, plus a lot of free time on her hands to be courting DMs and live chatting. (Of course, she never posted a single video response to any fan letters, ostensibly because she never received any.)

Going further back, Sam's MySpace profile was @Harley_Gurl14. It had 740 connections, not bad for social media in the early days before Facebook. Likely, the "14" in the handle referred to her age at the time she'd opened the account, while the rest is either a tribute to Harley Davidson motorcycles (improbable, considering her lack of interest in biker culture), or more plausibly, Harley Quinn—the violent right-hand girl to *Batman*'s fictional mass murdering clown, the Joker. Harley Quinn would have been a nod to Sam's love of makeup, goth culture, and violence, plus her often fickle desire to be seen as a "nerd girl." The nerd girl persona was one that Sam would struggle with in her future videos—attempting to cash in on comic book and video gaming culture, while in reality, almost reviling the people who enjoyed such media.

There's a discourse in gaming and comic book communities around the "fake gamer girl" or the "fake geek girl." It's a misogynistic purity test that often declares that women can't be into core "nerdy" fandoms, much less niche ones, and if they claim to be, they should be grilled on what games they've actually played, what trivia they know, or have imposed upon them whatever other litmus test the gatekeepers decide on—often, those gatekeepers being the men who take up more space in these communities. Women are often accused of *pretending* to enjoy "geeky" hobbies, in order to impress men. (It is not so different a tune in sports culture or band culture.)

In Sam's case, the distinction between seething incels banishing women from their platformers, and genuinely *being fake* was blurred. It's an important note—because Sam *saying* one thing and *doing* another becomes an inescapable pattern that one day would get Ernie Ibarra killed.

In fact, what she most *despised* about Ernie seemed to be how much he enjoyed video and computer gaming. She derided that in a lot of people. But it still didn't stop her from posting a series of videos to YouTube, trying out for *Maxim* magazine's "Maxim Gamer Girl." In the videos, she voiced platitudes about being an online gamer herself, while in reality, she gave Ernie an earful for his diversions.

To be crowned Maxim Gamer Girl, entrants were at the mercy of a public fan vote based on images and limited information. Sam made multiple posts explaining why she was the one worthy of the title, coaxing her audience to vote for her. In one such video, she called herself "Ridiculously obsessed!!"[191] with gaming, yet in another vlog admits, "Gaming has never really been my thing.... I was a social butterfly in high school, I went out all the time, had a lot of friends.... I thought gaming was *ridiculous*." She implies through

191 Simplymanic6075, "Brides and More," YouTube, November 18, 2011, https://www.youtube.com/watch?v=9HKYilWqQCc.

negative comparison that someone who is social or well-liked in high school can't also do something as innocuous as enjoy a night of cold pizza and *Smash Brothers* or *Mario Kart* with friends.

She goes on to claim that her brother got her into gaming, since he's always been such a hardcore gamer himself—a rather odd connotation considering her earlier statement, that she may have considered her beloved brother a ridiculous loser. For good measure, she throws in that her brother was recently diagnosed with a progressive condition that will cause him to be blind by age twenty, just one year later. She doesn't say this with concern, just as an aside to garner votes: she got into gaming so she could play with her younger brother, who was rapidly losing his vision and soon won't be able to play. (Her claim cannot be verified. She'd never bring it up again, nor discuss her feelings on it. There is a video of a family road trip years later, where someone who is seemingly her brother does not appear to be blind; and that brother was also filmed at a tattoo convention by Sam, still with sight.[192] Even if the statement were true, it was odd of her to bring up merely as an aside to help her win a competition.)

Sam also alleges that it was that same brother who encouraged her to try out for the Maxim Gamer Girl title. Another Sam-ism rife in her vlogging was the way she often surrenders her motivation to other people. It was never Sam who decided to do something; it was always that someone else had *asked* her to do it. She rarely took responsibility for those actions, waylaying the onus onto outsiders—as if her life were a series of burdens she was helpless to refuse.

"I wasn't really keen on the idea.... I haven't been a gamer that long ... only six months, before that I thought it was stupid and I could not understand why somebody would be a gamer." Again, an odd statement—she could have simply asked her brother or boyfriend what they found interesting about gaming and attempted to empathize and appreciate their hobbies rather than jumping to belittling conclusions. The two men closest to her in life enjoyed something she

192 Simplymanic6075, "Birthday," YouTube, December 24, 2012, https://www.youtube.com/watch?v=6CLHUBag574.

found ridiculous and incomprehensible—a sight harsher than simple disinterest.

Someone's little brother pushing them to become a Maxim model is also peculiar. *Maxim* magazine is a globally renown men's periodical, and while women are often featured as models and foldouts, they are generally relegated to sexy lingerie or swim shoots and steamy poses. A brother encouraging his sister to don a gaming controller and negligee for mass male consumption speaks to a confusing relationship. But Sam is determined not to take any credit for the idea, and when she begins losing the competition, her ire turns on the other participants. Falling back on moralistic outrage after receiving only sixty-nine votes mid-competition, she posted another video full of hateful snipes, accusing other women of being "half-naked" for votes, which she herself is too "respectful" to do (ignoring that this is what *Maxim* readers would like to see), and putting them down for sharing sexy photos.[193]

These jealous barbs precede, hypocritically, Sam showing off her own outfit, which she describes as modest: a tank top with a shiny martini glass over her breasts, which she then rubs on camera. Seated until this point in the video, Sam then gets to her feet for a full body shot, to prove she's *not like other girls*, because she is wearing a pair of jeans, unlike the "pick me" women. Sam, of course, cannot possibly be tone deaf to the fact that she's asking voters *to pick her* while actively making sure that the camera angle allows for only the curve of her backside to be visible, in cloyingly tight pants, for a protracted amount of time. Her unique blend of judgmental and two-faced has the tang of the classic gaslighter. The entire point of her rebuttal video is to attempt to do what she is tearing other women down for. She demonizes, sermonizes, and then prioritizes herself, not seeing the hypocrisy and hoping you don't either.

Sam then sits back down. Her kids can be overheard watching television in the background as she goes on to continue insulting other contestants' sensual poses, particularly annoyed that someone placed a gaming controller over their naked chest. But as she whines,

---

193 Simplymanic6075, "Maxim gamer girl voting!!" YouTube, April 25, 2012, https://www.youtube.com/watch?v=OE2qHly-WUo.

she shows off a tattoo of a dandelion that runs from her shoulder over her breast, tugging down her shirt a little to tease it. Then, perplexingly, she promises to show more if more people vote for her.

Despite not getting many more votes or, one imagines, having many requests to see her tattoos, she uploads not one, but two distinct tattoo videos to boost her chances for the *Maxim* competition. In these, she films her body slowly in front of one of her toddling babies while totally ignoring the child. She takes the audience on a tour of her more than twenty distinct tattoos; the "humble" and "respectful" Sam leaves little to the imagination, highlighting the same areas that lingerie might. "And here, right in my cleavage," she narrates, pulling her shirt down to show her chest, "I have some vampire bites."[194]

She curses quite openly, paying no mind to the angelic blond head of her child bobbling by, and proceeds to show off a tattoo in the *V* of her groin, pulling up her shirt and pulling down her pants for the camera. She tugs her waistband down to show the tattoos along her backside. Then, to show off her full back tattoo, she pulls her shirt clear off, leaving her wearing a bra after saying she would *never* don a bikini to impress voters; effectively, the same piece of clothing. She then removes her bra to reveal more of her back tattoo, which features a grim reaper and a half-naked woman with her own chest fully bared.

"Just because someone is beautiful doesn't mean their insides are beautiful," she warns, referring to the other, "less respectful" contestants. She shows off a hip piece by getting up on a chair and rubbing the area on camera. While rubbing her thigh, one of her children watches their mother film. Sam doesn't stop—merely moves the camera for a closer-up to cut the child out of the frame. Then she unbuttons her pants and pushes them partly down to show another tattoo. When she eventually uploads the video, she does nothing to hide the child's face or edit them out.

None of this was inherently evil, or even R-rated—it was simply hypocritical, proving that she only had a problem with someone doing these things when they were more successful or well-liked. If she were

194 Simplymanic6075, "Maxim tattoo request," YouTube, May 4, 2012, https://www.youtube.com/watch?v=4FYK8oocKyO.

truly shy about saucier content, she likely wouldn't have posted an additional video called "Phone sex," in which she complained that she'd been getting literally hundreds of emails asking her (again, through no onus of her own) to be a phone sex operator because of her sexy voice. She wanted her entire audience to know about it. It was, of course, a lie.

As in her initial *Maxim* video—in a move she would repeat with investigative detectives later—rather than relying on skill, she falls back on sob stories. Just as she casually mentioned her brother's severe illness on her first Gamer Girl upload, in Sam's tattoo video, she speaks in callous passing about a friend's suicide, followed by another story about a friend who she lost to a car crash. Car crashes are near-constant features in her online narratives, and while perhaps those stories had some truth, the tragic death of a loved one is certainly misused when pawned off for pity votes. But most of her content featured this thinly veiled kind of pretend-care.

@SimplyManic's first post to YouTube had come in late 2010, boasting nearly 27k views. Tellingly, it was entitled "Children die from CPS neglect..." In it, Sam details several chilling cases of kids who died at the hands of abusive caretakers, not helped by government services in time. She also linked to another video, entitled "Does child protective services hate children?" That video, about three dead young children, would check two big boxes for Sam: her hatred for Child Protective Services (CPS), and her macabre obsession with dead babies.

Unflinchingly, Sam narrated the gruesome deaths of small children. One of them, Michael Ibarra—unrelated to Ernie—died after his attempts to cover up the violence he faced at home. Sam then goes into graphic detail about a negligent mother whose toddler sustained wounds akin to being hit with a truck, mocking, "She claimed ... she found her lying on the floor. She just found her like that! *'We don't know how she got all bruised up and burned up and cut up.'*" Yet she chillingly was learning from these liars' playbooks to utilize later in her own family crime.

Her dislike of CPS was all-encompassing. The day before she had three men murder her own children's father, she did indeed visit her friend Sharla in the hospital—that part was not a lie—and they complained about the agency at length, while Sam's children were being babysat by her hit men. She hated CPS so fervently, she'd even bring those complaints with her into the interrogation room with police later. In her CPS video she claims, "People's kids get taken away *a lot*. For a lot of wrong reasons."[195] She then switches to detailing the death of an infant put on a laundry spin cycle. "How do you do that? How do you mistake your kid for clothes?"

Liars have a habit of telling on themselves. While perhaps her distaste for CPS was born from personal experience or that of friends like Sharla (or from reading about disastrous cases like the above in the news), Sam liked to position herself as a defender of children—after all, she was a mommy blogger, a mother of five!—while seemingly paying very little attention to her own children's health and welfare. In her videos, Sam neglects her children, sometimes openly and at other times backhandedly. She smokes in the house around babies with the windows shut; she, and family members smoke in a closed car with her children, all under age five. When there are the clear sounds of children calling for her attention off-screen, she ignores them and says casually to the camera that now she has free time. In one video, while filming with a baby in her lap, the baby spits up. She wipes it a little and keeps filming, not pausing at all to check on the baby, clean the child, or even toss the soiled napkin she'd used to dab at the baby.

Her seeming disenchantment with her own children becomes more obvious with the announcement of her third pregnancy and fifth birth. It was the kind of video a child should never have on their soul as an adult. Kids who feel wanted, loved, and welcomed by their parents tend to become healthier, more self-accepting adults. Instead of wanted, Sam holds the positive pregnancy stick up to the camera, recording for all time her flat expression, tone unenthusiastic. "No, I'm not exactly excited about this.... The dad's not excited either."[196]

---

195 Simplymanic6075, "Children Die from Cps Neglect...," YouTube, November 15, 2010, https://www.youtube.com/watch?v=OFpZl3yZDXE.

196 Simplymanic6075, "Pregnancy vlog!?!" YouTube, May 21, 2013, https://www.youtube.com/watch?v=VWAf9IRJenk.

In a vlog of hers where she is more heavily pregnant with that baby, she smokes a long cigarette. Of course, absolutely nothing compels her to film herself smoking—she mentions it as an afterthought, giving herself a free pass. She even goes so far as to extol her smoking as a *virtue*. "The fact that I cut back to 3 or 4 cigarettes a day is good but [my doctor] doesn't want me to completely quit cause, as much stress as I have? I might send myself into labor [by] having almost no vices. I don't play video games.... I don't go out, I don't vent to friends. I don't have any vices,"[197] she says, on a video displaying her vices to strangers—smoking, whining, lying.

Sam's assertion that doctor instructed her to smoke through her pregnancy is an obvious falsehood. Any medical professional would know that smoking carries the risk of low birth weight and premature birth—both of which her two earlier sets of twins suffered from, by Sam's own admission. It also adds the risk of birth defects and Sudden Infant Death Syndrome (SIDS). Cutting back on intake does not have any real benefit, as the chemicals are still entering the bloodstream, whereas quitting will have immediate health benefits to the unborn child. Additionally, any doctor can explain that the relaxation that comes from smoking is a placebo. It only resolves stress for a few moments before it speeds up heart rates and raises blood pressure—mimicking a stress response. No working physician could reasonably say that limiting consumption to four cigarettes a day for nine months was an acceptable middle ground.

Ironically, in a 2012 video, Sam explains why she's been trying to quit smoking. "Think about it. You smoke that cigarette and it's putting pollutants into the air. Do you want your children in the future to be smokers? 'Cause I don't.... That has to be affecting people."[198]

But smoking and disenchantment are not the only insults to baby number five. On video, Sam also offhandedly mentions that she'd totaled her car that week. She mentions it not as a frightening experience that made her worry for her baby's safety or her own, but as

197 Simplymanic6075, "32 week vlog," YouTube, November 9, 2013, https://www.youtube.com/watch?v=dpcC5Hq8RuU.

198 Simplymanic6075, "Ian somerhalder foundation," YouTube, April 25, 2012, https://www.youtube.com/watch?v=BQyDoLzlfMI.

an annoyance, because now she needed to rely on the help of family to ferry her around, for which she is ungrateful. She doesn't miss a chance to gripe about her other children, either. She mentions that her youngest has been sick with fever, diarrhea, and throwing up: "It sucked." She sympathizes—with herself.

And about Ernie, too, she barbs, "[The] dad's not having a whole lot to do with this pregnancy. And that sucks. We're still kinda working on things and trying to fix things but he hasn't had really anything to do with this pregnancy, which is hard on me because I'm doing it all alone." Despite saying so, she wears an engagement ring on her finger in this video, now the year 2014.

Her cawing refrain that she is a loving mother is sandpapered by how she puts down her children in videos, jokingly calling them brats and telling the world that they were slow to learn to walk and potty train. In another deplorable dig at both Ernie and her children, in a 2012 video called "Best day ever" she discussed what the best moment in her life so far had been:

> Most people would think [it] was the day my kids were born, and it wasn't.... [That] was kinda like, a letdown ... a sad day.[199]

Sam then goes on to describe meeting her "best friend," a man she met over Facebook, as the best day of her life. After chatting with him online for a while, they decided to meet up. She gave him her home address. Not a café, not a bar—her home, with her children, inviting a perfect stranger. He arrived with a hitchhiker. She admits that even though they "didn't really know each other," they partied and then went for a drive—just Sam, the man, and the hitchhiker. Once in the car, she notes with a giggle, he started taking sharp turns to scare her, since she'd been in so many car accidents.

It had been Fourth of July weekend, and straight from the post-partying joyride with dangerous driving, Sam introduces her new bestie to her extended family. Members of that family are Latin and she laughs that it "terrified him to death to have all these nonspeaking Spanish people running around, picking up [my] kids," as if somehow

---

199 Simplymanic6075, "Best day ever," YouTube, June 15, 2012, https://www.youtube.com/watch?v=A1k4o_BEDTM.

speaking another language was a cause for concern, or that speaking Spanish qualified as "nonspeaking."

The odd pranks carried on. Sam took him out on a boat and made him jump off to "exploit his fear of swimming." He got her back by saying that the hamburger she was eating at her family cookout was "made out of his ex-girlfriends, ground up," a jab at her fear of blood. From there, she decided to ruin his sleep in retribution. "He's terrified of dolls, so I made him watch a scary movie about dolls. And my sister put a big, tall Barbie doll of the girls' in my bed, it's one of those life-sized Barbies, so when he flipped the cover back to get in bed, he screamed."

After all the jump-scares, she let the man play with her kids. It is at this point in the story that Sam declares to the camera, "That made me fall in love with that man to death. That's my best day ever. The fourth of July I got to spend with him." At the time of posting, she was with Ernie.

"He still is my best friend. He wants to adopt my kids. He doesn't like the fact that their father's not on the birth certificate, the void on the birth certificate bugs him, and he wants [me] to allow him to put his name there. I mean he really is, he's just the greatest person ever." She would never mention him in another video ever again. But she would go on to marry Ernie.

In another display of hypocrisy, there is Sam's video about the show *Toddlers in Tiaras*. In it, she critiques a culture that puts young children through the ringer of beauty pageants, outraged by little girls wearing makeup. Plus, "Those kids are total brats."[200] She doesn't seem to see the irony in admitting she not only consumes this media, but is using it to create her own, while blasting little children. She says of one six-year-old who was given her own spin-off show, "It blows my mind, not that she's even really good.... *Way* too frilly.... I've watched little clips where she's like singing for these people, trying to get —record deals, I guess? She's not that good for the mom to be as involved in her daughter as she is.... she really can't sing."

---

200 Simplymanic6075, "Toddlers in Tiaras," YouTube, April 24, 2012, https://www.youtube.com/watch?v=efKt7RvdHd4.

She then admits that she's curled her kids' hair—they are four and younger at this point—and painted their nails and done their makeup. Why? "[I] put my kids in a pageant.... I had always wondered why my mother didn't put me in pageants.... When I got there, the way these other little girls looked, the way they were acting totally turned me off." She gripes about other children, before paradoxically gloating, "My six-month-old got first runner up."

It's Sam's usual zig-zagging road map. Children shouldn't be in pageants, she says, not out of concern for them—she openly rags on the kids herself—but because she's annoyed she was never entered in one. So naturally, after critiquing *other* moms for doing them, her *own* mother for not, and *kids* for participating, she enters her daughter in one—and gains bragging rights.

Sam also talks about dead children an inordinate amount on her Manic channel, covering news stories that almost exclusively have to do with the topic, or else other mass violence. Along with the anti-CPS videos, she covers a school shooting, discusses a two-year-old being mauled at the zoo, and reviews a disturbing story about babies being baked into pills for restorative skincare. In her review of *The Hunger Games*, a book and film whose central premise is children fighting to the death, she states, "in the book the deaths were a lot more gruesome than in the movie ... there's blood, gore, a love triangle."[201]

She also posted a video called "Army wife watches husband die on Skype," in which she narrates a horrific shooting while her baby is on her lap.[202] She playfully calls her baby a brat, then laments, "I cannot *imagine* going through this." It's chilling, considering what she'd then set it in motion for her own husband.

A key to unpicking liars is to believe what you see and *not* what you hear. Frequent liars will be inconsistent and defensive, embellishing their stories, peppering them with excessive or conflicting information for almost no reason. Keeping this in mind, almost all

---

201 Simplymanic6075, "Hunger games review," YouTube, May 28, 2012, https://www.youtube.com/watch?v=3tH3P4WGC18.

202 Simplymanic6075, "Army wife watches husband die on Skype," YouTube, May 7, 2012, https://www.youtube.com/watch?v=VJmIXA3OkOA.

of what Sam *says* in her videos is contradicted by what she *does* in reality.

She often classifies herself as a caring friend and family member. Yet, in her second-ever video, "Brides and Stupidity,"[203] she crows, "Hey YouTubers! Today, a lot of stuff pissed me off so you guys get to listen to it." She goes into avid detail about her cousin's wedding. About the venue, the dress, or the ceremony? Not quite.

She unpacks what upset *her* at the wedding, namely the number of people who simply stared at her as if they took issue but said nothing. "If you got something to say, say it.... I'm an approachable person. I'm not bitchy or gripey normally." She then proceeds to bitch and gripe that more women didn't compliment her. Which brings us to her second complaint—that her cousin's newly minted husband had told his bride following their vows that they'd gotten married too soon. This feels like an upsettingly intimate detail for her to air to strangers.

But not to worry! She moves on rapidly, letting her viewers know that many, many guests came up and told Sam she "looked really pretty." (Of course, this just moments after stating not enough people had done so.) She tosses out that she was Maid of Honor almost as an afterthought, then moves on to her third complaint: nearly hitting a deer on the way home. "I HATE deer!!!"

The animal lover and animal rights activist who hates deer then goes on to complain about motherhood, saying, "I damn sure don't get enough sleep to deal with stuff like this today."

But one video on this wasn't enough. It turned out, she'd forgotten some of her complaints, so later she uploaded part two of the screed.[204] It featured nothing positive about the wedding, nothing usual from a maid of honor about the joy or the décor, nor did it feature an apology for airing hurtful commentary about her cousin's husband for YouTube fodder just hours after they tied the knot. No, it was her taking advantage of having professional hair and makeup done up for the wedding to produce content. In part two, she negatively compares the ceremony to her own nuptial wishes: "I'm not

---

203 Simplymanic6075, "Brides and Stupidity," YouTube, November 11, 2011, https://www.youtube.com/watch?v=CZChkpq5avE.

204 Simplymanic6075, "Brides and More."

going to plan some big fancy wedding and wait six months when I find the person that I'm going to marry. It's going to be a spur of the moment—hey let's go to Vegas this weekend and get married."

This was two years after she'd met Ernie. She again seems to openly imply Ernie was *not* the man for her. In reality, she'd get married four years later, leaving the kids with Ernie's sister Abagail to go down to Hope, Arkansas, for the ceremony.

In yet another wedding vlog post, she talks about her best friend Amber's wedding this time, where she was a bridesmaid. "Everybody was so ecstatic." About the bride? Nope.... "The mom of the bride, every time she pointed [me] out,... She was like, isn't her hair beautiful, doesn't it go so well with her dress, isn't she cute? I felt so special. It was great. There was another girl there that was you know, [the bride's] hometown best friend, and I'm her best friend who lives ten hours away, heh. I think she was really jealous about it...." After the gloat comes the gripe. "Amber, the girl who got married, she told me [that the other best friend] was really jealous. Every little thing that went on she tried to step on my toes ... so it's frustrating but I think I got my vengeance when her mother was doting on me, and Amber was constantly wanting to take pictures together and telling everybody how we'd known each other our entire lives. So I was pretty excited about that, I was pretty happy. She made my night pretty special."[205]

Because the important part of a best friend's wedding is, of course, is how special and pretty the bride and mother of the bride make the bridesmaid feel.

Much of what Sam said back then, if posted today on social media, would get her analyzed brutally in the court of public opinion. The early days of the internet had more of a devil-may-care Wild West approach, and content was less curated, monitored, reported on, and reposted. Surprisingly, Sam's YouTube profile hasn't been taken down or privatized to this day.

---

205 Simplymanic6075, "Wedding," YouTube, July 5, 2012, https://www.youtube.com/watch?v=bo9VkVK247c.

In one old video, Sam says that she can "see both sides" of homophobia.[206] In another, she takes personal offense to someone being called a freak on a reality show, and naturally, relates it back to herself. "I've been called a freak.... But at the same time, I'm one of the most liked people around. A lot of people really like me." In yet another instance of touting herself, she croons, "[Being nice] is kind of one of my downfalls because people walk all over me and use me a lot." Yet in yet another video, she gives a chilling warning—"I can be the most horrible person you've ever met if you cross me."

The internet's memory is long, but its attention span is short. In a video titled "15 weird things about me"[207] Sam says, "I can't have a single birth. I can only have twins." This is disproven by the birth of her fifth—singular—child. No one calls her out on it. She also mentions she's been an extra on *numerous* films and has even had small acting parts, but the only part she's credited for on the International Movie Database is the nonspeaking role of "Zombie" in *Humans versus Zombies*, filmed in Pittsburg, Texas—a 2011 low-budget horror film based on a popular game played across college campuses. The film received almost no press and a 25% rating on Rotten Tomatoes. One reviewer wrote, "Pretty awful, it's like a college project in HD. It really sucks."

She uses her YouTube channel to complain of illnesses, accidents, morning sickness, weight loss, weight gain, medication, and death. These seem to cluster into her narratives like they are afterthoughts, rather than serious topics. They blister around her, her own crown of thorns.

But sometimes, a better part of Samantha is caught on tape. She seems genuinely delighted by her children when they are the focus of the video. She does seem to love animals, taking care of dogs, cats, and birds. Yet these bursts of kindness always seem to find threads that get picked at to pull them apart. She loves dogs, yet she surrendered her dog to her grandparents for no discrenible reason,

---

206 Simplymanic6075, "Freaks," YouTube, May 1, 2012, https://www.youtube.com/watch?v=Su6g2cgrA64.

207 Simplymanic6075, "15 weird things about me," YouTube, May 13, 2012, https://www.youtube.com/watch?v=UtuCn-YzzKI.

with her trademark lack of emotion. When in one video her young son spends almost the entire duration pleading for her, she laughs him off and continues talking about herself and how she had bronchitis. She doesn't cough, sniffle, look, or sound ill. In order to get his mother's attention, her little son Jareth cries and throws things and even manages to turn on a vacuum cleaner,[208] which she admits she left plugged in.

Then, in 2012, she shares the news that her house has burnt down.[209] She doesn't cry, seem distressed, discuss their escape, nor how anyone felt when they found out (in fact, it's not even clear if she was in the house at the time or alerted later), nor does she show any concern for her children. Instead, she talks about the "tons, and tons, and tons" of stuff they lost. Nothing of emotional resonance, nothing about safety, nothing about whether any pets are okay. Instead, in the video entitled "Totally homeless" she explains that they think the fire started because an air-conditioning unit overheated at night. Rather than *actually* homeless, she and the kids are staying with her aunt until she can move in with her mother, which she calls "boring." She at no point expresses thanks. This, of course, being the same aunt and mother who would run to her rescue when she called for help after Ernie's kidnapping.

She also uses the fire to explain why she hasn't updated in a while, though it's been less than a week since her last update—not an unusual gap for someone who, in another video, says her posting frequency is once every two weeks, thereabouts. Just as she manufactures vested interest from her audience, so, too, does she invent concern. Like people must be terribly *worried* that she hasn't posted to YouTube for six days. As usual, it's strange—if she wanted concern, a house fire burning everything she owned to cinders would be the place to find it. As would the terrible car accidents she'd claimed to have been in. Or, if she did *not* want concern, sharing those accidents publicly and with no real detail would also not have been the

208 Simplymanic6075, "8 week 5 day vlog," YouTube, June 8, 2013, https://www.youtube.com/watch?v=dUnWhAeYlfo.

209 Simplymanic6075, "Totally homeless," YouTube, May 20, 2012, https://www.youtube.com/watch?v=Tnm9OKQhN8k.

way to go. The logic is backwards. A fire is real cause for concern beyond not having "posted in a while."

No online record could be located about any major house fire in her area during the timeframe Sam claimed that it had happened. This may mean that it simply wasn't reported, or that the public information she gave was off. It may also mean that she simply hadn't told the truth. In any case, the background in her videos returns to being what it had been before moving to her aunt's house shortly thereafter. With her mother living quite a drive from her, and her own house gone, one wonders where she filmed so reliably if not her home. Perhaps a sibling's house. It also would not have been impossible for Samantha to have lied about something so major, with no worries about blowback or continuity—it didn't seem her family watched her videos, between her cruel and awkward remarks about her cousin, aunt, mother, brother, and husband, who admitted he didn't watch. Perhaps they knew her too well to assume they'd find anything they wanted to see there.

In that same "Totally homeless" video, she's in full makeup, rifling through DVDs and complaining about the loss, not of her house, but of her other DVDs. She provides only a vague and blurry timeline of events.

In another video, "Vampire diaries and batman :)," her idiosyncrasies are on full display again. She talks about how she got into the television show *The Vampire Diaries* when she bought season one—*purely* because it was cheap—as a relative's Christmas gift. She decided to watch it herself ahead of gifting it. She uses the show to take a jab at Ernie, whining, "I'm kind of screwed as far as dating goes because I date losers. I really do. I get into this ... darker-style guys who dress a little goth and stuff ... but then once I get involved with them, I realize most of them have no job.... They always want to sit around on the computer and play fucking games and it pisses me off, like hello, get a life."[210]

This was filmed on exactly the same month she was vying to be the Maxim Gamer Girl. She would also apply to work at Game Stop

---

210 Simplymanic6075, "Vampire diaries and batman :)," YouTube, May 29, 2012, https://www.youtube.com/watch?v=_N74BhQTnbc.

not four months after saying that people who play games should *get a life*.[211]

Later in that video she shows off her Batman-themed look, saying she's a fan. Yet in a video two months later entitled "Dark Night Rises Shooting," she is so unaware of the franchise, she doesn't spell "Knight" right for the duration, not realizing this is the central character's moniker *and* the name of the film itself. Instead, she comments on the then-recent 2012 shooting in Aurora, Colorado, at the midnight premier of the third film in Christopher Nolan's *Batman* series, blaming the shooting on the franchise itself, in the vein of "comics and games cause mass shootings"—a widely parroted theory that has been disproven. After panning the series' fans, she goes on to pan survivors for not protesting against police withholding the perpetrator's name from the public ahead of confirmation. "Personally, if I was a victim that got shot, I would be at that police station making sure every person in there knows my fucking name...."

As usual, she also hyperfocused on violence against children, stating, "There was a three-month-old that was wounded ... a six-year-old shot and killed, and a twelve-year-old. Let me take my kids to a movie ... and somebody gets shot? The police wouldn't have time to get to the guy doing the shooting, I would get to him first. Promise you that."[212] Yet she would be the very one to bring hit men into her home with her five children, to drag their father out to the slaughter. She lathers on the irony when she admits she wouldn't have any sympathy for a shooter, as a victim. Then, she switches to victim-*blaming*, and adds superiorly, "Well, I don't go to the movies *anyway*." A strange note from someone who purports to have been in films, and who wanted to be an actress.

In another video, her narcissistic tendencies are on full display as she demands that people not only send gifts to her PO box, but warns that if they want her to actually use the gifts, she requires a letter of explanation for why the items are special and why they wanted her to have them. She then points out the necklace she wears,

---

211 Simplymanic6075, "Phone sex...," YouTube, September 19, 2012, https://www.youtube.com/watch?v=-DGTG4CdELA.

212 Simplymanic6075, "Dark Night Rises Shooting," YouTube, July 21, 2012, https://www.youtube.com/watch?v=lQvDZsY_raI.

a black choker with a thin pendant on it. "This [necklace] was given to me by my kids' dad, and he's never really given me anything before, ever."[213] It's a backhanded compliment, ungrateful even as she shows it off. She wore the necklace constantly.

On *Ernie's* birthday in 2012, Sam posted a video entitled "Birthday"—saying it was *her* birthday and featuring her getting a cleavage piercing at a tattoo convention. Even if this video had been filmed on her August birthday and posted on Ernie's December birth date, it was still petty. She was refocusing his special day on herself, without viewers knowing that it *wasn't* her date of birth. It was also the date on which she would have been expected to get him both a birthday and a Christmas present, as a practicing Mormon; December 25. Instead, she shopped for herself.

The more one watches Sam, the more the contradictions pile up. She plays at popularity, yet in reality, seems very lonely. She begs her subscribers to leave feedback. "Please do that for me," she pleads at the end of one video, hoping for video responses. None come.

Not only does she seem to fabricate questions, but she uses the fabrications to chastise her partner publicly. "Something that bugs me about people asking me about how hard it is [to raise twins] is somehow they always seem to ask me when I have their asshole of a dad with me. Don't get me wrong, I love the boy to death. But he and I have a lot of problems.... He doesn't come around like he should and he's never done anything to support 'em. So when somebody asks me if it's hard he likes to pop off with 'oh, no, it's easy!' Well of course it's easy for him—I'm the one that does all the work, I'm the one who's there with them every day, I give them their bath, I put them to bed, I get up with them in the morning every morning. He's not here for any of it, he comes and sees them like once a month. So it's easy for him."[214]

While she would indeed *love Ernie to death*, she'd also display unfathomable callousness toward her children that same night. Courts

213 Simplymanic6075, "Necklace and fan mail," YouTube, May 29, 2012, https://www.youtube.com/watch?v=ir7L3bwY4Fg.

214 Simplymanic6075, "A little vlog and q&a," YouTube, July 15, 2012, https://www.youtube.com/watch?v=UKiDunMjuGE.

would later find that in order to kidnap Ernie without the children waking up, she'd drugged them.

When she and Ernie did get hitched, it was March of 2014. Their marriage was spur of the moment, just like she'd always dreamed, but its foundations were rotten. Ernie was an online gamer, and when Sam found out his character on one of his role-play forward MMORPGs—likely an avatar called Daegon—had married another character, she hit the roof. They got into a bad row about it, and Ernie promised that it was only fictional—that he'd marry *her* in reality.

Sam settled for reality.

They drove down to Hope, Arkansas. It was a far cry from Elvis's Graceland or Nevada's fringed look-alikes, home to the world's largest watermelons and not much else. TripAdvisor lists only two things to do there, one of which is to visit the house of former President Bill Clinton. The other is a museum that features a cardboard cutout of Clinton playing the sax and donning shades, plus some random information on old Amtrak trains. Hope's food is mostly big-plated Americana or Mexicana style. Why the couple decided to leap into marital bliss there is anyone's guess. But once married, naturally, their problems didn't magically resolve.

Ernie was known to friends as a "sweet father" and an "amazing person,"[215] but that didn't translate into nuptial bliss. In the one and only YouTube video that Sam posted with him in it, he seemed the opposite: grouchy and a little hostile. Entitled "Candid moments around my house," Sam films Ernie watching the anime *Soul Eater*. They have a short conversation:[216]

Ernie: "You're not going to light a cigarette?"

Sam: "Oh yeah, I forgot about that."

Ernie: "Cause you got that fucking iPad in your hands."

Sam: "Wah wah wah wah wha wha waaaah." (She makes baby noises, mocking him)

---

215 "Ernie Ibarra," BatesCooperLoanFuneralHome.com, accessed January 29, 2025, https://www.batescoopersloanfuneralhome.com/obituary/2975610.

216 Simplymanic6075, "Candid moments around my house," YouTube, January 1, 2013, https://www.youtube.com/watch?v=awuIICDFD8c.

Ernie: "At least you're paying attention. But only because it's a fucking hilarious-ass episode."

He smokes, too, implying he might have done the same thing as Sam, lighting up around the kids. For an aching amount of time, there is silence as he watches the show and she films him. Far from being "candid," he knows he is being filmed. He specifically did not want to be on Sam's YouTube channel. He put his frustration with Sam on display—that she wasn't in the moment.

The video can be read one of two ways. One, that Ernie was agitated by having his boundaries crossed, by his partner's lack of interest in the show he wanted to watch, and by the lack of respect for his boundaries, not letting him watch in peace. He was being filmed while grumpy to help sell her villainization of him. Or, it was a woman who wanted to involve her partner in what mattered to her—her videos—one whose partner had no intentions of supporting her channel and refused to even acknowledge her efforts, instead cursing at and belittling her. He was being filmed while grumpy to serve as proof of what Sam often had to put up with. Either way, it seems likely this was a two-way street of toxicity. But soon, Samantha would take to that street with a Mack truck.

If Ernie was physically or verbally abusive, then it seems Sam was emotionally abusive. Her videos show the public war she was willing to wage on Ernie, attacking everything from his hobbies to his gift-giving, often pulling her kids into the crosshairs and calling him an unfit father who did too little to raise them, never highlighting his work at two jobs to support them. Sam felt YouTube was akin to a job for her, though she put minimal effort into it and made little, if any, income. She also felt that motherhood was her job, which certainly felt true, with so many kids. As she said herself, "You do not have a life anymore after you have a baby." But how involved or effective she was as a mother is up to some debate.

Tellingly, in a video she posted about a school shooting, Sam says, "If I was gonna kill somebody it would definitely never be a kid."[217]

---

217 Simplymanic6075, "School shooting," YouTube, December 20, 2012, https://www.youtube.com/watch?v=Spqs13QR2-s.

In another, about shooters and murderers, she hauntingly remarks, "That's what all these psychos want. To be remembered forever."

These videos establish some facts of who Sam was. An attention-hungry liar with a mean streak and a lungful of complaints. Regardless of whatever else she was, she would let her own worst demons compel her into complicity—ending Ernie's life and ruining hers.

Have You Found My Husband?

So what did actually happen the night of the alleged break-in at Mount Pleasant?

The slow-burn romance of Ernie and Sam is often a muddled retelling that glosses over Sam seeing other men while they were together. It skirts past when and where they lived together, and sidles by why she went from having no intention of marrying him to dropping everything to do so. It's bewildering how they managed to co-parent. It's even unclear who abused whom, and to what degree.

Other points are unclear as well. Sensationalized articles would claim that Sam was more devoted to her YouTube stardom than her family, and that her thirst for attention led to her icing her husband—perhaps for eventual content. But the truth was, her rate of posting had dipped significantly from 2013 to the time of the murder in 2015; she had less of an online focus.

What we do know is that Sam's own actions led to Earnie's murder, and ahead of that night, she'd go on a vicious and targeted premeditated campaign to malign him to strangers and friends alike. Sam told her aunt Ginger she was sick of Ernie, and her childhood friend Stephen Patterson that she'd like him to "take care of him." She was vague on what that meant, but it was clearly a threat. We also know for sure that Ernie felt that Sam was a neglectful parent. But all of this discord still leaves us with a weak motive for murdering a husband.

An even weaker motive comes in the form of the three attackers who carried out the plan: Jonathan Sanford, Jose "JoJo" Ponse, and Octavius Rhymes—one a man Sam only met a month prior to the murder, another she'd just met just the *day* before, and the third one the father of one of her children's friends, whom she also barely knew.

What motive did *they* have for helping Sam? A thin one at best. Not promised money, sex, drugs, or anything else in return for the capital crime, yet they still carried it out—based on the alleged abuse alone, high on meth, and for no better reason than they wanted to.

Originally, the plan they hatched didn't involve murder. It morphed, in a series of hours, into something darker. According to trial testimony and the confessions of Sanford and Ponse, we can knit together how the bizarre scheme fomented. Sometime around Valentine's Day, Sam met Jonathon Sanford, the boyfriend of her pregnant friend Sharla. They spoke a few times between then and the night of the murder—"Johnny" had even been to her house.

Then, on March 19, Johnny was at the hospital and heard Sam complaining to Sharla about Ernie's alleged abuses. Johnny, newly out of jail himself, was there with his friends JoJo and Octavius. He asserted that no man ought to treat a woman that way and offered to "take care of him"—just what Sam had been fishing for from male friends for years.

She asked Johnny how he could accomplish that, and his idea was a simple one. They'd buy methamphetamines from one of Octavius's cousins that night, plant them in Ernie's truck, and call the police to snitch on him. When the police conducted the search and found Ernie in possession of meth, they'd take him to prison—and he'd be out of Sam's hair.

Sam would indeed give her children to the men to take to Walmart for a time so she could chat with Sharla, but upon their return, she did not go home. She piled the children into her car along with Johnny and Octavius, and they traveled to Mount Vernon, a charming Texas town with picturesque country-style stores. There, they met up with the cousin, purchasing the quantity of meth needed before journeying to Octavius's house in Pittsburg, Texas, where Jose Ponce and his wife were camping on the property.

Pittsburg is the hot links capital of Texas—hand-tied sausages popularized by the Pittsburg Hot Link Restaurant, which also serves Frito pies, keeping bellies full in Camp County. The town was also the filming location for *Humans versus Zombies*. Sam would later tell investigators that she didn't know a soul who lived there, and she herself had never been.

They passed the evening together. At some point, the idea of what they should do to Ernie began to shift. Wouldn't involving police as a key part of the plan be a dangerous move? Why not, they argued, just smoke the meth themselves? And then, Johnny amended, they could simply get rid of Ernie—*for good.* The men debated the merits of murdering Ernie under the same roof as his children. From Octavius's kitchen, where she was cooking enchiladas, JoJo's wife, Lacona Slaton, heard them talking in conspiratorial whispers. She'd met Sam that day for the first time. Then she clearly heard Sam tell the men: "I can make anyone believe anything; I'm an actress."

The children, Sam conceded, would be an issue. "I can give them something," Lacona heard her add. Something that would put them to sleep and keep them that way through any scuffle or noise. Johnny agreed, but gave her an out: If Sam decided she wanted Ernie gone that night, all she had to do was leave them a sign—leave her front door unlocked after getting home. If she didn't leave that signal for him, they wouldn't carry out the murder.

Around midnight, Johnny and Octavius drove Sam and her children back to the Mount Pleasant house. Sam gave the kids something to thrust them deep into the undertow of sleep and piled all five of them into the same room—something her aunt Ginger would later note as unusual when she came to their "rescue."

Sam let the men keep her car to outfit the next steps. They gutted the children's car seats and headed back to Walmart to purchase gloves, an easy way to mask their fingerprints. Then they picked up JoJo, who had a loaded gun to use for the foul business. The three men smoked more meth together on the car ride back to Sam's house. Now high, they tried the front door. Unlocked, it gave easily, so the plan was on. Sam had not taken the out—she wanted Ernie dead.

The men entered the premises, letting Octavius venture upstairs to the couple's bedroom to drag Ernie out. On the ground floor, JoJo and Johnny took turns beating Ernie with fists and with JoJo's pistol. When they were satisfied with the beatings, they rummaged around Ernie's truck and the house a bit. Sam, upstairs, was on her phone idly, not bothering to go downstairs and certainly not restrained in any way. Then, she made a call to her mother—putting on fake hysterics and mumbling as if through a gag.

When it was clear that Rosie was sending Ginger, who lived just ten minutes away, to come help, Johnny tied Sam up loosely on the floor and went downstairs to tell JoJo and Octavius it was time to hit the road. They had one last task: to shatter the front door into the living room to make it look as if they'd broken into the home. From there, they hoisted Ernie into Sam's car and began the drive back to Camp County, to a heavily wooded area.

Ginger went to her niece's aid with her partner in tow, and only called the police after arriving. In the 911 emergency call, Ginger reports, "My niece is tied up. I, I am, I am at the verge of untying my niece.... She is tied up and gagged.... We have five small infants asleep... ranging from seven to one."

911: "Can I talk to her? Is she able to speak?"

Sam: "Hello?"

911: "Do you need EMS?"

Sam: "No, they didn't do anything to me. They only hit me once."

The police were quick to arrive and begin their investigation. For them, it was immediately obvious that there weren't enough signs of struggle or bloodshed to support Sam's narrative. Similarly, she had none of the bruising or injuries consistent with her story, and the notion that she had so easily accessed her phone via her face came across as made-up. Though she had been untied by her aunt, the bindings found seemed flimsy and hadn't left her with any skirmish signs.

After looking through the house, police took Sam to the station, where she'd tread water, wasting their time and resources while Ernie was in his final moments. At one point during her police interview, she'd overhear Titus County Sheriff's Deputy Chris Durant asking the department's communication office to track Ernie's phone using cell provider service tower pings. It was at that point that she asked if they'd let her step outside to call her mother.

Once outside, she texted the men about what the police were up to, telling them to get rid of the phone, STAT. That was at 2:30 a.m. When police found a ping on Ernie's phone just a little bit past

3 a.m., close to the site of where he'd be murdered, they told Sam about it just to see her reaction. She quickly texted Octavius again: "Ditch phone, move." Ernie's signal disappeared, robbing police of their best chance at saving him. But confirming what they already suspected.

The men had parked Sam's car near a dense thicket of woodland and prodded Ernie, blindfolded and veiled, into leading his own death march into the thicket. Unseeing and barefoot, he slipped over a branch and took a hard fall.

Johnny had already determined that he'd be the one to kill him. But rather than shoot him, he'd decided he wanted to slit the man's throat. That was the plan, until Ernie nosedived. Taking the fall as a sign that this was the moment to end things, JoJo took out the gun and shot Ernie in the back of the head, ending his life instantly and frustrating Johnny's wish to do so himself. JoJo would later contest this to police, saying he hadn't been the one to fire, but investigators determined that he had indeed most likely dispatched the final blow.

The Wohlford kids were taken to their grandparents' house as police conducted an investigation that took three days, though it was clear to them that Sam was involved from day one. Investigators saw the house hadn't been robbed and that the front door's security chain and frame were intact—so the door had not been locked when it was smashed. Based on Sam's initial intel, they had driven out to meet Ernie's dad to see if the angry drug lord angle had any credibility, but by then Ernie's phone was pinging from Pittsburgh, Texas—nowhere near his father, who sat at home unmolested by double-crossed drug pushers, bewildered by the news.

In her subsequent police interviews, Sam wasted no time in casting herself as a saint. She said that the only reason she had even been discussing her alleged abuse at Ernie's hands with Sharla in the hospital was because Sharla was nervous about her baby's father—not boyfriend Johnny—finding her there. "[Sharla] was telling me what an angel I am for getting her to calm down." She then went on to reinforce for police her version of Ernie as a deadbeat, adding, "I'm the one paying the bills." How this was possible with no job to speak of wasn't clear. She attested that she'd bought Ernie his phone and his truck, a Dodge Ram, just weeks prior. It was all about her.

The detective pressed Sam, saying she must have some idea who'd taken Ernie away and why. She gave a line-up of false names—like Jeremy—and false leads, like maybe Ernie was cheating on her or dealing drugs himself. The detective coaxed her by saying that she wouldn't be considered criminally responsible for having withheld the names of Ernie's kidnappers if she'd known them. Armed with the idea that she could get out of a homicide blame-free, Sam then readily gave up some aliases—"John Rebel" and "Ty." She said there was a third man, but she didn't know who he was. She provided police with Sharla's first name and hospital number, saying that the men she'd met there yesterday seemed upset by her abusive situation; hence why she'd brought it up so randomly earlier in the interview; and she thought they might be involved, but didn't know their real names. But as she had already been setting the stage for a motive for them, and gave a fair amount of positive identifying information (three men, who'd visited Sharla the day before), it was clear that Sam was gearing up to sell her accomplices out to save her own skin.

But she kept up her charade and even laid it on thicker. She pretended not to know Sharla that well either, saying she was unsure even of her last name. Despite apparently knowing neither Sharla nor the men at the hospital, she'd lent the guys her Chevy and her key ring to be helpful—but her key ring, she "realized," also carried a copy of her house keys, and *that* must be how they'd gotten in. When asked why she didn't say so sooner, she simpered that they'd threatened to kill her kids if she spoke up. Another fiction that cast her as the victim, free of onus.

In fact, detectives handed her that excuse on a silver platter, implying she must just be a scared mother afraid for her kids. They wanted to see if she took the bait, and she did. She immediately switched tracks—taking on the mantle of the frightened maternal figure just trying to protect her young. It still didn't explain why the door chain hadn't been locked, even if they'd had her keys; maybe especially if they'd had her keys.

"They have a lot of friends around here, and my life will be in danger." She'd switch to insisting, once police seemed amenable to the sob story route. She didn't spot her own contradiction. It would be strange for her to fear for her life when the motive she gave for Johnny and "Ty" hunting Ernie is that *Ernie* had hurt *her*. She'd already claimed that they'd overheard her talking to Sharla about the abuse, and that inspired their violence. So why, then, would they kill Ernie for abusing a woman, only to turn around and also threaten her and her kids?

"Please don't let this come back on me," Sam begged police, after ratting on the others. "They did make it clear that if I called the police they would kill my kids." Another contradiction. She'd allowed Ginger to call the police, spoken with police openly that call, and was openly speaking with detectives now. Sam would slip up again when she admitted that she did in fact know the third person—that he was a man who was living with "Ty" alongside with his wife, and that his name was Jose.

Samantha not only turned on her co-conspirators right away, but her lies weren't even consistent. She said the men yelled that they'd never hurt kids, yet had threatened hers. She says the door was broken in, then says they'd used the house keys. She admits she also lent them her car—for Sharla's post-operation travel—yet didn't even know the names, much less the phone numbers, of the people she'd literally given her keys and vehicle to. The more detectives implied that helpful information would allow her to be found innocent of any misdeeds, the more she told them.

Her behavior became unhinged, though, whenever detectives left her alone in the interrogation room. At one point, on police footage, she's seen standing up abruptly, before going to doodle on a large whiteboard in the room, knowing full well she's being watched and filmed. In curly handwriting, she pens, "Hello my love." Next, she erases that to write "I hope you're hungry!" and "What's going on!" Finally, she shrugs aggressively at the camera, looking at it dead on. She erases the board again and writes,

HAVE YOU FOUND MY HUSBAND?

Police were able to find Johnny and JoJo right away, as soon as they had Sharla's hospital room number. They engaged in a quick chase through the facility before the suspects, on foot, surrendered to the police. Once at the station, they gave officers all the facts right away—Johnny even led police to Ernie's body, out in the deep copses of Sand's Crossing. For their cooperation, after they were found guilty of aggravated murder and kidnapping, they'd be given two *concurrent* fifty-year sentences—a bargain.

Octavius, who went on the run and, upon being caught later, pled innocent (perhaps not knowing Johnny had already given him up in full) would not be so lucky. He was sentenced to seventy-eight years in prison. The blanket placed briefly around Ernie's body, the veil and a bandana around his face at the time of his death, and the murder weapon itself were all found hidden under the crawlspace of Octavius's house.

Ultimately, Samantha would be sentenced to ninety-nine years on the same charges as the men.

The only details Johnny and JoJo had differed on were who shot Ernie and what Sam's level of involvement was. Police determined that JoJo was the shooter, as he had the gun and as Johnny was startlingly honest about his frustrations over not getting to stab Ernie to death himself.

> **Police:** "Who's got the gun?"
>
> **Johnny:** "JoJo does.... I know that sound by heart. I grew up with guns. My dad's 21 years Navy."

JoJo called Sam the "ringleader" of the plan, whereas Johnny would at first deny her involvement, trying to protect her even after she'd sold him out. At this point, Sam had even connected cops with his Facebook page after providing them with his girlfriend's birthing room number at the hospital, where he'd been found. Even up to the time of being a trial witness against Sam, Johnny would say that he thought Sam hadn't really understood he meant *murder* when he said he'd get rid of Ernie for good. No one else in the courtroom found this convincing.

During the subsequent trial, Sam admitted on the stand that she often vented about Ernie to other men and didn't want him in her life. Old friends of hers testified that Sam had adamantly insisted that Ernie was abusive and she wanted him pushed out of the family and gotten rid of, that she was actively looking for someone to harm him. Other corroborating factors popped up; Bret Webster, Ginger's boyfriend, said that two nights before the murder, Sam had left her children with him and told him that someone name John would pick them up.

But it is the police interviews that are the most telling—and the most chilling.[218] On them, Sam mimics crying as she speaks, her voice tight. In her initial interview she wears a red top and blue jeans, Ernie's necklace around her throat. Far from complaining about abuse, she paints a cheerful picture of their home life while also never failing to throw Ernie under the bus a little. She'd claim she only let him back into her heart after he successfully completed his anger management courses, and after the emergency protective order had been lifted. She said that since they'd been apart, they'd been sharing romantic phone calls, and that he'd become a better man who wanted to do right by her.

"I put it on my kids' life. I have not done anything. I did not have it done and I did not do anything," she said. She swears this lie to police on the lives of her innocent young children.

Though at first she gave very few details about her attacker, she manages to pepper a bit of racism in for good measure—though she "hadn't been able to see her attackers," she insisted they had "Hispanic" or "African-American voices," whatever that means. Her delivery goes from broken-down simpering to bordering on sociopathic levels of calm when detectives ask about any piece of the story she's unhappy to have deeply examined, or any methodologies she disapproved of. When asked to take a polygraph test, she refused on the grounds that she had nothing to hide. When that seemed like too much of a logic pretzel, she curtly switched to playing the blame

218 The Matthews Fam, "Stories that are Actually TRUE!" YouTube, November 10, 2021, https://www.youtube.com/watch?v=sxLysR9-mqk.

game, "Cops in general ... are not out to help you—CPS is the same way."[219]

When they finally have enough evidence, a detective finally lets Sam know, "I think it's not gonna be long before I'm gonna be locking your butt up.... I think you've been lying to me this whole thing.... I don't buy your freaking story for a minute. That's what I think."

The police point out that if things were so great with Ernie, it was odd that she was actively seeing other men. They'd make her run through her version of events again.

Sam would try the father angle once more. "I think it's something to do with [Ernie's] dad.... I hate, and I'm usually right and I hate that, but ... his dad has a problem with getting involved with things he don't need to be involved with."

In another room, JoJo was telling detectives, "Samantha is the one, and I can prove this.... Take me in front of my wife, and my wife will tell you a piece of what she overheard. And my wife will tell you: she's the one that orchestrated it."

Three days later, with JoJo and Johnny's confessions on the books, Sam would be asked back to the police station for a second interview. She'd return in a black hoodie and, ironically, a shirt with old school prison-style stripes. The police start easy on her, then rapidly amp up. They ask why she didn't confess that she knew who the killers were earlier in her first interview, so they could have had a chance of saving Ernie. She deflects with yet a new sob story, saying it's because her sister had been raped and police never found the man who did it, and therefore she doesn't trust cops.

"I'm going to show you what you could have stopped," a policeman says. Sam is then shown a photo of what she allowed to happen—Ernie, face down in his underwear, the back of his head partially obliterated, Sheetrock tape binding his mouth closed, blotchy injuries across his body from the beatings. Dead.

They tell her, finally, that they know she's guilty.

Sam finally cries.

---

219 Stranger Stories, "Evil Wife Realizing She's Going to Jail for 99 Years," YouTube, May 13, 2024, https://www.youtube.com/watch?v=i8jsNBJB8UI.

On February 26, police would catch Octavius in a Brookshire's grocery store parking lot in Pittsburg, Texas. He maintained that he thought they were all just hanging out and he was only there to be a lookout—that didn't know the plan was to *kill* Ernie. Jurors were not convinced.

In March of 2017, the last to have a hearing, Sam went down for aggravated kidnapping. Her defense team argued she hadn't known they'd really planned to murder Ernie, and that she shouldn't be liable for sending the text messages that she prevented his rescue because she was still addled from her Ambien pill. Prosecutors would claim her motive was fame. In September of 2017, she was additionally found guilty of murder.

By chance, there was also a witness to testify against Sam's claim she'd been too drugged to know better when she texted Octavius to ditch Ernie's phone. In Titus County jail on February 20, 2015, where Sam was being held, she'd told another detainee—Whitney Smith—that she'd be in the clear if she could just get rid of her texting records. Sam shared with Whitney that she had already deleted them from her phone.[220]

One person still does believe in her innocence, though. Samantha's mother told *Snapped*, the crime documentary show, "If she did do this? Then she's where she belongs. But a mother can tell, and she couldn't go through with a murder. There's no way. I'll never believe that.... Those kids lost everything." The five children were given to Sam's mother.

Jail Babes Seek Pen Pals!

Sam's original Jail Babes profile read, "There is never a dull moment with me. I am a caffeine-addicted Mormon who loves to laugh.... I'm not judgmental. I have a passion for anime, manga, cosplay, cosmetology, literature, gaming.... I'm a bit of a nerd, but I'm fun.... I work hard so I can play harder. Write me so we can play together. You won't be disappointed."

---

220 Samantha Nicole Wolhford V. The State of Texas, No. 06-19-00106-CR, accessed January 29, 2025, https://law.justia.com/cases/texas/sixth-court-of-appeals/2020/06-19-00106-cr.html.

The site then reminds mailers how to use JPay, the US prison mailing and phone system that can be prepaid from outside. Sam has recently updated her profile to be more enticing:

"My nickname is Firefly. I enjoy reading, laughing, listening to music, playing video games & spending time with those I care about.... I'm slightly nerdy and a bit of a country girl at heart, but you'd never know it by looking at me. I love to make people smile and I have a big heart.... I'm silly at times and can be outspoken. I love finding magic in the world around us. I'm looking for both legal help and people I can share letters and possibly phone calls with. If you feel like you might be interested, send me a letter and let's see how this turns out. You won't regret it."

CHAPTER 7

YUKA TAKAOKA, aka Yuyuyunochan/Uyupekochan

I'm getting a little turned on
Thanks to the actions of people around me
Stab you in the crown of your head
With your hair styled in a middle part
You saw, right?
That moron who coughed up blood.
So don't think you can win …
Viva Unhappy!
Nothing's ever enough, yeah? …
I'm gonna buy me some love.
—"HITO Mania," Sasuke Haraguchi

Yuka Takaoka dances to this song online in a video she uploaded to her socials, with her cosplaying as the devil-horned female Blood Fiend character named Power from the Japanese manga and anime series *Chainsaw Man*. Based on Eric Cartman from *South Park*, Power is a four-armed, sharp-toothed devil who "wears" the corpse of a cute, dead human girl. She's selfish and a habitual liar.

The Sleepless Town

It is May 23, 2019.

In the small hours of Thursday morning between 3 and 4 a.m., Tokyo is hushed. Even in Kabukicho, the red-light district, the streets begin to clear of their throngs of human traffic. Bars empty or shutter, neon signs flicker out, and only the most hardcore partiers and sex fiends remain in the bedazzled clubs. Just the biggest spenders, and therefore biggest drinkers, still lounge on the velveteen couches of host and hostess establishments, slashing open bottles of champagne.

In the lobby of an apartment building near the pleasure hub of East Shinjuku, Yuka Takaoka sits on the tile floor by the glass entryway. In front of her, policemen in bulletproof vests carrying saber-hilted batons hover around in a slim crowd. One officer, a middle-aged man in black-framed glasses, a white medical mask, and an orange arm band, squats down in front of her in his dress shoes, handcuffs clinking against his hip. He leans in close, presumably to speak with her, but Yuka seems otherwise absorbed.

She looks busy—but not anything like a threat. Slender, with long hair and a babydoll fringe bob, Yuka wears perforated Croc-type slippers, which are clunky on her, accentuating her smallness; the Japanese do not wear their outside shoes indoors, and she's had the foresight to hastily don house shoes, despite the chaos of the minutes before. Her knees are bent, feet pidgeon-toeing inward a little. Her thighs are bare and the long black button-down shirt over her frame pools into her lap, obscuring whether or not she is wearing underwear. She has on a thick black bracelet and similarly thick, dark glasses with sweet, overlarge frames, adding to her meek appearance. Her nails are neatly manicured, as all hostesses' are. In her left hand, she holds a lit cigarette, actively smoking. In her right, she holds a cellphone to her ear, mid-conversation.

The scene would seem badly juxtaposed just on that information alone. Police, who rarely have weapons drawn and ready in Japan, closing in on a girl who seems not to notice them from her roost on the floor, her bare skin to the ceramic tiling, puffing away at nicotine and chatting casually to a friend. But what turns the stomach in this off-kilter scene is what seems to be behind Yuka, and what she is covered in.

Obscured by the police and Yuka herself lies the body of twenty-year-old Phoenix Luna. He's seemingly naked below rows of mailboxes emblazoned with family names. He has a huge gash in his abdomen, which is half-hidden by Yuka, his right leg is akimbo, his left leg lame, and his bare chest is smothered in bright blood—his own. Yuka's legs, too, are splattered with enough of Luna's blood to be unnerving; one entire knee is red. The white tiles are streaked with gore, great smears and finger-painted bands, clotted up here and there in gnarly shoe prints. Luna wears no shoes. He is not conscious. He managed half an escape, getting out of the apartment he was stabbed in before blood loss felled him close to the lobby door, just paces away from freedom.

Yuka is less than half a foot from where he lies prone, facing demurely away from him with her back to his would-be corpse. Calm.

The stabbing of handsome, charming young for-hire club host Phoenix Luna by girly bar manager Yuka Takaoka in her dwelling that night took social and traditional media by storm, both in Japan and abroad. Much of what was reported has been confused and misinterpreted—that they were in a relationship, lovers, or roommates; that she had called the police, or a neighbor did; that he was staying there for one night, or many; that he loved her, or just pretended to. Japan's lock-and-key judicial system papered over a lot of the real story, burying it in breadcrumbs for netizens to fight over the salacious details.

What was reported correctly was the bizarre aftermath. Luna, who fell into a coma after Yuka's confirmed and confessed attempt to murder him, would beat his odds to survive—only to plead for a reduction in Yuka's sentence during her trial.

And Yuka, led away from his unconscious body by police—her premeditative handiwork—smiled an unnerving smile from the window of the squad car she was placed into at a gaggle of reporters and concerned citizens. It was a smile that witnesses described as *evil*.

Kiss Kiss, Fall in Love

To appreciate the unique relationship that formed between Phoenix Luna and Yuka requires an understanding of Japan's unique sex work industry—what it costs, and whom it's for.

Unlike the typical Western understanding of sex work, which veers more towards kink, prostitution, sensual dance, and sugar-babying, prostitution in Japan takes on a more cultural lilt. Coital prostitution is illegal, but anything outside the definition of "intercourse" (which discounts gay sex and fellatio) is allowed. But there are loopholes. If you pay for *conversation* and you give *gifts*, and that leads to sex outside of work ...? That's very much permissible—even if the expectation is built in all along.

The red-light districts of major cities in Japan cater to conversation and company more than they do to outright sex acts. In Japan, where the birth rate is negative and many describe sex as a chore, overwork is rampant, and men and women can find communication difficult, leading to social disorders like *hikikomori* (complete societal withdrawal), parasite singles, and the uptick in herbivorous (nonsexual) men. In a country trapped within these parameters, just talking with beautiful men and women paid to flatter you with attention and trained to pretend care about your life's wins and woes is considered a premium service.

Host bars, hostess bars, and snack bars profit on gorgeous bodies paired with made-to-order personae (each come with their own "look" and "personality") on a menu where one can order their company for the evening. You *keep* that company by ordering off the actual menu—purchasing food, and especially drinks. It costs a tremendous amount of money to keep a host's attention glued to you, for chatting, partying, and karaoke. Elegantly-dressed hosts—always in suits and ties for men, dresses and updos for women—serve you, pour for you, and become essentially your girlfriend or boyfriend for the evening—while usually providing the same service to others tangentially, at the same time.

Sex is, in fact, *not* guaranteed, but regular customers who buy expensive presents for their favorite host or hostess and spend enough money in the clubs to help them earn top billing might be favored with sex outside of work hours, at the worker's discretion. It's a legalized ambiguity—prostitution is expected, but not doled out by companies. Workers *can* technically say no—but saying "no" too often risks losing high-paying clientele, lowering a host's billing and wages.

As a result, hosts and hostesses often have many people they see at once, juggling and coaxing and then demurring their affections to keep the game in the green. If a host dates at all, it's often with other bar workers who can understand their lifestyle without judgment. *Usually* without judgment. Yuka would prove far outside the norm in terms of her expectations of Luna, yet colored within the lines of expectation when she became romantically attached to the beautiful host boy. While businessmen are the most common customers for hostesses, *hostesses* are the most common type of customer for male hosts—women who are up late, flush with cash, and sick of seeing to the needs of men. Hostesses often indulge at male clubs as a form of "me time" with boys who will wait on them, flatter them, and don't get resentful of their jobs. It's a vicious cycle of sex capitalism—women workers cash in on flings with men by paying other men.

This was the context in which Yuka really grew to know Luna, at the host club FUSION FOR YOUTH, inside a notorious building in the racy Kabukicho district of Shinjuku. It's so infamous that gamers will be able to spot its barely disguised twin in the hit video game *Yakuza 0*, renamed the *Maharaja*. In reality, it's the Number 6 TOA Building, and it is notorious for suicides—so many that locals call the place haunted. Its rooftop, previously a draw for its coveted views of Tokyo's downtown, is now permanently closed to the public after one too many lovelorn customers threw themselves from its heights. Once the rooftop locked and TOA 6 got its reputation as a suicide "hotspot," high schoolers began making pilgrimages to slit their wrists just outside of it, to become a part of its gritty lore.

To look at TOA 6 (TOA being the word for "tower," mimicking English) in the harsh glare of day is to be astounded by a building so peerlessly ugly and confused. The word "tacky" pole-vaults to mind. A monstrosity of mismatched architecture, its backside is decked out in black marble with Greco-Roman décor, its large windows are festooned with rainbow-colored glass in half-moons down its center, and adding to the mélange are round tiles, hot pink gating, and musty gold accenting. There is nothing in the way of a sidewalk on the streets it straddles, so it has made its own—a dizzying gray, black, and white diamond pattern that wraps around the building and plunges into an open-air ground floor lobby, which arrests breathing. The entryway is held aloft by two fat white stucco ionic columns, so poorly rendered you can trace the wide squares in their fragmented design. These are rimmed in about a foot of gold, which looks flashy at night, but cheap on a sunny day. At the front of the building, the first two floors have been walled off to create a grand staircase, roofed but otherwise open to the elements. White marble steps climb up into its guts, wreathed in red velvet carpeting down the center. Guests ascend the stairs through a stone-walled pilaster that looks almost medieval, up toward a cavalcade of bright lights, each one sticking out at a hard angle—like a million needles, suddenly ultramodern.

The hodgepodge is dizzying. A Willy Wonka nightmare ride that expels customers into a pantomime of luxury. The host clubs are almost all designed in the same way, with lots of low-hanging chandeliers and neon light fixtures, an abundance of leathery or embroidered upholstery, glitzy mirrors, and fairy lights.

Outside of TOA 6 are often the debris of bloody razors and sanitary napkins, used to try to sop up the bleeding of people who cut their wrists, only to think twice about ending their lives. Some women hurt themselves just lightly outside of TOA 6, so a host from within can dramatically fly out and "save" them. The space especially attracts those who feel rootless or who have faced adversity—offering a sort of for-rent glamor that ends in either a fairy-tale prince or a tragic twist. All the perfume and gloss of the host world hide the tinge of predatory underworld tactics at play here; emotional manipulation, addiction, kink, illness, and injury are all part of the story arc one gets to play out for a high price with pretty boys who encourage obsession while cajoling ladies into drinking exorbitantly, all so the "princess" can pretend: "This boy is *mine*."

Issues arise when customers tack onto that sentiment an *"At all costs"* or worse, an *"Or else."*

Women often think they can get their chosen host's full attention by taking things too far. That with enough money, alcohol, gifts, outbursts, or threats, they can claim ownership and take power where power was previously only a game of smoke and mirrors, a fictitious fantasy. When the game is played on a host's own turf and terms, it usually remains contained. It's when hosting spills outside of its clubs that matters can get dangerous.

Inside the clubs, the hosts have a playbook—literally—and they're expected to use it. One such playbook, or "host manual," teaches men how to employ "mind control," a set of power tactics that helps train new women visitors into becoming faithful consumers. Translating from a real guide that *The Japan Times* posted snippets of, instructions include:[221]

> The reason [women] come to a host club is to erase and fill the void in their heart.
>
> *MIND CONTROL:*
>
> 1. Make it difficult [for them] to get angry [with you].
>
> [Say often:] "You're great because you don't get unreasonably angry!"
>
> Praise them: "[NAME] can handle a lot of things!"
>
> 2. Don't let them go to other stores.

The manual goes on in the same vein. This kind of coercive control exploits, to a host's advantage, the four stages of psychological manipulation: flattery, isolation, devaluing, and gaslighting. A host reels a woman in by complimenting her and specifically pointing out the traits he wants her to have more of (such as being calm and taking care of him), builds up that praise, then makes sure she can't get the same emotional hit anywhere else by telling her not to visit other clubs or even other hosts, isolating her to him. Then, he devalues her when she cannot pay her tab or doesn't purchase enough drinks on visits by berating, whining, and even chasing her

221 Karin Kaneko, "How Japan's Host Clubs Trap Young Women Under Mountains of Debt," *The Japan Times*, December 26, 2023, https://www.japantimes.co.jp/news/2023/12/26/japan/society/host-club-pay-later-system-prostitution.

down. After all that, finally, he gaslights her by saying he loves her best and relies on her—thereby coaxing her back into the same cycle of drinking and spending for that feel-good moment at the finish line, the brief and fleeting feeling of *love*.

Host tactics also rely heavily on "planned complimenting," an emotional training method that praises the target not for who they are but for what they *do* that the manipulator wants positively reinforced. It focuses on praising the target when they are selfless, have fewer demands, don't get frustrated when it would be reasonable to, and act pliable, going with the flow of what the emotional manipulator asks for. It encourages the target not to share any thoughts or feelings that may be bothersome for the host, teaching women not to voice their authentic wants or needs but instead, that they are at their *most* worthy when their attention is on the needs of the *host*; when his needs are her duties. For example, if a woman is having monetary problems, he doesn't want to hear that. He wants her to be "cool," confident that she'll figure things out, and in the meantime, be "kind" enough to spend money she doesn't have on him without making *him* worry or changing *his* lifestyle. That's what garners his praise.

Some clubs are so specific in their parameters that they instruct hosts on how to escort women from the elevators: walk at her pace, be sure to call your meeting a "date" to give it a false sense of intimacy, move at a slower overall speed to look unbothered. It tells men to call out loudly when the woman's glass is empty (to make it too publicly embarrassing for the woman to deny a refill), to pay attention to which stories she enjoys and talk more deeply about those—that in feigning interest, the host must allow the women to talk more at the *beginning* of meeting to seem like an empathetic listener, but by the end of a date, he must almost fully dominate the conversation so she can't get much of a word in edgewise.[222] At that point she's being directed, since it's close to time to pay. Hosts must insist any payment to the club be by card, so women don't see the amount in cash and get sticker shock. (Many host bars, quite illegally, do not

222 みずきち（桐夜瑞紀）歌舞伎町 (@kubinimukade), "億ホストのエスコートはこうらしい。無理や。ストレス溜まる。諦めて皆でみずきちのエスコートにしよ。" X, July 5, 2024, https://x.com/kubinimukade/status/1809203188509319385.

advertise the price of alcohol on their menus, and the final tallying is nebulous. Some do not provide receipts; they "forget.")

The number one rule, though? Drinking. Hosts have to drink alcohol. If they work every day, they drink every day, almost to excess. In a documentary about hosting—called *The Floating World* after Japan's Edo period, where sex work was catered to on boats—one male host notes, "Our jobs are to sell happiness to the girls.... [but] it's like Mickey Mouse, it doesn't exist."[223] The admission price is far above that of a Disney cruise, though. The host in the documentary is a fashion plate. He wears $1,575 Tiffany's hardware earrings and sports a black Fendi Baguette bag, a model that starts at over $2,000 for a mini. It's very likely that these were gifts from his clientele, mainly hostesses and prostitutes themselves.

The host club featured in *The Floating World* is PLANTIA in Kabukicho, where its number one host made upwards of $95,000 in December of 2022 alone[224]—his total sales that year topped over $680,000. At a club like this, two bottles of André Roger Champagne (which costs between $30 and $90 at typical retail) and a bottle of Perrier Jouët Champagne (which can be costlier, ranging from $50 to $250) will cost a guest more than $13,000. The markups to drink with hosts are *insane*, yet giddily paid by customers, who have high expectations of a fun time and being made to feel special in return.

At PLANTIA, Ladoga Imperial Collection Vodka is on the menu. With lush 24-carat gold accents, a Venetian glass decanter, and a velvet box, a bottle at a liquor store can run all the way up to $5,000. The blue variety is in the lower range, about $1,000 to $1,500. For this experience with a host, a customer can expect to pay upwards of $14,000—a staggering 933% markup.

A YouTube mini-documentary by *Asian Boss* titled "Meet the Number 1 Hostess in Japan" introduces the feminine side of the

223 Nowness, "Inside Tokyo's host clubs and the interplay between self-realization and self-destruction," YouTube, November 27, 2022, https://www.youtube.com/watch?v=eF9oUdjgB_k.

224 "歌舞伎町の蘭社長【KG PRODUCE, "【ホストクラブの締め日】売上が命のNo.1ホストの戦略:歌舞伎町の蘭社長," YouTube, January 12, 2024, https://www.youtube.com/watch?v=DZDQbNiGKSk.

equation.[225] Lalah, working in the more upscale and high-rolling Roppongi, makes an average of $46,000 a month at a bar that features eighty girls. She easily admits to having sex with men she meets at work whom she likes, but laments the high costs of her job—plastic surgery, nail care, beautifully put-together outfits to wear to work, hours spent getting ready with hair and makeup teams, and the constant drinking.

A hostess fee for Lalah starts at just $27 an hour—extremely reasonable. But the champagne towers she sells to customers and receives commissions for? About $93,000. She talks men into buying them better than anyone else, as denoted by her fine jewelry; she dons a $14,200 Cartier Juste un Clou diamond bracelet with a matching $4,750 ring for a night of work. Part of being a good hostess, for her, is dedicating 40% of her salary back into the customers—giving them birthday gifts, remembering important occasions, and occasionally buying drinks for them, too.

It isn't uncommon, thus, for some women who visit host establishments who are *not* prostitutes to *become* prostitutes in order to pay for their habit after falling for a host. They may even be encouraged into it as hosts whine and cajole their "princesses," telling them they care about them but can't see them if they don't take care of them in turn, proving their love with gifts and alcohol.

Only recently have some Kabukicho clubs started to ban the dangerous "pay later" system, which encourages women to rack up a debt on the host's tab but then badgers them to pay it back because their host cannot afford it.[226] Many women feel safe spending on a tab that doesn't require a credit card to start—but with little insight into what they're being charged, they turn to whatever fast and lucrative work they can get to pay it off, which is how so many end up in sex work. Paying the host tab off then means being welcomed to return to the club to rack up debt again as their favorite boy, with whom they share a one-sided emotional bond, will pester them into sitting, talking, and then *drinking* with them—and more becomes owed.

---

225 Asian Boss, "Meet the Number 1 Hostess in Japan | ASIAN BOSS," YouTube, July 7, 2019, https://www.youtube.com/watch?v=u1xwLUjk1ul.

226 Kaneko, "How Japan's Host Clubs Trap."

In an unfortunate twist, lowering the age of majority to eighteen in Japan had an opposite effect on this. Debts used to be forgiven for minors (previously, up to age twenty) whose parents objected. Now, women can be disaffected at a younger age—though more recently, clubs have started pledging to ban entry to anyone under twenty. The younger the woman, the more susceptible she will be to scams that base self-worth and identity on the love and attention of attractive, charming men.

A major culprit for any host's harsh bullying of women to *buy buy buy* or settle up their old tabs is "tabulation day." Hosts are paid low fixed wages plus a commission based on what they sell. Their ranking per month determines their billing in the marketplace, and top-billed hosts get larger photos and better marketing upfront in the club and around Kabukicho—and are thus more easily sold to customers. Toward the end of each month, clubs calculate the winners and losers, and they award the top host with a trophy—but "unearned" wages, from unpaid tabs, are not counted in this tabulation, and thus, not included in rankings or salaries.

It isn't uncommon for anxiety over tremendous host debt to be so high that an already-drunk woman who has spent far beyond her means might try to slip the bill. At worst, she can't be held accountable for money that's due if she is hospitalized—so women may slit their wrists, sometimes to disastrous consequence, to escape into ambulances and be rendered unaccountable for payments.[227]

With women spending so much on the alcohol, hosts are expected to enjoy it, even to the point of illness or addiction. If a host throws up, he's expected to do so quickly and quietly and then move on, get back out there and binge drink, and not bring down the *vibe*. In this way, neither host nor customer is really looking out for the other person—any sense of care and concern is truly fake. It is all transactional.

Hosts are not expected to be good at anything beyond looking and acting their parts. They should be cute, conversational, and have a

227 Kenji Nakano, "Japan's 'Too Beautiful' Internet Sensation Product of Dark Industry," *Tokyo Reporter*, May 30, 2019, https://www.tokyoreporter.com/crime/japans-too-beautiful-internet-sensation-product-of-dark-industry.

"niche"—a personality that's easily defined or simple to understand. The cool guy, the baby, the quiet guy, the friendly guy. Hosts do a lot of karaoke with clients and are almost exclusively bad singers, which is not only forgiven but rather normal in Japan, where a performance is more about heart and energy than skill. Hosts don't usually make it beyond their mid-thirties in the profession, because their looks dwindle and the alcohol takes a heavy toll, so there's high pressure to earn and save while young. But it can take years to build up a roster of girls who will shell out big money, and hosts must reinvest earnings into appearance upkeep to remain enchanting.

It isn't uncommon, even knowing the way these games are played and playing them themselves, for girls to fall in love with their hosts—and to kill themselves when hosts are "unfaithful" and don't sincerely return that love. It's a difficult part of the job that many hosts endure; for some, it comes with a heavy sense of guilt, for others, puzzlement.

The tragic mystique has disturbingly led to a spate of high school and junior high students jumping off of a Kabukicho rooftop, following a deadly trend. At first, the deaths were attributed to hosts—committing suicide when a woman could not be with her preferred host, or else could not pay them their dues—and then it just became faddish. This idea of dying for love takes on an almost dreamy connotation for young women, and the types who were drawn to the "romantic" stories of lovelorn suicide in the news would eventually also be drawn in by Yuka Takaoka's famous motive for stabbing Phoenix Luna in her apartment: "I love you so much, I couldn't help it."

This phrase would become emblazoned across the internet and spend years festooning Japanese photo-sticker booths, called *purikura.*[228] *Purikura*, or Japanese photo-sticker booths, are an extremely popular activity for young women and groups of girls, where friends or lovers pose for photos in booths, then afterward decorate them on computers with art and phrases, then print them out as sharable stickers. Many booths don't allow men or boys to use them

228 Bunshun Online Editorial Department, "I Got Excited When He Licked My Blood"; "There Were Traces of Him Using a Sanitary Napkin to Stop the Bleeding…"; "What Are the Minors Who Gather in Kabukicho, Next to TOHO, Doing? 2021 BEST 5," Bunshun.jp, May 1, 2022, https://bunshun.jp/articles/-/50978?page=2.

unless they are with girls who have invited them, so it's a safe place for female-coded bonding—and the craze for bonding for a time revolved around Takaoka's chilling words.

After all, hosts sell bottled water for more than $40, thanks to the exploitation of feelings in a falsified relationship based on predatory pricing. Some hosts take their lies so far in the effort to turn a profit that they even promise their marks real relationships or marriage further down the line—always "one day." It gives women something to have to live up to, to aspire to, to keep clinging toward that promise of being special and unlike the other girls—to *one day* marry the prince. And it appealed to a lot of Japanese women, the idea that someone who tried so hard at that same goal—Yuka—and failed had taken back the power in that dynamic.

Despite all the markups and big-name brands, how much does the average host actually make? How much was Luna making when he first met Yuka? A newly minted host like Luna typically makes around $1,150 a month, but has to use a chunk of that to pay for club residence fees, taxes on wages, and hair styling.[229] Dorm fees (new hosts are compelled to stay in club dorms) are heavily subsidized to allow for the newest recruits to gain footing, but that still means at the end of the day, the greenest hosts earn—after paying host expenses—only about $830 a month in cash. The more their clients spend, the more they typically earn; if a client spends $50,000 on a bottle of alcohol, the host earns at least $20,000 on the purchase, heavily encouraging their upselling their host-patron bond. Women are *literally* supporting their boy of choice, the way parents might pay for the lifestyle of an especially spoiled child.

So why do women do it? What is the benefit in playing sugar momma to men who prey on emotional connection with only bouffant hair and a "how to" guide on coercion to show for it? In part, because it imparts a sense of purpose and continuity—someone to come back to, a routine, a feeling of importance women might not have in their own personal, social, or working relationships. Others enjoy getting to spoil someone beautiful and having a sense of

229 Kaneko, "How Japan's Host Clubs Trap."

ownership over them. Some women do it to play out their internalized fairy-tale romances, while still others do it to feel like a pinnacle of beauty themselves—they don't need romance, they need positive affirmation. After all, hosts—though loosely a brotherhood all working towards an individual club's good—*are* competitive. They vie for top spots and entice women away from other workers. That makes them pliable to doing what women want out of them in order to keep them spending. But that sense of competition seeps into the customers, too—very much like in gambling or sports, they *want* their team to win. They *want* their boy to come out on top, to be the most popular, the most handsome, the most special.

Yuka wanted Luna to *win*. And then, she wanted him to thank her properly for her efforts to get him there.

In comparison, for a more laid-back evening on the town, there exist Japan's lower-end "snack bars," catering to clientele willing to shell out—but not quite to the dizzying heights of a host or hostess establishment. They have a few seats at a bar, a karaoke machine, and a "Mama-san," or bar mother, who keeps track of things. A staple of the post-war era, such places cater mostly to locals, emphasizing socializing among patrons as well as with bar hosts and hostesses. Customers have their own bottles on tap and know how much they cost. "Snacks" sell off-the-cuff beer, whiskey, and sake, allow for smoking, and trade mostly in cash. It's a more honest, more hard-boiled version of the luxury that wrapped itself like a noose around Luna's neck.

Phoenix, Down

"Phoenix Luna" almost certainly isn't his real name. The moniker, cobbled together from a jumble of Japanese *kanji* and *kana*, mixing in English sounds, is supposed to be a trendy way to make the youth sound breezy and cool. A fake, jazzy alias is all part of the host persona.

He'd have little idea how precise his pseudonym would soon become following his move to Tokyo—the Phoenix, seemingly felled, before rising from its own ashes after a violent fall.

As a boy, Luna grew up in Nasukarasuyama City in the Tochigi Prefecture. The city crest is a cheerful sun, eyes crinkled in a smile, rising over green mountaintops. While a good representation of the area, Luna's childhood was not so sunny. One of eight siblings, his parents were eventually overwhelmed with the responsibilities of guardianship and derelict in their parental duties. They gave their children up to a local orphanage.

Nasukarasuyama, nestled in the Shiona Hills and shaded by the Yamizo Mountains, has its old town center directly on the banks of the Naka River—more of a wildly unkempt stream, at this part in its bend. Even the city's newer neighborhoods look wild with overgrowth and battered in rust, its commercial properties few and far between and its mostly old-style gabled homes imposing to trespassers. There are large swathes of woods cut across in hiking trails that feel as if you could get lost and never be found upon them.

Humid, the area gets a lot of snowfall in winter and a lot of rain in summer, a climate that allows it to sustain itself mostly through agricultural economy—dairy farms and vegetable produce. A far cry from the glitz and white-collar work of Tokyo, its single public high school concerns itself with teaching students how to use smartphones and warning against the dangers of poor posture while digesting subsidized school lunches. The municipal council warns citizens about wild dogs sighted in the city center and loans out ultrasonic cat-repellant devices to prevent strays from defecating in homes and cars.[230]

Nasukarasyuma has two social welfare buildings for children, with its home in Tochigi prefecture having many more, bestowed names like Neverland or Easter Village. Kikyo Ryo, one of the two homes in Nasukarasyuma, advises that the children living on that campus are unable to be with their families anymore—implying that many are not traditional orphans—and gives the foreboding counsel, "[Since] children living in the facility [have] been admitted for different reasons, they must make an effort to live an enjoyable life while being considerate and cooperative with each other."[231] The

230 Accessed on June 6, 2024, https://www-city-nasukarasuyama-lg-jp.

231 "Welcome to Kikyo Ryo, a social welfare corporation," Kikyou.org, accessed May 1, 2025, http://www.kikyou.org.

five dormitories are bleak, three-floor accommodations with a sand lot featuring four swings and a single set of monkey bars, donated. July is a difficult month for contributions to the facility and strange donations come in often enough the rest of the year: champagne, soil conditioner, plain taro root flour, a nonfiction book titled *Manga: The History of Japan*—donated on three separate occasions. Importantly, water was donated when a typhoon broke the dormitory's main lines and plunged the children into crisis.[232]

Meiwaen is another children's facility in Nasukarasyuma. Housed in austere concrete, the facility has a guiding philosophy of *gratitude* and *self-reliance*. Its campus lies up a wooded street, thickly overgrown, and is one of those rare places totally inaccessible by Google Earth. It does not accept the donation of goods and supplies, and it does not dole out candies, pears, and mandarin oranges to its children the way Kikyo Ryo does. Dwarfed by green hills, it is sequestered away with a small Buddhist temple in a complex with only one accessible road, so far outside the city center that running away would be laughable unless one planned to commune with bears.

While it's unclear which of these two facilities Luna was brought to with his siblings (the latter being more likely), or if they were even placed into these foster facilities all together, what can be extrapolated is the almost-total guarantee that once Luna was surrendered by his parents, he would fail to be a "successful" or "normal" member of Japanese civic society. Despite all the goodwill and best wishes of staff and supporters, Japanese orphanages are some of the bleakest in any first-world country. Because of old biases and the unique way the country handles the transition into adulthood, a considerable number of orphans and surrendered children become homeless adults or are forced to transition into sex work to stay off the streets. No clear statistics exist on the extent of homelessness for youth transitioning out of the care system. This means the true extent of the issue hasn't yet become *important* enough in the eyes of the government to pour funds into investigating.

232 "2024 Fiscal Year," Kikyou.org, accessed May 1, 2025, http://www.kikyou.org/custom.html.

Most orphans in Japan enter care facilities for one of three reasons. 1. They are not "true" orphans, but have parents who domestically abuse or neglect them. 2. Their parents have died, and their extended family is unable or unwilling to take them in. 3. They come from homes with mental illness or financial insecurity, and parents have asked for their children to become government wards. Over 38% of children who come to live in these group homes have suffered severe and repeated violence, and nearly 60% have been seriously neglected.[233]

In most first-world countries, such children would move into the foster care system as hastily as possible, where they'd live a family-style life, await possible adoption, and in the meantime, bond with foster parents and siblings. They'd live in regular city homes, have ordinary rooms and living rooms and kitchens, go to public schools, and receive personalized care. Foster care is already difficult for children, but in Japan, it's also inaccessible.

Some 82% of surrendered or parentless children in the US and 72% in Britain are placed with foster care families; in South Korea the statistic stands at 47%.[234] Yet in Japan, only a dismaying 16% of facility children are moved to foster care homes, a statistic that, as of 2017, was a massive improvement over historic numbers. While there is a governmental push through the Child Welfare Act to place a third of all facility children into foster homes by 2029, it's barreling against difficult odds. Stigma exists, not rooted in psychological and social science, but a pervasive general belief that fostered children will grow too attached to their temporary families and will find it impossible to relocate to a new family should they be adopted.

Research shows the opposite—that such children are more grounded in the idea of family and have an easier time communicating with and relying on adults than do their dormitory-held peers. Foster homing should be a priority, in fact, since Japanese youth face the calamitous reality that there is almost no hope of adoption for

233 Alexandra Hongo, "'3keys' NPO Founder Sheds Light on Japan's Poor Orphanage Conditions," *Japan Today*, May 26, 2016, https://japantoday.com/category/features/lifestyle/3-keys-npo-founder-sheds-light-on-japans-child-inequality-poor-orphanage-conditions.

234 Emile Shah, "Japan's Forgotten Children," *Berkeley Political Review*, October 29, 2023, https://bpr.studentorg.berkeley.edu/2023/10/29/japans-forgotten-children.

them. Japan's official naming registry makes it awkward for children to join a new family, but more than that, old-world ideas of *blood ties* being what makes family render adoption anathema in the country with one of the world's lowest birth rates. More traditional ideology snubs the idea of accepting into the family one who is not "your own."

Japan's statistics on the matter are skewed, though. Bizarrely, Japan has the second-highest adoption rate in the world, at roughly 80,000 adoptions per year. That's more than double the number of children in the care system currently—yet only 7% of Japanese children in need of families get adopted.[235] Compare that to the US, where 46% of foster children are reunited with their families and 27% are adopted.[236] So, who are the tens of thousands of people being adopted in Japan annually? They are adults in their late twenties and thirties, being made family by businesspeople who have no children of their own—so they can be named heirs of companies or land holdings and to avoid certain taxes that these turnovers would trigger, were they not related.[237] These are often transactional arrangements benefiting young adults who have "proven themselves," often by being already extensively educated, put together, and well-off.

Because of the lack of fostering or adoption of actual children, Japan's care facilities are overrun. Acting sometimes more as shelters than homes, they're a chilling echo of the fact that one in every six children in the country lives in poverty.[238] There aren't enough resources nor one-on-one time for individual children, who often have to share bedrooms and bathrooms and careworn toys with many others. Education—the hallmark of Japanese youth routine—is difficult for them, as upheaval has interrupted their schooling, they don't have quiet and clear spaces to study, and they don't have parents to pay for after-school study programs, which are often deeply neces-

235 Kelly Buchanan, "Many Adoptions in Japan Are Not About Raising Children," Library of Congress, April 5, 2017, https://blogs.loc.gov/law/2017/04/many-adoptions-in-japan-are-not-about-raising-children.

236 "Facts Sheet," CCAI, accessed June 10, 2024, https://www.ccainstitute.org/resources/fact-sheets.

237 Buchanan, "Many Adoptions in Japan Are Not About Raising Children."

238 Hongo, "'3keys' NPO Founder Sheds Light."

sary to pass the standardized testing to get into university, or to apply for high schools.

By age six, 80% of Japanese schoolchildren are usually attending additional after-school lessons.[239] In elementary school, that number slumps to 19%, then catapults to over 52% of students in late middle school attending *juku*, or after-school cram courses designed to prepare them for those entrance exams. Scores on the college exams determine which universities students may apply to. Which university they attend—its public ranking—has a huge impact on what full-time jobs students are able to access after graduation—which companies, and what ranks in those companies. *Baito*, or part-time work, is looked down on for adults. It all connects, and once someone steps a toe out of the line, they'll often trip when trying to rejoin the queue.

Another issue for system children is that school in Japan is only mandatory through junior high. High school is where many in the care system drop out, fully aware that they will have to immediately begin work upon leaving their dormitory, at age eighteen. They cannot afford college and feel pressure to start finding ways to save money as young teenagers to prevent the very real threat of oncoming homelessness. Even if such a student wanted to go to high school, despite the uphill battle, they'd still have to apply and be accepted—meaning that care-system students who want to continue their education, but who are at a disadvantage with study, may still find that junior high is their finish line, at age fifteen. High school is not necessarily promised to everyone who wants to go.

A staggering 71.6% of care-system children say they either don't plan to or don't want to engage in continuing education, mostly, one would think, because of how the systems fail to meet their needs.[240] Those who do manage to beat the odds and go to college don't have the same experience as other students. They rely on working at the same time as going to school, have no safety net at all, and often report that they're unable to socialize. It just takes too much time and

---

239 Yasuo Kojima, "After-School Activities of Japanese Elementary School Children: Comparison of Children Who Attend Lessons and Cram Schools with Those Who Do Not," *Journal of Physical Activity and Health* 21, no. 5 (2024): 472–80, https://doi.org/10.1123/jpah.2023-0642.

240 Hongo, "'3keys' NPO Founder Sheds Light."

money; meeting friends for coffee, spending a night singing karaoke, or joining a uniformed team is fiscally out of reach, a privilege that often leaves them embarrassed, asking others to cover their food or drink. They end up isolated, without the social bonds that help make college an important experience.

In addition to being significantly behind their peers in terms of education, many children experience neglect, bullying, and abuse *within* the system, and again once outside of it because of their status as "familyless." These are lost children who face ire from all sides. It is already assumed by society that they will be a societal burden and will ultimately work in "unimportant" sectors, being less accomplished than their peers—it is expected that they may turn to gang life, thievery, or prostitution.

The odds are stacked against them; it is extremely difficult to emerge from this system victorious over one's circumstances. And the final nail in that coffin is the age at which the system spits youngsters out.

As previously mentioned, in Japan, the historic age of majority is twenty years old. The age that children are pushed out of the care system? Eighteen.

A large part of the recent change in the Japanese Civil Code to shift the age of majority down to eighteen in the spring of 2022 was the disastrous effect that being twenty was having on care-system youth. When Luna was shoved into the world, not yet an adult in the eyes of the law in 2017, it was because the care facilities could no longer afford to keep anyone in his age bracket. On paper he couldn't legally drink, smoke, vote, or enter into contracts without parental consent. At eighteen he *could* get a driver's license to help him get a job, but that would cost between $2,000 and $3,000. (Government subsidization for licenses for care-system youth is another only recent development, with a subsidy of just $550,[241] making affording a license—much less the driving lessons to apply for one, or renting or owning personal transport for work at just eighteen—laughably out of reach.)

241 Amy Braunschweiger,"Witness: Lack of Support in Japanese Orphanages," HRW.org, May 1, 2014, https://www.hrw.org/news/2014/05/01/witness-lack-support-japanese-orphanages.

Before the legislative change, Japan—which is home to more than 34,000 care-facility children, with numbers on a steep year-by-year rise—was churning out children to compete with adults in the job market. Literally, by definition *legal*, children. The first thing these children had to do was find a place to live. But Japanese apartments are notoriously difficult to rent. In addition to being unable to get the required parental "consent" for a lot of the forms, system children often wouldn't typically have the down payment required (usually three months' rent), and certainly no guarantor—often a requirement. The orphanage could only fulfil the guarantor requirement for a child's first contract, if they chose to do so at all—but as care facilities are strictly unable to take these children back in and cannot pay if the child fails to make rent, landlords view such applications with a wary eye.

In addition, these youngsters couldn't independently register their needs with the government for relief, nor sign up for cell phones, passports, credit cards, loans, or bank savings accounts, stymied by being unable to enter into contracts without parental consent for two whole years after leaving the facilities. Only recently have orphanages and care facilities been trying to provide better transitional help. Previously, they were simply too strapped to support the huge number of floundering young men and women pushed outside their walls against the tide of government regulation. Many children who still had living parents would return to them to beg for help, only to be abused, exploited, and let down by the families that had already abandoned them, finding themselves even worse off than before.

All of this amounted to the hardest part of turning eighteen in the system being the need for *immediate* housing—being kicked out of your dorm just one day after your birthday, yet having little recourse for getting a place to live, even if by some miracle you'd saved up enough money for down payments by starting work at the age of fifteen. Thus, the key type of job these teenagers often looked for was one that provided dormitory housing to workers—construction work, farm work, factory work, and nightlife or sex work—with many of these jobs favoring men over women. Kids who can't land or hack these jobs will often get *baito* and pay small amounts to stay overnight in cubicles at manga or internet cafés, or else they sneak in to sleep in public parks. (Sleeping rough is barred by some local ordinances, and bigger Japanese cities employ "hostile" anti-homeless architecture.[242] Japan boasts an almost 0% homelessness rate, the best in the world, but this statistic doesn't take into account the "hidden homeless" who scrape enough together to wash up and sleep in computer or comic cafés, where an overnight stay for eight hours can cost as little as $10 a night, allowing them to shuttle between part-time work and their rest cubicle. Just as artificially high adoption statistics hide abandoned children, so, too, do homelessness statistics.)

Luna was placed in the system during elementary school. When he graduated junior high, he was unable to get a spot in a high school, and so, at fifteen years old, he began working a job in construction. After being fired for being too difficult to get along with, now eighteen and newly unable to stay at his work dormitory or his youth facility, he found himself homeless and living on the street. So, he turned to sex work.

Luna made his way to Tokyo and then to Kabukicho, to its infamous Host Club Street, known for its pretty boys on demand. In November, with the city newly bursting into autumn leaves and its thoroughfares coming alive with *yosakoi* dancers, Luna interviewed at a bar called FUSION BY YOUTH and was accepted as a host trainee.

Though this put him automatically in debt to the bar—a debt he'd work off—they gave him a place in their dormitory and got him set up there, filled up his belly with hot food and tea, and gave him a "family" of older brothers to look after him, teach him, style him, and help him adjust. It was the first time in his life he'd felt a real sense of *home*. Luna was desperately thin and fragile by then, but had a comely face and good hair, wide eyes easily accentuated by colored contact lenses, and big lips that gave him a bone-warm smile. They got him dyed and dressed, taught him the ropes of being charming and convincing, and set him on his way.

---

242 Philip Brasor, "How Hostile Design Keeps Japan's Homeless at Arm's Length," *The Japan Times*, December 12, 2020, https://www.japantimes.co.jp/news/2020/12/12/national/media-national/homeless-bench-designs.

At this job—being a host—one gets personal attention, has their food and drink paid for by those renting their time, invests in self-image, and has a support system of other men to fall back on—all the things Luna lacked before. Hosts who are too easily embarrassed by being used, have too much pride to whine and cajole girls into paying for them, or can't handle the dog-eat-dog competition in the higher ranks don't find success. A lack of pretension, a focus on being engaging and mysterious, and not having too much of an authentic identity to share with strangers is a plus. Luna was built for it.

The persona he'd chosen for himself, despite the fiery name, was based on the idea of darkness, of pain. A catchphrase of his, used on all of his marketing when he made it to the club's #4 spot, would become "Luna gives into the pain." His look, carefully curated, featured wide sweeping bangs dyed dark brown, textured hair, fitted black suits with dark mottled ties, and silver earrings. A *cool* look.

Having also lost track of his siblings, with no way to contact them since they had also largely been expelled from their facilities, this new life would have to do. He'd already been separated from some of them for a long time, and now he had new "siblings"—he was their precious *kohai*, their younger brother in the chain of command.

At twenty years old, Luna was finally ready to tackle a roster of guests, becoming popular very quickly for his amiable personality and tapered good looks. As far as he was concerned, FUSION BY YOUTH was "The only place I could return to. I grew up in an orphanage.... So it was like the seniors in this restaurant were my first real family."[243]

For the almost full year Luna worked there, the club did well in its space in the TOA 6 building, with its stunning view from the sixth floor. It oozed a welcoming feeling with its stylish open floor plan and advertised aggressively both on the streets and on social media via online blogs. Hosts were especially needed for the early morning shifts, around 6 a.m.—when a lot of hostesses finish up, but hosts

243 "Host Stabbed by Woman Confesses, 'I Love You So Much,' What Happened That Day?" News Post Seven, September 7, 2019, https://www.news-postseven.com/archives/20190709_1408290.html?DETAIL.

catering to them are hard at work. And that is how Luna and Yuka began to spend time together in earnest.

Not only did Luna rise in the individual host ranks speedily, but he rose to the position of executive assistant at the club quickly as well. Women did love him; he often received the most nominations for special ranks, more than even the head host at the club or whichever host got the #1 spot month to month. He climbed his way into second place in terms of overall earnings and then, in May of 2019, into first place. This was largely thanks to Yuka's help. And this would be part of what triggered her explosive outrage.

FUSION BY YOUTH wasn't all songs and games. Even outside of the incident that would nearly claim Luna's life, other occurrences would land it in hot water and on the news. In one such episode, another FUSION hosts—a man named Hiro Kawakami—punched a customer just six months after Luna was stabbed in Yuka's apartment.[244] Hiro was told by a female customer that he was a bad singer (not unusual), and she poured a drink on him after the diss. He went to hit the woman who'd insulted him and ended up instead fracturing the interior surface of another woman's eye, a young lady who'd stepped up to beg a stop to the fight.[245] He split her retina, optic disc, macula, and fovea—and was immediately arrested.

Hiro, like Luna, was a newer host, but much less popular. Stout and a bit unruly-looking, with blond-dyed spikes in a close-crop fade hairstyle, the Kanagawa-born host assaulted the woman at an after-hours karaoke bar called Uta Hiro (ironically located on Godzilla Road, and certainly qualifying as a rampage in Tokyo), not actually on site at FUSION. But it's likely that one or more of the women were customers, to be hanging out with Hiro after hours.

After numerous incidents, Luna's being the most famous, FUSION BY YOUTH would be forced to close its doors.

244 "「FUSION ByYouth」 ホスト比呂が音痴とディスられ客を殴り逮捕," Gekiura.com, June 11, 2019, https://gekiura.com/post/33149.

245 "「FUSION ByYouth」," Gekiura.com.

ConFUSION Brewing

Yuka was a year older than Luna, which made the slim and sweet boy seem even more pleasant. One of the most attractive "types" in Japan—where people are sorted into buckets for their looks and attitude to determine their appeal to prospective partners—is "refreshing." A tidy, clean, and youthful appearance is often the most favored for men.

Not much about Yuka before her move to Tokyo, or before Luna, is really public knowledge. She was an obstinate only child, not originally from the area. She did well enough on the college entrance exams to place into university, only to drop out in her first year for the purpose of taking up work at a Girls Bar in Tokyo, to start her career early and shed her training wheels.[246]

Girls Bars are a hostess-adjacent concept. Again, it's the murky idea of sex work: It's not on the official menu, and in no way promised, but flirtation is at a premium in terms of service, and especially good regulars might expect more out of the working women there. It costs money per hour or half-hour to even sit in such a bar, considered the entertainment fee, and from there the cocktails and champagne result in extra, run-up charges. Rules-wise, sex is a complete no-no; in reality, the lines blur.

These bars exclusively feature young, attractive female bartenders who sling marked-up drinks and provide banter and companionship to male buyers. While women aren't barred from entry, they are actively discouraged, gay or not. Female staffers are the main attraction; depending on the bar, they will dress up for men, sing for them, drink with them, light their cigarettes, give them hugs, perform skits, or serve as DJs. Some bars allow girls to brazenly exchange numbers or email addresses with men, while others don't. They're usually small spaces with single countertops lined by bar stools, sometimes with side tables hugging close to the action. The point is for the atmosphere to be intimate, and women have to be near enough to all of the customers to chat with them.

246 Nakano, "Japan's 'Too Beautiful' Internet Sensation."

Yuka, though achieving a higher position than most of the other girls, would still have been expected to sing, flirt, and mix highballs most days of the week, dolled up in cutesy outfits. Her original Instagram profile noted one of the Girls Bars she'd worked at was "New Sensation Girl's Bar, Tokimeki BinBim," a 1980s-themed affair in Kabukicho's Arai building.

She was almost immediately promoted to management. Her job allowed her freedom in the daytime and a large amount of disposable income, a chunk of which she'd spend on her fifth-floor apartment in the Plaire Deuxq building in Shinjuku, a luxury rental spot. Her apartment was all white marble tile, with good light and handsome balconies with stunning views of Tokyo, especially at night, when she'd least get to enjoy them. Rent there for a one-bedroom ran about $1,600 a month,[247] which may seem cheap to Western urban dwellers, but a one-bedroom apartment in Tokyo averaged just $730 a month, with even three-bedroom apartments typically costing less than what she was paying.[248]

At the time, Yuka was gaining renown online via her Instagram, where she posted cute photos of herself dolled up for work in Shinjuku, or sometimes wearing cosplay. As with Snow, the character she liked to portray online was *yandere*: cute and cuddly on the outside, jealous and vicious on the inside. Yuka would even go so far as to note this was her favorite "type" in any story, and that she related strongly to them.

Yuka was a big fan of manga, anime, and video games. Especially the aesthetic. She liked to wear maid outfits or don ultra-cute oversized cardigans, then take silly photos to post online that highlighted her big eyes (made wider with unnaturally large Circle-brand contact lenses), her thin lips lilting into her favorite keen cat-like smile. When not wearing a wig, she had babydoll-style fringed bangs and often curled her bottle-dyed rusty brown hair. A favorite character of hers to cosplay was Himiko Toga—again, in a callback to the Snow case,

247 "Plaire Deuxq Shinjuku West," Plaza Homes, accessed July 10, 2024, https://www.realestate-tokyo.com/rent/B0023144/plaire-deuxq-shinjuku-west.

248 Alex Shapiro, "Cost to Rent an Apartment in Tokyo," TokyoPortfolio.com, last updated March 17, 2025, https://tokyoportfolio.com/tokyo-apartment-rent-cost.

this was the *My Hero Academia* villain who uses blood to mimic others and shows her love through violence and murder.

In addition to being small, cute, and apparently a little dark, Yuka had a soft, sweet voice, lyrically high-pitched, with a slow, deliberate way of speaking. These traits made her increasingly popular online as well as with men at the bar. People liked to talk with her.

Yuka truly fit the part of both elegant bar manager and slightly off-beat *yandere*. Her own personality was typically quiet and mawkish, but was often perforated by *bursts* of agitated energy. She could be impulsive, peculiar, and had a barbed sense of humor. At other times, she played the unassailable part of the honeyed good girl, the composed older sister to the other working girls, then unruffled leader.

She posted her content—mainly endearing, filtered, often wildly-angled and grainy photos, decorated with things like mustaches and cat whiskers—to her Instagram, her Twitter (mostly in cosplay), and a now somewhat-defunct YouTube profile. For someone merely dabbling in content creation without dedicating a huge amount of time or effort to it, she had a solid amount of engagement. But soon—after plunging a knife into Phoenix Luna—she'd become an online *sensation*, a hashtag, and an unapologetic starlet.

Luna met her the opposite way that most people in the red-light industry meet—*he* stumbled upon *her* rather than the other way around. Around January 9, just after the Christmas season (considered a romantic holiday in Japan, one for lovers and city light-ups) and the long spate of New Year's celebrations, Luna wandered into Yuka's bar.[249] They chatted for a while, exchanged information, and that was that.

That was Luna's version of the story. Yuka's version was that they had met a year before that at her bar, in October of 2018.[250] Either way, radio silence followed.

249 "Host Stabbed by Woman Confesses," News Post Seven.

250 "Shinjuku Yandere Knife Bread Recent News," J-Cast.com, April 12, 2019, https://www.j-cast.com/tv/2019/12/04374268.html.

At the initial meeting, Luna had spoken about his new life in the environs of Tokyo, explaining to her, "I'm hosting now."[251] Luna didn't visit her establishment after that. They wouldn't cross paths again until months later, when Yuka located Luna's club. She ordered him off the menu as her host, then rapidly became a frequent customer of his, visiting FUSION once or twice a week.[252] She had actually been immediately smitten with Luna and had tracked him down.

From there, the tango of host and customer began, creating a lot of confusion for the eventual media circus—and for Yuka herself. Originally described as "dating," it would seem that was a one-sided impression, a fantasy Luna was selling Yuka rather than based in any sincere feelings he had—he was just a host doing his best job to keep her coming back for more. As with many hosts and their women, Yuka and Luna even began to see each other a bit outside of work—though Luna would insist this was harmless and friendly. In subtle ways, Yuka began to pressure him to move in with her, viewing her apartment as *their* eventual apartment—later, even reporters would be confused about whether they were living together (they were not).

She was almost always the one making the overtures and extending invitations. They went to movies together and visited one of her favorite spots, the local cat café, a popular date location where customers can order cutesy coffees and play with kittens. She was dedicated to supporting Luna. She did so with advice and direction. Luna wasn't a big drinker, despite his profession, so she taught him tricks on how to avoid alcohol himself by letting others drink more, and how also to make the biggest impact on a small number of customers during a slow day.[253]

She knew how the host system worked, of course, but she wanted to help him at his game. She nominated him rigorously for FUSION's number one host spot, and with her dedication—her enthusiasm, time, and especially money—he finally clinched first place for the first time in May of 2019, thanks to a hefty April tabulation largely paid for by Yuka.

---

251 Accessed on June 6, 2024, https://x.com/kawaiiguccigang/status/1153239545720131584.

252 "Host Stabbed by Woman Confesses," News Post Seven.

253 "Host Stabbed by Woman Confesses," News Post Seven.

Yuka felt comfortable being her truest self, her most frantic self, in front of Luna. This was worth its weight in yen—and a sizable weight it was. On every visit she'd spend between $3,200 and $3,900.[254] That would mean that she spent more than $21,000 getting Luna into first place in May alone. In response—direct from the host playbook—Luna had responded with, "Let's get married in the future. I'll quit hosting in September."[255]

There is a lack of clarity around their relationship they shared outside of FUSION. Luna was certainly flirting with her, but he also must have thought that as a Kabukicho worker herself, she understood it was a fiction. As friends, they were seeing one another outside of work more frequently, and it's unclear whether Yuka had already had her Plaire Deuxq apartment when she'd met Luna, or if she'd moved into it to have a crash space closer to FUSION, so he could drop by more regularly after work. Whatever the case, she seemed to think that the next natural step toward marriage was living together, and Luna seemed comfortable sleeping over at her place when the need arose. Still, he'd later *insist*, "We didn't live together, we weren't dating—just good friends."[256]

Yuka was intent on marrying him but content just to love him—jealously, though. He was her only love, and so, she must be his. Luna, for his part, saw no warning signs. He assumed they had the typical association between host and customer—fake intimacy, false promises, an understanding that this was a fairy tale bound to curdle.

Because she'd done so much to help him, though, when she asked him to visit her apartment to help her clean up the place, he readily accepted.[257] She was expecting a big delivery and needed a second person to tidy the place up. Luna could absolutely do that.

I Like You, Too!

Yuka's apartment building sets the scene. The building was no stranger to tragedy.

254 "Shinjuku Yandere Knife Bread Recent News," J-Cast.com.

255 "Shinjuku Yandere Knife Bread Recent News," J-Cast.com.

256 @kawaiiguccigang, accessed June 6, 2024.

257 "Host Stabbed by Woman Confesses," News Post Seven.

The complex houses mainly red-light district workers and high rollers who can afford to rent a second or third apartment close to the city's epicenter of fun. So it's par for the course that fights break out around it, street-side or in the units, from jealous lovers finding cheating spouses, to hosts and hostesses giving frustrated customers the pointy end of a hard "no."

In the last decade and a half, the building has seen its fair share of bloodshed, too. There was a stabbing once; a suicide, where a woman who was in steep debt to a host bounded to her death from the balcony of a high floor; and then there was the murder of the seventy-seven-year-old playboy, the "Don Juan of Kishu." Kosuke Nozaki, said playboy, boasted of sleeping with over 4,000 women in the Tokyo red-light district and also bragged that he paid to maintain all those women, despite being married to twenty-two-year-old Saki Sudo. He was found dead of poisoning in connection to the apartment building, but his murderer was never found—Sudo, who maintained her innocence, was acquitted.[258]

It was the perfect place for a *yandere* princess.

After Yuka had invited Luna over to help her clean, she was a little annoyed when he ran late, held up by work. Already extremely possessive of him, she was on edge, resentful of the long hours he was putting in entertaining other women. That was a massive "no-no" in the world they lived in, letting jealousy bleed over onto the profession.

When Luna finally arrived at the apartment, it was 3 p.m. She'd expected him at around noon, when his shift usually wrapped up, but he'd been up all night and into the day first working, and then helping staff clean up. His hours had run well into overtime and he was exhausted.[259] Still, because she had a delivery coming, Luna stepped in and helped her neaten the place up. Once that task was cleared, on the back of his full morning, Luna was *beyond* exhausted. He asked if he could take a bath to wash himself up in order to take a nap at the apartment, wanting to be clean before borrowing her

---

258 Nakano, "Japan's 'Too Beautiful' Internet Sensation."

259 "Host Stabbed by Woman Confesses," News Post Seven.

bed for a few hours' sleep. He only had underwear to wear to bed, since his clothes were dirty, but that wasn't a problem. Yuka agreed.

While Luna was bathing, she picked up his phone and began to scroll through it. Inside, of course, were flirtatious and coaxing messages from other women, other customers. But he couldn't help what women texted him. What was worse, inexcusable to her, was what she found on his camera roll. It was suffused with photos of him with other women at the club—photos not purely for the women's sake but for himself, photos that he'd *kept* of himself with other girls.[260] This, she concluded, was proof that he was stepping outside their promise—that he was being emotionally and physically intimate with other women.

She instantly became wildly envious and decided she only had one recourse. While he slept, she would just have to kill him. If they couldn't be together in life, then he'd just have to die; maybe then they could be together in death.

At around 3:50 a.m., when Luna was deep into the throes of REM sleep, lying neatly in her sheets in just a pair of boxer shorts, his chest and torso naked, Yuka grabbed a kitchen knife. She sat on the edge of the bed, then suddenly straddled him and thrust the blade down hard into the soft side of his belly, to its hilt.

The sudden plunge of the knife into his guts woke Luna with a start. The first thing he remembers is feeling confusion—and fear. Nerves alight, mind groggy, he didn't yet feel the hurt of his wound as he processed the image before him, laser-focusing on the knife jutting straight up from out of him. Luna, then wide-eyed, would shove Yuka off as she lunged to grab at him.

She began to babble to him that she liked him and wanted to be with him, thinking this was the way to bond them, the correct thing to do. "Do you like *me*? Tell me you love me!"[261]

---

260 "Yuka Takaoka," Wikipedia.

261 "Host Stabbed by Woman Confesses," News Post Seven.

He shouted back at her, "Yes, I like you!"[262] His motive was simple: survival. He was hoping she'd have a sudden stroke of empathy and would stop trying to hurt him and instead call for an ambulance. Even then, his mind worked in quick ticks of manipulation. *She likes me, so she'll help me if I say I like her back.*

Colloquially, the word "like" is the same as the word "love" in Japanese. Luna knew that, even in his state, just as Yuka knew it was time for them to die together. "I don't want you to go.... I love you so much," Yuka would narrate to him as he bled out ... then fled out.

"I was in a panic and thought I would die.... I was desperately running away."[263] Luna would later describe the scene.

The knife clattered out of him at some point in the scuffle around the apartment, with her chasing, and him dancing away in a flail of gore-slicked limbs. Luna ran, wildly, and Yuka pursued, just as hectic. He didn't have a destination in mind as he flitted around furniture, dodging her—he just knew he had to get *away* from her, in any direction, now desperate with the idea that he was going to be killed. Finally, gaining some semblance of a plan, he made a beeline for the front door, where she would try to claw him back inside. Luna threw her off.

He somehow found the strength to fling himself into the hall, holding his gurgling wound as he went. He pressed to call the elevator, and mercifully, its arrival would beat his attacker. Yuka, held up by losing a contact lens tussle, had paused to remove the other one and switch to her glasses.[264] She wanted to see him die, with perfect vision. So, like a serial killer in a '90s movie, she'd stalk very slowly after her prey.

In fact, in a deeply unhurried move, she'd grab cigarettes, a lighter, and Luna's phone.[265] Later, the walls of the elevator would be found smeared with his blood, the floor soaked with it, the buttons

---

262 Tokyo Reporter Staff, "Yuka Takaoka Incident: Gruesome Details Emerge About 'Crime of Passion,'" *Tokyo Reporter*, June 4, 2019, https://www.tokyoreporter.com/crime/yuka-takaoka-incident-gruesome-details-emerge-about-crime-of-passion.

263 @kawaiiguccigang, accessed June 6, 2024.

264 Coffeehouse Crime, "The Real Life Yandere Girl | The Strange Case of Yuka Takaoka," YouTube, March 2, 2021, https://www.youtube.com/watch?v=UgBFeZXQwoO.

265 "Shinjuku Yandere Knife Bread Recent News," J-Cast.com.

for the third and fourth floors hastily and deliriously pressed with mired hands. She'd ride in it after him, paying the scene no mind. He'd have made it down into the lobby, hoping to burst forth onto the street to beg for help—but he'd only make it to the entryway, where he'd be felled by blood loss, and would collapse unconscious—not to wake again for nearly a week.

Yuka daintily sat down beside him when she caught up, wishing to stay with him while he died, wanting them to be together in those final, precious moments. "I did not want to go anywhere.... I did not call emergency services [for Luna] because I intended to die after watching him die.... Since I loved him so much, I just couldn't help it," she said.[266]

"Since I loved him so much, I just couldn't help it" would become a catchphrase that teen girls around Japan would hail as a symbol of purest love, echoing it in pop culture. A *yandere* love. Killing and dying for what you wanted, to be together in the afterlife, somehow became an esteemed version of romance for jilted teenagers, moved by both Yuka's beauty and twisted devotion as much as they were by Luna's handsomeness. 'I did it for love' was instantly transformed from a sickly justification for attempted murder into a movement around Japan concerning feelings—their depth, their capacities. So very like *Romeo and Juliet*—only very much not.

Yuka, who an hour later was photographed grinning in the backseat of a police car, her teeth glinting in the newly risen morning light, would become a venerated celebrity.

At some point in all of this, she'd even idly written *I love you, I love you, I love you* ... in his blood.

A neighbor called the police.

That is what saved Luna's life. Spotting him as they were coming inside, they'd call for ambulatory services and police officers, who arrived just in time.

As the news stories began to go viral, bloodied and grinning photos of Yuka started capturing national attention and a bizarre level of admiration. More and more netizens began looking Yuka

266 Nakano, "Japan's 'Too Beautiful' Internet Sensation."

Takaoka up online. Then, they began to empathize with her, drawing parallels between her story and their own lives—their own traumas over emotional or romantic rejection. People felt she was a "true *yandere*," a real-life example of some of their favorite characters brought to life. Many women idolized the *yandere* type for their unflinching ability to both conform to norms while, inwardly, violently rejecting them. Many men admired the trope because it presented the type of woman they'd want to date: beautiful, obsessed with their man, devastatingly loyal in love, even willing to die for their partner. This characterization, paired with Yuka's classic hostess good looks—natural in the light of day in those photographs, without any makeup or styling, her hair back in a short ponytail in the cop car, wispy, her posture upright in an oversized gray sweater that helps her look smaller, poised and demure, then wildly cheerful—men began to fall for how attractive and dedicated she was, while women were enticed by her commitment to love. A fandom sprouted around her.

She began to trend on Instagram, with people calling her the "too-beautiful criminal."[267] Fan websites began to pop up, social media handles dedicated to her began to collect photos, people began making art of her, students began mimicking her voice and poses, poems were penned in her name. Yuka had struck a national nerve—rather than it simply affecting people on the fringe, a specific set of marginal *otaku* of true crime or animanga, Yuka hit public interest dead on, a bullseye. She was popular with teenagers torn up after being overlooked by a love interest. She was popular with young adult men who wanted someone cute and devoted like her, imagining that they would have treated her better. She was popular with adults who espoused that her story showed the dangers of red-light work, a poor victim who had fallen prey to Kabukicho.

She was adored by the anime and cosplay communities, who saw her dedication to the *yandere* trope as admirable. She interested elderly people who liked stories of the underworld, because the crime had involved a host and a Girls Bar manager. She also interested that enraged set of women who had been done wrong by

---

267 Nakano, "Japan's 'Too Beautiful' Internet Sensation."

hosts, starting up a national conversation on predatory pricing. It was a potent blend of celebrity worship, parasocial relationship-building, and natural sympathy people feel in greater measure for attractive young people.

Somewhere in all the fanfare, the plot was lost.

She's stabbed a man with intent to kill who had come over to help tidy up after his long workday. She never shied away from that, eventually stating, "I felt a strong desire to die. I wanted to kill him and die, too. It was very hard, and the only way to be with him was to kill him and die."[268]

The prosecution leaned into that during her trial in December of 2019, demanding she get five years in prison for attempted murder. She was found guilty, which may illicit a *Well, naturally!* What followed was less expected.

Phoenix Luna, when he woke from the coma she'd put him in, would argue in favor of a lesser sentence for her, telling the judge, "If possible, I want [her] to be able to lead a normal life rather than paying for her sins." He even filed a petition to that effect and submitted it to the court.

The judge agreed that, despite the obvious nature of the crime, she should only face three and a half years of prison time for coming a hair's breadth away from remorselessly costing Luna his life—she had not even called for emergency services, after all, unlike Snow or even Abigail White. She was also ordered by the court to continue to support Luna, this time to the tune of nearly $40,000 in medical fees and lost wages, as restitution for her crime.[269]

She went to serve her sentence on December 5, 2019, and was released in 2023. Members of both legal teams found it odd, the forthright manner in which Luna described the sequence of events, as well as his easy forgiveness of his assailant.

When he'd reached the hospital, sometime between 4 and 5 a.m. that day in May of 2019, Luna had only a 20% chance of survival. He'd been stabbed in the liver, an organ very much needed for his alcohol-soaked profession, and the injury was so serious that

268 "Host Stabbed by Woman Confesses," News Post Seven.

269 Nakano, "Japan's 'Too Beautiful' Internet Sensation."

he remained unconscious for five days after collapsing in the lobby. When he woke up, the pain was intolerable, and he found it difficult to move or speak for weeks, his weight melting off of him and leaving him reedy again as he languished in a hospital bed.[270]

Upon her release, Yuka took to social media like a fish to water and began her new career as a professional livestreamer and influencer.

Luna's New Dawn

> It's a shame, but I'm back alive.[271]

That's how Luna reentered the social media world in July of 2019. Still in recovery, he'd begin taking interviews, pale and very thin, with his bleached blond hair and a quieter demeanor. If he'd had a dark persona before, that darkness was amplified by what he'd been through, but softened by his being so tongue-in-cheek about it. He even returned, miraculously, to hosting while still in recovery. His first tweet back at FUSION went:

> I'll be at work tomorrow too, so I'll be waiting for my first appointment. #Kabukicho #6TOA #host

This was accompanied by a picture of him with half-closed eyes and a sleepy smile, hoisting a gold champagne bottle and flanked by cheerful friends crowding into the frame—fellow hosts.

A large portion of the internet reacted violently—against the victim.

On July 1, 2019, Luna revealed he was back to regularly hosting, this time at a new bar.[272] Along with that announcement, he posted a photo of himself to SNS with a thin, pained smile across his mouth, tagging himself "LUNA THE PHOENIX," and explaining, "Luna [had been] defeated by pain. I cannot drink alcohol for a while because I was stabbed in the liver."[273]

---

270 "'I Loved Him So Much I Couldn't Help It'–Host Stabbed, Promoted to 'Executive Assistant' In Kabukicho," News Post Seven, July 8, 2022, https://www.news-postseven.com/archives/20220807_1782373.html?DETAIL#google_vignette.

271 "Host Stabbed by Woman Confesses," News Post Seven.

272 "Host Stabbed by Woman Confesses," News Post Seven.

273 "Host Stabbed by Woman Confesses," News Post Seven.

There's a pervasive cultural thought that hosts are opportunistic to the point of malevolence, using charm to exploit customers, where every woman is a potential target—that hosts will even encourage poor women to spend to extremes. That they'll convince women that to love them enough means prostitute themselves or become hostesses to feed their habit and support their boy—so why, society asks, wouldn't such women also be willing to go to the extreme of killing or dying for him? That's what a lot of those giving Luna backlash were espousing, anyway. The comments came in swiftly—harsh, bullying, and full of vitriol and blame. "Don't you know why you were stabbed?"

But Luna was no stranger to online hate. One day after the trial verdict was handed down, an especially prolific user using a sock account at handle @CgJZ5XQQgwDooTm would comment directly to Luna's Twitter/X, "If you don't want people to comment on the incident, why use account names like 'Phoenix' or saying 'Give yourself up to the pain' that exploit it? ... Return that 5 million yen settlement money to your parents. It is a fact that you legally defrauded a total of 8 million yen, robbed a woman of her promising life, [set] to spend more than three years in prison."[274]

After his return, another comment read, "You are horribly evil. [This man] glorified the profession of deceiving women and then returned to being a host.... The perpetrator ... is the true victim. How long will you continue to hurt people? I have never seen such an ugly, money-grubbing man. You are a disgrace to Japan."[275]

Continuing to be a host, the online discourse raged, meant continuing to sacrifice women. As if Luna were single-handedly at the root of female prostitution.

But Luna didn't totally disagree, saying, "Sometimes [Yuka] would spend more than [$6,400 on me] ... I think some of those girls [I

274 北辰一刀流免許皆伝 (@CgJZ5XQQgwDooTm), "事件についてコメントして欲しくないなら なぜ「不死鳥」「痛みに負け」などど事件を利用するようなアカウント名を名乗りますか。ほとぼりが覚めたら示談金500万円は親に返してやって下さい。あなたが計800万円を合法的に詐取し、一人の未来ある女性の人生を奪い刑務所に３年以上入れたのは事実です," X, December 6, 2019, https://x.com/CgJZ5XQQgwDooTm/status/1202895840114659329.

275 北辰一刀流免許皆伝, December 6, 2019.

hosted] had reasons to stab me in the back. I'd been a host for less than a year, and then it was thanks to Yuka I was able to accomplish such good sales results. Maybe I didn't reward her enough for her hard work for me...."[276]

Of Yuka, he held firm in saying, "I don't hold a grudge." In fact, in a news interview in July of 2019, he calmly stated, "The number one most important thing to me was that Yuka had always loved me.... Of course I don't hate her. After all, she helped support me. I truly owe to her who I am today. I was about to improve my rank and received praise from my peers [as a result of her support]. All I can say is thank you."[277]

It's an oddly sunny comment about his assailant, and much like the logo of the city of his birth, Luna would be like a sun struggling uphill, trying to keep a smile on.

Yuka wasn't the only thing he remained positive about.

The news of the stabbing went so viral, and the race to find next of kin became so uproarious with his tenuous condition, that Luna managed to actually reconnect with both a blood brother and a sister of his—two of his seven missing siblings. Police had searched until they found them. Luna had not seen them in at least five years, not since before he was fired from construction work as a teenager. For Luna, this was a great blessing, the reunification a precious outcome of a disturbing ordeal.

Almost unnervingly upbeat, he also had praise to heap upon his host brothers after the incident. He was tired after his time in the hospital—of course he was—and his brave face for news cameras didn't betray some of the harsher realities. Outside of his makeup and host persona, just as Yuka became volatile outside of hers, Luna was, in fact, meek, quiet, and really seemed his age—very young. He was still faced with having no parents to support him, no education, and no experience outside of hosting or construction—and his now-lifelong injuries and long recovery rendered the latter impossible. He naturally went back to the only job he knew, one that would

---

276 "'I Loved Him So Much I Couldn't Help It,'" News Post Seven.

277 @kawaiiguccigang, accessed June 6, 2024.

give him room and board while he recovered—he knew nothing but hosting, his found family were in Kabukicho.

And indeed, his adopted brotherhood clamored to help. Being unable to drink with a ruined liver—the *key* job of the host—his fellow hosts at the club offered to take his drinks for him—no small measure, when hosts already often have to drink until they're ill.

He really would need to rely on their kindness. He'd been bedridden for a while, unable to speak or eat properly for weeks. He was underweight and suffering under a blanket of PTSD that rendered him unable to sleep, too deeply gripped by anxiety over both slipping back into a coma and the horrifying way he'd woken up to a knife inside his body. To try to cope with the fear, he began going to counseling—much less common in Japan than in the West, showing how truly daunting his issues were.[278]

Hosting was a return to some normalcy and a way to take back his life, now that he indeed was going to live. He was welcomed back to that space with heavy praise and support from coworkers and customers alike. At first, he confessed that he was actually a little afraid of the customers, too nervous to speak with them, petrified of being encouraged to drink. His body was in ruins, which would make progressing to true "romance"—having sex with high-paying women—difficult. The wound Yuka gave him was not only deep but had mutilated his flesh in a jagged pattern, and emergency rescue procedures had left even more intense scarring from his chest to his naval, leaving a sunken and puckered well in the area by his liver.[279] Luna was embarrassed by it and still largely refuses to show anyone, even now that the angry red lines have healed. He'd spent over a month in an ICU unit, accumulating sores and weakening muscles. But his work brothers consoled him, reassured that he was stronger than his fears and offered him a place to go home to—a place that *still* felt like family.

Luna was also struggling with some of the sensationalist news media, which had spun stories that were either lies or had been taken from the perspective of Yuka only, who had owned the narrative

278 "Host Stabbed by Woman Confesses," News Post Seven.

279 "Host Stabbed by Woman Confesses," News Post Seven.

when he'd been in a coma. She had said that the two of them had been dating and living together. So, once recovered a little, he began doing interviews to try to set the story straight. Quiet interviews that never laid blame at the feet of his attacker, always taking the high road, but which strove to amend the idea that they'd shared anything but friendship.

When FUSION shut down, he had moved over to a club called Servant of EVE. His official profile listed his birthday as February 23 and his blood type as AB (associated in Japan with either a "genius or psycho" personality, often assigned to villainous characters), and his new persona as being a "healing type" and a "cute type." The profile, still active in mid-2024, could not be found by early 2025.[280]

When Luna moved to Servant of EVE, he totally revamped his socials, going with the Instagram handle @runaruna_0000 and a matching Twitter/X handle—both now defunct ... sort of. His friends and fellow EVE hosts would post photos and videos together with him, all very positive social media blasts. Keeping his new blond look, now in a mawkish bob and still thinner than he'd been his first year at FUSION, he'd be given the cutesy nickname Lunapiyo by his friends. In the videos, heavily filtered, he flashes playful peace signs and giggles with them, bundled up outside in the Kabukicho district.

EVE was certainly a different vibe. One of its #1 hosts is a chubby boy named Nagomi who brags about being over 200 pounds while he hyper-cheerfully dons a Snorlax onesie from the cartoon *Pokémon*. Fatphobia is typically rife in Japan, so Nagomi stands in sweet relief to this. EVE also is more focused on holiday marketing, celebrating Christmas illuminations, Halloween (not typically recognized in Japan), and hosts' birthdays. Hosts do group cosplays together and post silly jokes and memes of each other online. EVE is a member of the LUMINOUS group, which owns many host clubs, and even does a monthly ranking that includes *all* of its Kabukicho hosts.

Luna did well at first, and by the summer of 2022 he'd been promoted to assistant executive officer. The club threw a birthday

---

280 Accessed on June 6, 2024, https://host-kabukicho.com/profile/218.

party for him in the winter, producing bottles of champagne commemoratively featuring his image, along with a $22,000 champagne tower purchased by a customer. Everything was decked out in purple, Luna's favorite.[281] Ironically, he still couldn't drink, but there was no need; the girls who came to party and celebrate him drank straight from the bottles bearing his face. At his party, Luna wore lots of makeup to accentuate his eyes and lip gloss to frame his mouth, trying to look less gaunt. Dressed in a casual and loose-fitting sports jersey instead of the usual scripted attire of a suit, his celebration featured labels on the champagne bottles showing him in a smart black fedora and a clear blue sky behind him. If he'd been trying to look more mature and suave at FUSION, he now looked no older than sixteen at EVE, to match his "endearing" new style.

To help achieve this look, he went under the knife again, this time with plastic surgery to give him double eyelids. He wanted it to widen his eyes, to make him look more innocent. That look helped him avoid tight clothes, fast sex, and hard liquor. And the shift worked—his customers at EVE would easily spend more on him than Yuka ever had, and his job title there was also more impressive. His rank, too, was consistently in the top five for over a year.

He'd seemingly taken nothing from the backlash he'd received, even if he'd partly agreed with it. "If I can sell, I'll do whatever it takes," he told *News Post Seven* in an interview. "I've decided I have no choice but to make my living in the nightlife district."[282] If he couldn't let go of hosting, he *was* slowly giving up Yuka, feeling that he was finally past her with his growth at EVE—that he didn't have to rely on being the "stabbing victim" to attract interest anymore.

As recently as January of 2024, Luna was on LUMINOUS's public rankings, posted to their Twitter/X channel at @Eluminous38b. By the time he made the #5 spot across all clubs, his look had changed again—now with dusty gray textured hair and a slouchier, more intense look—and he held the more elevated title of "manager." His subtitle was that same "gives in to the pain" line. He continually made the impressive top lists across clubs in 2023, but seems to have fallen

281 "'I Loved Him So Much I Couldn't Help It,'" News Post Seven.

282 "'I Loved Him So Much I Couldn't Help It,'" News Post Seven.

off the wagon sometime after April of 2024. On April 3, 2024, the group Twitter/X account posted that Luna had finally nabbed the #1 spot *overall* since joining EVE, out of all the LUMINOUS clubs.

But after April 3, he was gone, a phantom—no more mentions, no more rankings. And then, abruptly, he began deleting all his old replies to people on socials regarding Yuka—and most anything else, too.

Sometime in November of 2024, in a disturbing twist, Luna's previously scrubbed Twitter/X account came back online. Now it had two extra 0s tacked onto it—@runaruna_000000—but all previous tags by his friends online had been updated to reflect the change. This means it's likely that it's still Luna behind the account (though it cannot be 100% confirmed) and he simply changed his handle a little. Before this, briefly, the profile had been named "sarin inhaler," a reference to the sarin gas attacks on the Japanese subway systems in 1995. The name is so morbid that it was questionable if the owner of that handle had been authentically Luna at the time, or if he'd been hacked.

But the handle's current feed, if indeed this is Luna—which remains likely, as the user joined in May of 2019 and was linked thereafter to footage of Luna in other hosts' videos *and* on vetted retweets of television news spots with his interviews—is especially disturbing. On April 12, 2024, about the time his hosting profile was taken down by LUMINOUS and he disappeared from EVE's feeds, Luna posted to this handle, "I'm alive!"[283]

From there, the timeline descends into horror.

Between April and September of 2024, there were no posts. Then, from September to November of 2024, all of the posts were retweeted art—*ominous* art. A pair of twins covered in blood standing over a bound torture victim. A woman who had sliced off her own hand with a knife. A disembodied grinning head floating eyeless over a town in black and white. A man being hanged as a representation of "mundane life." A series of stills from the horror video games *Silent Hill* and *Resident Evil*. A painting of a live surgery in the 1800s, with

283 レスリー(@runaruna_000000)," 俺は生きているぞ！" X, April 12, 2024, https://x.com/runaruna_000000/status/1778745485156655105.

a close-up of bloodied hands and the patient splayed on a table with an open torso as the physicians sweat around him. A series of off-kilter white doorframes, a shattered mask, a video of a game character holding a knife, a woman cleaning intestines off the floor, a child hanging themself, cats eating a woman alive, suicide by gun, monstrous black growths sprouting from a man's face, the distressing missive that there's "No Way Out of Your Own Skin & Bones" over a video of creepy smiles, a CD made of meat, an apple made of meat, someone pulling red thread—the symbol of love and fate—from their eyes.

His profile was updated to just one word—*misanthrope*.

He had wanted Yuka to live a normal life. If this is still Luna posting, it would seem he was not given the same mercy.

Nonexistent, Starving

During Yuka's trial, even the court drawings of her were beautiful. In what is probably the most famous of them, she sits on the left side of the courtroom, her hair longer now and free flowing, framing her face in a pretty cascade. Her nose and lips, drawn upturned, are full; she is given wide eyes and an accentuated chest, neatly dressed in a white button-up blouse and a form-fitting black suit jacket. Her glasses have slid down her nose to reveal an enigmatic gaze, which she bestows in a half turn on Luna, who sits turned away from her on the right side.

Luna, by contrast, is faceless and foreign. His hair is a mess of off-green blond; the cleave of his left cheekbone—the only visible part of his face—looks skeletal, and he swims in a sloppy cross-hatched hoodie in his favorite shade of purple. In the background, a lawyer with an upturned brow is gesturing at him.

The effect is almost backwards. Yuka looks put together, tranquil, and soft, while Luna looks like he's the target of legal ire—sloppy, blank, ill-postured. It draws immediate sympathy for Yuka. Most parts of the case, shockingly, did just that. This is likely what led to her decision to immediately go online when she was released from prison in 2023.

With her previous profiles scrubbed from the internet, she made her new debut as @uyupekochan on Twitter/X, Instagram, YouTube, TikTok, Twitch, and BIGOLIVE—with the latter two being livestreaming websites. On Instagram she'd previously gone by @Yuyuyunochan, and her old account now promotes her new ones with links to all her updated socials. Her main focus? Cosplay photos—dressing up as winsome heroines and *yanderes* alike—and livestreaming her play of various video and computer games.

Her online handles are an amalgamation of words. *Uyu* can mean "nothingness" or "nonexistence," but it's most often used in the set phrase *uyu ni kisu*, meaning to be "burned to ashes" or to "come to nothing." It's an interesting call to Phoenix's own moniker. *Peko* is part of the onomatopoeia *pekopeko*, the sound for being very hungry. *Chan* is simply a cutesy addition to tack onto the end of a woman's name, usually a younger girl or someone well-known to you, inviting her audience into a sort of easy familiarity.

Yuka's return proved that public fascination hadn't diminished. On Instagram, across both her new and her original handles, she had almost 100k followers, and on YouTube 11.4k subscribers.[284] On Twitter/X she had 19.7k followers in January of 2025 and 40k followers by June of 2025,[285] on TikTok 43.7k followers,[286] and on Twitch 3.9k followers[287]—each a different revenue stream.

Yuka's fan base began growing while she was in prison. Along with the cult of celebrity and horror worship that grew around her—including a movement of fan art and fan pages that left many in Japanese society worried and disheartened about the state of young people celebrating a would-be murderer—her fans wanted to *actively* help her as well. A GoFundMe campaign was started in South America, entitled "Help Yuka Takaoka (yandere girl) bail out." Its profile read that she had only "allegedly" stabbed Luna and lamented that she was "not in the best place right now," encouraging the public to "do our part to make the whole ordeal a little

284 "うゆ," YouTube, accessed May 1, 2025, https://www.youtube.com/@uyupekochan.

285 "うゆ (@uyupekochan)" X, accessed May 1, 2025, https://x.com/uyupekochan.

286 "うゆ (@uyupekochan)" accessed May 1, 2025.

287 "うゆぺこちゃん," Twitch, accessed May 1, 2025, https://www.twitch.tv/uyupekochan.

less stressful for her <3 ....FREE OUR GIRL." It received sixty-nine contributions totaling 38k, mostly foreign donors, before being shut down for violating the website's terms of use.[288]

Anyone who has ever struggled or watched loved ones struggle with trying to meet goals on GoFundMe for a friend or family's urgent medical care or a sick pet's vet bill will know how difficult it can be to get donations on crowdfunding sites like this. That makes Yuka's number *staggering* for someone who'd committed a crime so red-handed that she was covered in the gore of it and didn't bother moving more than a foot away from the body as it bled out on her. A woman who'd smoked a cigarette while a young man fell into a coma.

On that GoFundMe page, a photo of Yuka shows her looking sweetly confused and fragile with her messy ponytail, big glasses, a wide wondering look, and oversized gray sweatshirt. *Parasocial* sells.

A quick look at her socials shows us what else sells.

On Instagram, where her profile simply says "I love *Pokemon*, all I do is play games" she posts big-eyed, Circle-lensed, decora-filled selfies, same as before. Fans readily chime in their adoration, and GIFs of yandere anime characters. In one post she makes what is perhaps even a reference to Luna, after a long break from content:[289]

> *One day early.* I kind of understand Christmas Eve, but recently it seems that there is something called Eve Eve, so today is going to be Eve Eve, so then yesterday would be Eve Eve Eve, right? That said, I thought then maybe any day of the year can be Christmas Eve x (many Eves).
>
> ...#EveEve #WhatisEveEve.

And the replies come in:

> **@kidlaroi:** omg youre back! merry christmas cutiee!! i need a killer like this in my life this christmas.

288 Coffeehouse Crime, "The Real Life Yandere Girl."

289 @ uyupekochan, Instagram, "1日早いね なんかクリスマスイブは分かるんだけど最近はイブイブなるものが存在するらしくて、じゃあ今日はイブイブになるんだけどそうしたら昨日はイブイブイブになるという訳でしょ？そんなことを言ってしまったら一年中どの日でもクリスマスのイブ×(たくさんのイブ)になるよねって思いました。#うゆ #クリスマス #クリスマスイブ #イブイブ #イブイブってなんだよ," December 23, 2024, https://www.instagram.com/p/DD6ox0WSbzc.

@lazuphy: ...hope you are enjoying these days, Ilove you!

@dafyolivs: I love you, you look beautiful. <3

She also posts her cosplays, *Pokémon* game content, makeup looks, and dance videos. Fans greet her mostly in Japanese, English, and Spanish. They call her "baby," "my wife," "divine," and "cute." Men offer to "meet you, date you" and cry out "CAN WE MARRY?" They remind her to keep eating her fruits and veggies and to be well. When people bring up the stabbing and say she should be more ashamed, Yuka's fans bite back with "the dude gained fame" and "he thanked her."

She's a lot more talkative on Twitter, which she mainly uses to post her Twitch schedule, show off her fan art, and celebrate he fandoms like *Oshi no Ko* and *My Hero Academia*. She also posts injury and illness content. She shows her finger, purple and blowing up after being slammed in a metal door, and asks fans if it's bad; herself at the hospital, letting fans know she's dangerously thin and frail; and many more selfies and cosplay photos, food photos, and ambling thoughts. She is, apparently, an open book.

On September 9, 2024, Yuka used her X/Twitter profile to put out something of a statement, asking people in Japan and abroad, "whether you like me or not," to read it before commenting. It describes why, instead of suicide, she has turned to living an honest life and enjoying her time online with the people there who love her:[290]

> I am so grateful that you say you like me, follow me, watch me, and support me always. I also get a lot of comments about mistakes I've made in the past.... I make no excuses.... [The case] has helped people get to know me.... I live with that mistake for the rest of my life and I will never be forgiven. It's not just me [involved], so I don't have anything more to say about it. As I reflected deeply, I wondered a lot about whether I should continue my online activities. But people are supporting and waiting on me here.... I have no desire to justify myself.

---

290 うゆ (@uyupekochan) "遅くなってしまい申し訳ありません、私を好きで居てくれる方も、嫌いな方も、何かコメントをする前にお手数ですが一読頂けると幸いです。海外にお住みの日本語が分からない方で、それでも読んでいただけるという方は、写真から翻訳できるアプリがあるのでそちらを活用いただけると幸いです。," X, September 9, 2024, https://x.com/uyupekochan/status/1833049784296624134.

> If you don't like me or think I'm not serious, please block me so I don't have to see you. I have been deleting slanderous comments because there are people who support me and care for me.... I would be very happy [if those who love me] will stay with me and continue to love me.

People replied en masse, with a wave of sympathy and support. And in a rare show, Yuka herself replied to many of the comments.

Her Twitter profile, in addition to sharing her love of *Pokémon*, additionally notes that she's hooked on the *Persona* gaming series. Perhaps Yuka's revival, her redemption arc, is relatable and appealing to anime and gaming *otaku*.

Her TikTok is more of the same—aimless music videos pulling cute faces that fans reply to almost rabidly, her *Pokémon* playthroughs, dance videos, and cosplay footage. Replies included, "the person you love will be really lucky" and "they will never get me to hate you."

Luna's empathy for her seems again to be lost in the narrative, while Yuka is often recast as the adorable victim. In fact, just three months after the crime, horror fetish accounts online took their worship of her beyond fan art—they started recreating photoshoots of the crime using live models, and reached out to Luna, saying they'd love it if he would pose for them.[291] There was no outrage or backlash in that comment section.

The judge presiding over Yuka's case hadn't allowed Luna's soft words to be the final ones. He called Yuka "selfish" and reminded everyone of her "strong intent to kill." It was also revealed during the trial how much premeditation went into her crime in the time when Luna was peacefully asleep. In a memo pad on her phone, the same memo pad in which she'd tell fans she was uninterested in judgment or negative feedback, she'd made a note just before the stabbing. It was read to the court and later publicized by *Tokyo Reporter*. It went,

291 チェルシーひよこ (@hiyococoro), "るなさん応援してます！やりたいです！ぜひ撮らせて欲しいです！ご本人で再現写真撮りたいです。," X, August 24, 2019, https://x.com/hiyococoro/status/1161588657989414917.

> I want to be the tragic heroine. How is it possible for him to look at a woman other than me? I know killing [him] is for the best. If I kill [him], it will be eternal.[292]

She cried as it was read aloud.

To the public, Yuka remains the real-life yandere. An idea that in reality should generate loathing and disgust, but instead, people are relating to, celebrating, and engaging with. Tragedy rubbernecking strikes again as the dark fantasy of Yuka gains her more and more followers. (Her latest cosplay photoshoot on Instagram, dated May 8, 2025, is of a knife-happy *yandere* maid from the "bullet hell shoot 'em up" video game, *Tohou Project*. As of June of 2025, it has been viewed over 800k times, liked over 10k times, bookmarked over 5k times, and has hundreds of deeply fawning comments.[293] She admits the photos are heavily edited.)

In a surprising move, in September of 2024, in the trendy and fashion-forward district of Tokyo known as Ikebukuro, Yuka decided to do a live meet-up where fans could purchase tickets to come see her in person.[294] Taking a Polaroid or selfie with her ran about $10, talking with her for five minutes cost about $30, and additional talking time was $10 per five minutes. Everything had to be prepaid in full, and any lateness meant cancellation without refund. She didn't allow any filming, and a bit humorously (though understandably), bag checks were conducted—to ensure her safety and make sure that no one brought, say, a knife.

After all, fans can be so *obsessed*.

---

292 Tokyo Reporter Staff, "Real Life Yandere: Yuka Takaoka Handed Prison Term for Attempted Murder," *Tokyo Reporter*, December 6, 2019, https://www.tokyoreporter.com/crime/real-life-yandere-yuka-takaoka-handed-prison-term-for-attempted-murder.

293 うゆ (@uyupekochan) "イベントのお知らせ日付→2024年9月7日場所→池袋に行うイベントの詳細です場所と時間は予約確定後にチケット配布と一緒に伝えます！もしかしたら何か少し変更になるかもしれないのでその時はまた告知しますリプライまたはDMにて予約受付開始しますので参加希望の方は教えて下さい！" X, June 30, 2024, https://x.com/uyupekochan/status/1807657574982193594.

294 うゆ (@uyupekochan) "もう前回分は完売してしまったんですが、再販予定なので、いつになるかはわからないんですけどその時に注文して頂けると嬉しいです！！" X, September 21, 2024, https://x.com/uyupekochan/status/1837467719438160107.

At that meetup, she also sold key chains and acrylic stands of herself, plus printed versions of her cosplay photos. (She was willing to ship such items, too, so long as orders were over $100.)

All of Yuka's merchandise sold out.[295]

295 うゆ (@uyupekochan), X, September 21, 2024.

CHAPTER 8

RANDY STAIR,
aka Andrew Blaze/ PioneersProductions

They all say, I'm broken
They never meant anything to me
Can't they just leave me be
To follow my own fantasy

I'm lost here
I'm jaded
Stuck in my own misery

This is my comeback song
It's only meant to fucking prove you wrong
I am so far from being famous
I know you're not the same as me and that's the way I want—
That's the way I want it to be!
—"Comeback Song," Send Request

The opening theme song used for Ember's Ghost Squad in 2015, featured an overlay of Ember McLain and several *Danny Phantom*-themed original characters rocking out. It opens with Randy Stair, also known as Andrew Blaze, announcing that a war was on in the afterlife. A bloodied still photo of Randy is overlaid on animated tombstones as Randy narrates, "They say that God takes young souls because of their purity ... that's a *Squad* recruiting their newest member ... all souls are fair game."

A note on pronouns, sexual identification, and warnings for this chapter: Randy Stair privately identified as a woman's soul trapped in a man's body. He did not agree with the term "transgender" to describe himself. He used "he/him" pronouns in his everyday life and "she/her" occasionally in private reference to his soul. Because he identified with his feminine spirit almost entirely on the pages of his journals and in his art, there is some confusion over proper pronouns. That said, outwardly Randy identified as "he/him." He resisted the term "gay" and never once referred to himself as a "lesbian," despite identifying as a woman's spirit who loved other women in the pages of his personal journal. Though he claimed to love women, was attracted to them, and got off on fantasies of them—even desired to "brainwash" specific girls to suit his needs—he said he had no desire to have sex with women. He was not asexual, as he experienced almost violent physical attraction, but instead was either involuntarily or voluntarily celibate. He patently *hated* men, in his own words, but contradictorily mostly admired and was inspired by men in his life. So, in his own personal concept of sex and gender, Randy self-classified himself as divinely female but irrevocably physically male, in fact "doomed" to be male on earth. He felt there was nothing he or anyone could do to make their earthly body correspond with their soul if they were mismatched. In a sense, he felt that being transgender wasn't possible in life, only in death. But he did not identify as transgender. If anything, his point of view was confusingly transphobic.

The name he gave to himself online and to his female spirit was Andrew Blaze, and he often referenced himself this way while also going by Randy. He split his understanding of himself into two: Randy, as a male body, and Andrew, as the female spirit with "she/her" pronouns. The following narrative uses "Andrew" as "she/her" to reference his "ghost" personality (the one he felt he'd achieve after death, that interacted with the other "ghost" characters he communed with and wrote stories about) and "Randy" as "he/him" (his physical self outside his ghost persona). This is how he used the names, to differentiate his inner and outer selves. Randy is *not* a dead name.

Very important for understanding his particular case, Randy firmly believed he could *not* be a woman until he "purged" his male body by suicide and became his feminine higher self.

Randy left hundreds and hundreds of pages of notes and self-obsessed diary entries that cover this understanding of his own identity in detail, often contradicting himself from day to day.

While Randy's understanding of himself might have changed over time had he lived, with the rise in global activism and conversations around gender identity, this chapter discusses him *in his own words*. It's important to note that many of Randy's thoughts regarding sexuality, gender, and age are extremely sickening. He thought bisexuals were "cursed" and that gay men were "disgusting." He felt it was impossible for anyone to be gender fluid or outside the binary—"you're STILL a Male or a Female, you can't be neutral," he wrote of nonbinaryism or gender fluidity.

Many of his own views were transphobic, homophobic, misogynistic, ageist, and racist, with screeds so horrific they could not be printed here. What remains is truly horrifying in its own right.

Autopsy Report

RANDY ROBERT STAIR

<u>EXTERNAL EXAMINATION:</u>

Intraoral shotgun wound of entrance...

Black make-up lateral orbits and lips.

Shaved body and extremity hair.

<u>MEDICATIONS:</u>

None known at time of autopsy.

CAUSE OF DEATH: Shotgun Wound of Head (Entrance Mouth)

MANNER OF DEATH: Suicide

FINAL SUMMARY: The decedent was a 24-year-old white male who shot three coworkers at Weiss Market in Tunkhannock, Pennsylvania, then shot himself.... Extrusion of copious brain matter occipitally.... Two upper front teeth are absent.... massive exit occipitally 5 x 4'.... skull extruded.... This wound was lethal in and of itself.

BRIAN HAYES

EXTERNAL EXAMINATION:

Multiple shotgun wounds x5

Poor dentition.

CAUSE OF DEATH: Multiple Shotgun Wounds (Five)

MANNER OF DEATH: Homicide

FINAL SUMMARY: The decedent was a 47-year-old white male night manager at Weiss Market.... [He] sustained shot wounds to his head, chest, right flank, groin, and left arm. Wounds were lethal.

TERRY LEE STERLING

EXTERNAL EXAMINATION:

Shotgun wounds x2

Edentulous (Lacking Teeth)

CAUSE OF DEATH: Multiple Shotgun Wounds (Two)

MANNER OF DEATH: Homicide

FINAL SUMMARY: The decedent was a 63-year-old white male ... co-worker at Weiss Market.... [He] sustained two shotgun wounds. One to the upper back and a second to the left shoulder. Multiple exit wounds in neck. Multiple pellets in head, neck, and chest.... no defensive injuries. Each of these wounds was lethal.

VICTORIA TODD BRONG

EXTERNAL EXAMINATION:

Shotgun wounds x4

CAUSE OF DEATH: Multiple Shotgun Wounds (Four)

MANNER OF DEATH: Homicide

FINAL SUMMARY: The decedent was a 25-year-old white female shot four times with a pistol shotgun ... a co-worker at Weiss Market.... [She] sustained shotgun wounds to the left hip x2, anterior chest x1, and to the back of the head x1. All wounds distant. All through clothing. No defensive type injuries.[296]

---

296 "Randy Robert Stair," Forensic Associates of Nepa, June 8, 2017, https://randystair.com/sites/default/files/2024-10/stair_autopsy.pdf.

In 1912, the Weis Markets brand was founded in Pennsylvania by Weis brothers Harry and Sigmund. The store didn't allow for credit to be used, which at the time came as a surprise for shoppers. It was risky not to allow for families to run up tabs, but no tabs meant that grocery prices didn't have to be marked up to accommodate for late payments or defaults. The low cost to consumers helped Weis expand to 115 storefronts across just that single state in twenty-one years, making the Weis brothers rich men. Today it's still a mainstay along the east coast of the United States, though still mostly situated in Pennsylvania.

The Weis Market in Tunkhannock, Pennsylvania, is close to the banks of the Susquehanna River, the longest in the States to be free of commercial boat traffic. It's bordered by a small, public-use landing strip for aircrafts, frequented by adrenaline junkies for skydiving. Workers at Weis can stop over at neighboring Antonino's Pizza for a shrimp and garlic slice with white sauce on their break. The strip mall they share is on a secluded plot of land but kept busy by the comings and goings of customers. There's plenty of free blacktop parking in the wide front lot to accommodate late afternoon crowds on their supper runs after work.

Just before 1 a.m. on Thursday, June 8, 2017, the throngs had long since cleared out, and the deep red Weis sign glowed neon against the accumulated fog gathering outside. It was unseasonably cold, a chilly fifty-two degrees, and the moon was high and full. Workers who'd begun a long night shift after the store's closing at 10 p.m. were dutifully restocking shelves, eager to get the job done and be on their way home around daybreak. Unbeknownst to them, Randy Stair—also on duty for a late-night stocking shift, clocking in at 11 p.m.—had slipped out to his car when he should have been stocking shelves.

Or maybe someone had seen but hadn't thought much of it. Randy was an unsociable night stock manager, avoiding the more talkative morning shifts. Since he was a supervisor—the only one on staff that night besides Brian Hayes—most coworkers wouldn't have had the authority to question his comings and goings even if they had spotted his bizarre mid-shift exit.

Randy ambled out into the expanse of the parking lot early into his shift and took a duffel bag containing two pistol-grip shotguns from his gray 2013 Hyundai Sonata. One gun he'd named Rachel, the other Mackenzie. He felt a little bad about naming the latter Mackenzie, as that was the name of his favorite original character, a cartoon ghost he'd fallen in love with, a gentle and bright soul. Rachel, on the other hand—named for another cartoon ghost he communed with—was a bloodthirsty murderer who would help guide his hand in the gory deeds ahead.

This would be Randy's last time feeling the outside air, the nascent summer snuffed back into the sensation of early spring by the unusual cold front. But he'd been planning something like this for years and, with more dedicated effort, he'd been at this *particular* plan for weeks. He'd even flipped a coin—heads, he'd kill himself privately in his bedroom; tails, he'd shoot up his workplace. He filmed the coin flip and posted it to YouTube before the shooting, seemingly unedited. Tails won out. While it's likely he'd simply reshot the video until he had his desired result, posting it online before heading to his shift meant there was no turning back now.

His car, decorated in stickers of his favorite animated characters—a dead punk rocker and her band, whom he devoted himself obsessively to—was parked outside the Tunkhannock Weis so often that, as recently as 2020, Google Earth still showed it parked out front, a phantom.[297] Randy entered the car one last time that evening, to snap down the driver's-side mirror and apply a smear of makeup around his eyes, pitch black. Satisfied with the look, he re-parked outside a Weis emergency exit—to block it—and commenced with his plan.

Randy wandered back inside the grocery store and calmly blocked the remaining exit doors with various large objects and paraphernalia, mostly palette boards. He was feeling secure as he moved, dressed for the occasion. Under his clothes, he'd meticulously

297 "R/Masskillers," Reddit, accessed June 1, 2024, https://www.reddit.com/r/masskillers/comments/ohsdxs/fun_fact_if_you_google_the_supermarket_randy.

trimmed and shaved every bit of body hair from every inch of his skin, donned his favorite black bra, and worn his special pair of deep purple silk panties. He also wore the black beanie he used for filming YouTube videos and a black wristband he felt would identify him to other ghosts in the afterlife.

This was his uniform for death, expertly and painstakingly selected, a soft and comforting hug against his bare skin. He'd always hated his body hair—and his skin color, too, though he'd opted not to make himself whiter than he already was on that night. He'd tried that in the past, to mediocre results; he'd have to wait for death to make him pale.

Randy's plan was to murder his coworkers before taking his own life, assuring that those who'd clocked in that day would not be clocking out. He thought *four* murders was a relatively low number, nothing spectacular, when he'd wanted chaos and *mass* slaughter for so long—but he didn't see any better alternative. Shooting up the more crowded and central Weis store in Dallas, closer to his home, would have seen too many gun-toting Pennsylvanians ready to take him down. Pennsylvania ranks fifth in the United States on registered gun ownership—over 40% of households have a gun registered to an adult. As it was, Randy worried that Brian might have an opportunity to rush back to his own car and arm himself, so obstructing the emergency exits was meant to curtail those heroics. As it turned out, he'd never give Brian the chance.

When it came to motive, Randy had been carrying the heavy burden of his own mind for too long. Bored with his life, full of malaise and fascinated by death, he'd receded into a fictional world partly of his own creation. He believed in death he'd ascend, becoming an apparition capable of interacting with the cartoon characters he'd come to treat as friends—his "Squad." To get into the ghost Squad (an idea he'd hijacked from the cartoon series *Danny Phantom*), he felt he had to do something worthy of its attention—multiple murders.

Randy's collapse into these delusions was heralded by his difficulties with his own reality—he'd suffered the loss of several acquaintances to tragic accidents, had a severe phobia of aging, and was experiencing gender dysphoria. He welcomed suicide as an escape hatch to becoming his spirit-self, who he called Andrew: an ultra-white, gigantically tall, forever young woman.

But he wasn't delusional to the point of not understanding the task he chose to undertake. Randy was simply malevolent: not a young person suffering, but someone who wanted, *needed* others to suffer, too. He'd dreamt of committing violent murder for years and reveled in all forms of slaughter, admiring serial killers and celebrating natural disasters. He patently *hated* humans, especially the old, blue collar workers, anyone non-white, and *especially* those who mildly inconvenienced him. He claimed that in the whole cesspool of humanity, he loathed men the most. Yet his casual, vehement misogyny aimed at "bitches" in his life, how he'd taught himself to quietly jerk off to women during his high school classes to degrade them, spoke otherwise.

Randy had never been bullied, nor even faced any great outward adversity to bring on these revulsions. The colleagues he targeted hadn't done anything to him—hadn't terrorized him, weren't unkind. They even *liked* him, at least in the case of Brian, who'd tried to give Randy pep talks to help with his loneliness. Randy simply wanted to commit homicide, and Weis would have to do. He wrote giddily in his journal about killing his coworkers of many years, just *because*. He only lamented that some shooters had entire schools as their playgrounds, while he was stuck with only killing grocery staffers. His final YouTube video upload, just ahead of the Weis shooting, was an animated fantasy of him and his imaginary Squad shooting up a school.

His father had gotten him the Weis job, but Randy wasn't grateful. Hypocritically, he often veered between holding his immediate family in high esteem and reviling them simply for living life—going to work, disagreeing with him, not amusing him enough. He couldn't help himself; his thoughts always deviated to the cruel and vile. Though he and his mother laughed and joked, and he seemed to love her, he also wished she would stab herself. With his father, he was harsher. Randy felt that the man who was so famously *kind* to everyone must secretly be a raging sleazeball who held his true nasty personality hostage because he'd been "programmed" by society. Though

Randy shared a close bond with his brother Jeremy, he fumed over the peace-loving boy calling guns idiotic. He wrote in his diary, "Let's see how stupid they are when you're staring at a barrel an inch away from your face."[298]

Aside from the job and family he took little interest in, Randy's age dysphoria had gotten more intense with every new birthday. With his twenty-fifth on the horizon in September, he felt it was time to exit Earth. "Honestly, I'm just ready to die.... I'm rapidly running out of youth." He felt his soul was perpetually sixteen to nineteen years old.

His main driver for suicide, though, was his desire to become his ideal ghost woman and to join an undead assassination force. He truly believed that by committing murder and killing himself, he'd be able to enter the animated world of the Nickelodeon cartoon series *Danny Phantom* as a punk rock goth, part of an all-girl "Ghost Squad," with his perfect body: a busty, ten-foot-tall, paper-white member of a group of spirits that would enslave "putrid" living humans. He believed that to earn placement in such a squad, you had to be exceptional, which is what his killings would prove—along with being wish-fulfillment for himself.

Randy felt sure that Ember McLain—a *Danny Phantom* character who'd died in a house fire after being stood up on a date—not only spoke to him, but was with him in spirit to help commit the murders. So were a number of other girls in Ember's "Squad"—original characters ("OCs") that Randy himself had developed. While a minor side character on the *Danny Phantom* show, Ember and her crew were the main characters in all of Randy's hopes, dreams, and fantasies.

The final motive was that same supervisor, Brian. Brain had several vacation days left to schedule, and his being out of the office would delay or ruin Randy's plans. Worse, he had begun talking about switching to the day shift or changing jobs altogether, and if he did that, Randy would miss his opportunity to kill him. That was *unacceptable*. Brian hadn't done anything to Randy, of course. He just wanted his full roster of kills.

---

298 Peter Langman, "Randy Stair's Journal," SchoolShooters.info, March 14, 2023, https://schoolshooters.info/sites/default/files/stair_journal_1.0.pdf.

In March, about three months ahead of carrying out his plan, Randy laid it all out in his journal, much the way it would eventually happen:[299]

> [I am] full of fantasies of storming into a supermarket.... and shooting everybody; ending with me blowing my head off in Aisle 1. That could easily become a reality, but killing two, three people is nowhere near satisfying.... (it) would have to be when I'm working (overnight). No one would see it coming ... Including me there's only a MAX of 4 people on overnight, Brian would get shot first; neutralize the biggest threat.... I don't hate Victoria but ya gotta go. The biggest problem is the supermarket has too many exits. If you hear gunfire, you're gone, as long as you're not two ais ais asis, how the fuck do you spell asle AISLES....
>
> I wish I could have.... a bunch of teenagers to shoot at.... [But] nowadays you shoot in a school and I see it all being over within 10–15 minutes * *sad face** It sucks. I wish there'd be more people to kill besides Brian, Victoria, maybe Will, and the floor guy. Hey, better than nothing.... I'd do it after our 1 am break, probably. That way the store's long closed and everyone's focused on work. We'd come back inside, I'd act like I'm putting stock up, sneak back outside, gear up and have fun.

Here, he included diagrams of the asiles, showing where he and his colleagues would be.

> The biggest problem though is there'd be no witnesses; no one to say what happened or what was said.... Again, I'd do it on a day shift but you could easily be overpowered. The last thing I'd want is to A.) Survive, and B.) have the customers "fight back"; those headlines would make me sick.... unless I miraculously learned how to make bombs. They're sitting ducks HAHAHA! ... Wow ... I could legit do this shit.... [Brian] might hire people ... make it even funner.

Stair was a popular YouTuber with almost 9,000 followers, including a handful of zealously devoted super-fans and over a thousand views on most uploads—some with over a million. He'd been liked and

299 Langman, "Randy Stair's Journal."

name-dropped by some fairly big-time YouTubers for his blend of bizarre skits and game play-alongs. Eventually though, he'd abandon all that for his "EGS" series and channels—Ember's Ghost Squad would bring him increasing fame but also isolation.

In his final video upload, entitled "The Westborough High Massacre," Randy gives a sonorous monologue over an animation of himself and his Squad butchering a school, while thanking fans and followers. The feed flashes to the *My Little Pony* wall posters in his bedroom, a tribute to the Columbine school shooters ("our heroes"), followed by unhinged laughter and then odd animated weeping—all of it ending awkwardly with the song "Together Forever" from the children's animated series *Pokémon*. The video disconcertingly juxtaposes Randy asking, "What is the point in living in a world where you can't have everything you truly want?" with these lyrics from the upbeat pocket monster cartoon, "You've been such a good friend ... We've got lots of friends, but they come and go. Even though we've never said it, there's something that the two of us both know: Together forever, no matter how long...."

Randy was ready for suicide and ready to sow bedlam before he went. Since he'd hated his seven long years at Weis, he'd turn his ire on the symbols that represented the system he felt oppressed by: corporations and their servile shift workers. His coworkers felt so differently toward Weis. Diligent in their duties, long shifts together made them feel like forged family. The Weis community was a close-knit one, looking after and supporting one another. Had Randy engaged more, they would have done the same for him. In fact, Randy in his diary mostly accused them of only their *best* traits—and as with his family—he pointed out why that goodness was so obnoxious to him. Brian, the hero. Victoria, boringly inoffensive. Terry, strong. Kristin, whose name he could never bother to spell right, innocent. And condemned for it.

In that same diary, he listed his objectives for the evening. He marked Brian as his "number one target"—"He's fucking dead no matter what.... Consider it a token of my appreciation.... I want Brian to die the fastest; he's been through enough." What he'd "been through," to Randy's twisted mind, was middle age and the

Weis job itself. He marked Kristin as "impossible to miss, weights [sic] like 300 lbs," seething in fatphobic fragments. Victoria was an "easy target" whom he alternately said he'd only wound, then gleefully changed tune to "I'm gonna destroy Victoria's head. She'll be completely beyond recognition." Finally, he mentioned "Floor Guy" (who is possibly Terry, but more likely someone who didn't clock in that night) as a "worthless fuck who should be burned alive." He felt the most likely scenario was that he'd kill the two women and that the two men would escape—"But I ain't leaving this world without bringing someone down with me."

He wrote that his final goals were to scare the world, die in the Aisle 1, and have fun.

That night, when Randy entered the Weis facility for the final time, he was armed with 100 rounds of ammunition. Rather than his intended primary target, Brian, he began his onslaught by shooting Victoria Brong while she stacked items in Aisle 16. He fired four rounds. They would be his worst shots—the only ones that were initially nonlethal, fired from further away. She wasn't killed by the first bullet, but by the fourth, she was gone.

Victoria, with her wide warm brown eyes and a short bob of brown hair left behind a young son named Kevin whom she'd worked to support, and a loving partner named Bill. From Factoryville, she'd been a big fan of YA novels, music, and magazines, and she loved spending time with her wide web of family. The tribute posted online includes a photo reel more than ten minutes long of her smiling, surrounded by warmth, and resplendent, especially around Christmastime, when she always dressed up and helped trim the tree.

When Randy shot Victoria, the noise caught the ear of Kristin Newell over her headphones. The gunshots sounded like a small series of *pops* as they blitzed through the music, reminding her of balloons. Curious as to what could have happened, she took an earbud out and turned from her perpendicular aisle to ask Victoria if she'd heard the noise, too—only to see her friend on the floor, bleeding out, and Randy with his guns. They made eye contact. For a long moment, the two stood staring. Then, Randy moved on. He walked directly to the next aisle and shot Terry.

Terry Sterling, of South Montrose, was a devout Christian who liked jokes and stories. A ready conversationalist, he'd chat with anyone, no matter their walk of life, and was known for treating everyone with kindness. A proud grandfather to his only son, Terry Jr.'s two girls, Carmen and Kylee, he was known as "Pops" to family and friends—of which he had so very many.

Finally, Randy went looking for Brian. Kristen, meanwhile, daringly called 911 still in plain view at the mouth of Aisle 16. She'd witnessed Terry's fate, but in a bid to save Brian, she spoke to a police dispatcher while still easy prey. Police instructed her to flee or hide; easier said than done in a market designed for clear views and wide-load cart traffic. Kristin made her way to the entry doors, and in a moment of blind panic—she says she can't recall how she did it, or even the *act* of doing it—dismantled Randy's barricade. She got the doors open and, per instruction, ran.

Police soon made it to the scene, and as they did, more gunfire sounded. Brian was dead. He'd been shot several times, though the first bullet had ended him, as with Terry. Brian Hayes, whose oft-smiling face was softened by a pair of frequently askew wire-rimmed glasses, was originally from East Orange, New Jersey. A Navy veteran, he left behind a wife, Tina; a daughter, Caitlyn; and a stepdaughter, Rachel. He was a brother and had a sprawling family who adored him.

Finally, Randy slid the shotgun into his own mouth and shot himself. He died instantly.

He'd fired fifty-nine rounds in total. Mostly at the shelving, shattering bottles and blitzing racks. A search warrant was soon issued for his place of residence in Dallas—his family home—and his grim messaging over social media was quickly discovered. Perhaps Randy had left Kristin alive for the same reason he sent out a digital archive on his crime: He *required* an audience.

Ghost Stories

Randy Robert Stair was born on September 17, 1992, the first child of Lori-Anne and Robert Stair. For a time, he'd be the toddling only child in their ranch-style home, nestled into a thicket of woods on the bend of Ransom Road in Dallas, Pennsylvania. Two years later, filling the home's third and final bedroom, his brother Jeremy arrived.

The Stair home was a somewhat desolate one-story residence described by realtors as a "country property, yet close to town." The town in question, Dallas, is populated by only about 715 families, mostly with a low to median household income some $20,000 below the national average. Its main thoroughfare, the Memorial Highway, boasts most of its commercial properties, from one or two cute coffee shops to Fat Mike's Texas Wieners and the Weis Supermarket—the very one that Randy had wished he could have shot up instead of the Tunkhannock branch. It had better foot traffic, a bigger staff, and his *father* worked there.

While Lori-Ann was employed in biomedical equipment technology, Robert Stair was a manager over at Weis. He'd worked there since before Randy was born, from 1989 until even present day.[300] So when Randy needed extra money in high school and some real money thereafter, Robert had helped get his son hired with the company he'd dedicated his career to.

Randy never appreciated his father's profession, despite Robert impressively making manager in his first year. Instead, he viewed his career as cripplingly sad and meaningless. He rarely saw the irony in his doing the same job only through the benefit of nepotism, because of Robert's hard work and good standing. Randy never appreciated jobs in general; he took one at McDonald's, only to quit after just one day before accepting his father's handout. Eventually tiring of Weis, he'd quit to work instead with his mother at her start-up business—before promptly and thanklessly quitting on her as well. His reason for quitting the stocking job at the Wilkes-Barre General Hospital—the job his mother Lori-Ann had gotten him—was that the facility was too large. He simply didn't feel like stocking sixteen or more floors or going all the way to the basement to load a large cart when, even when broke, he could simply leach off his parents.

300 "Robert Stair," LinkedIn, accessed July 10, 2024, https://www.linkedin.com/in/robert-stair-b09122125.

Of course, he'd finally crawl right back to the Weis opportunity provided by his father, but the 360 didn't make him any more appreciative. He wrote in his journal, "I don't want to work anymore. I don't want to deal with anyone anymore.... It's fucking bullshit! If I didn't need to hold down a goddamn full-time fucking job I'd be cranking out the best content on the planet. Okay, that's a little egotistical but still. I'm superior to these humans. I'm fucking evolved. I deserve better than this never-ending nightmare of 'reality.'"

By the time he was working at Weis again, he was an adult, 6'4" with ruddy blond hair, an unnervingly upturned smile, and bags under his eyes that he played up with makeup. He was wiry on purpose, severely underweight for his height, as he felt that was more feminine, referring to himself as "134 lbs of plasma." He kept his thinning hair shaggy, constantly tossing his head to retain a punkish side part when he wasn't donning a beanie.

As a child, Randy's life had been relatively normal. His room was his haven, all the way up through adulthood, with very few changes: he kept it dark, curtains drawn, bedsheets opaque, walls papered in framed art. There was an askew keyboard with gleaming keys, a photo of the Beatles on Abbey Road, and a wraparound poster of WWII B-52 bombers littering the skyline in attack formation above his bed to lull him to dreamland. His preference for inky blacks and neon-adjacent purples made the space look like goth-rock potpourri had exploded everywhere. He housed a riot of DVDs, Post-It notes, bottle caps, and actual refuse—gummy wrappers and plastic labels. His closet was part time capsule, party hobby-shop hodgepodge, bloated with My Little Pony figurines, Dallas Cowboys' helmets, tangled wires from old tech, and his cigarettes of choice, Marlboro Skylines. His room was like a household junk drawer, but supersized.

As he grew older, the room's walls would become dominated by more self-obsessed media—his favorite cartoon characters, art of his original characters, and art of himself *with* his original characters. From high school onward, video equipment, DVDs, crafting and writing supplies, tributes to his fandoms, and a generous number of stuffed animals would be added to the general pandemonium. The stuffed animals, disturbingly, would be used to ill purpose online.

His family were staunch Dallas Cowboys football fans—perhaps in a subtle nod to living in Dallas, just not *the* Dallas of the Lone Star State—and despite Randy's overall distaste for anything masculine-coded, a favorite blanket of his for years to come would be a woolly NFL one with the Cowboys logo blaring across its center. He also littered his shelves with his own sports trophies and even made his favorite original character a basketball star.

Randy's parents were typical American hard workers, with a good sense of humor and a firm moral compass, trying to juggle careers with raising two kids, as one grew stranger and further from them. Lori-Ann, blond with a full halo of hair, a mellow smile, and an honest face, is a graduate of Penn State at Wilkes-Barre. She'd been a biomedical technician at Wilkes-Bar General Hospital for thirty-three years before deciding to go solo—starting her own company in 2010, the eponymous Stair Biomedical, Inc.,[301] where she was responsible for the maintenance of medical equipment for surgery centers and nursing homes. She'd described herself as dependable and flexible. Randy described her as *stupid*, despite her technical degree, and too laid-back; he'd preferred she be more hysterical. He wanted her to be more *upset* about things.

He was always harsher with his mother when she didn't notice him the way he wanted her to. He was more hateful toward his father on the whole, but when it came to Lori-Ann, he willfully hid parts of his personality and smothered his inner demons, then blamed her for not guessing at them. Since he expected nothing of his father, Robert was in the clear. But when Randy began losing significant weight—something he wanted to do for his own sense of body positivity—he was astounded that Lori-Ann didn't try to get him to eat more. Then when he began plotting mass murder, he privately sneered at her ignorance to the dark thoughts lurking behind his eclectic smile. Randy did show rare bursts of affection for his mother in writing, calling her "great" and that hanging out with her "was nice" when they'd laugh and joke around.

301 "Lori Stair," LinkedIn, accessed May 1, 2025, https://www.linkedin.com/in/lori-stair-43489189.

Robert rarely made enough of an impression on Randy to land in his journal. Known for being unflappably helpful, he'd gotten his second son, Jeremy, a position at Weis markets also, working as a stocking clerk while he studied to be a graphic designer in college. Robert was consistently lauded for his keen customer service and adored by all departments.[302]

Finally, there was little brother Jeremy, a visual artist who'd sometimes helped Randy with his YouTube videos. Diligent and bright, with a love for designing graphics and logos as well as editing and producing videos, he was mostly self-taught ahead of college. His never-give-up attitude earned him a spot at Luzern Community College, where he began a side business in T-shirt design.. Jeremy was a loyal boyfriend to his long-term sweetheart and a pacifist. Unlike Randy, who wrote privately "I love the darkness, the sadness, the abyss of it all ... it's literally a drug," Jeremy wrote online missives like, "In a world full of violence and hate, and pessimism and depression, try to smile and be happy.... Spread Peace, Love, and Positivity."[303]

Jeremy and his father looked alike, with the younger Stair one day growing up to his father's build, with his same wide, friendly face, low brow, strong jaw, and tenderhearted smile.

The boys had a family dog growing up. Ginger, a beautiful tricolor Beagle, lugubriously overweight and often seen panting, tongue lolling, while she took on the wilderness just beyond their front door in the surrounding environs of Abrahams Creek and the Francis Slocum State Park. Ginger was much more interesting than the tank full of colorful fish sitting adjacent to the living room. The house had its share of pets, with Randy getting his own handsome blond Labrador retriever, Bruno, down the line as well.

An uncle lived nearby, and the family traveled and took trips together, went to sporting events, practiced at the shooting range, and helped one another with their projects. They even shared friends

302 "Robert Stair," LinkedIn.

303 Jeremy Stair (@unconsciousartdesign) Instagram, "By far my most favorite shirt I've ever made. 'Peace' Filled with the American flag. In a world full of violence and hate, and pessimism and depression, try to smile and be happy. Happiness is as contagious as sadness but sadness is easier to feel. Spread Peace, Love, and Positivity. #peace," November 29, 2016, https://www.instagram.com/p/BNaGaMHgvJB.

in some cases, with Randy especially impressed by his younger brother's male friends.

Randy also had a regular time in school. Though he wasn't popular, he also wasn't picked on. He remarked that the middle school class bully left him alone after stealing his lunch once, only to find Randy didn't care at all. This made the bully laugh at how aloof he was, returning the lunch. By high school, the key reason Randy didn't fit in was his disdain for his peers. For sitting near him in art class, he felt one classmate should "fucking burn to death." In his journal, he described his dislike for the growing racial diversity of Dallas classrooms, especially its Black students. He loathed locker room talk and seethed when other teens joked about sex. He didn't like it when anyone touched his things, hated taking tests, and was bothered by even physically *being* in a classroom—which, like working, he viewed as a waste of his time and talents. He despised alarm clocks, the "attention seeking whores" he sat near, and was even furious at graduation when the students threw their caps into the air and one of them clipped him harmlessly on the way down.

He also considered himself, first and foremost, a "wimp" in high school, unable to speak his mind. But by degrees, he did like the sense of camaraderie other students gave off, and their youthfulness—their aura of naivety. He'd even one day manage a sort of nostalgia for it. After all, high school kids were the age he wanted to be perpetually—older teens.

In middle school, he'd had two close friends, James and Chris, but by high school he stopped making any effort at real connection, transforming his "desperate" need for an in-group into a casual nihilism. He knew his entire graduating class, spoke with them, but didn't engage deeply. They occasionally would josh him, hiding his books or taking his pencils to get a reaction, but he was never really annoyed by harmless pranks in the volatile way other things annoyed him—words, phrases, ideas, *people*. People were able to play little tricks on him, in fact, *because* he took it so well—and they never took these jokes too far. Randy typically replied playfully back.

Randy was also a devoted hypocrite. No matter what he wrote, he did enjoy elements of school. He even became wistful when just months after graduation his alma mater was torn down—Dallas High School in all its 1960s glamour reduced to rubble to make way for a modernized update to the institution. The wing he'd studied in became the parking lot for a shiny, new three-story building. Randy was heartbroken there'd be no new students in his old haunt. A big part of that melancholy came from his tremendous need to be remembered. A self-described ultra-egotist, despite not feeling that he had many friends or remarkable memories from school, Randy had a robust general friend group. Despite his attested abhorrence of men, his closest associates were mostly male: James, Chris, Tim, Paul, Henry, Dalton, Morgan, Zach. His "group" was fifteen students large and, in their senior year, they went on a trip to Cleveland, Ohio. They had a laughably bad time, which became a bonding moment. James, who posted collabs and comedic sketches with Randy through his own eventual YouTube handle (@Freakshow180) and on their shared one (@LowBudgetVideo), would even describe himself as Randy's *best* friend. So Randy was not exactly the "loner" he wanted to be seen as.

From late high school into early college, Randy was coming into his own. Despite calling men "literally the most disgusting thing on earth," aiming particular ire at macho men ("jacked, hairy, tough, and in charge [men can] kiss my white ass"), he actually admired and looked up to males close to his age and preferred the company and philosophy of men. Inconsistent as always, he favored burly men as soon as they picked up a bat or a ball, as much as when they picked up a rifle. He adored professional athletes and shooters, always impressed by men who were physically powerful in games. He even liked playing team sports, for someone who otherwise was so against being in groups. Two men in particular would ultimately change Randy's life—by dying, and in dying, becoming cemented in his imagination as forever-young touchstones.

In addition to men he knew personally, Eric Harris and Dylan Klebold were Randy's absolute idols. He related to the two Columbine High School shooters on almost every level, poring over their diaries openly celebrating their schematics for mass murder. Randy even donned a Natural Selection T-shirt, matching both Eric Harris and Pekka-Erik Auvinen.

For someone who purported to love women, Randy objectified them. He had rape fantasies, despite his distaste for sex, jerking off at school and at the Weis marketplace to unsuspecting, unconsenting women. "Been using moisturizer lotion ... it feels amazing," he wrote. "I must have jerked off at work 10 times ... in the car, bathroom, or the back manager's office :)." For him, men were friends, and women were objects of beauty that had to be *more*.

Around this time, he began writing gory stories about murdering his classmates and doodling nihilistic artwork rife with obscenities during classes. He got pissed off when his *female* teachers didn't notice—he wanted them to be frightened of him, to worry. He complained in an online video, "Yeah, the teacher like never felt *concerned* or anything." He was similarly incensed *only* at his mother for not identifying that he suffered from an eating disorder and self-diagnosed depression—despite lauding himself as a pathological liar and refusing to attend therapy or take medications.

Randy, though, unlike most mass shooters, was never threatened, never physically or mentally targeted or harmed in high school, and seems to have drifted through that period of time at relative ease with everything but his own skin (and any other skin types that he took prejudicial issue with). He even got good enough grades to attend Luzerne Community College.

His family supported him through Luzerne, allowing him to live at home, make his YouTube videos, work at Weis, and complete his two-year associate's degree in applied sciences by 2014. He wasn't sure what he'd do with his degree, but he wanted it to involve cameras. Unfortunately, that conflicted with his desire not to hold any kind of real job. He disdained the media, politics, music, movies—the majority of roles that involved filming—and the "dissatisfied faggots" in those corners of life. But oddly, college—far from being the tipping point it is for many mass shooters, the plunge into further social isolation—was a boon for him. The best years of his life.

Randy's closest friendships outside of his computer were somewhat half-baked and full-gleaned. For someone nearly heartless, he poured a tremendous amount of energy into two specific men—but only once they were lost, cementing his worship of death.

Tom's death sucked the life out of me. Matt's death killed me.

Tom Lynch was a friend of Jeremy's; they'd known each other their whole lives. At Dallas High, Randy had shared only a single class with Tom, since he was an underclassman. They'd chat sometimes when they'd see each other in town. One day, during a free period, Tom approached Randy to inquire about his stint of less than twenty-four hours as a McDonald's cashier—Tom was a part-timer at the same location and was confused when they didn't wind up as coworkers. Such low-input general nicety isn't usually enough to forge loyalty, but for Randy, it was less Tom's life and more his passing that made him a defining figure.

On Monday, February 13, 2012, Tom was in a car accident.

Randy's mother texted him and Jeremy, both at their respective schools in the midday, about the crash. Jeremy was devastated. Randy felt himself go numb. He'd later attribute this as his first step towards "EGS"—the story he'd narrate to himself, animate for YouTube, and eventually believe was reality. Despite not knowing Tom very deeply, Randy made it a tradition to drive past the site of his accident every February 13. It seemed Randy *almost* had a crush on Tom—or on the idea of his ghost, which he also believed was female. "I'll never forget it and never truly will move on from it. There are some things a girl's heart just can't let go of," he'd written.

"From that point on, I was just fascinated by death.... I'd never dealt with anyone who is you know a year younger than me dying."

The second blow also came during college, making quick work of those best years of his life. Randy had newly become friends with a boy at his school named Matt Murray. After the short winter holiday break, Randy returned to campus in January only to learn that Matt had died in December—also in a car crash. In Matt's case, the tragedy was compounded by the fact that it happened close to where Randy had physically been, without his knowing about it for weeks.

Randy, working at Weis over the Christmas holiday, heard chatter in the aisles; apparently, someone had died just a mile and a half from the market. They were saying that it was a local kid. Matt didn't do a lot of online communication, so it wasn't until a teacher took Randy aside in the new semester and told him of Matt's passing that he found out that the boy dying just minutes from where he was stocking cans was his closest campus friend.

December 20, 2012, was the date of that fatality. "That was it. That was the moment that everything changed. I was never the same since. Literally something just short-circuited in my head, something completely broke, something shut down. It just completely fucked me up."[304]

Thomas Edward Lynch was popular around town, a Boy Scout who'd made Eagle Scout and pre-enlisted with the armed forces, hoping to become a Cavalry Scout. Matthew John Murray had been a devastatingly handsome graphic designer and a guitarist. Both were only children, the losses gutting to their families.

After losing Matt, Randy stopped believing in God and let go of his flimsy hold on the Christian faith altogether. His total change in his philosophy, based on two tenuous relationships to men he found charming and beautiful, shines light on his own inner contradictions. Good-looking, popular men preoccupied Randy, a trait that would follow him onto his socials.

In 2014, Randy lost his Labrador retriever, the sweet, gentle old dog, Bruno, who was put to rest after suffering from a breathing issue. This hit Randy hard enough to vlog about it.

On June 23, 2015, yet another tragedy occurred. Keith Zapoticky was one of the few guys who could make Randy laugh, born in the very hospital that Randy had quit work at. An old high school classmate, Randy heard that Keith had died from an anaphylactic reaction at twenty-two. A kind young man and an organ donor, Keith was yet another attractive, affable, and intelligent boy who should have had a bright future ahead of him.[305] At this point, disillusioned, Randy could only say that those who died so young were "better off."

---

304 AndrewBlaze.com, accessed May 1, 2025, https://andrewblaze.com/suicide-tapes.

305 "Keith A. Zapoticky," Legacy.com, accessed May 1, 2025, https://www.legacy.com/us/obituaries/citizensvoice/name/keith-zapoticky-obituary?id=17698996.

Randy's fixation around suicide and the afterlife began in high school, with the losses in college only amplifying his fascination. But he was gung-ho about *murder* long before those tragic accidents, even if his grief worsened or twisted that dark epicenter.

Randy was a ball of contradictions. Despite being so callous toward others, he took any slight against himself badly and felt betrayals and losses deeply. His definition of friendship, rarely bestowed, was ultra-precious to him. *Loving* people apparently meant *losing* people—or was it the other way around? Those who passed were elevated to precious places in his heart because he loved *ghosts* instead of humans—and very specifically, cartoon ghosts.

He found solace in two places—on YouTube and in the Nickelodeon cartoon *Danny Phantom*.

Blazing onto the Scene

Randy created his primary YouTube channel, @PioneersProductions, in June of 2008, when he was sixteen. Before that, he'd been posting content online under the handle @Point2122, mostly videos of goofing off with his friends—flashlight tag, catch, and nighttime dodgeball. It showcased his burgeoning sense of ironic humor, with one dodgeball game being filmed entirely in the dark, the screen literally black.

@PioneersProductions was home to a series of dark skits featuring his toy animals—a plastic frog and a stuffed whale. Froggy—orange, black, and rather rough-looking—was an open-mouthed amphibian doll he'd found abandoned in a Weis shopping cart. Whale, beat-up and mottled, was a predatory stuffed animal—and despite Randy's attested distaste for sex jokes, Whale was characterized as a pervert, often aiming his perversions at Randy in particular. Froggy had a high, sassy voice paired with a slick attitude and a biting tongue; Whale had a distressingly deep and distorted timbre. Randy voiced both of them.

By 2011, he'd amass enough of a following to achieve his dream of becoming a paid YouTube partner, with over 8,000 followers—a solid number for that time. From there, he'd court the attention of bigger YouTubers he admired. One was @Makemebad35, a young man named Damian whom he *fixated* on. He would eventually score a collab with him, which sent Randy over the moon, until Damian made him wait for his half of the video. Randy showed unbridled, unusual restraint for Damian, even privately. A nicety he afforded no one else.

He also netted positive comments from @PlasmaMasterDon, who at well over sixty years of age, had over 400k followers. This was unusual, since Randy despised the elderly; and so did Don, it turned out. He was later outed as a sexual predator, Tier I sex offender, and pedophile who had inappropriately touched a young boy. On one of Randy's videos, Don had commented,

> OMG, 24 wow you're getting old, Randy, lol![306]

Don's own birthday was just two days before Randy's. In a reply, he glibly mentioned, "Yeah, 69, everyone's favorite number, lol! Thanks so much Randy (hug)." From this man, a sick person who hurt children, Randy appreciated the innuendo.

They'd discovered one another through Damian, who they both were dedicated fans of. Damian had just over 30k followers in YouTube's early days but today boasts nearly two million, despite having stopped actively posting to his channel in 2016 with the video "This Is Not Goodbye." Randy worshipped Damian and gave him slack where he gave others only a rope to hang themselves with. He wrote in his diary, "The night of my death I'll send some final goodbyes to people like ... Damian (makemebad35), David and Hobo Deadfish (Xbox), Andrew B (which will most likely be a heated email, fucker), James (Freakshow180), and anyone else who I deem worthy enough."

He did, at one point, get mad at Damian for failing to deem *him* important enough for his attention. But even in writing he almost immediately retracted his harsher sentiments:

> I'm fucking done with EVERYONE! Slit your fucking throats! You're worthless! Laura, Reira, the animators, Damian, EVERYONE CAN

306 Dire Trip, "The Delusional World of Randy Stair–The Whole Story," YouTube, November 1, 2024, https://www.youtube.com/watch?v=D4q_-BJwG5A.

FUCK OFF! You're so goddamn 'busy' aren't ya?? You're fucking pathetic.... I wrote loving/caring emails for you's (Damian/ Laura) but now I feel like I wasted an hour of my life typing them. Damian I can still forgive and respect but Laura [no].

He and Damian had met through Randy's unpopular gaming blog, and Damian, sensing he was lonely and appreciating Randy's offbeat sense of humor, reached out. He had no idea how dark Randy actually was—the eventual suicide letter that he would receive shocked him. As usual, Randy's distaste for men was hypocritically confounded by his simpering desire to be accepted by them—especially famous or conventionally attractive ones. He was much harsher toward women. His "final goodbyes" to those "worthy enough" were all male. To Damian, he'd mete forgiveness for being eight months late recording a few lines; to Laura, the loyal animator on some of his most beloved videos, he would not. It's the same old casual misogyny and double standards observable time and again in mass shooters.

Randy seethed when men ignored him, however. After all, as his diary stated: "I'm egotistical; if you don't know that by now.... you're fucking retarded." About @Markiplier (who in 2025 had over 37 million followers), @JackSepticeye (at almost 31 million subscribers), and @PewDiePie (with over 110 million followers), he wrote, "You humans make all of these losers who overreact to video game footage out to be fucking gods. THEY SIT IN FRONT OF A SCREEN PLAYING VIDEO GAMES. They're worthless." He even mocked Markiplier's charity work. Then, two-faced to the core, he reached out to Markiplier with a gift and a coquettish note. The gift was a Slender Man shot glass—a fictional towering, faceless creature that stalks and hunts humans. Born of online lore, Slender Man's mythos inspired the stabbing of a child in Wisconsin in 2014. Attached to this gift, Randy backpeddled and wrote, "Hi Mark, I've been watching your videos ever since I came across your slendyman [sic] elementary videos in November and I was HOOKED. I think it's great you use your audience for good, raising money for charity."

Social media giants mattered to him, because he craved to become one. Randy was extremely active across all his handles, of which he had a staggering fifteen at minimum on YouTube alone, to varying degrees of fanfare. They were horror-based, offbeat sketch comedy, skits, and finally, animations on his beloved Andrew Blaze/@EmbersGhostSquad channel. He was also active on Blog TV, Facebook, DeviantArt, and Instagram. His most popular channel was his main @PioneersProductions handle, but Randy slowly detached from it as he fell further into obsession with "Ember's Ghost Squad," eventually viewing his animated content as factual and biographical.

In his final six-part video upload to @PioneersProductions—alternatively titled either "EGS Prologue" or "PioneerProductions Finale," signaling the end of one channel and the rise of the other—Randy included an episode called "Amnesia Rape." It features Randy, in a stupor and tied to a chair, being videotaped by his toy Froggy as he is sexually assaulted by his Whale plushie. Whale croons, "I've waited three years for this moment." Froggy encourages, "Amazing footage! Come on, score!" With Randy helpless on the floor, Whale cheerfully notes, "I came."

The vulgarity continued to episode three, where Randy finds the video of his assault leaked and uploaded to YouTube. Randy confronts Whale, spitting, "All these years I've put up with your shit, your homosexuality." He then stabs the stuffie "to death" with a real knife, splashes of red blood gushing out as he plunges the weapon down over and over. He murders Froggy next, who begs to know why he's doing this, and Randy says it's "because she told me to."

Ember appears behind him. Randy slices Froggy through his plastic head and drops his "corpse" onto Whale's. Randy stabbed at his toys so violently, he broke his pinky finger while filming.

View a World Unseen

The show *Danny Phantom* aired on Nickelodeon from 2003 to 2007. Despite its short run of just fifty-three episodes, it has a cult following to this day. Creator and director Butch Hartman graduated his successful elementary-grade *Fairly OddParents* show run to high school, swapping up to the growing pains of a teenage protagonist, Danny Fenton. Danny, who is accidentally turned into a half-ghost hybrid, teams up with his two human besties to help keep their world safe from the demon-like phantoms from the Ghost Zone. The only complication? Danny's parents are ghost hunters who don't know his secret. "Ghosts," in Danny's world, are poltergeist-like manifestations. Most live in the Ghost Zone with no connection to the human world.

Randy could not have cared less about Danny and his workaday hero problems. Randy cared about *Ember*. Ember McClain was a side character featured in just ten episodes of the show, and mostly as an afterthought. She is central to the plot of only two episodes. That didn't deter Randy's instantanious spiritual connection to her when she first aired in 2004. But it wasn't until late 2010 that the *connection* would bloom into a full-fledged obsession.

In a suicide video he posted in May of 2017, Randy rambled about his first time seeing Ember: "It was like my first crush. And it's a cartoon, you know. It's kind of crazy to think that way, but it's the truth." He'd first seen her in her introductory story, "Fanning the Flames," airing on October 8, 2004. Randy would have been newly a teenager himself at the time.

Even within the *Danny Phantom* universe, Ember was special and different. She was one of the show's few ghosts whose past human life mattered to the plot. Her tragic backstory involved waiting so long for her popular crush to take her on the date as promised that she fell into an exhausted sleep after his no-show. Her fatigue means she sleeps through the house fire that claims her life. In the afterlife, she comes into her own, becoming a ghost rock star. Her sad end, her disillusionment with society, her nihilism, her desire for celebrity—all of this resonated with Randy. In the show, when crowds of concert-going fans scream, "We love you, Ember!" she replies, "That's because I filled a void in your empty lives!" They return, "You're right, Ember!"

Randy wrote, "From the very instant I first saw Ember.... I instantly felt something change on the inside. NO, it wasn't puberty, it was the ember igniting inside of my soul. I couldn't take my eyes off of her, nor could I get her off of my mind.... She never went away after that. Ember completely overtook my mind ... bringing me into the darkest days of my life."

It was his final year of high school when she became important to him again, right around the time his self-diagnosed depression began to worsen. Ember's song "Remember," written after the character died in the house fire and performed by Robbyn Kirmssé for the show, was something Randy described as hypnotizing, playing it over and over again, singing along to the lyrics: "Your heart has rendered your loss, now bear the shame. Like dead trees, in cold December, nothing but ashes remain. Oh, Ember, you will remember. Ember, one thing remains. Ember, so warm and tender! **You will remember my name.**"

He became so absorbed by it that he posted a long version of the song on his @WorthlessToaster YouTube page and it would be the first Ember-themed video of his to hit over one million views.[307] He didn't care that its musical artist hadn't given permission for this version to be tracked down, dug up, and released—hijacked musical content would be a mainstay for Randy. He even made fun of the female artist for "losing" to him when he took the song against her will.

From there, emboldened by cracking a million views, Randy opened an @EGSWorld handle for his creations on YouTube, Instagram, and Twitter/X, and even created an EGS Wiki page for his original characters.[308] Now fully in the grips of fixation, he'd devote time and energy to his EGS channel and backstories for his own characters, set to the backdrop of concepts from the *Danny Phantom* world, but horribly twisted. As he created, a burgeoning issue emerged: Randy began to think that this "afterlife"—half his creation and half that of Nickelodeon—was *real*.

In Randy's version of the hereafter, people who were exceptional in life—which he defined as either dying wretchedly or committing an atrocity—were "recruited" into "Ghost Squads." These Squads could have hundreds of ghosts, but *all* of them were female. Men who died but had female souls could be recruited. The Squads were built as friendship clubhouses whose main activity was destroying and

307 WorthlessToaster, "Ember McLain-Remember (Official Soundtrack Version) [Robbyn Kirmssé]," YouTube, April 6, 2014, https://www.youtube.com/watch?v=wBMOc24_alw.

308 "Home," The-EGS.Fandom.com, accessed May 1, 2025, https://the-egs.fandom.com/wiki/The_EGS_Wiki.

enslaving humankind through murder, chaos, and brainwashing. Of all the Squads in the afterlife, Ember's Ghost Squad—EGS—was the highest ranking.

He began to fill those ranks with his own creations—drawing, animating, voicing, and penning stories for them. He posted videos about his ghost girls, who to him, really existed, padding their world with convoluted lore. His most important girls had the most excruciating histories.

There was **Madison McBride**, a sixteen-year-old girl who'd died by hanging herself from a tree. Falsely accused of witchcraft and the murder of her school bully, her father had beaten her senseless for the crimes, forcing her to flee her home and live on the streets. Turning to prostitution to survive, she would be used and abused by men until she decided to end her life. There was **Alex Gebhart**, a man in life but a woman in the afterlife, Alex had been killed in a traffic accident in college, distracted at the wheel by a recent breakup with his girlfriend. Then **Celesta Reynolds**: a trouble-making high school dropout who died accidentally after mixing heroin, alcohol, and antidepressants. **Rachael Shadows**, whom he'd name one of his shotguns after, tried to kill a classmate with rat poison, only to be found out and have students spraypaint her locker with the words "Rachael deep-throats homeless child porn addicts on the street for a living." In retribution, she planned a school massacre. **Harmony Ingram** had been a kind soul who killed herself by slitting her wrists after three boyfriends in a row used and then dumped her. Almost all his stories involved some kind of assault by men on young girls. His singular male-in-life, female-in-afterlife character, Alex, mimics the deaths of friends Matt and Tom.

Mackenzie West would become Randy's favorite EGS girl by far, overtaking even Ember. It's not clear whether Randy fell in love *with* Mackenzie or felt that he *was* Mackenzie. A self-aggrandizer in the extreme, completely self-obsessed, it isn't beyond the pale to think Randy could be in love with an idealized version of himself. He often said that Mackenzie and he (as Randy, not as Andrew Blaze, his ghostly female counterpart) looked exactly alike, so to prevent confusion, he couldn't dye his hair a dark color even though he wanted to.

Aside from looking nothing like the character (who was over nine feet tall, had hot pink eyes, and extremely long purple-and-black hair), the disturbing video of himself being sexually assaulted by his whale character bears some striking similarities to the backstory he gave to this fictional girl.

Randy considered Mackenzie his soulmate. And to his soulmate, he gave the following backstory: Mackenzie was a kind youngster, well-liked with good grades, a talented athlete. But she began to sense someone was stalking her. When she fled a basketball court mid-game, spooked by seemingly paranormal activity, she was captured, kidnapped, and drugged by a man in all black who hauled her back to a safe house in the trunk of his car. There, he'd proceed to repeatedly drug, rape, and torture her, all while—like Randy in the video—she was tied to a chair. The torture this character endured—though fictional—is, in fact, too disturbing to recount, featuring some of the most gruesome mercilessness. After days of endurance, Mackenzie would be brutally murdered, her body dumped in a bog, her killer never found.

In 2017, Randy wrote in his diary, "Whenever I close my eyes, [Mackenzie] is there.... She's right by my side at all hours of the night and day. Although Rachael and I connect on so many levels, Mackenzie is my girl. The innocence.... her slender body and smooth white skin.... I'd do anything to hold her ... Soon, soon it will happen.... she'll wait for me." He had invented his own child bride in the afterlife.

Andrew Blaze was the name of the ghost spirit Randy Stair knew he would become upon death—a blue-eyed, purple-haired female guitarist. The name came from Hurricane Andrew, which had killed sixty-five people in August of 1992, a month before Randy's birth; "Blaze" was clearly a link to Ember's manner of death. He drew and animated Andrew Blaze so she could interact with Ember and her Squad. Andrew was a woman who towered over other women, with bright neon eyes, black hair, a huge bust, a thin waist, and pale white skin.

Randy was obsessed with sexually and physically violent backstories for his more than 1,000 characters. The women all looked alike—pallid white with dark hair, light eyes, and goth clothing. He wove Andrew Blaze into several of their backstories, and he made himself the physically largest of all his ghosts. Froggy, his rubber frog toy, also joined EGS. In Randy's mind, it was Andrew Blaze herself who'd stabbed Froggy, and in death the toy became an avid murderess.

In total, the Squad boasted upwards of 1,700 recruits. Each newbie was given an identification bracelet and a booklet entitled "So, You're No Longer Living; the EGS Guide to the Afterlife." Sometimes recruits were scouted among the living and the Squad waited for them, others were murdered *by* EGS so they could more quickly join the superior ghostly ranks.

As Randy fell more in love with EGS as not only a reality, but as the Squad he was destined for upon death, he began to plan his sweeping final act in earnest. Again from his diary:

> What makes someone as innocent-looking as me want to cause mass devastation and manipulation? I have my reasons; some more morbid than the others. I've hated humans my entire life. I hated making friends, 'socializing' amongst my classmates, and just overall being spoken to. Humans are WORTHLESS. We are living, breathing, moving trash.... What is there even to be remotely happy about in this shithole of a planet?? You are a dead man the instant you're conceived by your parents. You don't even have a say in your own name!
>
> I can't stop envisioning myself in the ghost squad; being one of them ... being happy ... killing humans after returning from the grave. Manipulating and seducing humans with my feminine charm, and then brutally attacking and killing them with a huge grin on my face. The power. The revenge. The ghost squad. I FUCKING WANT IT ... and soon ... it will be a reality.
>
> I probably won't make it to see 30. I NEED to die young. Wish I could've as a teenager.... But it wasn't meant to be. All I know is each day I get that much closer to her..... Ember.... And Mackenzie.

Around this time, he also became fixated on Sonata Dusk, an antagonist from the *My Little Pony: Equestria Girls* animated television series.

Sonata was very much like Ember—teal hair, wide eyes, pale bluish skin, and a member of a rock band. But in his pantheon of obsessions, he could have only one mania.

Randy was starting to grow anxious about aging too far beyond Ember and Mackenzie, even though in death he'd be given a new and timeless body. "I wouldn't mind being permanently stuck between the age of 16 and 24.... You don't want to get old, trust me. Anything beyond 55 is just borrowed time," he wrote. "Here's to never growing up."

He also began writing stories about what his life would be like after death more earnestly. In one, featuring himself and Mackenzie, Andrew wakes up after dying to her love waiting for her:

> *"An-An-Andrew-Drew-Drew-Ew-w-w???," her voice echoes. "Can you hear me??"*
>
> *I somewhat know where I am but feel half confused.*
>
> *"You made it back!" or "You did it," something to that effect. That's how I envision it. M will be the first to greet me....*

Unfortunately for Randy, he wasn't the only one writing fan fiction ...

Called "Randygate" for how it all culminated, a mega-fan of @PioneersProductions named Dave wrote a steamy fanfiction piece about Randy, entitled *A Gift for Randy*. It features a *Scooby Doo*-esque mystery wherein Randy is forced to admit to himself that he is gay. Creepy in the extreme, attributing a sexuality to Randy that he not only didn't identify with, but actively hated (he did not identify love for Mackenzie as the female Andrew was "gay"), it featured audaciously graphic pornographic scenes. It was Dave's well-meaning but extremely twisted attempt to get Randy to notice that his fanbase wanted him to be healthy—to Dave, that meant Randy admitting he liked men. Jeremy also appears in the story, saying, "I've never seen anyone work as hard at being miserable [because] you don't even try to get a job in the field you studied [and] you couldn't do your dream job of living off YouTube videos ... no, you wanted people to feel sorry for yourself."[309] It was a bizarre look at what people who had parasocial relationships with Randy may have thought, and what they hoped for their idol. At the end of the story, Randy lets go of being a child and decides to focus his energy on improving himself and having a good future—to work every day to make himself happy.

At first, Randy praised the fanfiction before slowly becoming so disgusted by it that it triggered his decision to quit the @PioneersProductions channel. He often had similarly conflicting relationships with his fans. He blocked two particular fans online at his on-again, off-again whims, a pair of devotees named Haley and Sammy. In his diary, he fantasized about murdering them. He even debated turning his supporters into a cult, to "spread EGS around the globe and to perform mass suicides, sacrificing their lives for the Squad," but ultimately didn't appreciate the type of people that suicide cults attracted—cloying believers. He couldn't tolerate admirers long-term. Randy was obsessed with controlling his image and forcing others to conform to his idea of himself as the dangerous genius loner—so runaway opinions and unapproved stories by fans threatened to hijack *his* narrative. (He didn't see the dark irony in writing and thinking much worse about others.) Part of that image was his extremely curated aesthetic. "I care a Lot about how I look," he wrote. "My hair is never perfect; I'm ALWAYS adjusting it or looking in the mirror. I can never pose for pictures because I'm never satisfied with my looks.... I could post a 'selfie' but the one you see is almost always between pic number 20 or even 50."

Control over the "canon" around himself—what was true of him and what wasn't, especially in his EGS world—became paramount. In his EGS, bewilderingly, some souls were ghosts *before* they became human, though not all souls became ghosts *afterward*. Naturally, he was one such rare recycled soul, stating, "I can't wait to be a fuckin' girl again. I can't get the thoughts off my mind. Every time I see hot girls I say 'I used to have that'.... I guess you can say I think about dying and being female just as much if not more than the average

309 Mike [Phantom Phoenix], "A Gift For Randy Audio book - Reading a Randy Stair Fanfic (Not by me)," YouTube, July 2, 2024, https://www.youtube.com/watch?v=h26XmoNv9lU&.

male human thinks about sex...." He did not identify as transgender and was, in fact, openly transphobic.

Despite his pearl-clutching over sex, sex occupied Randy's thoughts constantly, too. "I'm officially dubbing ✳March 14th✳ as 'Mackenzie West Day'.... I love you so fucking much, M.... I'd plow you in the middle of the fucking street if I could.... Love, Andrew Blaze."

He was also obsessed with what he perceived should be both the purpose and the popularity of Ember's Ghost Squad. "I fucking live for catastrophic disasters.... I love hearing enormous crowds of people screaming and dying, and envisioning the EGS being the cause of it all. The *Titanic* soundtrack and EGS must become one." He drew a crude picture of EGS being the reason for the infamous ship hitting an iceberg in 1912, killing more than 1,500 people.

His spiral into EGS lore went hand in hand with his descent into a malaise he would not recover from. In 2013, a year before he became deeply Ember-focused, he'd had the worst months of his life. He'd been recovering from his grandfather's death when their family home's basement flooded, leading to the loss of a great deal of significant personal items. He totaled his car, Jeremy totaled *his* car, and Randy's iMac hard drive fried, destroying his video material and costing $700 to fix. He documented these losses across his vlogs. In 2012, his videos were offbeat and heavy on violence, but largely cheerful—nothing to hoist a red flag over. But by 2014, the red flags would be a parade. In 2014, the EGS videos began in earnest, and that became his favorite year as a YouTuber. By 2017, EGS had gained an enthusiastic following, built up by individual Twitter accounts for many of his EGS characters and dozens of pages of wiki lore he'd written.

Around this time, Randy also got more into drinking. Beer was his alcohol of choice, and he could throw beers back rapidly for his build. At nearly twenty-five, but with no clear life trajectory, the buzz became a boon. In his diary on April 6, 2017, Randy crooned, "Happy Emberversary! Crazy to think 3 years ago today I got word that the HD version of '*Remember*' surfaced on the internet.... It was the best feeling I had ever had in my life; nothing has ever come close before or since. I remember being up until 6:30 in the morning uploading it to YouTube and having three Budweisers. Even saved one of the bottles and wrote the date on it. It was the happiest I had ever felt in my life and it will never be topped." Brewskie in hand, his fascination with the Columbine mass shooters also rekindled during his EGS heyday.

Besides EGS, alcohol, and violence, he'd lost interest in much else, writing, "By mid 2014 I didn't want to work anymore. I constantly envisioned hurting customers ... [then] I got offered the night shift position (full-time). Jeff signed the death warrants for Victoria and Christan [sic] that day."

It was on his EGS channel where he'd post his final videos, the prelude to his murder-suicide, just before the Weis marketplace shooting. One video flashed footage of the Weis Market, outside, then of the aisles, then of Randy stalking the aisles, all to No Doubt's "Hella Good":

> A performance deserving of standing ovations....

His character Rachael asks on that video, "What is the point in living in a world where you can't have everything you truly want?" Randy left the world with that foreshadowing, attached to some of his final thoughts:

> I always envisioned the afterlife as being this magical place where you could do like whatever you wanted and be whoever you wanted, and, you know, just be happy, be around things that you like and not have to worry about any bullshit that you deal with here on Earth.

He'd soon find out.

Dearest Diary ...

There is a large mythos built around Randy Stair, surviving to this day. His wild persona in videos, his off-kilter humor in skits, his talent in storyboarding EGS, his dexterous voice acting, and his blunt livestreams appealed to teens lost in dark places who found him comforting—in the same boat, disillusioned and relatably furious with the state of the world. Audiences liked his struggles with his sense of self and his openness. He didn't flinch away from describing the type of body modifications he wanted (including dripping pale liquid latex all over to make himself as "white as possible," to look like Ember), or the fact that he was desperately in love with cartoon characters—he took pride in that. People thought he was charming, talented, and attractive.

Certainly, he had his skills. But his videos gave glimpses, through fissures and fault lines, of his inner world. His dislike of body hair, for instance, belied his scorn for adults, while craving to be *whiter* spoke to a deep-seated racism. The violent skits he performed with his stuffies were stand-ins for the violence he craved to enact on human bodies. But his diary was the epicenter for his most gratuitous—and honest—thoughts.

On YouTube, he was to some extent performing. He knew he had an audience, and that he was limited by certain rules and expectations. But in the pages of his two journals, college-ruled, black and purple, he jotted more than 270 pages of screeds in black ink, his letters looping sideways across some of the worst paragraphs fathomable. Perhaps that was performative, too—surely he had some inkling that his journals would be found after he'd made the decision to commit mass murder. Perhaps he hoped they would be viewed as something of an autobiography or a manifesto, edgy and full of malevolent prose, spittle-foam dripping over each word. And perhaps he knew it would all be digitized, uploaded, pored over—villainized, yes, but just *maybe* also lauded by people who felt like he did. Who felt humanity *sucked*, without looking inward.

He kept these candid diaries from November of 2016 to June of 2017. There is no better insight into who Randy was than his own words—which ought to dismantle any hero worship of him, or the pity for a lost soul who "just needed help." More than most shooters, Randy embodied truly *malignant* evil that reveled in itself.

His diary, in fact, is so foul and vile that the worst passages are not fit for print. Instead, as a sampling, to show the core of who Randy was without giving too much screen time to the worst scrapings of the gutter of his thoughts, here are a few passages in his own words, on various topics. Randy Stair was not edgy. Not a martyr. He was a deeply disturbed bigot, violently racist, homophobic, sexist, and misanthropic. His words didn't exist in an angry void—he went to school with the people he talks about, he worked with them, he killed them.

Be advised that these passages are disturbing and abhorrent. Please skip to the next section if you would like to continue Randy's story without sampling his diatribes. If you decide to continue, note that in the primary source material, his words were monstrously *worse*.

Regarding race, where Randy was his most repugnant, he wrote:[310]

> Let's talk about Black people. Okay, first off, one, you're not "black," you're fucking "brown." Secondly, white people aren't "white," who's the retard who coined those terms? Black people should all be [killed] ... for even existing in this fucking world. They dress like complete fucking retarded homosexuals from another galaxy, their hair is a fucking disgrace to the shitskid on the underwear that is the human race, their voices are worse than ... Donald Trump.... They almost all do hard drugs.... Fuck black people."

He goes on to degrade Japanese and Hispanic people as well, but *always* in comparison to Black Americans. He details his plans for the murder of Black people and his white supremacist eugenicist views on racial genocide in nauseating detail.

Regarding men, Randy wrote:

> She asked me once as an "end all be all" way of "Are you gay?" and I said "No." because I'm not gay. Guys who are "gay" are attracted to men (the same sex). I despise men, I hate them, they're disgusting.... All men are ... lazy sacks of shit OR cry baby whores who want you to get a job and work a slave job to "build character" and "be a man." FUCK ... OFF!

On transgenderism and nonbinarism:

> I guess the proper term would be 'transgender' but I don't even fully agree on that. I'm legit a girl trapped inside a boy's body. I'm a feminine soul.... On Earth you're born as either a male or a female, there's no in-between. Yes, you are born with a sexual preference (straight, bisexual, gay, lesbian, transgender, etc.) but you're STILL a male OR a female, you can't be neutral. Your 'spiritual' sex is what you

310 Langman, "Randy Stair's Journal."

truly are. My soul is female but my mortal body is male, which is what I had to be sent here as in order to realize how 'wrong' it was.

Of women, he wrote:

I just became [so] OBSESSED with fantasizing about girls in 10th and 11th grade that the hormones were impossible to ignore. I jerked off in class.... for sometimes as long as 25–40 mins until lo and behold there was success.... I have fantasies of killing girls and laying their corpse on top of me and fusing into their bodies, absorbing their feminine traits and absorbing what little life is left inside of them. I'm a ghoul, a girly, feminine ghoul. I want girls' bodies. I want to become them, overshadow them, and eventually discard them for something better and more satisfying. The smooth skin, the curves, the stomach (exterior), the chest, the silky moist smooth arms and legs, the long hair on the head, this I how I'm meant to be but I'm not; not yet.... Dead girls are perfect.

On mental health:

If you cut yourself then you're fucking retarded. You deserve to die. "It helps get the pain out" BULLFUCKING-SHIT! You're unbelievable. Just end your life if you frequently cut yourself. You'll be happier, trust me. Just die.

About the people in his life:

[Haley] I mean HOPE to Goddess that you fuck up your life so badly that one day you end up getting hunted down, beaten, drugged, raped, tortured, and locked up in someone's basement.... I would shoot you to death if you were on my property.

Sammy is a fucking 5-year-old who needs everything handed to her OR she's just a lazy cunt bitch who feeds off of people for attention. She dragged me into her depression and 'tried' to take her life.... I wish you fucking had.

I would've killed dad but he needs to suffer. What the fuck is he even doing with his life? NOTHING! He's a manager at a fucking supermarket, that's one of the lamest, worthless, pathetic jobs on Earth! .... Who is he to tell me how I should live when he works a job at the bottom of the shit barrel?? Fucking kill yourself. You can take all of your life/parenting lectures and shove them down your throat.... My fucking dad is a worthless faggot.

It's not my fault [Tim] can't drive! He's a worthless fucking faggot!... I'm going to pull your fucking tongue out through your worthless pathetic face and watch you choke on your own blood and bodily fluids. KILL YOURSELF YOU SACK OF SHIT OF WORTHLESS SHIT! If you ever speak to me again, I WILL kill you.

This is who Randy was. These words, his own, encapsulate his extremely unglamorous thought process about humanity, gender, race, and sexuality. His words go further, get worse, glamorize torture, revel in belittling people in his day-to-day, and fetishize gore. Randy was hypocritical, twisted, and fanatical about physical and sexual violence. A final passage from his diary, regarding coworkers who escaped his wrath by the miracle of scheduling:

I WILL TORTURE YOUR SAD PATHETIC EXCUSES FOR HUMAN BODIES SO BADLY THAT YOU'LL BE COUGHING UP BLOOD AND SHITTING YOUR ORGANS OUT FOR 7 MONTHS STRAIGHT!!!! KILL YOURSELF OR I'LL DO IT FOR YOU.

Ashes to Ashes

From in front of their two-acre lot in Dallas, Lori-Ann and Robert made a statement of condolence after the Weis shooting. "Our thoughts and prayers are with the victims and their families. We are so sorry for all the pain and loss of life this has caused everyone involved."[311]

Even as flowers, electric votive candles, and makeshift cardboard signs began to litter the outside of the Weis Market, the general sentiment of the town was that it wasn't the parents' fault. "You've Got a Friend in Pennsylvania" is more than a slogan; people in PA have a firmer sense of neighborly empathy than almost anywhere in the States.[312] The people of Dallas saw the Stairs as victims, too. They'd tried everything to help their son, to steer him right, give him a sense of purpose, direction, and belonging. They were good people, and

311 Peggy Lee, "Search Warrant Shows Chilling Account of Weis Shooting from Sole Survivor," *WNEP*, last updated June 9, 2017, https://www.wnep.com/article/news/local/wyoming-county/psp-search-warrant-shows-chilling-account-of-weis-shooting-from-sole-survivor/523-0928a4ef-3667-4b98-a788-6c2e914b84e5.

312 Chris Hopkins, "How Friendly is Pennsylvania? Apparently We're not as Nice as the Buckeyes," PennLive.com, August 22, 2019, https://www.pennlive.com/life/2019/08/how-friendly-is-pennsylvania-apparently-were-not-as-nice-as-the-buckeyes.html.

Jeremy stood as proof. Randy, with his Peter Pan complex, had no interest in improvement.

Yet despite his childish antics, at the point of these murders, he was very much an adult.

His diary got in one last taunt at his family. "How does it feel knowing you wasted a shitload of money on giving me an education? What are you gonna do now, Bob? Huh? What are you gonna do now to keep the three of you remaining afloat? What's your plan? I got news for ya, it's nowhere near your time; you're gonna suffer for at least a decade and a half over this," with "this" being the Weis murders, "and I'll enjoy every nervewracking [sic] minute of it." Dallas wasn't going to let Randy have his final three victims, insomuch as possible.

As Randy *would* have wanted, his family had him cremated. In a suicide note he left them, he admitted, "I know you might be thinking you could have gotten [me] help. Getting medication, going [to] therapy, he says—"That's not me, never would be."

Despite all of this evidence of who he was, Randy's online obituary is suffused with sycophants. They *did* blame the Stairs for Randy's loss. People who never met him gushed:[313]

> I hope the ghost squad is treating you well. Forever 24.
>
> What struck me about him was his natural charisma and creativity.
>
> Rest in peace my fav girl you will forever be missed, I hope your doing better with the EGS ♡♡♡
>
> Forever missing you pretty girl....<3

Additional tributes poured in as the Weis news went viral. On YouTube, user @deepdarkdown posted a video playlist dedicated to Randy titled "Ember's Ghost Squad."[314] One music video highlights the Tunkhannock Weis in short, dark clips, spliced with images of fire, Ember, the Weis parking lot, stuffed animals, and butt plugs. @Deepdarkdown offers free "Ember's Ghost Squad" stickers

313 "Randy Robert Stair," ForeverMissed.com, accessed May 1, 2025, https://www.forevermissed.com/randy-robert-stair/about.

314 Deep down, "ember's ghost squad, hope they're ready :(" YouTube, July 16, 2022, https://www.youtube.com/watch?v=yiVe0lcLZcM&list=PL5YzulWPObdmxRw_cUo8SUMXE4qrzDAoM.

emblazoned with the Weis logo to the first fifty people to message him.

A tribute site to Andrew titled "My Eternal Shrine to Mommy"[315] calls Andy a "Prophet" and the "O.G. Working Class Hero," laughably misunderstanding Randy's thoughts on the working class. The site "nominates new members"—a thinly veiled way of suggesting targets for murder.

In a video posted a month before the shooting, Randy asked in a moment of introspection, "What's ... to prevent this from happening again?... you can't prevent it. You can only endure."

Survivor Kristin touchingly has the date of the massacre tattooed on her arm, along with a mourning flower and an owl, Victoria's favorite animal—in honor of hope, and in honor of her lost friends. She has found a way to forgive Randy for that day, for her own well-being.

And yet he wouldn't have asked for forgiveness. Inside the front cover of one of his journals, he'd written, "I have no regrets for what I may do or what I have done. I am who I am, and no fucking human shit can take that away from me. I'm an 'EGS' recruit; you're worthless fucking humans. One day you'll all see things my way; especially when our ghost squad invades your pathetic putrid planet and [you] become our slaves for the rest of your lives. I will not stop. I will not change. I will not cower. I will fight for the squad and do what I've set out to do. I am Andrew Fucking Blaze."

He threatened privately to haunt anybody who didn't remember him, saying, "the last thing I'd ever want is to be forgotten." He thought of himself as one of Earth's "greatest minds" and hoped that Weis would "permanently close" thanks to him. He thought staff should thank him for the day off they'd get after the murders. "You're welcome."

In an episode of *Danny Phantom* where Ember is defeated and sent back to the Ghost Zone, she begs, "Say my name! Say it!" Much like Ember, Randy wanted people to remember him—to say his name. Remember his victims instead—Victoria. Terry. Brian.

315 AndrewBlaze.com, accessed May 1, 2025, https://andrewblaze.com.

CHAPTER 9

DAVID KATZ,
aka Bread

Whatever I downed, it got me goin' crazy
Psychedelics got me goin' crazy
I was hot as hell out in the heat
And then this storm came in to save my life
Look up to the sky, down on my knees
Out of nowhere, you came in to save the night
In the nighttime
Got me goin' crazy
Okay, I been up for some days, I ain't got time to lay
Just to drown out all these thoughts, I tried all kind of things
If I take you to my past you will be traumatized.
—"Stargazing," Travis Scott

This song's notes, eerily discordant, floated up through the haze of gun smoke, playing over a pair of fallen headphones lying still on a blood-slick floor in the otherwise silent moments after the shooting stopped. It was loud enough for victims to make it out as they waited, injured, for help or absolution.

Get That Bread!

Over 400 million viewers, one billion dollars in revenue, sold-out arenas, franchised leagues, newscasts, trophies, television spots, terse salary negotiations, and performance-enhancing drug scandals: just your average sports season. Except these sports aren't played on the pitch—they're tethered to a joystick in the exciting world of esports. After booming onto the global marketplace in the 1990s, esports has matured into a competitive industry with tournament winner pots in millions of dollars and finals matches that sell out 20,000-capacity stadiums. Esports has become such a dominant form of entertainment, it's even begun to demand Olympic consideration.

Esports are played through gaming systems such as Xbox, PlayStation, and Nintendo Switch, and "e-athletes" have become big-time household names among gamers and streaming fans, gaining online followings and gaggles of admirers, especially those players who make it into the international tournaments that pull big crowds both online *and* in person. Esports can be played individually or as a team, but competitions are always showdowns where the fastest, shrewdest, and most skilled are hoisted to the victor's podium. Though one joy of *online* gaming is competing or cooperating with strangers from the comfort of one's own home, celebrity players elevated to the ranks of "world's greatest" are trotted out to live venues. They're on cheered by real crowds, have their moves covered by genuine sports commentators, and are livestreamed to thousands of viewers across the globe during play.

Gaming's rapid professionalization in the early 2000s grew alongside popular easy-streaming platforms such as Twitch and YouTube. By the 2010s, game companies were developing their platforms with multiplayer tournaments in mind, the viewership of which was sometimes more lucrative than the games themselves.

A hallmark of esports is its worldwide appeal, thanks in part to its being open to players from any country, and also partly due to the likelihood of fans *also* being players—a common barrier in contact sports. For example, although someone may love watching hockey, it wouldn't be unusual if they'd never *played* hockey before—maybe because they don't live near a rink, or have the physical build or level of skill needed. But all it takes to play the *NHL '25* game is owning the game itself—and its console. It also helps that tournaments are not localized to individual nations or states. Add that to the popularity and accessibility of gaming and streaming and it's little wonder that esports have gone global.

Cost is another major factor in esports' popularity. The lowest-cost ticket to the NFL Super Bowl final comes in at a whopping $8,000—whereas spectator passes to *Madden* football gaming tournaments start at just $5. Equipment for playing tackle football—the full padding, cleats, helmets—costs between $700 and $2,200 on average. The most expensive version of *Madden '24*, the deluxe edition, clocks in at $99, with infinite replayability.

Esports doesn't lose out on the cool factor, either. Its origins were a little bit rock 'n' roll, with the first acknowledged competitive tournament taking place on October 19, 1972, at Stanford University in California. Players faced off at *Spacewar!*, the first video game that could be played simultaneously from multiple computer ports. Each port looked like a vintage projector—in actuality, they were cathode-ray tube displays—with combat simulations glowing in shades of green against the viewport window. Touted as "The Intergalactic *Spacewar!* Olympics," the tourney was an all-out dog fight against gravity, pitfalls, and fellow computer science students, featuring clashing egos and that eternal college event staple, *free beer*.

Surrounded by viewers in a room plastered with antiwar posters and elven script from *The Lord of the Rings*, five students vied for the top spot, firing sluggish torpedoes and out-maneuvering orbital gravity. From the fray, esports' first grand champion emerged: Bruce Baumgart, with free-flowing wavy blond locks, unobtrusive wire-framed glasses, and a wide and jubilant smile. The hippie youth had taken a break from homework in the AI lab to crush the competition. His prize? A year's subscription to *Rolling Stone*, a counterculture music and political rag plugging gonzo journalism. Through an alumnus, it was also the *Spacewar!* tournament's sponsor.

Then-*Rolling Stone* sportswriter Stewart Brand—a Stanford biology graduate himself—covered the event in a wash of sci-fi tropes and real sports commentary. "Ready or not, computers are coming to the people.... an irrepressible midnight phenomenon known as *Spacewar* [has].... hundreds of computer technicians ... locked in life-or-death space combat ... for hours at a time, ruining their eyes, numbing their fingers in frenzied mashing of control buttons, joyously slaying their friends, and wasting their employers' valuable computer time.

"Personalities begin to establish themselves in the maneuvering spaceships: The pilot of the ship called *Pointy Fins* is a dead shot but panics easily in crossfire. *Roundback* tries to avoid early dueling and routinely fires two torpedoes.... *Birdie* drives for the sun and a fast orbit, has excellent agility.... *Funny Fins* shouts a lot.... *Flatback* is silent and maintains an uncanny field-sense of the whole battlesky, impervious to surprise attack."[316]

The event was photographed by Annie Leibovitz, a staffer at the nascent *Rolling Stone*, her prints appearing in *Stone*'s newspaper leaflet printout, which typically sold for twenty-five cents a pop. *Rolling Stone* was not yet the glossy magazine offered at newsstands from New York to LA, and Leibovitz had not yet snapped shots of John Lennon curled naked around Yoko Ono just hours before his assassination. Like esports, they'd both be household names soon enough.

While esports has "sports" in its name, many of the games defined by this term are first-person shooters, real-time strategy games, or battle royale games, like the popular *Smash Brothers* series. In 2000, there were only a dozen pro tournaments for players to clash at, versus a staggering 260 just a decade later, with some international prize pots climbing to $2.8 million. Unique viewership of the biggest events has surpassed 4.5 million for finals' matches.[317] They've become a way for those skilled in hand-eye coordination and mental flexibility to *get that bread*—slang for working hard to make that money.

---

316 Stewart Brand, "Spacewar," Wheels.org, accessed May 1, 2025, https://wheels.org/spacewar/stone/rolling_stone.html.

317 Ben Popper, "Field of Streams: How Twitch Made Video Games a Spectator Sport," *The Verge*, September 30, 2013, https://www.theverge.com/2013/9/30/4719766/twitch-raises-20-million-esports-market-booming.

And that's just what one user, who went by the online handle @Bread, would do.

David Katz's—@Bread's—esport of choice was based on a real sport: *Madden*, the National Football League game. A regular on the competition circuit and a finalist at major regional tournaments, Bread cemented his fame in the 2017 *Madden* NFL Buffalo Bills tournament, hosted in part by the Buffalo Bills professional league team, where he'd snipe the lead on a final buzzer, producing one of the most sensational finishing flourishes in esports history.

He'd make the news again soon after. This time, at the *Madden '19* NFL tournament, and for a darker reason. On August 26, 2018, the bowels of the GLHF (Good Luck, Have Fun) pizza parlor at Jacksonville Landing in Florida was teeming. 150 guests crammed around gaming rigs, families enjoyed lunch, and friends flagged bartenders for beer. That peace was shattered when David entered at 1:30 p.m., opening fire on the throngs. He'd shoot thirteen innocent victims, some even execution-style, with a red laser sight. Mirthlessly and methodically, he turned his last bullet on his fourteenth and final victim—himself.

The attack on his peers seemed senseless and random, especially after the celebration of the previous year and the joy—to the point of obsession—that gaming gave David. But what emerges when digging into David's past is a history checkered with abuse and bullying—but on whose part, it's hard to say.

Grossly shy with wide, bulging eyes and an unerring stare that led people to feel he was looking *through* them, David was often perceived as aloof. In hindsight, his quietness was touted by mobs of press as proof of his monsterhood and sociopathy. This was the version of David that his mother, Elizabeth Katz, consistently painted for courts and police—depressed, violent, disrespectful, schizophrenic, and dirty.

But the David that his father, Richard Katz, knew read much differently—maltreated, misdiagnosed, and neglected, but also normal, self-aware, sometimes joyful. A regular kid who liked to play baseball outside, adored games, and needed, but rarely received, peer support. A lonely young man who took his woes out on those he felt wronged by.

Boom! It's in the Game

Hosts complained that David had been standoffish at the *Madden '17* tourney in Buffalo. He was accused of not looking his opponents in the eye, and commentators whined in retrospect that getting him to open up to them in post-game interviews had been like "pulling teeth."[318]

But viewing the livestream, David seems very different than in the press sensationalism. During tournament play, David *is* happy, and though he is not chatty, he's quick to respond in interviews. He appears uncomfortable in his own skin at times, but certainly not devoid of emotion. He is not a sore and boastful winner, and his shy gaze doesn't seem to be malignant. In fact, across esports, not meeting your opponents' eye seems par for the course where egos lock in virtual battle over real money. Carlos Yancy Jr., who ended up coming in second to Katz in 2017, would do the same exact thing when they went to shake hands—look away.

Though the tournament featured just eight players, David's seventh-seed position was a Hail Mary. Prizes on the line were steep: almost $10,000, US tournament ranking points, and a spot at the national final in Burbank, California. The first seed was Carlos, considered the front-runner and an easy favorite. It should have been a stress-free finish for Yancy, known by his screen name @Los, against a disfavored dark horse. But after Carlos lapsed against his first and second opponents, Bread was in the hot seat for the prize pot.

EA Games provided live coverage of the stream, commentated by Larry Riddley, a CBS sports host, and Zach Farley, now *EA Games*' senior communications manager for North American football. One announcer proudly declared that Bread had had "the gunslinger mentality to go for it," as he climbed ranks in his first two games, but still, no one really thought he had a chance of pulling off a hat-trick

318 Eyewitness News ABC7NY, "David Katz identified as shooter at Madden tournament in Jacksonville," YouTube, August 27, 2018, https://www.youtube.com/watch?v=GG02oGdg46A.

of wins to take it all. He'd blown out the second-seed player, Cino, with a 41 to 7 win first, but his second game against Nova was a narrower 25 to 22 victory.

Wide C-shaped booths, juicy notes of chopped meat and wing sauce on the air, enviously large television sets casting a blue glow over white barstools—these were the hallmarks of 716 Food and Sport in Buffalo, the overachieving older brother of sports bars everywhere. Decked out with Buffalo Bills NFL backdrops, decals, and helmets, the scene was all set for its final battle: spectators were introduced to Bread versus Los. The underdog situation was double-underlined Riddley and Farley, who almost cattily narrated,

> Los, Lesotho the God, his real name Carlos Yancy Jr., you might know that name, I mean he's got athletic genes, he's got athletic blood in his family. His father played for the New England Patriots back in the early '90s ... his granddad played ... major league baseball, [he's] got a sister that's playing softball currently down in Tampa at the University of South Florida ... and when you look at Bread? He used to have a pet rabbit.... Because he couldn't get a dog.... But now he's got a chance to be the big dog.
>
> The two best players in this tournament so far. Will we break Bread, or will it be Big Los?[319]

David, then just twenty-three compared to Los's twenty-eight, was considered amateurish against Los's "veteran" status. Until the game began. Los would do a lot of moving and obvious strategizing as the two duked it out, whereas Katz sat quietly and stared ahead with those bulging, bright eyes, a little unnerving for their lack of blinking. Farley noted "that *stare*," saying he'd seen Katz smile earlier in the tourney when he made his second-round comeback. But Bread wasn't all chill: He came across as nervous when his plays didn't work out, relieved when he scored, and annoyed when his offensive line got tackled.

Only eight gamers would get to compete in Burbank. He *needed* this win to be one of them.

---

319 Joman66, "Madden 17 Club Series Bills Championship Bread vs Los," YouTube, August 26, 2018, https://www.youtube.com/watch?v=G4Zuwd5EW64.

In the fourth quarter, with just under four minutes left in the game, Los would storm into the lead from the icy grip of a long tie, notching the score to 20–17 after his field goal attempt cleared, all while he chewed on blue gum. Bread would wet his lips, refocusing.

Just under the three-minute mark, Bread threw too low. He was visibly frustrated and disappointed. Then, he'd manage a forty-six-yard field goal, tying the game up again. Los would cover his mouth in horror and sit back. Bread stared unblinkingly ahead, without celebration.

Bread had played *Madden* thousands of times. Los was returning to the scene after a three-year break, drawn in by the promise of a million-dollar prize pool for the winner in California.

With 2:26 left on the clock, the ball went to Los. Time ticked down. Hands shaking, Los made a wild throw when less than fifty seconds were on the clock. When the throw was picked off by Bread's squad, Los tossed up his arms in frustration, before touching his head in disbelief. Los sat back in his gaming chair as Bread pitched forward in his, mouth open in a smile of relief.

He could *not* believe it.

The ball went back to Bread. With thirty seconds left in the game, Bread touched his hair nervously after he played a bad second down. He'd fail the third, too. At fourth down and five, back on his own end of the field, around the forty-yard line with twenty-eight seconds left to play, he made a pass he couldn't complete, turning the offense over to Los in Bread's own defensive zone—and Los did a literal happy dance. It should've been all over now. Los could score.

Bread's mouth flickered; his eyes grew moist. Los was set up for the win if he took any points, and with seconds left, there would be no recourse for rebuttal. But then, amazingly, Bread's team knocked the ball out of his opponent's hands—David celebrated in his seat. Tensions ramped. Los messed up his second down, too, then dropped his pass on third, and Bread shouted "YES!" With the quarter almost up and the game tied, Los figured he'd see Bread in overtime. Los would punt downfield to force that overtime. A literal throwaway move, with eight seconds left to waste.

But miraculously, Bread *caught* it, and inconceivably, his team passed down to the fifty-yard line. The catch was completed, so he ran. And ran. And *ran*. With *one* second left, he was twenty-five yards from a touchdown. "Does he have enough juice?!" Larry cried out as Bread began openly, warmly laughing and Los pressed his lips.

Touchdown. With zero seconds left on the clock.

Los dropped his headphones into his lap, shaken. Bread grinned from ear to ear, toothy and thrilled, and rocked back and forth with glee. It was a legendary upset, this sterling final buzzer win.

Bread even made his field goal. The final score stood at 27 to 20 after a run of more than seventy yards. Following the win, Bread and Los shook hands, with Bread readily making eye contact, smile studded with blindingly white teeth, looking cheerful and clean—a far cry from the unwashed man who reviled a toothbrush and rewore the same stinking clothes every day of his final tournament at GLHF in Florida.

One of the hosts, Steve Tasker, would also shake David's hand. David grinned, electrified and bashful.

What seemed to off-put people about Bread was the wideness of his almost lidless eyes. If not for their unerringness, so deeply set that he almost seemed to be wearing makeup, he'd have been considered conventionally handsome. He had curved, thin brows, and a slender mouth, often pressed. Reasonably tall, he was reedy for his age, middling around 120 pounds, with a mop of ruddy brown hair and sunken cheekbones. He gave the impression of a Tim Burton claymation character. He also had some trouble communicating, stumbling over his words, restarting often. He didn't have a winning personality, but he didn't need to. Not for esports.

While much of the media storm that would follow his GLHF shooting would call David arrogant, at *Madden '17* in Buffalo David seemed humble, saying he "got lucky" that Los fumbled an easy play and that he had managed a difficult one. He refers four times to luck being the main factor. Though he'd call himself "the best," he'd mean that particular day, never wearing the moniker like a crown.

Often replayed after his mass murder was the soundbite of Bread telling Stever Tasker, "Um, yeah, I don't think of myself as seventh seed. I think, personally, I'm one of the better players."[320] Left out was: "I was glad I was able to play a good game, and lucky...."

Low-ranked or not, he would be bound for the Burbank games on April 15. There, he'd find defeat, but that eventual overthrow did not detract from that fantastic moment: the underdog taking the top spot. Also going by handles like @MrSlicedBread and @RavensChamp online, that clutch victory put him on the map in esports. The winner's pot of $3,500 wasn't bad either.

His moment in Buffalo influenced viewership globally. No one could believe how extraordinarily exciting David's win was—both its cinematic, last-moment triumph and the impressive pole-vault over the odds set against him. *Bread* became a household name for those in the know, and his performance would be heavily praised by game companies and announcers, his livestream and clips viewed hundreds of times a day.

After his eventual loss at the 2017 grand finals, and despite his burgeoning fame, he'd go on to have a disappointing run a year later, losing early at a big tournament in Tampa, Florida. It looked like his luck had run out.

Little known to them at the time, it had run out for the other players, too.

As if foreshadowing, in LA at the 2017 finals, Bread was knocked out by an opponent named Misery—exactly what he'd eventually lose himself to in real life.

Bad Seed

Many Miles Mews is a leafy cul-de-sac with manicured stretches of front lawn and fulsome white oaks shading the pavement. It's a safe place for children to throw a ball or ride a bike, with little traffic. The sameness of its many two-story, brick-faced houses gives it a friendly, same-team air, while garages pregnant with automobiles flash upper-middle-class wealth.

This is a street of neighbors who wave to one another, whose children tumble from one yard into the next with easy abandon,

320 Eyewitness News ABC7NY, "David Katz identified as shooter."

where family dogs lope around vast hydrangea bushes. Unlike most avenues of affluence, here the lawns mostly flow into each other, back terraces left unhidden, property lines unmarked by fences—forgoing America's typical privacy policy.

Maybe it was that lack of privacy that led neighbors to notice when police cars were parked outside the home of Richard and Elizabeth Katz. Or maybe it was the sheer frequency of it.

From 1993 through 2009, some twenty-six calls to authorities were recorded by authorities in Columbus, Maryland.[321] Mostly. it was Elizabeth Katz calling to report her son, David Katz, for minor infractions; sometimes it was David calling, begging relief from his mother.

The Katz family should have had the sort of easy living promised by impressive institutional degrees and fantastic jobs. Richard Katz worked for NASA at the Goddard Space Flight Center in its Instrument Electronic Development branch, just outside of Washington, DC. With a master's in electrical engineering, he was expected to help design, test, and deliver systems for space flight, from temperature control electronics to data processors. Award-winning, he chaired the Military and Aerospace Programmable Logic Device International Conference in 2004.

Elizabeth was equally a success, with a PhD in toxicology and a job with the US Food and Drug Administration (FDA). She helped coauthor seven papers on topics ranging from the "excitation of primary afferent neurons by near-infrared light in vitro" to "fiber-optic nerve integration with optical coherence tomography distance sensors."

Both job tracks came with the potential of six-figure salaries, achieved by at least one parent, and the Katzes raised a family on a street where homes—mostly four-bedroom newish builds from the 1980s—cost $600,000 to $700,000. They had the money to pay Homeowners Association fees and property taxes that were generally higher than elsewhere in Maryland.[322] The area they settled was

321 Jose Pagliery, Curt Devine, and Drew Griffin, "Jacksonville Shooter had History of Mental Illness and Police Visits to Family Home," CNN, last updated August 28, 2018, https://www.cnn.com/2018/08/28/us/jacksonville-madden-shooter-katz-mental-health-invs/index.html.

322 "Overview of Maryland Taxes," SmartAsset.com, accessed May 1, 2025, https://smartasset.com/taxes/maryland-property-tax-calculator#jIVfDPIFsL.

extremely car-dependent, not lending itself to families who rely on walking or public transport. Children were extremely dependent on parents to get further afield than the Mews.

The Katz family had two sons—Brandon, born in 1990, and David, who came along three years later. They stuck together until 2005, when Richard and Elizabeth separated, before filing for divorce in 2007. The acrimonious suit would last for almost a decade. At the center of it were allegations of infidelity, alcoholism, adultery,[323] verbal abuse, and negligence toward the children. Most accusations were on the part of Richard toward Elizabeth.

By 2007, it was noted in court that both Katz boys had what was termed "significant healthcare needs."[324] But David and Elizabeth were at odds about *how* significant, and whether those needs even existed at all. Ninety-six pages of their divorce filings were devoted to the bitter back-and-forth over Brandon and especially David.

Elizabeth's point of view was put forth by her lawyers: David suffered from great mental stress and needed continued treatment for emotional and psychological issues. He was on antipsychotic pills for schizophrenia and also taking antidepressants. She wanted her boys to go through dedicated psychiatric evaluations and to continue on robust, steady medications.

From Richard's point of view, that was absurd. In a motion filed by his lawyer, he communicated that he "has seen no evidence whatsoever of schizophrenia in David Katz. David seems aware of reality at all times."[325] As for the antidepressants, in court filings Richard worried that they "posed significant and unknown risks to the children," though both his sons—aged twelve and fifteen—had already been placed on medication at that time. His fears revolved around

323 Louise Boyle and Ben Ashford, "Jacksonville Gamer Gunman's Parents Battled Over Whether He Was Schizophrenic During Bitter Divorce—and Mom Claimed His Dad Stopped Him Getting Therapy," *Daily Mail*, last updated August 28, 2018, https://www.dailymail.co.uk/news/article-6106961/Jacksonville-gaming-gunmans-parents-battled-schizophrenic-bitter-divorce.html.

324 Stephanie Dube Dwilson, "David Katz's Parents & Family: 5 Fast Facts You Need to Know," Heavy.com, August 27, 2018, https://heavy.com/news/2018/08/david-katz-family-parents-richard-elizabeth.

325 Curt Devine, Jose Pagliery, Drew Griffin, Joe Sterling, and Susannah Cullinane, "What We Know about Jacksonville Shooting Suspect David Katz," CNN, last updated August 28, 2018, https://www.cnn.com/2018/08/27/us/jacksonville-madden-tournament-suspect/index.html.

some evidence that antidepressants could created suicidal ideation in teens. Richard's approach leaned more holistic: He preferred for David to attend support groups specifically geared toward children in middle school before jumping into pharmaceuticals.

In 2006, Elizabeth would try to block Richard from legally accessing either of their children's future medical records; Richard would insist that same year that his ex-wife was "not a mental health expert" and said, "[David] informed me that he does not want to take the psychiatric drugs, they make him feel worse, and is making efforts to refuse them. I was unaware of David's efforts ... [but] Elizabeth Katz purchased medications for David after a single visit with a prescribing doctor, during which the doctor was given information that was not correct or [was] significantly exaggerated.... [She's] not acting in the actual best interests of the children."[326] Then he accused her of possibly having a mental disorder herself.

The divorce became so bitter and rancorous that, in the midst of the custody battle in 2006, both Richard and Elizabeth filed a request that David be given over to a judge-appointed guardian *ad litem*—someone to effectively advocate for David so he wouldn't have to make appearances in court or represent his own desires in the crosshairs of their profound disagreement. He was not even a teenager yet during this upheaval—his parents so unable to agree on how he should be supported that his needs and advocacy were trusted to outside legal professionals.

Was his mother an overreactive alcoholic, or was his father not facing up to reality? Mud was slung in both directions. Did David's issues mainly develop after the divorce was triggered, when he was left adrift with his mother, or did they just grow along with him? Regardless of who was right, Elizabeth was granted full custody, with Richard being given visitation rights only. For David, this was a nightmare—and it turned out to be no picnic for Elizabeth, either.

By the time he reached middle school, David was receiving psychiatric treatment at the behest of his mother. He'd seen multiple doctors and therapists, which his father derisively referred to as "a succession

326 Boyle and Ashford, "Jacksonville Gamer Gunman's Parents Battled."

of psychiatrists,"[327] including an art therapist and a social worker, all by 2006. One of these specialists agreed that David was in "psychiatric crisis."[328] While still in middle school, David became so distressed by the idea of any more mental health appointments that he locked himself in his mother's Volkswagen Jetta, frantic, to try to escape going to one. His mother then threatened through the door to have him arrested. She'd call the cops, leaving the frightened boy; just twelve years old; with "the prospect of being put in handcuffs by police."[329]

Birthdays were also hectic time, put mildly. The day after David turned thirteen, Elizabeth called the cops on him again. This time, for the television volume being too loud and for being disrespectful toward her and his grandmother, the police report reflected.[330] The authorities were called the day after his fourteenth birthday, too, this time with the caller being David, who complained that his mother "keeps punishing [me] by taking away [my] video games."

Another fraught holiday was Mother's Day. Elizabeth kicked David out of the house twice as a minor, once at around the age of fourteen on Mother's Day itself.[331] She'd packed his clothes right into a suitcase and sent him out.[332]

When things were as normal as they ever got, David attended Hammond High School in Columbia, Maryland, where, as a shy loner, he was sometimes bullied. Peers recall him as quiet and strange, but also kind. A few former classmates would even admit he sometimes came off as *cool* because he was so unflappable. Nonetheless, David spent much of his academic life mentally suffering. At different points during high school, he was on Risperidone, an antipsychotic

---

327 Devine et al., "Jacksonville Shooter Had History."

328 David Fleming, "The Madden Tournament Shooting in Jacksonville–An Inside Look at What Happened," *ESPN*, September 19, 2018, https://www.espn.com/esports/story/_/id/24686074/the-madden-tournament-shooting-jacksonville-look-happened.

329 Devine et al., "Jacksonville Shooter Had History."

330 Devine et al., "Jacksonville Shooter Had History."

331 Chris Perez, "Madden Shooter Constantly Fought with Mom, Refused to Bathe," *New York Post*, last updated August 28, 2018, https://nypost.com/2018/08/27/madden-shooter-constantly-fought-with-mom-refused-to-bathe.

332 Michael Biesecker and David McFadden, "Florida Shooting Suspect had History of Mental Illness," *Times of Israel*, August 28, 2018, https://www.timesofisrael.com/florida-shooting-suspect-had-history-of-mental-illness.

used also to treat schizophrenia, and Lexapro, to treat depression. His mother, as a toxicologist, certainly would have had some insight into how these chemicals would affect him.

Richard balked at all of this, saying his former wife had "an obsession with using mental health professionals and, in particular, psychiatric drugs to perform the work that parents should naturally do."[333] Ironically, part of what he entered as evidence to the court was a study showing a link between people under the age of eighteen taking certain antidepressant medications and increased levels of suicidal ideation—a study by the FDA. He insisted that a psychiatrist had also told David to *stop* taking the drugs he was using, as they were too potent or not working. Richard attested that David was "physically strong and mentally does not need drugs."[334]

Court findings from 2006 summarized, "There are serious issues regarding the children upon which the parties have fundamental difference of opinion ... [such as] the children's mental health needs and educational needs.... It is unfortunate for the children that both parents are so focused on litigation that the children's needs seem to be taking a back seat."

The calls to the police continued even after the divorce was finalized. Elizabeth reported David for a number of infractions, ranging from mental unwellness to alleged abuse. No police recording or filing, though, actually attests to any physical violence David committed against his mother.

From the number of incidences noted across police reports and court filings emerges a picture of a fraught relationship. Elizabeth was reliant on punishment for what she saw as David's disrespectful behavior, and she seemed to feel that he was too dependent on video games for escapism. David complained that she'd often lock away his games to discipline him for staying up late to play since those late hours made him listless for morning classes. In one instance, after his mother locked up his Xbox controllers in her own room to keep them from him, he punched a hole through her bedroom door in his frustrated attempt to get them back. At this time, a therapist noted that

333 Fleming, "The Madden Tournament Shooting in Jacksonville."

334 Fleming, "The Madden Tournament Shooting in Jacksonville."

David's depression was worsening, making him less motivated to eat, sleep, bathe, or have the motivation to leave his room.

After the separation, either David's mental health deteriorated rapidly, or Elizabeth's ability to deal with it was diminished. At the age of thirteen, David was sent to a psychiatric care facility called Sheppard and Enoch Pratt Hospital in Towson, Maryland. A sprawling brick campus, lively with greenery at first glance, yet its imposing size, high walls, and littering of black gates might whisper of spookier fates to a young onlooker. Its Gothic-style gatehouse was a design from the 1860s, arresting and archaic, with a main campus designed originally as an asylum in the Kirkbride style: uncoiling from a hard center, spreading like wings, adding irony to the term "medical wing," so strongly did the layout of wards resemble a bat in flight. Modernized heavily, however, the Pratt facility is a venerated hospital for care and treatment of mental health disorders. David's stay was involuntary, but taking place in August of 2007, at least he did not miss much school, nor did it give classmates an opportunity to notice and question his absence.

His next stay at a mental health facility was in December of 2007, again around the holidays, when school could not provide a buffer of relief for Elizabeth. Perhaps Richard was right, and there was a lack of want or desire to parent David when he was home more often. According to affidavit records, Elizabeth made him an inpatient because he was skipping school and seemed despondent. This stay would have pockmarked David's fourteenth birthday on December 22.

He stayed at the Potomac Ridge Behavioral Health clinic, a faith-based organization in Rockville, Maryland, for adolescents. As of 2025, it has a chilly 1.9 stars on Google Reviews, with reviewers stating, "As a young one, being put in here was not helpful for me.... I was forced in a wheelchair and rolled through the super dark and cold outside.... [they] put an ankle monitor on me.... put me in the room with the boys and I immediately got made fun of for 'looking gay'.... As the days went on the bullying about my weight [continued]...."

Another reviewer laments, "The nurses, staff, and even other patients are bullies. They will make you feel worse." The reviews continue chillingly:

> If you, or your family member/loved one, is given the option to go to any other inpatient psychiatric hospital, take it and run from this place.
>
> For the most vulnerable, this is dangerous care.
>
> [I] never took a shower or changed clothes while I was there.... they stole my shorts, books, shoes, and deodorant.
>
> My son is here.... no natural light, no fresh air or able to go outside.... this is the biggest regret of my life.
>
> I left with ... fleas.... [Food was] two years past the expiration date.... shower water was dark brown and they did nothing about the patients pooping in and all around it.... very pushy with religion.
>
> .... some of the girls said one of the male nurses inappropriately touched them.
>
> Punishment for not complying includes a full-body straight jacket.... Four men tackled my 14-year-old self to the ground and forcefully pulled my pants down to be injected.
>
> Perishable foods ALWAYS had an expiration date of one day later than served.... Others received moldy fruit, nuts when allergic to nuts.... They gave our daughter someone else's meds once.
>
> There is something deeply wrong with this place.
>
> It was hell on earth.... May God forgive the people that work here.

Again and again, former patients mention no heat in the facility in winter. While David was confined there, temperatures in Rockville reached lows of 23 degrees Fahrenheit. This experience for a young person can easily be understood as traumatizing. But was it also necessary?

Richard, naturally, took a dim view of it, telling the court, "Instead of going to school, David was placed in psychiatric day-care."[335]

David's most enduring and difficult stay came in 2008, when he was sent to a therapeutic wilderness school. Located in Enterprise,

---

335 Bill Hutchinson and Marissa Parra, "Suspect in Madden 19 Tournament Shooting Targeted Gamers: Sheriff," *ABC News*, August 27, 2018, https://abcnews.go.com/US/suspect-madden-19-tournament-shooting-targeted-gamers-sheriff/story?id=57423449.

Utah, the facility for thirteen- to seventeen-year-olds—called Redcliff Ascent—is nestled into rural farm country that boasts of fishing lakes, hiking trails, and an annual Corn Fest. Redcliff Ascent has a sunny 4.5/5 rating on Google reviews. It might not have been the care that was arduous, but the length of stay: nearly 100 days.

One hundred days in his freshman year of high school. One hundred days, which may have cost over $40,000 in fees. And one hundred days away from the games that gave him comfort. Redcliff Ascent would try to mold him into something different—better—than his mother felt he was.[336]

Redcliff Ascent is modeled on behavioral modification practices. It begins with isolation until a youngster can conform to the facility's rules, then promotes personal value-building and survivalism. The program ends with group work. According to Breaking Code Silence, a group that explores abuses in institutions in the "Troubled Teen Industry" (TTI), punishments employed by Redcliff Ascent included solitary confinement and socially exiling individuals. Abuse allegations included "denial of medical attention," "physical punishment, restriction of food and water, forced labor, and emotional abuse ... [and] sexual abuse."[337]

Redcliff Ascent was featured on the UK version of *Brat Camp*, a television show that ran from 2005 through 2007 in which troubled teens were blindfolded and led to their new home to do trekking and soul-searching. The show won an International Emmy. Paris Hilton, hotel heiress and icon of the early aughts, made Western American TTI institutions her political cause, having been committed involuntarily herself as a teen and surviving a dehumanizing experience at a similar Utah Ascent program. She helped promote the Breaking Code Silence. Her own hellish experiences, widely known to the public, may have paralleled some of what David endured.

---

336 "RedCliff Ascent Tuition Information," Imgur.com, accessed May 1, 2025, https://imgur.com/a/redcliff-ascent-tuition-information-shUV2FZ.

337 "Redcliff Ascent Wilderness Program (1993–present) Enterprise, UT," BreakingCodeSilence.org, accessed May 1, 2025, https://www.breakingcodesilence.org/redcliff-ascent-wilderness-program.

In total, David was committed against his will six times as a minor.[338]

David's home life with Elizabeth can be cobbled together from records and transcripts. When agitated, the boy would collapse to the floor and curl up, lock himself away, weep, or beat his hands against his face. If his games—a source of joy—were taken away in punishment, he'd stagger around the house doing bizarre concentric circles into the wee hours of the morning.

In a 2009 police call, Elizabeth tells the dispatching operator, "He's sitting here, wrestling me with the cable chord to the TV. I've had enough with this child. He has been abusive for almost two years." David apparently rolled his eyes at this characterization. Elizabeth snaps back, "Roll your eyes. Fine. You'll pay. Where are you going to be tomorrow?"[339]

She also called the police in 2010 to claim that David being home late home from a visit with his father constituted abuse toward her.[340] Richard insisted the majority of her contact with the police was over "trivial matters." On the other hand, David once called the police himself to report, "I was trying to watch TV and [my mom] came in and tried to cut the cord because she thought I wasn't being fair to my brother or something.... Then I just like stood in her way and she just came in with like scissors and I took the scissors and then she came with a knife."[341]

Many of their fights seemed to revolve around control of the television set. Their arguments over possession of his gaming system became so fraught and furied that a lawyer had to remind the family, "This is not *Xbox court*."

By the end of 2009, after Redcliff Ascent, David had had enough. He wrote to a judge on loose-leaf paper, in blocky graphite letters,

---

338 Kate Amara and Vanessa Herring, "Court Documents Shed New Light on Accused Jacksonville Mass Shooter," WBALTV.com, last updated August 28, 2018, https://www.wbaltv.com/article/27-volumes-of-official-documents-shed-new-light-on-accused-jacksonville-mass-shooter/22843359.

339 Biesecker, *Times of Israel*.

340 Accessed on June 6, 2024, https://heavy.com/news/2018/08/david-katz-family-parents-richard-elizabeth.

341 Prudente et al., "Parents Sought Psychiatric Help for Shooting Suspect," *The Baltimore Sun*, accessed May 1, 2025, https://digitaledition.baltimoresun.com/tribune/article_popover.aspx?guid=162585a6-8b15-43e0-9e7d-899166586c7e.

begging to be allowed to live with his father. "Today is my birthday and I'm turning 16.... My mom is pretty crazy. She's called the police on me about 20 times for pretty much nothing, like coming home a little late or something. She also gets drunk and starts yelling at me and poking me and doesn't leave me alone. She has hit me before and always takes my stuff because she feels like it.... I hate her more than anything in the world. I hate everything about her."

Four months later, David wrote again, beseeching the same. This 2010 letter to the magistrate judge would also call his mother "pretty crazy," again accusing her of alcoholism and unjust calls to the authorities. He pointed to Elizabeth's behavior as the reason for his weak school performance, rather than his own sleepless nights.[342]

It seems bizarre that Elizabeth should request full custody of David when she seemed so little equipped to cope with what she characterized as his many mental disorders, aggression, and disrespect. There is bitter irony in the fact that, in a sense, both of David's parents were right—once David became a young adult and moved in with Richard, he settled down and grew more normalized, outgoing, and cheerful. But free of Elizabeth's supervision, he also went on a mass shooting rampage. It is likely that both parents saw different, equally real, sides of their son.

If his home life was fraught, then David's life in high school was no reprieve either. At Hammond High School in Columbia, Maryland—sometimes called "the Zoo on 32"—he was an odd duck. He never quite fit in with any group or forged a band of friends—little wonder, with the looming upheavals of repeated, humiliating institutionalizations at his back. So despite the school motto "Where People Are Important," David faded into the background. When peers noticed him, it was for his baby face. They liked that he looked like Jim Halpert, the popular character played by John Krasinski on the TV show *The Office*.

When his mother didn't take his systems away, David's main focus as a teen was in staying up until 3 or 4 a.m. to game, honing his craft. He'd nap during classes and began to fail in some subjects. He also began foregoing showers and personal hygiene to play, play,

342 Biesecker and McFadden, "Florida Shooting Suspect had History."

play. "His hair would very often go unwashed for days," said his mother. The problem had begun at about the time of the separation: middle school. At Glenelg Country School, the middle school David attended—posh, uniformed, and private—his principal had said that David ought not to return until he'd "straightened himself out."[343] At *that* school, David was bullied for being *weird*. Glenelg was a little too blue for his blood, despite his family's money.

Hammond High School was kinder to him. In his yearbook photo, though unsmiling, David is striking in a suit and black bow tie, his blue eyes piercing, his face more filled out than it would become in later footage, growing lankier and gaunt once he no longer had Elizabeth to feed him.

Three years after high school ended, in 2014, he'd gain admission to the University of Maryland as an environmental science and technology major. Despite it being a four-year degree, he was not enrolled in any classes by August of 2018—the month of the shooting. One of his early TAs characterized him as silent and blank-faced, worrying he struggled to retain information or didn't submit materials. She'd tried to chat with him privately, wanting to offer help, but found him unresponsive. Yet, he didn't forget her attempt at outreach. At year's end, he visited her office to thank her personally for her help, mystifying her.[344]

In adulthood, David finally got his wish to live with his father, moving in with him for a time and often visiting for long stretches at his home in Baltimore's posh Inner Harbor area. They warmed the bleachers at Bowie Baysox ball games, played catch outside on the green in front of Richard's townhouse, and took trips to the batting cages. With Richard, David was less angry, more athletic and outgoing, and his father saw him as the "lively, communicative [and] playful" boy he remembered.[345] Richard displayed David's childhood art in his home, warm and supportive, and encouraged his son to abandon any psychiatric medications he didn't like taking.

---

343 Boyle and Ashford, "Jacksonville Gamer Gunman's Parents Battled."

344 Prudente et al., "Parents Sought Psychiatric Help."

345 Biesecker and McFadden, "Florida Shooting Suspect had History."

It's unclear when David quietly dropped out of university, failing to register for any upcoming classes. Perhaps it was a sign of premeditation; perhaps he knew he would not be returning; or perhaps it simply denoted a tired young man who wasn't very interested in achieving academics, who wanted to be a pro gamer. No one seeming to notice, though, meant that David was no more socially prolific in college than he had been in high school or middle school. No friends called to ask where he was. David still mainly kept to himself and his games, even with his father's nurturing touch and the extra freedom of choice that adulthood provided.

This meant that by the time David was truly embroiled in professional esports, he wasn't prepared for the loud and raucous friend groups that characterize it—having never had one of his own. Esports, in fact, combined a number of discomforts for David. The anonymity of online practice play could lead to brutal verbal bullying. Competition could be cutthroat. But online, as Bread, he was usually lauded for his play style. In person, his shy and peculiar personality made him a target. With the most important esports events being live all across the country and world, players form an ecosystem in a tightly knit "bro culture." Circuit players get to know one another personally, almost better than they know each other's styles and stats. It's something of an open-enrollment frat squad—a family, a band of brothers. And as with any large grouping of people, some members were *in* and some were out.

Online, in viewer counts, David was a superstar. But in person, David was on the social fringe.

On the Fringe

David should have been hard to ignore. EA Sports called his on-the-buzzer victory the "most exciting moment in all the 2017 NFL Club Series Championships." But other gamers mostly ignored him at events, and when he did garner attention, it's possible it was negative.

Most tournaments weren't just big cash prize pulls for the competitors; they were like mini-vacations for the squads who traveled to contend. The players consider themselves a brotherhood. They hit the road for a few days, jetting away from work, school, and domestic chores for a weekend of shooting the breeze—win or lose. Usually tournaments span a full weekend, so even if a player is felled early, he's booked for the full time and sticks around to cheer on friends and learn new moves. Players go for beers together, laugh at in-jokes, play pranks on each other, ask after one another's families, and make a lot of noise. In the after-hours, as the excitement ebbs a little, they filter into quieter, deeper conversations. On the whole, it's very much a male bonding zone—it's estimated that female viewership and participation sits at just 15%.[346] This comes with its own brand of trash-talk and brash-talk. David engaged with almost none of it, not even the small talk. Other gamers didn't appreciate Katz's habit of looking past people rather than at them. But some still tried to be inclusive and gregarious, or else the few that matched David's quiet, sheepish vibe would sidle up to him to engage. These guys were largely stonewalled—chatting wasn't David's forté. The big crowds and loud participants were alienating for him. He already had to swallow his pride when he lost in front of a huge audience—it felt absurd to also be expected to swallow hot wings and gossip thereafter.

But between most players, teasing was expected, extracurricular activities anticipated, and getting personal was de rigueur. To get along in that troop meant catching up on real *life* after the day's main events: work, school, sex, family. Getting real created long, stable, and lasting friendships. But they were topics David couldn't relate to. A lot of the players were also military, or real athletes on top of e-athletes, and so David also would have felt physically outclassed.

But on rare occasions, Katz did join in. In one instance, he texted a fellow player he'd heard was struggling with depression and offered solace and a listening ear. By contrast, none of the gaming group were really aware of Katz's *own* mental health struggles.[347] Outside

346 GameSpot Staff, "Major League Gaming Reports 334 Percent Growth in Live Video," GameSpot .com, November 14, 2012, https://www.gamespot.com/articles/major-league-gaming-reports -334-percent-growth-in-live-video/1100-6400010.

347 Steve Patterson, "Did Grudge Push Gunman in Jacksonville Landing Mass Shooting?" Jacksonville .com, last updated August 25, 2019, https://www.jacksonville.com/story/news/2019/08/25/did -grudge-push-gunman-in-jacksonville-landing-mass-shooting/4383323007/did-grudge-push -gunman-in-jacksonville-landing-mass-shooting/4383323007.

of major tournaments, he only dropped in regularly at small-scale and more socially manageable game nights at a sports bar near Baltimore's M&T Bank Stadium.[348] At the big tournaments, with so many of the competitors being older family men or else energetic college guys, Katz didn't have lot of common ground on which to establish himself.

The 2018 *Madden '19* tournament in Florida was shaping up to be especially exciting for these players. The new game had only been out a couple of weeks, so the updated mechanics and refreshed style felt crisp and helped level the playing field as competitors adjusted the tweaked controls. They'd have to remaster their automatic reflexes around the buttons—and what better way to sharpen up those skills than with a tournament? A $5,000 prize plus a spot at the Madden Classic in Las Vegas in the autumn were up for grabs, too—nice incentivization.

David had come a long way to participate, as Jacksonville was an eleven-hour road trip from Maryland. He packed abnormally light for someone intending to be away from home for days. He didn't pack changes of clothes or a toothbrush. Instead, he'd stuffed a random assortment of knickknacks into a Baltimore Ravens backpack—including a neutral plaid overshirt, high-shine sunglasses, and two handguns. With extra ammunition.

At the event, one player would attempt to strike up a conversation with Katz, asking what other upcoming *Madden* events he had on the horizon. Before he could finish asking the question, David turned away sharply and said, "Don't worry about it."[349] He perhaps already knew that there wouldn't be any future *Madden* events for him.

Mean as Motive

Police would announce after the violent events of August 26, 2018, that David Kazt's murders and subsequent suicide did not appear to be premeditated. But that is incongruous with the facts.

---

348 Prudente et al., Miller, and Richman, "Parents Sought Psychiatric Help."

349 Prudente et al., "Parents Sought Psychiatric Help."

David purposefully demurred from class enrollment at his university—either because he'd become disenchanted with his lack of success, or because he'd taken future planning off the table. Despite his love of gaming, he'd recently told a fellow gamer that he had no plans for further tournaments after Jacksonville. David was calculated in his purchase of guns right before the GLHF event—and methodical in his use of them. He also would have known ahead of time who else would be taking part in the tournament. Specifically, he'd have known that Elijah Clayton and Taylor Robertson were queued up to take on matches. There was bad blood between them and Kazt.[350] He didn't like them—and the feeling was mutual, especially on the part of Elijah. Where Robertson was concerned, there was maybe only a clumsy dislike and a feeling of being overlooked. With Elijah, those livid feelings took on concrete shapes.

As with the students at Glenelg Country School, Clayton felt that Katz presented gawkily and would begin to poke fun at the awkward Katz, increasingly mocking his social ineptitudes, other gamers noticed. One player would later tell *The Florida Times Union* that they were locked in a feud that had been going on for years—ever since Katz had put together a book (its topic unspecified, but very likely a gaming guide) meant to bring him clout and money, and Clayton had purchased it. Rather than reading it, though, he ripped its contents to post online for free, cutting Katz off at his knees, dooming the project, and dealing him an embarrassing blow.[351]

In another incident, David complained that Elijah had offered to share a taxi with him to get back to the hotel they both were rooming at following a tournament. When the cab arrived, however, Elijah got in—and slammed the door on David, instructing the driver to leave without him. At that tournament, to add insult to injury, Elijah had beaten David and eliminated him from play.

Whether due to a sense of loyalty as a member of that brotherhood, out of respect to the dead, or because David was truly making mountains out of mole hills, other gamers disagreed that the taxi

350 Fleming, "The Madden Tournament Shooting in Jacksonville."

351 Patterson, "Did Grudge Push Gunman?"

incident ever happened. But no one was in disagreement about the book. Clayton and Katz were not destined to be friends.

Very much cognizant of that fact, David would go to purchase two handguns while living in Baltimore, ahead of the tournament. In Maryland, gun purchase has a higher bar than in other parts of the US. Federal regulations require that anyone with serious mental health issues be denied gun ownership. The Old Line State has the added qualification that the purchaser must have no history of violent behavior *nor* have spent more than thirty days voluntarily committed in a mental health facility. In a sad bit of irony, had Elizabeth's claims about David being violent with her ever been on official record and verified, he would not have been given a gun license.

Also, a bitter irony was the fact that David had always been committed to facilities *against* his will, so he didn't fail Maryland's voluntary institutionalization restriction. At twenty-four years of age and no longer on medication or seeing doctors, he did not legally qualify as "mentally defective" under federal law.[352] By regulation, he may have had to disclose his involuntary entry into institutes like Redcliff Ascent as a minor—but it wouldn't have mattered much.

Further in the column of premeditation, to obtain the guns he eventually took on his road trip, David would have needed to apply for a handgun qualification license in his home state. For this, he would have undergone a background check, passed a safety and training course, and submitted his fingerprints for filing. Maryland is one of the toughest states to get such a license, and the sixth most difficult state overall in which to achieve gun ownership.[353] He'd never shown interest in gun ownership before, but after passing with flying colors, got a 9mm pistol, a .45 caliber handgun, and extra ammunition just weeks ahead of his Jacksonville trip.[354]

Even if Elizabeth had been on the nose about the mental health issues her son suffered from—chronic low-grade depression,

352 Marco della Cava, "Jacksonville Shooter Legally Armed Himself in State with One of USA's Toughest Gun Laws," *USA Today*, last updated August 29, 2018, https://www.usatoday.com/story/news/2018/08/29/madden-killer-katz-legally-armed-himself-maryland/1127528002.

353 della Cava, "Jacksonville Shooter Legally Armed."

354 Boyle and Ashford, "Jacksonville Gamer Gunman's Parents Battled."

schizophrenia, disaffected disorder, unspecified oppositional disorder—*none* of these would have been an indicator that David would commit an act of violence. People who suffer from mental health issues are more often the *targets* of violence and bullying. And perhaps David was, and felt he had been for long enough.

On August 13—more than a *week* ahead of the *Madden '19* tournament he'd be participating in—and with no clothes or toiletries, Katz made his way down to Florida, shacking up in a Motel 6 just ten days after his firearm purchases.[355] Arriving so early and only hitting the road *after* receiving deadly weapons does have at least the tang of premeditation.

Good Luck, Have Fun!

The Jacksonville Landing was a cultural landmark for a brief flash-in-the-pan of time. Huge and horseshoe-shaped, it straddled the St. John River and dominated the Riverfront Walk with its iconic burnt orange roofing. A staple of the late eighties, by the 2010s, it had less of a reputation as "the place to be" and more of a status as "the place people don't go."

The company that built the superstructure, Rouse, was notable for the development of Faneuil Hall in Boston and South Street Seaport in New York City. Change was supposed to bring new life to the core of Jacksonville during a spate of urban renewal and cleanup projects. And at first, it worked. They built it and people came, for the mall shopping (The Gap, Victoria's Secret, Brookstone, The Limited) and—even more popular—the mall *grub*. Its "Founders Food Hall" took up the second floor with eighteen restaurants and a food court. But chain shopping couldn't sustain the waterfront property and little by little, tenants left, stores shuttered, restaurants were replaced by arcades, then those closed their doors, too. It became a *bad* hangout spot. Thefts, assaults, drug use, and petty crime began to plague the area—homelessness was rife.

One bright spot was GLHF—a pizza parlor and beer-slinging sports bar whose name was an abbreviation for "good luck, have

355 Patterson, "Did Grudge Push Gunman?"

fun," a common gaming phrase. Outside, hand-drawn graffiti advertised "GAME BAR" over a hand-painted mural of Sub-Zero, a player-favorite from the *Mortal Kombat* fighting series. Its heavy arcade elements were a main pull, but so were the neon signs celebrating hops and southern culture. Local IPAs were advertised as being on tap, and its wide windows, framed by friendly red awnings, were papered over in colorful ads for community events around Jacksonville. Sub-Zero was flanked on either side by towering graffiti of Mario, Boba Fett, Wolverine, and Samus Aran, all by different Florida artists. Inside, visitors could enjoy *classic* games, like the *Back to the Future* pinball machine or the *Frogger* arcade edition, while sampling Chicago Deep Dish. They had retro nights where they rigged up old SEGA and Nintendo systems for *Mario Bros.* and *Sonic the Hedgehog* free play. They sold nerd-chic merch—*Rick and Morty* pins, *Ninja Turtles* movie cards, *Rock 'Em Sock 'Em Robots*.

There was a wooden baby grand piano where guests could tickle the ivories beneath a *Street Fighter* mural. GLHF teamed up with local anime and gaming cons, hosted outdoor food trucks, served cocktails with a waterfront view, and hosted watch parties for esports and regular sports alike. From *League of Legends* to WrestleMania, this is where you came to be a fan.

Naturally, it hosted competitive tournaments, too. But while the *Madden '19* contest was a big fish for GLHF to land, GLHF was a shallow pool for esports. Only fitting about 150 people, its relatively unimportant crowd size and comparably small time winner's pot might not have turned too many heads. But for GLHF, it was a massive boon—150 people meant a packed house across multiple days, plus solid cash flow in the flagging Landing building.

On tourney days, there were more people than there were chairs, by a significant number. Crowds milled and flowed, and the vibe was energetic, frenetic across both days of play. David spent the majority of the tournament inside GLHF, but in a strange move, despite its darkened interior suffused with bursts of flashing neon from the machines, David opted to wear his heavily mirrored sunglasses indoors the entire time, obscuring his notably unnerving stare. Players who knew him thought something was more off than usual. He kept his Ravens backpack close (guns loaded inside) and rebuffed most conversation, aside from one chilling exception. For a little while on the second day, David went around asking where Shay "Young Kiv" Kivlen was. Shay, who'd just retired back to his room, was a friend of Elijah and Taylor's. This would later haunt Shay, who ended up hearing and seeing what would happen live on the EA stream.[356]

Players noticed something else amiss, too. Over the two days, David didn't seem to wash himself or change clothes. He came back in the same exact outfit on day two, now smelling of stale BO. Players were perplexed as to why he'd want to represent himself in such an aggressively slipshod manner on livestream. David had a motel room and access to a shower, but hygiene was perhaps the least of his concerns that weekend.

During pool play, Katz won a game and then lost to a New Jersian going by the moniker of "Evil Ken." The victor went to shake his hand after the match, but Katz ignored him, refusing to complete the gesture. It confused Evil Ken—he knew Katz, and while he'd noticed he wasn't especially talkative that weekend, it was strange for such a famous player, well-known in the circuit and heavily watched online, to suddenly be a sore loser.

On day two, Katz received a second "L," this time to a player nicknamed "Boogz." Forgoing his usual "Bread" title in this tourney, Katz had given himself the new moniker "SatiricBulb"—a red flag. Boogz had been in the lead until Katz tied it up with a curious play that Boogz pressed *pause* over, requesting an official call on it—he thought it was an illegal move. It turned out that Boogz was a victim of the new rules; the play was cleared, and rather than throw a tizzy over it, Boogz said "good stuff" and carried on with a nod and calm acceptance. He thought Katz had been pretty cool to recognize the loophole.[357]

But Boogz scored again, and that was it for David in the tournament. And, apparently, in life. About ten minutes later, chaos erupted.

---

356 Fleming, "The Madden Tournament Shooting in Jacksonville."

357 Fleming, "The Madden Tournament Shooting in Jacksonville."

Just One Bad Day

At 1:30 p.m. on August 28, 2018, David surged past the host's stand and the family-style tables that lined the mall entry to GLHF. He headed with unflappable determination towards the back of the room, where the tournament consoles and televisions were set up. Just ten minutes later, three people would be dead and eleven more injured.

That weekend, game announcers and participants called David's behavior all the usual adjectives: He was "stoic" and "cool." That was a total mischaracterization. What was deemed unflappable chill was actually seething ire and unkempt resentment. Beneath the mask, under the pretentious set of shades, David was *roiling*, a ball of unsteady petulant emotion.

He ducked back out of GLHF briefly, as if changing his mind, only to circle back, reentering. He'd set his sunglasses down on a random tabletop with a deliberate movement. Then, he'd unzip his Ravens bag and pulled out the .45 caliber.

Elijah Clayton, known by the handle "True Boy" or @True 818 (818 being both an "angel number," signifying abundance, and the area code of his home state of California), was playing a match against Drini Gjoka on livestream. In the livestream footage, a red dot briefly appears on Elijah's chest. It disappears quickly, flickering, as kickoff begins on their Falcons match. Then, it finds the spot over his heart. Shots follow, and the livestream abruptly ends.

Elijah died right away in the gaming chair, ensconced in his maroon Adidas hoodie, grinning with delight and glinting with keenness just a breath before. Three bullets hit him, one shattering his right eye, one finding his forehead, and one entering his chest.

David would ultimately only use one of his two guns in the attack, but he didn't leave the 9mm handgun in the Ravens bag, which he'd abandoned, crumpled, on the floor of the entry. He had it tucked into his waistband as he fired, as backup. At first, he fired with one steady hand as the crowd struggled to register their new reality, using his red laser sight to aim. When panic set in and movement flurried, he braced his first hand with a second to steady his fire.

From there, he began "popping off shots" one after the other in chilling succession, but almost always taking the time to train his muzzle at someone in particular. Under his breath, he was keeping a whispered tally, and some witnesses thought he was counting the number of people he had volleyed. The muzzle flashed successively. Loud bangs punctuated the sudden roar of the crowd like an exclamation point—a din of screams, crashing furniture, splitting upholstery, shattering glass, and weeping, set to the spooky undertone of live arcade games looping chipper jingles. At first, patrons mistook the gunshots for balloons popping or fireworks. Quickly enough, though, shouts of concern began to cut the thick rancour of confusion:

What'd he shoot you with?!

I told y'all that guy was coming back!

Oh, *fuck*, what *did* he shoot me with?!

David walked backward as he fired, one hand stabilizing the other still, seeming typically "aloof" amid the panic. He was still aiming with intention, and that frightened witnesses, especially those who felt he might target them as payback for an errant comment, a sideways glance, or winning a match—anything that might have wounded David's pride. David's pride, now armed to the teeth, was a chilling opponent.

It was clear he had predetermined some of his targets and was cherry-picking the rest. Not everyone he shot would be an intentional hit—the throngs became much too disorderly for that—but he was methodical, and his two kill shots had almost certainly been on a mental checklist.

Taylor Robertson, known by the handle @SpotMePlzzz, was the second person David murdered. He fired into the twenty-eight-year-old West Virginian's back and once was enough. The bullet exploded frontward, exiting his chest, and Taylor died almost instantly. He'd done nothing to harm or insult David, nothing that should have earned his ire. It's unknown why David had targeted him—maybe for something he'd done that weekend, or hadn't done, or maybe just because Taylor was everything David was not. Taylor was known for his saintly kindness. A sweet, sociable man with a rakish smile who never raised his voice and never bragged.

Taylor's body pitched and fell face up. His mouth and eyes were wide open, ossified in horrific shock. His body, dead where he lay, would unfortunately help to block an exit route.

David moved on, looking for his third kill—Shay. Shay, fortunately, was no longer on the premises, instead at a hotel with only snippets of audio to relay the nightmare happening at GLHD. With that plan spoiled, David began to widen his net.

Acerbic smoke and gunpowder, bright flashes of barrel spark, the squelch of sneakers on bloodied tiles, exploding windows belching shards over shrieking masses as they sought to hide or escape. Furniture toppled as bullets roared and the wounded added a groaning layer to the cacophony. People trampled over one another to make for the riverfront, then became confused about where the shots were coming from and rounded back inside, creating gridlocks. Others who'd hunkered down guarded their hiding places jealously, shooing away runners who begged to share prime spots behind arcade games or in locked bathroom stalls.

The list of injuries was long. Nine of the eleven wounded eventually needed stabilization measures. Tony Montenina was shot in the lower back and leg. Alexander Madunic was shot in the foot. Chris McFarland and George Amadeo both sustained bullet wounds that would send them to the ICU. Timothy Anselimo was hit in the chest and the wrist, with the latter bullet ripping through his hand and leaving his middle finger hanging on only by its skin. David would shoot Tim a third time, wounding his hip, when he tried to push past his injuries toward escape.

Nonetheless, these men considered themselves blessed to be counted among the walking wounded, rather than in the morgue alongside their friends. Drini, the gamer who'd been sitting beside Elijah, later noted, "I am literally so lucky. The bullet hit my thumb. I will never take anything for granted ever again. Life can be cut short in a second."[358]

358 Josh Fiallo, "Who Was David Katz, the Jacksonville Mass Shooter?" Tampabay.com, August 27, 2018, https://www.tampabay.com/news/publicsafety/Who-was-David-Katz-the-Jacksonville-mass-shooter-_171249699.

Finally, David was coming close to the end of the tally he'd been keeping under his breath during his rampage. He was counting bullets. He needed to save one—the final one in the magazine—for himself. He put the muzzle of the gun into his mouth and fired.

The assault that had seemed to go on forever it was over in just twenty seconds.[359]

Someone's tricked-out Xbox controller had fallen onto the blood-slicked floor. From its custom skin, *Batman*'s the Joker grinned on a sea of floating *HAHAHAs*, asking victim Tony Montagnino as he struggled to stay conscious on the floor beside it, "*Why So Serious*"?[360] A gore-smattered poster on the wall declared, "There are shortcuts to happiness and *dancing* is one of them!"[361] *Stargazing* played eerily over a pair of abandoned headphones, audible in the sudden quiet.

Tony Montagnino survived and would have "Why So Serious?" tattooed onto his arm, the same way it had been seared into his brain in that moment, marking his journey against a tide of PTSD and physical recovery. *HAHAHA* glides around his forearm, obscured by body hair, with a wide, white-toothed and red-lipped grin inked beneath the words. By 2024, he'd have at least three Joker-themed tattoos, including one full backpiece. Victims coped in their own way: Timothy Anselimo took a photo giving a *thumbs* up from his ICU bed alongside the governor of Florida.

There were many survivors, thanks largely to a rapid rescue. Fortuitously, a gaggle of first responders—mostly firefighters—had been practicing training drills across the street. They heard the gunfire and rushed to the scene, beginning to stabilize victims by 1:36 p.m. The incident itself had only begun at 1:34 p.m. They ran in headlong, without protective gear, with no thought of their own safety, unaware as of yet that the *active* shooter was now *inactive*. The day had its share of everyday heroes, too. Victim Timothy Anselimo, who would be unable to have the bullet that hit his chest removed (too dangerous), would have had the gushing from his ruined hand stoppered by a brave Hooter's chef who refused to let him bleed

359 Patterson, "Did Grudge Push Gunman?"

360 Fleming, "The Madden Tournament Shooting in Jacksonville."

361 Fleming, "The Madden Tournament Shooting in Jacksonville."

out, hugging him hard enough to stem his chest wound, too, until help arrived. Attending Sheriff Mike Williams would later note on his press release, "As bad as this is, it could have been much worse."[362]

And indeed, even without the savvy rescue, it could have been. David opted not to use both guns, nor his extra ammo. Police also confirmed that David strode past anyone not of interest to him, leaving women, children, and families alone. This seemed personal, earmarked; though again, assuredly, some of the injured were casualties of chaos and misfiring.

Katz didn't seem to target people who'd beaten him, either. Jax, someone who'd done so in the past, Boogz, and Evil Ken were all unharmed. The motives here ran deeper than gameplay, though losing the tournament may have been his cue to carry out the deed.

Toshiba Sharon, one of the announcers that day on the livestream who hid behind a table he'd overturned for safety when the violence began, tearfully noted on *Good Morning America* that Clayton and Taylor hadn't died alone: "They died with family ... with a brotherhood ... loving what they do."[363]

Distressingly, while the Twitch TV livestream had gone off-air when Clayton was shot, the audio feed from within GLHF continued to be broadcast. Just screaming, screaming, screaming. And the relentless sound of merciless gunfire.

Student, Father, Brother, Friend

Elijah "TrueBoy" Clayton had won at *Madden* tournaments before, earning sums in the tens of thousands. He strove to win not out of ego—but as a means of future planning. He was saving up his pro gaming profits to pay his way through a college education.

Elijah was only twenty-two when he was murdered. Handsome, boisterous, and popular, he was either someone you loved or someone who

---

362 "Jacksonville Shooting Suspect David Katz Obtained Guns Legally, Police Say,". *ABC7NY*, August 28, 2018, https://abc7ny.com/jacksonville-shooting-david-katz-shooter-madden/4065537.

363 Bill Hutchinson, Mark Osborne, and Kelly McCarthy, "Florida Esports Shooting Survivors Describe Mad Rush to Escape Gunman: 'Went Into Survival Mode,'" *ABC News*, August 27, 2018, https://abcnews.go.com/US/florida-esports-shooting-survivors-describe-mad-rush-escape/story?id=57420411.

rubbed people the wrong way, right away. Either way, he was well-known, talkative, and emoted easily. He was a big, shining personality.

From Woodland Hills, California, Elijah had made a lasting impression on his community. The principal of Chaminade College Preparatory, the high school he'd attended for three years in the West Hills, said of him: "Elijah [was] ... a sweet, mild-mannered young man who always showed great respect for his peers... a dedicated student, doing his best in the classroom while being a great teammate to his football family."[364] In his final year, he'd transferred to Calabasas High.

His obituary[365] sheds light on the life that was and what could have been.

Elijah left behind a huge, close-knit family who thought the world of him. He loved to "harass his loved ones" and "play the dozens"—a game where you take turns insulting one another to try to make someone angry or upset. His family was playful and thick-skinned, not minding a few buttons pushed. They described Elijah as "well-regarded," "extraordinary," and as a natural leader. He was a firstborn son with a gift for STEM and he *adored* sports—playing, watching, and gaming. He played basketball, football, and ran track, all while keeping a 3.2 GPA. He'd earned his associate's degree in computer science at Pierce College in 2016.

He'd been playing *Madden* since he was six. He'd made it to the semifinals of the 2018 Ultimate League, had ranked as *Madden*'s sixth-highest earner, and was selected to serve as an esport representative to the NFL. His decision to join the Jacksonville tournament was last-minute.

Elijah left behind his parents and nine siblings—seven brothers and three sisters. A family devastated.

Taylor Robertson was twenty-seven years old and hailed from Ballard, West Virginia. Married, he and his wife, Holly, shared a two-year-old son, Reed, at the time of his death. He was an impressive

---

364 Hutchinson and Parra, "Suspect in Madden 19 Tournament Shooting Targeted Gamers."

365 "Elijah Michael Clayton," UtterMcKinley.com, accessed May 1, 2025, https://www.uttermckinley.com/obituaries/Elijah-Clayton/#!/Obituary.

Madden player, the defending champ of the most recent Madden Classic.[366]

He'd attended James Monroe High School, where he'd been an honor student and an athlete, making it to the all-state football competition two times, and even named his senior class's Athlete of the Year. As a graduate, he went on to get his BA in accounting and worked to support his growing family with a role at a local First Community Bank.

In addition to his young son, he left behind a brother, Andrew, and a whole mess of family, close-knit like Elijah's. He had so many friends you could toss a pebble in Ballard and hit one. His family selflessly requested that any donations made in his honor at or following his funeral go not to them, but to a sports charity Taylor had cared about in life.

His online obituary[367] is utterly suffused with comments of grief and comfort. Thronged with observations about what a good man he had been, his warm smile, his unwavering friendship:

> He was the nicest, easiest person to get along with. Taylor had a huge heart and would help anyone ...
>
> He truly was an awesome husband [and] Daddy ...
>
> Taylor was such a good student ... In the classroom he was such a positive influence to his peers. Always ready to help ... with a smile.... Parents, well done raising him to be the Taylor everyone loves. Holly and Reed, you gave him a desire to be an even better person. Andrew, you set a high bar for your little brother ... May peace be with you all.

Demolished

Police barricaded the streets near Jacksonville Landing immediately following the shooting, leaving the Landing in unnerving silence against a setting of still river waters and barren, glass-shot roads crisscrossed with vicious neon caution tape. GLHF's jolly storefront would be swathed in biohazard tape, a whisper of what was to come—that GLHF would not survive the shooting. It shuttered its doors,

366 Hutchinson and Parra, "Suspect in Madden 19 Tournament Shooting Targeted Gamers."

367 "Taylor Mack Robertson," Broyles-Shrewsbury.com, accessed May 1, 2025, https://www.broyles-shrewsbury.com/obituaries/Taylor-Mack-Robertson?obId=27779216.

and the community lost a space that should have been dedicated to joy and play. In the investigation that followed, police found that its game room had violated emergency code: its exits were obstructed, making evacuation dangerously restrictive.

From there, the Jacksonville Landing lost more tenants. In an odd added security measure, it stopped allowing its elevators to run. Five years later, to the day, there would be another mass shooting in Jacksonville. An article ran about it in *Rolling Stone* magazine.

EA Sports, *Madden*'s owner company, would put out a message of condolence following the GLHF incident. Angry families sued—EA Sports, GLHF, the Jacksonville Landing—for lack of security and bag checks. That quick, twenty seconds of devastation led to court dockets being filled with about fifty lawsuits in total, as grief-stricken families rushed to assign blame to make sense of it all, the deaths, wounds, and traumas of the day—the physical and emotional ramifications of a shooting spree. The claims were found to be unsubstantial—no one could have known what Katz had planned.

Richard Katz's home in Baltimore would be combed over by FBI. They wouldn't find anything vital or illuminating regarding the case, which ultimately was rather cut-and-dry. Elizabeth and Richard both cooperated with authorities straight away. During their divorce proceedings, it had been asked through a pychologist if Richard thought David had the capacity to become violent. Only, the response came, if his mother made him *so* angry that he'd lose his cool. Anyone else, the inquiry pressed? "No.."[368]

Floral bouquets, wooden crosses, necklaces, and candles were placed as a vigil in front of GLHF. The Jacksonville Landing was demolished in October of 2019, the sight of all that bloodshed churned into rubble.

---

368 Prudente, *The Baltimore Sun.*

ACKNOWLEDGMENTS

I would like to give thanks to the following people who helped to make this book what it is through one of the most hectic periods of my life. First to Shelona Belfon for selecting me for this project—getting to dive back into true crime but in the crosshairs of pop culture (my forté, I hope!) was a real honor. Then, to Kierra Sondereker for picking up the project, and for her Mariana's Trench of patience with me. To editor Renee Rutledge, for her keen eye and truly astounding knowledge of grammar and style. (If Kierra has a Mariana's Trench of patience, then Renee went *through* the trenches with this book.) To Zeynep Ozturk, for the hard and mucky job of end noting (and understanding my appalling shorthand throughout)—we survived the TikTok Broken Links Apocaly-Blips of 2025 together. To Nevi Ozturk, for helping pull me through the Randy Stair and Pekka Eric Auvinen chapters to the finish line—and for the multiple cups of coffee. To Brent Mayr, Franklin Blazik, and Dolly Lace for agreeing to be interviewed about their firsthand knowledge. To Zach and Rachel, for sharing their personal experiences and insights for these pages. To Susan Mary Rosenberg, for her kind reply. To TJ, for yet again being the first to preorder my book, the first to tell me it was *up* for preorder, the first to tell me it was delayed (my fault!!)—and for offering a sensitivity read of some chapters.

To all my friends and family who were excited for this book and whose enthusiasm kept me going through the darkest parts of investigating, all my love. Steeping yourself in some of the most gruesome realities doesn't wash off as easily as fiction does, but good friends help.

And honestly, speaking of fiction, thank you to Ceri Young and Ann Lemay for writing the game *Gotham Knights*. My escapism from these pages was, ironically, entering your world of vigilantism and saving the day on those fantastical city streets. To Colin, Henry, Rob, and now Jason, too, thank you for letting me be Fynn at you when I needed a break—the Barb, and its Oatmeal Tao, are forever. Thank you also to Megan Buxton, for the chocolate chip fuel.

Finally, I want to thank the 318 squad. You know who you are. You're probably eating free bagels right now. Your coffee is late. You're screaming BABADOOOOOOOOK!! into the middle distance. (I redacted his actual name, don't worry. His secret is safe with me!) What you are *not* doing is taping an episode of the podcast "More or Lester" (#DownTheRabbitHole), and I find that regrettable. Get on that! But really, I was astounded by what an exceptional group of people you are. Our time together changed how I went about my final edits and how I thought about these cases. I hope that group text keeps us laughing for a long time to come. Now that the book is done, I *guess* I have time to make a cheesecake. Correct? Correct.

And thank *you* for reading this. Be good to each other out there.

ABOUT THE AUTHOR

Madison Jayne Salters is a journalist, writer, editor, and translator who has lived all over the globe, only to settle back at her starting line: New York City. She works in publishing as a content leader for works in translation from Japanese for the US and European markets. She loves a good investigative deep dive, drinking too much coffee, her two little epileptic sausage dogs, and her partner—not necessarily in that order. Highly awarded for her work, she was once named "Top 30 Under 30" by *Westchester Magazine*, which her family found hilarious. This is her third book.